FOLKTALES OF *India*

FOLKTALES OF THE WORLD

GENERAL EDITOR: *Richard M. Dorson*

FOLKTALES OF
India

EDITED BY
Brenda E. F. Beck
Peter J. Claus
Praphulladatta Goswami
Jawaharlal Handoo

FOREWORD BY
A. K. Ramanujan

THE UNIVERSITY OF CHICAGO PRESS
Chicago and London

The University of Chicago Press, Chicago 60637
The University of Chicago Press, Ltd., London
© 1987 by The University of Chicago
All rights reserved. Published 1987
Paperback edition 1989
Printed in the United States Of America
96 95 94 93 92 91 90   5 4 3 2

Library of Congress Cataloging-in-Publication Data

Folktales of India.

(Folktales of the world)
Bibliography: p.
Includes indexes.
1. Tales—India.   2. Legends—India.   I. Beck,
Brenda E. F.   II. Series: Folktales of the world
(Chicago, Ill.)
GR305.F65   1987   398.2'0954   86–7112
ISBN 0-226-04080-1 (cloth)
ISBN 0-226-04082-8 (pbk.)

BRENDA E. F. BECK is professor of anthropology
at the University of Toronto. PETER J. CLAUS is
professor of anthropology at California State
University, Hayward. PRAPHULLADATTA GOSWAMI
is professor emeritus in the Department of Folklore
at the University of Gauhati, Assam. JAWAHARAL
HANDOO is director of the Folklore Unit at the
Central Institute of Indian Languages in Mysore.

Contents

III   PARENTS AND CHILDREN

IV   SISTERS AND BROTHERS

VII   KNOWLEDGE AND THE FOOL

THE STATES OF INDIA

KASHMIR

HIMACHAL
PRADESH

PUNJAB

HARYANA

UTTAR
PRADESH

ARUNACHAL
PRADESH

SIKKIM

RAJASTHAN

ASSAM

NAGALAND

BIHAR

MAGHA-
LAYA

MANIPUR

GUJARAT

MADHYA PRADESH

WEST
BENGAL

MIZORAM

TRIPURA

ORISSA

MAHARASHTRA

ANDHRA

GOA

KARNATAKA

KERALA

TAMIL
NADU

Foreword

This collection of Indian folktales is quite unusual. The late Richard Dorson, doyen of modern folktale collections from all over the world and the founding editor of the Chicago series, initiated this collection twenty years ago knowing full well what he was getting into when he said, "We will have to do this [India] volume one tale at a time." The ninety-nine tales presented here were collected by eighteen regional folklorists from fourteen different languages. They have been edited by four folklorists, two of whom are North American anthropologists and two of whom are Indian experts from two regions in India separated by 1,000 miles.

The Indian subcontinent is vast and various, containing many Indias represented by over 100 living languages, each with its social and territorial dialects, its cultural niches, attendant traditions (oral and otherwise), ten writing systems and over a dozen literary languages. All these have dwelled together for several millennia in what we call India today. Even in such a country of multilinguals, few people know, let alone command, more than a couple of languages. And authentic folklore cannot be collected secondhand without a knowledge of the many speech varieties of each region. Therefore, making a book of "representative," "Indian" folktales is a venture of long and varied cooperation—as the present book has been. There have been one or two smaller collections representing more than one language, but they have been retellings of other published or literary materials. The present book brings together the work of several local folklorists in English translation. Though the representation here is still understandably uneven, it is a first effort to present freshly collected oral tales from the many regions of India within the covers of a single book. We must remember, however, that "representativeness" is a chimerical ideal; in the study of a culture, one does not look for a ratio between sample and bulk but for a holograph where every part is a true representative of a whole which can never be seen whole. Or, as in a dream, every section is a cross section that tells us something about the whole which cannot be grasped directly.

Earlier Collections

The collection and translation of Indian oral tales began over a hundred years ago. W. Norman Brown, in a classic essay (Brown, "Panchatantra," 1919), estimated that some 3,000 oral tales from the Indic region (including Sri Lanka, Pakistan, and Bangladesh) were available in translation to the English reader, and that was in 1919.

A few tales had been reported in travel books and such, but the first considerable collection of a region's oral tales was Mary Frere's *Old Deccan Days* (1868). The book was published in England and in the United States and was soon translated into several European languages. Three years later, G. H. Damant began to publish a series of Bengali tales in the *The Indian Antiquary*, a series that ended only in 1880. Others followed suit and published tales from many provinces in *The Indian Antiquary*, *The Journal of the Asiatic Society of Bengal*, *Folk-Lore*, *North Indian Notes and Queries*, *Man in India*, and other such learned journals. Stokes's *Indian Fairy Tales* appeared in 1879; in 1883, L. B. Day's *Folk-Tales of Bengal;* in 1884, Temple's *Legends of the Punjab* in three volumes. Temple and F. A. Steel's *Wide-Awake Stories* (1884) was a landmark, for it also surveyed and classified incidents found in most of the tales published up to that time. In 1909, C. H. Bompas translated the admirable collections of Rev. O. Bodding among the Santal tribes. In 1914 the third and last volume of H. Parker's important three-volume *Village Tales of Ceylon* appeared. Others not mentioned here may be found in bibliographies like Kirkland's (1966) or the more recent one by Handoo (1977).

Since W. N. Brown's 1919 survey, dozens of books and scores of tales have been published. (Sterling, a Delhi publisher, has put

out over twenty small collections in English—but alas, they are
mostly unreliable and poorly written.) Of the collections made in
the last few decades, probably the most authentic and noteworthy
are M. B. Emeneau's *Kota Texts* in three volumes (1944–46) and
Verrier Elwin's *Folktales of Mahakoshal* (1944). The latter is especially valuable for its comparative notes.

Yet, as others have pointed out (Elwin 1944, xiv), with the
exception of a few reliable collections like Bodding's, Emeneau's,
and Elwin's, most of these works bowdlerize, "Victorianize," and
sentimentalize the earthy, often bawdy, Indian tales and render
them fit for middle-class English nurseries. In fact, we owe the
bulk of our collections in this period to five missionaries (Rever-
ends Bodding, Campbell, Day, Knowles, and Swynnerton) and
to five English ladies (Frere, Dracott, Steel, Stokes, Thornhill).
With the exception of Frere, the collectors say little about their
methods of collecting and recording, or about the caste, class, or
place of their tellers. Rev. L. B. Day's vagueness is quite typical:
he had heard the tales from a Bengali Christian woman who as "a
little girl and living in her heathen home had heard many stories
from her old grandmother." He himself had heard "thousands" of
stories in his youth from an old woman, but "they had all got
confused in his head, the tail of one story being conjoined to
another and the head of the third to the tail of the fourth." Others
speak of tales collected "down country," or in an "extremely out
of the way village," and "not a few [from] a blind man" (Elwin
1944, xiv).

And in the case of Indian collections like that of the learned
Natesa Sastri (1884–88), old Tamil and Sanskrit texts are often
retold in English as folktales. In the hands of ethnographers like
Sarat Chandra Roy or Parker, the tale loses its style and spunk
and acquires "italics and brackets." When professional writers
like F. A. Steel (a popular Victorian novelist on Indian themes)
turn on the charm and turn the tales into English kindergarten,
words (and concepts) like "honeymoon," "dinner," "breakfast,"
and titles like "Prince Lionheart" and "Princess Pepperina" pepper the pages.

So they returned to the cage, by which the tiger was waiting for
the Brâhman, and sharpening his teeth and claws.

'You've been away a long time!' growled the savage beast, 'but
now let us begin our dinner.'
'*Our* dinner!' thought the wretched Brâhman, as his knees
knocked together with fright; 'what a remarkably delicate way of
putting it!'
'Give me five minutes, my lord!' he pleaded, 'in order that I may
explain matters to the jackal here, who is somewhat slow in his wits.'

(Steel 1894, p. 109)

It must be remembered, however, that these kinds of treatment were not the special fate of the Indian tales. We know now
that even the great Grimm Brothers elaborated, rewrote, and em-
broidered their "household tales" (Ellis 1983). Both the zeal for
folklore collection and the attitudes toward it in India reflected
larger movements in the field of folklore studies in England and
Europe. This was the period when the word "folklore" itself was
invented; in countries like Finland this was also the period when
nationalist movements made folklore a part of their self-discovery
and self-expression. The study of Indian folklore and mythology
fit very well into nineteenth-century European ideologies: scholars researched "peasant traditions and savage customs" for data to
buttress evolutionary theories of society or for the excitement of
worldwide foraging in comparative mythology and anthropology.
Darwin, Marx, and Freud were all in different ways heirs to such
nineteenth-century preoccupations. Indian materials were also
grist for that mill. Indeed, the study of Indian folktales and
myths was one of the early and central inspirations of the international discipline of "folklore" itself. India was thought to be the
original motherland of all European folk narrative (Benfey 1859).
Ancient Indian literary collections like the *Panchatantra* had been
translated and retold through the medieval centuries in a wide
variety of non-Indian languages (Persian, Arabic, Latin, and from
Latin into the languages of Europe). In the other important medieval Indian collection, the *Kathasaritsagara*, "The Ocean of the
Streams of Story," (Penzer 1924) one could find parallels (if not
sources) for many of the great tales in *The Arabian Nights, The
Decameron,* etc. Well-known European stories that became the
bases of Shakespeare's *Cymbeline,* or *All's Well That Ends Well,* for
instance, can be found in the early Indian collections. With the

rise of Indo-European studies, following the discovery of the relations of Sanskrit to Greek and Latin, J. Grimm (1935) also proposed a kinship between Indian and European mythology, and Max Müller (1856) elaborated on it. Dumezil's monumental work (1968–73) on Indo-European mythology in the last few decades is a direct heir to that heritage.

So, what began with travelers, missionaries, civil servants, and their enterprising wives and daughters was later seriously undertaken by philologists and comparativists, finally becoming a part of ethnographic research and most recently part of a separate discipline called "folklore." The present collection is a combination of the last two approaches.

The thousands of tales collected since the 1850s, with all their flaws, were nevertheless valuable data as narratives for the growing international study of folktales. The comparative notes of writers like Temple, Steel, and Parker, the articles of Brown, Bloomfield, Crooke (who later became the President of the Folklore Society of London) and S. C. Roy, and the voluminous notes, indexes, and appendices of Penzer to the enormous literary collection, *The Ocean of Story,* translated by Tawney in ten volumes (1924–28), provided the bases for all later studies and classifications. Especially in the late 1950s, three important indexes were made for India modeled on and yet feeding into the international motif-and-type indexes of Aarne and Thompson: L. Bødker's *Indian Animal Tales: A Preliminary Survey* (Folklore Fellows Communications 170, Helsinki, 1957); S. Thompson and J. Balys's motif-index, misleadingly titled *The Oral Tales of India* (Bloomington: Indiana University Press, 1958); and S. Thompson and W. E. Roberts's *Types of Indic Oral Tales* (FFC, 180, Helsinki, 1960). If we set aside the by now well-known theoretical problems that all such motif and type indexes raise and cannot solve, these are still the most useful bibliographic tools a folklorist could wish for. But they are already a quarter of a century old, and they understandably include only materials available to them in English and nothing of untranslated materials from native Indian languages. However, Edwin C. Kirkland's *A Bibliography of South Asian Folklore* (1966) does make a serious attempt to include the latter.

After 1960, a new regionalist interest in folk materials

blossomed in Indian languages. While good amateur collections
had been made several decades earlier, they were not part of any
institutional enterprise. Since the 1960s, several Indian univer-
sities, literary academies, and the Central Institute of Indian Languages have devoted time, attention, and money to folklore.
Speaking only of folktales, in the Kannada language alone, over
3,000 tales have been collected (some of it, alas, fakelore) from
towns and villages, and two reliable type-indexes have been
compiled.

"Classical" and "Folk"

In an ancient, widespread, palimpsest-like, yet living civilization
like India's, traditions are organized in many and complex ways.
Anthropologists have offered rubrics, like the Great and Little
Traditions, for describing these complexities. They are sug-
gestive, if taken with the necessary pinches of salt. Roughly
speaking, the Great Tradition (this too ought to be plural) is
carried by Sanskrit; it is pan-Indian and consists of things like the
Vedic texts and sacrificial rituals, the epics, the mythologies of
the pan-Indian divinities like Vishnu, Siva, and the Goddess.
The Little Traditions are carried by the hundreds of regional languages and dialects with their own literatures, folk traditions,
local gods, and sacrifices (often assimilated or connected by new
myths to the pan-Indian ones) and so on. But we must remember
that the two traditions are entirely permeable to each other, or are
often versions of each other, and are constantly interfused. For
one thing, all Sanskrit authors were, of necessity, bilingual:
Sanskrit was their formally learned father tongue, and the language of their home and region was their mother tongue. So, in
addition to creating original Sanskrit works, authors were trans-
ferring and archiving (often unawares) whatever was considered
memorable or valuable in the mother tongues for posterity and
for others outside their regions. In folklore studies, which is our
present concern, the greatest early collections were clearly of this
nature. *The Panchatantra* and *The Ocean of Story* (Penzer 1924–28)
and the earlier Buddhist birth stories, *The Jatakas*, (Rhys Davids
1925) and the epics, are our richest ancient narrative en-
cyclopedias. Even the oldest religious "scriptures" contain recog-
nizable folktale types. Composed around 900 B.C. by priests in

order to explain the esoteric meanings of Vedic ritual, the obscure Brahmana texts preserve, as in amber, tales like "The Youth on a Quest for His Lost Father" (tale type 369)—many versions of which have been collected in our times not only in the literary languages but also among Santal and Gond tribes. As Wendy O'Flaherty rightly says,

> If it can be established (as I think it can) that the Brahmanas, so long accused of being the private property of the most elite and obfuscating textualists who ever lived, are in fact the vehicle for a great deal of material virtually indistinguishable in tone and plot from the stories collected by the Brothers Grimm in German farmhouses, how can one possibly separate the "folk" materials from the "classical" materials? (1985, 11)

Yet, while the great myths and the local tales share similar structures and motifs, we must not imagine they are put to the same uses or carry the same unchanging meanings. Motifs do not predict structures, and structures do not predict functions, nor functions meanings. An animal tale like type 175, "The Tar Baby and the Rabbit," may be told to little children as a cute little tale, read in a comic book on Brer Rabbit's adventures as told by Uncle Remus, or be part of the Buddha myth in a Jataka tale. A tale like "The Pursuit of the Heavenly Maiden" (type 306A) may occur as a Vedic myth and recur in the ritual texts, in the epics, and also in a grandmother's tale told in a South Indian kitchen to coax a naughty child to eat more. The aesthetics, ethos, and the worldviews in each context will be different and should be described differently in each instance. Comparative mythology and folkloristics may begin with shared features and comparisons, but their end, ultimately, has to be contrasts. We have hardly begun.

The plurality of cultures and subcultures that compose Indian civilization is also expressed in the narratives by versions and meanings that change from region to region, from community to community, and certainly from period to period. The same narrative materials may function differently in different genres and present different concerns. For example, the myths and folktales may have much in common but use the materials very differently. Myths are replete with proper names of places and persons; they deal largely with public events like wars, origins of worlds, and foundings of communities. Folktale characters and locales rarely have names and deal with familial themes (as the organization of this book demonstrates vividly)—not a region's famine, but a couple's childlessness, not the ancient and recurring war between gods and antigods, but the equally ancient and recurring quarrels between siblings or in-laws. The supernatural in folktales is not divine and cosmic but magical and worldly, frequently comic. Indeed, when the great gods and heroes appear in folktales, as they may, they are thoroughly humanized, given bodies that sweat, sneeze, and shit—the gods of Hindu mythology mostly do nothing of the sort, their eyes do not blink, their feet do not touch the ground. Myths, by and large, divinize the human; folktales humanize the divine. As genres, they have ecological niches in the culture. If the one functions in ritual contexts, the other indirectly regulates social forms; if one is a public genre in performance, the other is, by and large, domestic. When what began as a domestic folktale becomes part of a ritual (for the "same" structure may have many functions as we said earlier), the tale acquires the properties of a myth: e.g. sonorous names, formulaic styles, even verse, royal or supernatural characters, incidents that link many worlds. In women's ritual tales, *vratakatha,* tales about the ritual are told ceremonially as part of a ritual. They acquire reflexivity as a special structural property, for such a ritual has a narrative function within the tale, and the tale functions as part of the ritual. Thus the skeletal structure might still be the same, but the shape, the costume, the status, the style and magical powers that flesh it out and give it life may be utterly different. A tale like "The Jealous Queens" (type 707), told in South India by grandmothers to little children, is also elaborated and recited by professional bards to a village assembly. And its telling is central to a possession ritual in Himalayan villages— the characters possess selected members of the audience who then become vehicles of prophecy.

Thus, tales have to be studied not merely to extract a taxonomy or a structure, but in relation to other genres in the repertoire of the region. Tales and myths, to return to that pair again, are told in the same community in appropriately different contexts; they may express different worldviews. Mythologies, especially Sanskritic ones, are imbued with philosophies and metaphysics, while folktales present deep yet homely paradigms, psychological problems and resolutions, childhood fears and consolations, the poetry and prose of daily living—though the materials of the one may be transformed into that of the other in given contexts. For instance, while Sanskritic epics and myths and even literary retellings of tales propose Karmic philosophies, or play with questions of illusion and reality, folktales tend to ignore karma or illusion (*māyā*). Folktales rarely speak of lives before birth and after death.

Thus in the civilizations of India, myth and folktale, two instances of the so-called classical and folk expressions, are intermeshed yet distinct; they should be studied together and seen as complementary traditions. Their continuities and contrasts within individual psyches as well as in communal expressions (like art and ritual) make the culture what it is. One cannot study an Indian painting, or a piece of music, or a temple, a wedding or a death ritual without attending to both the classical and folk forms they evoke, combine, and rework. (I have not spoken here of the "popular" and "tribal" strands which too are part of the intricate cultural web.)

Indian Tales and Worldwide Types

That Indian tales share motifs and structures with tales all over the world is obvious; leafing through an index of tale types and motifs will clear any doubts one may have. For instance, tale 83 in this book is type 57A, "Fox Flatters Crow into Dropping the Meat"; it is not only an Aesop tale retold by Chaucer and La Fontaine, it has been collected as an oral tale in Finnish, Latvian, Lithuanian, Irish, Spanish, Dutch, German, Russian, Korean, and North American Indian, as well as in several Indian languages. Cinderella tales, tales of Lear and his daughters, Oedipus, etc., all have their variants in India.

Then what is Indian about the Indian tales? For one thing, the motifs participate in Indian (and regional) lexicons; the tales bear Indian names, are enacted by personae who make Indian faces, wear Indian expressions, speak Indian commonplaces, dream Indian nightmares. Indian tales may be different from similar ones found elsewhere at different levels. They may have the same motifs in different variants; favored motif clusters; the same tale types, different variants; the same tale types but in different combinations; the same tale types, but with different meanings and contexts. Archetypes there may be, but they are steeped in, and express, Indian culture and history.

Or there may be unique motifs and types that occur only in Indian tales. The last claim is the most difficult to make, for it implies an exhaustive collection of tales all over the world so that one may say decisively that a tale is found only in an Indian region. One may isolate some "oikotypes" by comparing the world index and the Indian index; but every new index changes the count. The recent Chinese tale index lists a number of tales (Nai-Tung Ting 1978, 18) that were thought to be special to the Indian regions. So we can say, as far as we know now, stories like "The Crocodile Carries the Jackal" (type 58), "Cunning Jackal and Foolish Fox" (59A), "The Pursuit of the Heavenly Maiden" (306A), and "The Lecherous Holy Man and the Maiden in a Box" (896) have been recorded as exclusively Indian by the indexes. Also, some stories have greater currency in India than elsewhere. For instance, "The Thief and the Tiger" (type 177) has been reported 25 times in India but only once in Spain and once in Korea.

Depending on which area of India one is examining, the tales demonstrate different connections with the non-Indian world. The tales of Goa, a former Portuguese colony, naturally show Christian influences; the tales of the northeastern regions are akin to those of Tibeto-Chinese Buddhist countries; and the tales of the northwestern regions are akin to those found in the Middle East. Religions like Islam, Buddhism, and Christianity have brought their own tales and carried folklore into new regions with their migrations. Indian connections with Arabia, China, Southeast Asia, not to mention the West, have all been registered in the annals of Indian fiction. So it would be trivial to seek out what is particularly "Indian" in the tales by looking into the origins or unique distributions of certain tales. It would be more important to ask what the Indian tellers do to the tales (worldwide as the types may be) to make them different; how they use the language of motif, sequence, and structure that they share with other parts of the world; and how they invariably say characteristic "Indian" things which have deep connections with other parts of Indian cultural expression. Detailed studies of single tales in context, comparing their Indian and non-Indian variants, can yield new insights and lead to new fruitful discussions of the Indian folktale.

I shall leave the reader with the following Indian tale a half-blind Kannada woman once told me in a South Indian village (Ramanujan 1983). One may ponder the startling similarities and telling differences between the Oedipus myth and this Indian village tale:

A girl is born with a curse on her head that she would marry her own son and beget a son by him. As soon as she hears of the curse, she wilfully vows she'd try and escape it: she secludes herself in a dense forest, eating only fruit, forswearing all male company. But when she attains puberty, as fate would have it, she eats a mango from a tree under which a passing king has urinated. The mango impregnates her; bewildered, she gives birth to a male child; she wraps him in a piece of her sari and throws him in a nearby stream. The child is picked up by the king of the next kingdom, and he grows up to be a handsome young adventurous prince. He comes hunting to the same forest, and the cursed woman falls in love with the stranger, telling herself she is not in danger any more as she has no son alive. She marries him and bears him a child. According to custom, the father's swaddling clothes are preserved and brought out for the newborn son. The woman recognizes at once the piece of sari with which she had swaddled her first son, now her husband, and understands that her fate has really caught up with her. She waits till everyone is asleep and sings a lullaby to her newborn baby:
Sleep
O son
O grandson
O brother to my husband
sleep O sleep
sleep well
Then she hangs herself from the rafter with her sari twisted to a rope.*

A. K. RAMANUJAN

*From "The Indian Oedipus" by A. K. Ramanujan. In *Oedipus: A Folklore Casebook,* edited by Lowell Edmunds and Alan Dundes, 234–66. New York: Garland, 1983.

Acknowledgments

This volume has a long and complex history. Richard Dorson was already director of the Folklore Institute at Indiana University and general editor of this series when Professor B. K. Barua of Gauhati, Assam, first visited Bloomington in 1964. Dorson had wanted to develop a volume on Indian folktales for some time and he initially commissioned Barua to prepare the manuscript. This hopeful start was brought to an unfortunate halt, however, with Barua's sudden death in 1964. Praphulladatta Goswami was one of his colleagues in Gauhati, and at that point responsibility for the volume passed to him. An invitation to visit the Folklore Institute just a few years later soon allowed for his close collaboration with persons at Indiana University. Jawaharlal Handoo, Peter Claus, and Brenda Beck joined the project in 1979. From then on the work became a collaborative effort.

India, however, has many languages and cultures and even the collaborative efforts of several scholars are insufficient to collect material representative of India as a whole. Fortunately, we were able to elicit the aid of many fine collectors all over the country. We would like to express our appreciation to them, not only for their excellent work, but also for their care and promptness in fulfilling our needs. Their names, along with short biographical sketches, are listed in a separate section at the end of the volume.

It was to our immense delight that Professor A. K. Ramanujan graced our collection with his sensitive and thought-provoking Foreword. The North American editors acknowledge their further thanks to him: he was their teacher at the University of Chicago and inspired their interest in Indian folklore from the beginning. He has helped to guide their work on Indian folklore and culture throughout their careers.

Stuart Blackburn and Marci Williams worked at different times to produce the tale type and motif indices. Blackburn also read the full manuscript at various stages of its completion and provided valuable comments for revision. He also did the majority of the work on the bibliography, much of which appeared in *Another Harmony: New Essays on the Folklore of India,* edited by Blackburn and A. K. Ramanujan. We would like to thank the University of California Press for allowing its inclusion here.

The very idea for the collection, of course, came from the late Professor Richard Dorson. He inspired, encouraged, guided, and supported each of us, individually and as a group, in countless ways.

In December of 1978 Dorson visited India for the first time. In conjunction with the 10th International Congress of Anthropological and Ethnological Sciences he participated in a special Folklore Conference in Calcutta. During this trip Goswami arranged a reception at the University of Gauhati. Upon his return to the United States, Richard Dorson wrote about his impressions as follows:

> . . . The principle of the Chicago [folktale] series is to present authentic, traditional accounts recorded directly from story tellers, and to support these tale texts with a proper scholarly apparatus: data on the informant, on the collector, and on the translator, plus comparative annotation and analysis of a tale's function and cultural meaning. This is a tall order, and I think that we will have to build this [India] volume one tale at a time.

Professor Dorson wanted each volume in his series to represent the finest possible collection of materials. It is tragic that death came before the final fruit of so many years of effort and prevented his celebration of its publication.

Introduction

Although generations of folklorists have recognized India as one of the world's richest sources of folktales, India's tales remain remarkably understudied and underutilized. They are underrepresented in many worldwide collections and indices and are frequently misrepresented by stories drawn from ancient literary sources rather than oral sources. At present, the English translations which exist are scattered throughout hundreds of discrete sources, many of them obscure and all but inaccessible today. What we have tried to do with this book is fill a gap in our current knowledge of folklore by providing a collection of tales representative of the numerous regions and languages of India.

Each of the ninety-nine tales in this collection—an auspicious number in India—was recorded from oral sources. There are notes for each tale which enable the reader to locate and interpret it in the context of local culture. The tales, taken as a whole, contrast sharply with those found in literary sources. Different readers will discover different aspects which characterize the distinctions, and it is unnecessary to belabor this point before the tales themselves are read. The tales in this collection revolve around lived-in images and domestic scenes. They suggest interpretations in line with everyday life.

The classification scheme used is arbitrary. Such schemes always are. In this case, given the manner of collection and potential scope, it was unlikely that a "natural order" would emerge. It is doubtful that a single "emic" classification exists across the cultural and linguistic boundaries of India. It is certain that not every kind of story to be found in India is represented in this collection. Another set of ninety-nine tales might well have led us to a different pattern and a different classification.

The classification scheme does, however, have a certain natural logic. The majority of tales in the collection revolve around family relationships, and so the first five sections are based on types of family ties and on the logic of the domestic cycle. These sections separate the tales into several types of familial concerns. Each section is thematically consistent, although not always what the Western reader might expect. Two of the remaining three sections deal with personality characteristics. The final section presents origin tales, a common story type found in most cultures.

On the whole, the classification scheme we have used is not strictly geared to "what the tale is about" (usually a highly disputable claim), or to genre, or to a commonality of form. Instead, we have taken considerable liberties in order to arrange these tales in such a way as to provide the greatest insights and be most useful. The classification scheme was, in fact, decided on early in the collection process. It was based more on our intuitive feelings about Indian folk culture and society than on a firm prescience of an inherent order into which the tales would coalesce. In a sense, then, we were asking that the tales provide us with a commentary on aspects of Indian culture we felt (from altogether different sources) would be important. This is not to say, however, that we have imposed Western tale-type concepts, or even Western family concepts, on the tales. Our impetus was, rather, questions such as, "Given the universality of the family in human societies, how do Indian folktales portray this social unit? How do they characterize family bonds? What is emphasized in family relationships?"

Often several themes, motifs, family ties, personality types, and so on are found in a single tale. All tales can be related in some way to others in other categories. Many could have been placed in other sections as well as the ones in which they are found here. In such cases, we have tried to cross-reference the tales. Furthermore, we have found this classification useful and stimulating. It has served to highlight particular everyday aspects of these tales that could otherwise have been overlooked.

Other collections in the *Folktales of the World* series have notes to the tales at the end of the book. Some of the editors have restrained their remarks to matters of purely folkloristic interest (information about the narrator and tale type and motif information), while others have also included notes to help the reader interpret the tales in terms of the local culture. We favored the latter approach, but moved the cultural notes up to the body of the text and often added suggestions on how to interpret the tales which go beyond commentary on individual motifs. We utilized the note section at the end of the book to provide information about the narrators and collectors. We also placed notes concerning the translation of Indian words and the specific meaning certain images convey in that section. Tale type and motif identification is left to the tabular indices. There we provide three, rather than the usual two, lists. The first identifies type and motif information for the tales in the order that they occur in the collection, while the second and third list the tale types and motifs found in the collection in the order of the Aarne-Thompson system.

Thus, each tale in the collection is placed in context with a short introductory note. These commentaries try to address questions the reader might have about that account: Is the ending formulaic? Are the characters typical? Does the story have a deeper meaning? This discussion, in both the introductions to the sections and to the tales, covers a range of theoretical perspectives. Some editorial interpretations focus on tale structures, some on tale functions, and some on historical or cultural issues. Our range of suggestion is intended as a practical guide. Selected commentaries can be used together, therefore, as an illustration of differing interpretations or points of view.

We made our final tale selections with several factors in mind, including the need for a wide geographic spread, the collector's knowledge of the local language and general experience with folktale materials, and the willingness to submit specific story texts on schedule. Fortunately, most of our contributors were also able to meet at an all-India folklore conference that took place at the Central Institute of Indian Languages, Mysore City, in August of 1980. At that time, we held a long discussion with many persons who later became contributors to our project. That face-to-face meeting greatly helped to get the work of story collection started. Our volume now contains tales provided by eighteen different collectors, all of whom (with one exception) are still active folklorists. The exception is William Wiser, a distinguished field-worker who studied a small village in Uttar Pradesh in the 1920s. Wiser's complete fieldnotes were acquired by Susan Wadley who studied the same settlement a few years ago. Wadley's efforts to interpret Wiser's records have helped link the work of this "grandfather" figure to contemporary storytelling patterns generally.

Every effort has been made to use newly collected, well-documented materials as opposed to out-of-date or previously published tales. Indeed, the majority of accounts herein have never been published. All have been unavailable in North America.

Tribal areas and peasant groups, urban areas and remote villages, all have provided materials. North and south India, two very different subcultural areas, have been equally represented. Folktales from Kashmir, Assam, and Manipur—each a distinctive boundary region—have all found a place. Even eastern and western India can be compared, as these two sides of the subcontinent may each lay claim to having a significant presence in this collection.

The oral tale is the only genre of Indian folk material that we claim to survey. But genre boundaries are always difficult, perhaps impossible, to draw with firm authority. A few of the items tales we have chosen could be said to link this corpus to other genre categories. Several are accounts of creation, for example, or concern the origin of some particular custom. Such stories could easily be called myths. Others involve divine personages in one form or another and therefore touch on the religious domain. In India, this type of story fills great collections called *puranas,* a special name for a vast body of devotional writings. Sometimes, these more literary materials are said to represent a separate genre. Similarly, several of our very short folktales are used as jokes, while a few longer items resemble ballads or legends. For example, one story was taken from a narrative chanted by women working in the fields. Another models itself after an imagined scene in the *Mahabharata,* one of India's great epics. This present collection of folktales, therefore, has a strong genre focus without insisting on any rigid definitions. Indeed, perhaps such categories are always best understood by reference to their fuzzy boundaries. If so, this volume allows for, even encourages, typological debate.

Encounters with professional storytellers are much less common now in India than was the case in previous decades. The competition with radio and the cinema has lowered the demand for such services. Young apprentices, furthermore, are nowadays drawn to seek their niche in salaried posts. They are attracted to newer professions, based on educational achievement, which carry with them higher status. A trend away from employing bards is already well known in the West. Modern transport, a high standard of living, and the communications revolution have come more slowly to India and thus have retarded a basically similar shift in amusement tastes. Folktales, because they are told by nonprofessionals, have survived in greater profusion than have oral legends, ballads, and folk epics. Even so, folktales are becoming less popular as family recreation patterns change. Some of these traditional forms, however, now thrive in new settings. Factories have their heroic legends, companies have their myths about a founding entrepreneur, and folktales about waste baskets and locked safes circulate in bank offices. A shift in emphasis toward the joke is now occurring both in India and in the West. Tales that an average urban, educated person remembers are the short, witty ones. We have consciously included a representative selection of these in the present volume.

Written manuscripts often start with the description of a storyteller who (within that account) then begins to tell a longer tale. Oral stories, such as those contained in this collection, have no such references to tellers. Instead they use event or scene repetition to increase story depth. A similar pattern is found in many temple sculptures. These small figures which decorate the base of a major one sometimes cleverly reflect a human gesture or activity also important to the central scene. Frequently, women in such sculptures view themselves in mirrors, another way artists incorporate the important reflection theme.

One interesting feature of Indian folktales, then, is structural subtlety. Such devices are often employed instead of didactic commentaries, horrific outcomes, or bold verbal statements as ways of getting an important idea across. The model is that of epic storytelling. Each separate episode in an epic usually has a partially independent status. Yet, told in sequence, such segments pose philosophical questions, highlighting larger issues such as fate, or the parallels between various stages of human life. It is also common to find a tale within a tale. The internal story then mirrors, like a little crystal, a larger progression of events. Sometimes one even sees fate operating from the outside, and then in parallel fashion, from within.

In sum, most Indian folktales are intellectually sophisticated, philosophically rich accounts. This can be seen, in part, through the sheer number of tales where heroes and heroines use strategy to outwit their protagonists. Many tales also focus on situational logic, using such givens to the underdog's advantage. All these traits of the Indian folktale might seem to build on Brahmanical notions about the value of intellect. In fact, Brahmans bear the brunt of heavy criticism in these stories. They are the unfortunate dupes, the egotistical fools, who lose each story contest. Cunning, rather than outright intellect, is thus a key concept. It provides the subversive undercurrent, a hidden power which often enables lower ranking persons to triumph. In general, the losers are hereditary priests, powerful landlords, influential kinsmen, or wealthy rulers. Many Indian folktales, furthermore, contain trickster characters. Some of these take on an animal form and some take on a human form. This great emphasis on cunning or intelligence, furthermore, is neatly balanced by the position of the fool. The Indian corpus is full of "numskull" stories, tales that highlight the importance of clear reasoning through a comical insistence on its blatant absence.

Women's roles in these folktales also deserve special note. Females frequently appear in semimagical roles, employing some kind of disguise. Often they shift back and forth between human, vegetal, animal, and divine forms. Key female characters, furthermore, are often like tricksters in that they hold underdog positions. Many triumph against great odds (for example, against less virtuous women) by combining selflessness with moral courage and religious dedication. Like tricksters, these heroines often are in touch with extrahuman forces. Thus they are closely linked to other realms of being. Women are also not cast in fools' roles very often. That indignity is left to men. Specific caste identities, too, are generally defined by male figures. Women, by contrast, project more universal roles. They are known by their femaleness in general rather than by their specific position in life. Their basic sexual identity is also often linked to hidden psychological strengths, to their willingness to act on impulse, and to their courage to stick to their personal convictions. Females come through as influential figures in these tales. They are not the milksop characters some suggest Indian women to be.

Untouchable and outcaste roles are absent from this tale collection, though Brahman figures are prevalent. The two ends of India's social hierarchy, therefore, are unequally portrayed. The overall perspective, as in most folk literature, takes existence for persons with lowly callings very much for granted. The thrust of these tales is upward; more fun can be had symbolically unseating the high and mighty than by describing the lot of the poor. If humbleness is the issue, a person's specific caste status always seems to be vague. It is not an individual of a specific caste, but rather the generalized hard worker who attains a wished-for prosperity in the end. In keeping with this theme, most of these tales end happily. The morally better characters are the ones who succeed most often.

Like other universal human characteristics, truthfulness, modesty, loyalty, courage, generosity, and honest effort are greatly valued in these folktales. The cultural uniqueness of this collection, then, will come across to readers in subtle ways. Newcomers to Indian folklore are encouraged to enjoy the flavor of each story, noting the great range of tale motifs presented and the many distinct narrative styles employed. While important abstract issues can be discussed by using these materials, the individual color and detail embedded in each story is what counts most. Each tale should be savored as an experience in itself.

BRENDA E. F. BECK
PETER J. CLAUS

Part I
Suitors and Maidens

*I*NDIAN FOLKTALES make the period of courtship romantic and exciting. Such interest is universal, but the widespread practice of arranged marriage in South Asia tends to heighten the strong sense of fantasy that surrounds amorous adventures. Indeed, only one story in this section (tale 5) has a relatively practical and down-to-earth lover as its hero. Significantly, that is also the only story from an area of the subcontinent (a small part of Nagaland) where premarital sexual experimentation is condoned. All the other seekers described here, male or female, are either nonhuman or control extrahuman powers.

All these lovers are courageous in confronting social norms. Several suffer painfully or even lose their lives attempting to challenge the status quo. Some succeed, but never without cleverness or some magical aid. In other words, the love object sought is always guarded and hard to obtain. The suitor's task is to overcome all manner of obstacles. Furthermore, the common goal of these arduous attempts is always marriage. Only one of these seven stories does not mention that great event. It, too, is from Assam, and even that tale involves a symbolic joining of lovers, only this time it is through their simultaneous death.

Temporary affairs have a much more humorous status in Indian folklore than do romantic love and marriage. That kind of story appears in our collection under a different section heading: marital strife. Sexually adventurous demons also frequent Indian folktales. They can be of either sex but always have a cross-sex preference in their selection of love objects. In such cases, furthermore, the courtship is strictly unidirectional, and outright aggression dominates. Also, persons who are objects of demonic affection generally escape unharmed. Unlike the folktales in this section, demons embody perversity and thus help confirm the importance of ordinary social norms. True lovers are never so twisted or so immoral. Instead, Indian romantic tales subtly challenge social givens by pointing to overly rigid boundaries that govern day-to-day events.

It is important to note that romantic attraction is often linked to natural imagery in Indian folktales. Thus our first three tales concern a river, a tree spirit, and the thunder-lightening bond respectively. Each has strong expressive overtones and points to hidden powers or to superhuman bonding mechanisms. These stories also share the theme of love and death and, through that imagery, depict subsequent transformations of being. A river looses its force and the sea its resistance, for example, when they join. Similarly, to cross the divide between what is human and what is not, a tree and a girl must first lose their lives. A handsome prince and a hunter's daughter reject their earthly differences when they merge electrically in the sky. What ordinary life holds separate, therefore, secret sympathies and hidden powers rush to unite.

Another pair of tales contrasts with these first three by exhibiting relative realism. One concerns a traditional marriage right, the other a traditional behavioral norm. In the first, a sage's ritual power helps reassert the equal status of two related families after their social balance has been threatened by increasing differences in wealth. Thus, an impoverished suitor manages to win the hand of the prosperous bride against a moneyed rival. Following this is a second tale where two potential brides, one rich and one poor, compete for the hand of the same groom. Again the poorer contestant wins, this time by establishing superiority over her wealthy opponent by using a straightforward manner and plain honesty.

The final three tales placed in this section all depict a woman who must choose between several male lovers. Each illustrates the female's important role in determining the outcome of a courtship sequence. In the first tale an attractive bride waits too long, so that excessive self-esteem eventually leaves her a spinster. In two others a woman chooses her eventual life-style in other ways. In the first she consults her father, in the second she makes her choice alone. In all three stories, however, the spatial placement of each of the main characters plays a special role. Thus ritual considerations, even those due to chance, serve as effective social levelers. After all, romance is a game of chance. Physical and psychic attractions are mysterious forces which often force parental and social logic to retreat.

· 1 · The Goddess of Mahi River (Gujarat)

This tale is a kind of origin story. It portrays the great Mahi river of Gujarat as a goddess who boldly sets off from her father, the Satpura hills, to find a lover in the sea. Like many Indian goddesses, Mahi is a lovely but fierce young girl. She has a warrior personality and an independent temperament. This associates her with the women of the forest or tribal areas, and by implication sets her in opposition to the more placid and submissive women of the plains. Her dark complexion also fits this ensemble of associations. Unable to convince her heart's desire to accept her on her first visit, she later returns to the sea with an army of pebbles to wage war. She wins her battle but is tamed into submission in the process, never to be a fierce goddess again. Mahi's military style reminds one of the popular Hindu dieties, Durga and Kali. This local tale, therefore, fits with much wider mythical traditions. But the theme of her being tamed through marriage also reminds one of other stories. The goddess Minakshi of Madurai, for example, is said to have been tamed through her marriage to a local form of Lord Siva. Finally, it is significant that the goddess in this tale is a river. This waterway flows between her parental home in the mountains and her place of marriage, the sea, much as a human would move between her natal and nuptial families in real life.

THE EASTERN PART of Gujarat contains a lovely area known as the Satpura hills. The Mahi river flows out of these hills and is said to be their daughter. This watercourse flows down toward the central area of the state. The hills themselves are often spoken of as a kind of parental house for the river. The Mahi is wide and strong. It is also somewhat blackish in color. The hills, too, are dark colored, and they serve as a home for the Dharala, Bhil, Baraiya, and Patanwadi tribes. These people are known for their dark complexion. So too, the Mahi river is seen to be a dark-skinned girl.

People say that when the Mahi river first matured she wanted to marry the sea. Because this river is a woman of Herculean strength and strong will, she left no path untried in her efforts to

5

fulfil her cherished desire. However, Mahi's father, the Satpura hills, never favored such a wedding for his daughter. Unsympathetic, he did not even try to understand the reasoning of his willful daughter. Still, Mahi was an independent woman. So she ultimately left her father's house to fulfil her heart's desire on her own. First she traveled to the West in her attempt to embrace the sea. The way was strewn with thorns and stones, and she had to pass through many jungles. She met ferocious tigers and leopards. Still, Mahi longed for the sea. Along the way she met the Gulf of Cambay. Dissatisfied and still eager to meet her true lover, she began to dream about him. Then she continued her search, crossing the rocky lands of eastern Gujarat and showing the energy and spirit of a true jungle maiden. Mahi was confident that she would finally be warmly welcomed by her lover and embraced by the arms of the sea.

By the time the river finally found the sea, however, she was exhausted. Her face was covered with dust and she had a strange, dark look. Beads of perspiration dropped from her forehead. Seeing this dark-complexioned maiden, the sea turned his face away. He rejected the offer of marriage. So the Mahi river, being a woman who valued self-respect, left the house of her lover in anger. She recrossed the dusty, thorny, and stony regions of Gujarat with great speed. Daring this wild and hazardous course once again, she returned to her father's house as quickly as she could. Now she entered her home with a sad look on her face. Seeing this her father tried to comfort her saying, "Oh pupil, the center of my eye, do not look so dejected! Turn your face toward me and tell me what you have experienced. Do not hold back any details." Hearing the soft words of her father, tears began to roll from the eyes of the Mahi river. These droplets looked like dew on the cotton leaves in the hills on a sunny morning. But the river concealed her mind. She asked her father only for an army to wage war against her lover. Her father tried his best to calm his daughter's wrath but he did not succeed. When he questioned her, she simply replied, "Father! If you love me, if you at least feel sympathy for me in your heart, then lend me your army."

Finally the hill-father made up his mind to assist his daughter, and he put his army at her disposal. The Mahi river was extremely pleased. She now led her warriors and marched back through the jungles like the commander of an invading force.

First she crossed Madhya Pradesh, a state in central India, and then she entered the Gujarat hills. Next she passed through a large area of rocky land and approached the sea. Finally she called out, "Oh, Lord of the sea waters, be ready with your army! Open your arms and accept my challenge of war." The stones of the Mahi river were now in an excited mood. Their din and the sound of their movements terrified the sea. The Mahi river, on the other hand, had confidence in her army. She looked forward to the battle. But she had a surprise. The sea soon surrendered unconditionally. He married her, and her army of stones was laid to rest in the bed of the river, forever.

· 2 ·   *The Girl Who Was Loved by a Tree Spirit*
        (Nagaland)

This touching Naga love story compares nicely with the preceding tale. Both are about the dual identity of a passionate lover. In the first case the seeker was a daughter, the lovely river Mahi, who seeks union with the sea. Her double personality, both watery and human, is evident throughout the tale. By contrast, the seeker is male in this case. If anything, his dual identity as a tree spirit and a man is even more explicit. Furthermore, the secret sympathy between these two worlds of being finds support in the tale outcome. A dual death joins the loving couple and surrounds them with a masterful blend of physical and emotional images. If the flowing and babbling of a river is seen as female, so the shape of the tree here blends with that of the man. His body becomes the trunk, his arms the limbs, and his hair the leaves. Tale 41 features a woman who can transform herself into a tree, but she is more passive. In that account another person must pour water over her to achieve each transformation. The tree described here finds itself at the scene of a girl's daily bath. This erotic scenario is generally very popular in Indian mythology.

IN CHUNGLIYIMTI VILLAGE there once lived a beautiful girl, the daughter of a rich family. Many young men came to her dormitory (*morung*) at night to court her. But she gave all her attention to one particular young man, the most handsome of them all. He came to her every night and went away before dawn. But he could never be found during the daytime. The girl looked for him among the village bachelors in the fields, in people's private houses, and in many other places. But her search was always in vain. At last she reported her experiences to her father and mother. On the advice of her parents, she tied a new *dao* belt around her lover's waist one night. He departed with it at the usual time. To the girl's surprise, when she went out for a walk the next morning, she found the *dao* belt tied around a tree that was standing below her house near the bank of a stream. The family now began to suspect that the young man was not a human being at all but the spirit of that tree.

To confirm their suspicions, the girl put an indigo-dyed shawl on the man's shoulders the following night in the same manner as she had tied the dao on him during his previous visit. He departed as usual. In the morning they found that same shawl hanging from a forked branch of the special tree. It stood near the edge of a well where the girl often went for water. Then the daughter remembered that she had gone to that well often during the period of courtship with her lover. She had washed her hands, and legs, and face daily and had liked to sing as she bathed. She now remembered that the branches of the tree above her used to move up and down, as if blown by the wind, whenever she came to that spot and realized that the spirit of this particular tree had come to court her in the form of a handsome bachelor.

The girl's father soon decided to see these mysterious happenings for himself and so kept a watch one night outside the girl's dormitory. When the stranger left before dawn, he secretly followed him. Instead of going to the young men's dormitory, as all the other youths did, this man went straight to the stream. There he stood at the side of the well and quickly transformed himself into an ordinary tree. His body turned into the trunk, his arms into branches, and his hair into leaves. And behold, there stood a big tree in place of the youth!

The father then decided to cut this mysterious tree down. He called the villagers together and asked their help in felling it, after telling the whole story to explain his concern. He also asked his daughter to remain inside the house, just in case anything dangerous happened. The men cut and cut, but the tree would not fall. And as they chopped, a small chip of wood flew toward the girl's house. At that very moment the girl was watching the cutters by peeping through a small hole in the wall. The flying wood chip entered the hole and struck her in the eye. It moved with such speed that it damaged her brain and the girl died instantly.

At the same moment that the girl fell to the floor, the tree also fell with a huge crash. The father was now happy. He came home rejoicing, relieved at the thought that the tree spirit would no longer chase and haunt his lovely daughter. To his utter shock and horror, he found his daughter dead. The two lovers had died together.

· 3 · *The Rain Prince's Bride (Gujarat)*

As Western commentators have often mentioned, Indians have a "desire-dread" attitude toward the rains. Some years the monsoons will pass over a given region without yielding a single drop. On these occasions the hopes of the farmers wither with the crops in their fields. Other years, in the same region, awesome storms wash away house and field. Max Müller made much of the "mythopoeic" way the ancient Indians personified storms in their Vedic hymns (Müller 1907). While not necessarily adhering to this view, the idea that one can witness the birth of primitive religion in such events, this story does illustrate that folk literature continues to involve human relationships in natural events.

ONCE UPON A TIME, a poor man lived with his wife and daughter in the heart of a dense forest. He was so poor that he could not support his family. He roamed the forest from dawn till dusk searching for food. His daughter was very beautiful, in radiant health, and very smart as well. She worried about her father wandering all day in the forest. He would rise very early in the morning and return late in the evening, exhausted from his search for food. Whenever she saw his tired face, wrinkled from worries and concern, she was moved with pity. She wondered how she could be of help to him.

One morning, as the father left the hut with his bow and arrows to go to the forest to hunt, the daughter decided to follow him without his knowing about it. But once in the forest the father moved quickly and stealthily. Soon he blended with the forest so that she lost sight of him. The daughter lost her way, yet she walked on and on until she was exhausted. Then she rested under the shade of a huge Mahua tree, gazed around, and to her surprise she saw a vast field of maize. The ripe kernels shone like pearls in the sun. Her heart danced with joy. The girl leapt to her feet and ran toward the field. There she saw two old men working the soil. Astonished, she approached them and inquired, "What a fine harvest! How do you grow this crop? It is so wonderful."

The old men looked up and replied, "First we remove the trees and then we cultivate with a hoe for several days. Later we plant the seeds and finally we harvest the crop." "Is it so? Such a marvelous crop?" she asked again and again. "It is so," they replied, "and why not? The forest is very fertile. Only there must be no trees on the land you wish to plant." So saying, the men resumed their work.

The young girl was delighted with the knowledge the farmers had given her. She made up her mind that when she got home she would clear a small piece of land in the forest and cultivate maize herself. This was how she could help ease her father's burden. When she eventually found her way home, she told her mother what the farmers had taught her. She asked her parents to make a small plot near the cabin for cultivation. So, the next morning, father and daughter went into the forest with an axe, selected a piece of land, and cut down all of the trees and shrubs. They spent the next few days clearing this land for sowing. The daughter looked anxiously toward the sky for clouds. Without rain all of their work would be for nothing.

On the day set aside for sowing, the girl came to the small field. In the sky she saw many clouds. She was overjoyed. She waited for many hours as these clouds passed by, hoping one of them would rain on their farm. But instead of rain, she saw a young man emerge from the forest. His bearing and his dress were that of a prince. Seeing him, the girl's heart danced with excitement. She had never encountered such a handsome man. "Why do you look toward the sky?" he asked as he approached her. "I need rain for my field. The rain brings rich harvests," she replied.

"And what will you give me if I bring you rain?" the prince asked her. She did not know what to say. "Will you marry me?" he asked, finally. "With pleasure," she replied, blushing. "You are a handsome man; I love you from the bottom of my heart." "I will leave, now, and within an hour's time a cloud will come which will give water to your farm. But you must remember your promise to marry me," said the prince. The girl thanked the prince and renewed her promise. "But," the prince added, "I must warn you. My appearance is not always as you see it now, at the beginning of the rainy season. At other times I am quite ugly and fearsome. Will you not be afraid to look at me then?" "No," said the girl, "I will always love you." "So much the better," said the prince. "But there is yet one more condition. Wherever I go, you will have to guide me. Do you accept this?" "I swear I shall," replied the girl. "If you fail me, it will cost you your life," warned the prince. And with that he left. Within an hour's time it rained heavily on the field. The girl was overjoyed and happily thought of the seeds they would sow the next day and of the harvest they would reap.

As she worked in the field the next day her prince emerged from the forest in his finest clothes. She smiled at him and asked that she be allowed to bid goodbye to her mother before they left together. Having said her farewells, she went with the prince. He took her skyward on the wings of clouds to where his own home lay. They lived there together in happiness and pleasure. But, after some days, when the young bride was asleep the prince took on a new and horrible appearance. The girl awoke to see a naked man, with mud on his arms. His skin was crawling with scorpions and snakes and other terrible creatures. The man's hair flew to and fro. His eyes were red. Seeing him she became faint with fear. Thinking that her reaction to his fearsome form was a breach of her promise, the man took his knife and plunged it into her

breast. As he did so, the girl streaked across the sky as a flash of
lightning. He followed her as thunder. And thus they became the
Lord of Rain and the Queen of Lightning.

· 4 · *A Farmer's Son*
     (Tamilnadu)

This story provides a third example of a tale about groom selection. It depicts the customary claim, expressed in a ritual, that
some men have over marriageable female relatives, in particular
their elder sisters' daughters. This is not only a legitimate form
of marriage in many areas of southern India, it is a preferred
form (see also tale 8). Several other issues are also treated
openly. For one, the potential groom is clearly poor, while the
sister and her daughter are well-to-do. Yet most Indians feel
that siblings should remain relative equals throughout life. This
is one reason given for the ritualistic claims described. Such
marriage rights help counteract the development of economic or
social discrepancies. As is typical in real life, the parents of the
rich girl in this tale at first want to find a groom of high status.
Hence they ignore the mother's brother. With the help of a
magical ascetic figure met in a wasteland or semisacred area,
however, the maternal uncle in the story finally gains access to
special powers that allow him to assert his true marriage rights.
He does this at the wedding ceremony itself, which is typical in
such tales. The high status groom must now back down in favor
of the poor man's prior claim. Weddings often provide the
setting where such disputes get adjudicated. The guests are
present to testify to any accord that is reached, and the rituals
never proceed until things are finalized. This places a final
stamp of sacred authority on any key decisions.

A VILLAGE. In it there lived a farmer, his son, and his daughter.
The daughter was married and had a girl of her own. The mother
of this girl was very rich, but her brother was not well off. He had
to tend the sheep that belonged to his father. After a time the
sister's daughter matured, and it was time for her marriage. But

because her mother's brother was so poor the family settled on a different groom. The day of the wedding was set.

It was the rainy season and the boy was grazing his sheep. Each day he would carry a noon meal with him and return home at about five in the evening. One day it rained, so he took off his lower cloth and put it in the empty pot in which he had carried his food. He then turned this pot upside down and stood in the rain wearing only a tiny loin cloth. After the downpour stopped he took his cloth out of the pot and used it as a towel. He then put it on. A little later the boy met an ascetic with long hair. He was also wandering in this forested area. The ascetic was amazed at the shepherd, for the young boy looked dry while he, himself, was shivering and wet. So the ascetic said, "How is it that I have learned so many magical verses and yet I get wet while you stand here quite dry?"

The shepherd boy answered, "If you teach me your magical verses, I will teach you my secret in return. But you must first help me with my problem. I have a sister who has refused to let me marry her daughter. She says I am too poor." The ascetic agreed to help. He taught the boy a magical verse and gave him three stones. Then he said, "When you throw the first stone the marriage will be prevented. When you throw the second stone everyone will sit still. When you throw the third stone everyone will be fed." The shepherd boy tied the three stones in his lower cloth. In return he told the ascetic how he had kept himself dry in the rain.

Two days before the wedding was to take place an invitation arrived from the boy's sister. He decided to go. So he set off, taking the three stones with him. As the crowd gathered for the ceremonies the boy sat down in the audience. A Brahman arrived and performed the necessary rituals. The bridegroom lifted the wedding necklace. But at this very moment the boy threw his first stone saying, "This wedding must be prevented." The crowd gasped. Everyone wondered why. Then they realized that the bride was not being given to the groom who could rightfully demand her. Soon the father of the girl announced that he would instead give his daughter to his wife's brother, the man who had a right to demand her. He then called the shepherd boy forward. Soon the former bridegroom left the bride's side and the rightful

groom took his place. Next the boy threw his second stone saying, "No one may move." Not a person stirred from their seat.
Then the boy tied the lovely wedding necklace on the bride.
Finally the boy threw his third stone and said, "All the guests
shall be fed." So the wedding was completed and the new groom
and his wife lived together happily.

· 5 ·   The Man Who Was in Love with Two Girls (Nagaland)

This story depicts a clever lover who sets out to test the character of two would-be brides. The contrast between these
women is cast in a rich-poor framework common to many Indian folktales. The rich girl turns out to be deceitful, gluttonous,
and selfish, while the poor one is honest and straightforward.
Not surprisingly, she wins the hidden contest. This outcome,
which favors the underdog, does not set this story apart. However, the poor girl is also a self-confident woman, an unusual
quality for most Indian men to seek in a bride. In other ways,
too, this tale is atypical. For one thing, the man selects a bride
by himself. He also subjects a series of females to his own tests,
without reference to parental wishes or to more formal customs
of marriage arrangement. Furthermore, he is able to take wom-
en alone to a riverbank for a picnic and to serve them wine and
meat. All these actions would appear socially unrealistic (even
immoral) to most Indian audiences. But the giveaway clue to
this story's origin is the presence of a male dormitory (*morung*)
for adolescent youths. There is also one reference to couples
sleeping together before marriage. These customs are practiced
in some parts of Nagaland but would be considered shocking
elsewhere on the subcontinent. Hence this tale helps to define
the boundaries of a Hindu India culture area by highlighting its
outer limits.

AT ONE TIME there lived a young man in a certain village who
was in love with two girls at the same time. One woman was
from a rich family and the other from a very poor one. The man

was both smart and handsome. Both girls wanted to marry him and he could not make up his mind. Finally he decided to test their characters and to choose the one who came out best.

One day the man took both girls to a river. He said they would go fishing and have some small refreshments, a kind of picnic. After doing a little work in the fields near the riverbank he invited both girls to sit down. He asked them to accept some wine which he had brought along and urged them to drink as much as they could. The rich girl picked up a small bamboo leaf, folded it into a conical shape, and put a few drops of wine in this container. She then drank with style and told her friend that she had been completely satisfied by these few drops of wine. But the poor girl drank freely. She took as much as she could, and she told her friend that she could have drunk even more if she had wanted to. Meanwhile the rich girl laughed at the greediness of her poor companion.

After a while it was time for the midday meal. The young man then told his two girlfriends to eat some of the rice and meat which he had brought along. He asked each to take as much as she could and to enjoy herself. The rich girl ate only one handful of rice and a very small piece of meat. But the poor girl ate a very large helping and took as much as was available. In this way the two girls spent their day in the company of one another.

In the evening the young man took the two girls back home and pretended to go to his own male sleeping quarters. But instead of going to the adolescent dormitory, he quietly went back to the rich girl's house. There he hid in a dark corner and found a way to look through a hole in a wall. The rich girl had reached home very tired and very hungry. As soon as she arrived, she asked her parents to give her a meal of rice. Not satisfied with using her own hands, she then asked her mother to put rice into her mouth for her. Her mother began to feed her like a baby. But the girl's hunger was not satisfied by the rice alone. So she asked her father and mother to feed her boiled arum roots. Both were kept busy peeling the skin of these roots and placing them one by one in her mouth, as if she were a baby bird in a nest. She also drank a huge quantity of wine, emptying an entire pot that normally kept all the members of the family satisfied. She was behaving like a small child. Unknown to her, her lover was watch-

ing throughout this period. For every mouthful of rice she ate,
her lover picked up a handful of sand and placed it in a large cloth
that he had brought with him. For every piece of arum root the
girl ate, he also picked up a small pebble and placed this in his
makeshift sack. After the meal he left silently, carrying his heavy
load with him.

The next night the young man met both his girlfriends, together with a large group of other girls and boys. They had all
come to his dormitory where the young men and young women
sometimes slept together. In the company of these many youths
the young man opened his sack. As he laid out his large collection
he asked, "Is there anyone in the group who can eat as much rice
and arum root as I have sand and stones?" The rich girl quickly
answered, "Ah! My goodness! Who could possibly eat such quantity of food? I think it must be impossible for any human being to
eat so much. For myself I could scarcely eat a handful of what is
there." Then the poor girl replied shyly, "Had I had such an
opportunity I could eat at least that much. Indeed I believe I
could eat even more." The other girls in the group each gave an
opinion in turn. But the young man was only interested in the
answers of the first two women. He did not pay much attention
to the other replies. He then left the dormitory and said goodbye
to the girls. The following day the young man chose the poor girl
to be his bride. He had been greatly pleased by her straightforward, frank and open manner. She had passed his test.

· 6 · *Love between Two Birds*
       (Nagaland)

This next tale (like tale 2) is from the Ao, a tribe in northern
Nagaland. It also describes lovers, but here they are separate
species of birds. The story has a clear moral to it, namely that a
young and beautiful girl should not pass up adolescent oppor-
tunities to make a good marriage. Later, as a less attractive
older woman, she may lose her bargaining powers and live to
regret her youthful indecision. Indeed, this story goes so far as
to make an unwed old maid the laughingstock of other birds.

Several additional symbolic details are also quite prominent. The most handsome lover lives on top of the highest tree, while the old and rejected woman prefers to burrow in the ground. She lives in the roots of small shrubs and plants, or even in a heap of weeds. The male gradually blossoms into a fine singer, while the female reaps a lifelong harvest of humiliation due to one youthful moment of excessive pride. The story also has poignancy in the way it projects human emotions onto various birds. Its overt purpose is to explain why two particular species have such distinct nesting habits. In this sense it is a "just-so" story. Though not the exclusive property of tribal groups, such origin tales are particularly popular among those who inhabit India's more forested and remote areas.

THE LITTLE BUTTON QUAIL was once a beautiful bird. She was a charming young thing with a voice that soon had all the young male birds excited. One by one they came and asked to marry her. But the button quail became so proud that she refused them all. She kept her nest to herself, choosing to live in a short tree located near the rice paddies of a particular local farmer.

At last a young barbet, just reaching adulthood, came down from a high branch in the nearby forest. This barbet also began to court the button quail. But he had just come out of his nest-hole and was not very trim or attractive. His feathers were not fully grown and his voice did not yet have the practiced pitch of a fine singer. Meanwhile, the cute little quail found it a humiliation to be courted by such an ugly male bird. She treated her suitor very badly and flatly rejected his offer of marriage. She told him outright that he looked ugly, that he was untrim, and that he was unsuitable for someone of her elevated status.

So the young barbet returned to his forest nest full of sadness. Nonetheless, within a few weeks his feathers grew out fully and his green color became so bright that he outshone even the fresh leaves on the evergreen trees. Now the barbet recovered from his grief. Indeed, one day he began singing just for the joy of it. He also hopped from branch to branch on the top of a very tall tree. This meant that his voice could be heard throughout the countryside. It broke the silence and the tranquillity of the rice fields and even penetrated the surrounding wilderness.

When the tiny quail heard this lovely song she looked up from her lower perch and found her rejected lover looking so resplendent that she changed her mind about his courtship. Indeed, she now fell in love. She found the barbet's voice so enchanting that she longed to hear it over and over again. But at the same time all the other female barbets also began enjoying this new male presence. They too began singing from their respective nests, each one trying to make her voice more beautiful than the next. Each wanted the handsome male to notice her. The little button quail also sang loudly, inviting the barbet to court her. But the emerald barbet now spoke frankly. His words were, "It is too late." The tiny quail felt ashamed of what she had done and covered her face in despair.

Within a short period the marriageable age for the button quail passed. No more birds came to ask for her hand. Now she was willing to marry any bird at all, no matter how lowly or ugly he might be. But no male was interested in her. Instead the birds, and even the insects, regularly began to humiliate her. They spoke about her foolishness and she became the laughingstock of her generation. The little quail no longer dared to fly in the air because of her shame. At last, however, she found a small heap of vegetation that a farmer had forgotten in the midst of his rice plants. She now built a new nest there, below the weeds. This place was covered from the view of other birds and was well hidden among the paddy plants.

The little quail was confident that no one could find her in her new nest. She thus hoped to save herself from further humiliation. But a grasshopper, whose eyes looked in every direction, soon found her and loudly sang this song:

Oh foolish button quail, oh short-tree nester,
Here is the bird who refused to be a treetop dweller
But instead built her nest on the solid ground,
Under the farmer's pile of weeds.

So to this day the Ao people say that the little button quail can be found only in the rice fields, where her nest lies beneath the roots of weeds. This little quail roams under the paddy plants and around small shrubs. But it never flies in the air above, since it

feels shy in the presence of other birds and animals. The elegant
barbet, on the other hand, is a treetop dweller. He can be found
singing on the highest branches of the tallest trees. The fine barbet regularly makes its existence known through its song, even
the wretched quail who lives below it on the ground must listen
to it.

· 7 · Four Clever Men (Tamilnadu)

Tale 5, from Nagaland, described a groom's test of the personalities of several potential brides. The next two stories reverse
this situation and describe various means of deciding between
grooms. Significantly, perhaps, both focus on the ingenuity or
magical skills of the groom rather than on his psychological or
social traits. They also make a man's social and physical placement in life key factors in determining the outcome of events.
In the first tale, four very skilled men join together as suitors of
a king's daughter. Despite the obvious potential for trouble, all
four men cooperate in trying to win the girl. In this they behave
like brothers. Finally, the girl's father steps in and assigns each
man a ritual position. The bride's choice of the man standing in
front of her thus occurs in cooperation with her father's wishes.
It is somewhat surprising that the groom chosen is the elderly
suitor in the group. However, there are also subtle images associated with the skills of each man which make the elder one the
likely choice. The physical prowess of the other men make them
ideal consanguineal kin, but the man who can find the beautiful
flower, an image associated with femininity in many other tales
(see tales 41 and 44), is the better choice for a husband. The
story was told by a professional bard, and the imagery it contains is highly traditional. Readers are encouraged to contrast
these features with parallel details in the following tale. A comparison with tale no. 13 is also suggested.

A KING ONCE SAID to his wife, "I can shoot an arrow so straight
that it will hit a man in the middle of his forehead. I can bring

down crows, small birds, and even little ground animals with my
bow. No one can match me for skill in archery." "Oh, come, my
lord," answered his wife. "there must be many men in the world
as skilled with a bow and arrow as you are." "All right. If you say
so, let me see if I can find them." Saying this, the king set off in
search of an equal, taking some cold rice tied in a cloth with him.

After the king had walked a short distance, he found a man
lying on his back in the middle of the path. He had his bow
drawn and his arrow aimed at the sky. "Hey! What are you doing
there?" cried out the king. "What could possibly be grazing in
the sky?" "There are a male and a female deer up there," he
answered, "and the female is pregnant with two fawns. One fetus
is male and the other is female. I can hit the female with my
arrow without damaging the male." "Well, I guess you are as
clever as I am," said the king. "I want to continue my search. Let
us see if together we can find a third man as skillful as we two
are." So the two men began traveling together.

A short while later the two men came to a big riverbed, but
there was no water to be seen. Then they found a man standing at
a distance and holding the water back with one big toe as he
brushed his teeth. "My goodness," exclaimed the king. "There is
a man as clever as we are. We are all three clever men." So the
three men joined together and set off in search of a fourth. After a
time, in another area, these three wanderers came across an old
man carrying a lovely flower. "Hey, old man! Hey grandfather,"
they called. "Where did you find that lovely flower to pick?" "I
found it in a country that stretches from where the sun rises to
where the sun sets," replied the stranger. The three travelers
agreed that the old man was clever too. So all four men decided to
stay together. One could shoot a man in the middle of the forehead, another could shoot a fawn in the womb of a deer, a third
could hold back a river with his big toe and the fourth knew
where to find an extraordinarily beautiful flower. All four now
admitted that they wanted to impress a lovely girl with their
cleverness and eventually marry her. They then heard about such
a girl, the daughter of a king, and they set off together for her
father's palace.

As the four clever men approached the house of the bride-to-be
they were stopped. The man who met them said, "He who wins

her hand will have to bring with him a very special flower." The old man in the group said "I can do that," and the king quickly sent him off on a quest. The other three men stayed behind. The old man traveled alone from country to country. Finally he found a lovely lotus flower with a five-headed cobra asleep on its leaves. He went and carefully lifted up the plant, cobra and all. But as he started his return journey, the smell of the flower made the old man dizzy and he lay down for a nap. As he slept, the cobra woke up and awaited some movement so that he might bite the man. The cobra was the flower's faithful guardian.

Meanwhile, the old man's three friends waited at the king's palace. When their companion did not return they began to worry. Then the fellow who could hold back a river with his big toe claimed that he could also see things at a distance. So he closed his eyes and soon saw the old man asleep under a tree. He could also see a cobra lying beside the man just waiting to bite him. Next the fellow who could shoot a deer in the sky drew his bow. His arrow flew through the air and landed on the cobra. There was a great sound. The cobra died and the old man awoke with a start. He then made his way back to his three friends, carrying the lovely flower. They greeted the old man and the four set off to present the king with their beautiful plant. The king took the flower, and in return he presented his daughter to the four men.

As the king handed over his daughter, the four friends began to fight. Who would have the girl? So the king broke up the argument. He said, "Stop fighting. Go and bathe. When you come back you are each to take your place next to my daughter. The man who can shoot and hit the center of a man's forehead is to stand in back of her. The man who can hold a river back with his big toe is to stand on her left side. The man who can lie on his back and shoot a fawn in the sky is to stand on her right side. The man who brought the flower from a faraway place is to stand in front of her."

The four men went to bathe. When they returned they each took up their assigned place. But then they began to fight all over again. This time the girl herself interrupted the argument. She said, "He who stands behind me is my father. He who stands on either side is like a brother. And he who stands in front of me shall be my husband." Having said this, the girl took the old

man who had brought the flower as her husband. The three other
men each returned home. The old man and the girl then left
together and lived happily with one another.

· 8 · *A Poor Man*
          (Tamilnadu)

This next story is a modernized version of the previous tale. It
was told by a thirteen-year-old village girl during a story-swap-
ping session in the collector's home. The two tellers concerned
are from very distant villages, from different castes, of opposite
sex, and of different ages. Each generated the story without
prompting. It is, therefore, interesting to note certain parallels
and shifts in emphasis. In this tale there are three suitors, not
four, and they are real brothers. As in the last story, the men
cooperate to woo a girl. This tale is much shorter, perhaps
reflecting the inexperience of a young teller. It also focuses on a
traditional marriage partner, an elder sister's daughter, rather
than on an exotic princess. According to the social traditions of
this particular region, all three men have a special ritual claim
on this niece. Their rights are reflected in their magical ability
to restore the girl to life after her death. When the men arrange
themselves around her, as in the previous story, the bride again
chooses the man who will face her (as she stands up). The theme
of having parents at one's back and siblings at one's side thus
provides continuity with the previous tale, but this time the
young girl makes her decision without the intervention of a
father (a choice that might, in part, reflect the age and sex of
the tale teller). Her choice of the senior man now reflects his
strong claim on her as the eldest sibling, not as a display of
special skills. This story is also more materialistic than the last
in that each potential groom is asked to bring an object worth
"a thousand rupees." The introduction of an airplane, alongside
the magic carpet, also gives it a special contemporary flavor.

A VILLAGE. In it there lived a poor man with three sons and one
daughter. The daughter was married and had a daughter of her

own. Soon all three sons went to their sister's home to ask for the hand of their niece in marriage. The young niece replied, "Each of you must bring me something worth a thousand rupees. I promise to marry the man whose gift I like the best." The youngest brother returned after some time with an airplane. The eldest brother brough a magic mirror. And the middle brother brought a magic carpet. Looking into the magic mirror, the three men knew their niece was doomed to die because they could see her being carried to the graveyard on a funeral bier. A little later the three men arrived at her funeral in the airplane. Then all three men stood by her side. The eldest brother placed himself near her legs. The middle brother waited near her head. And the youngest brother stood by her side. Then the three men brought the girl back to life using their magic carpet. As she revived she said to the three, "The one nearest my head is my father. The one nearest my side is my brother. And the one at my feet is my husband."

Part II
New Brides and Grooms

MARRIAGES in most parts of India are arranged by family elders. Brides and grooms often have never talked to one another and sometimes have never even seen one another until the beginning of their marriage ceremony. The Westerner, who increasingly feels that marriage must be based on prior love and familiarity, often wonders how an Indian can enter such an important relationship without knowing exactly what he or she is getting into. From our perspective, we might expect tales about new brides and grooms to revolve around anxiety over the unknown. Actually, only two tales even suggest this problem. In tale 9 the groom is married to a girl fated to die by snakebite, but he was made aware of this fact by the bride's father before the nuptial ceremony occurred. Only in tale 10 is the strange character of the bride revealed after her marriage is consummated, and in this case the marriage was not an arranged one but one of free choice.

So, instead of looking at these tales with Western expectations, let us see what the texts reveal in their own statements. One theme which runs through all of these accounts is separation. Life presents many hardships, and various forces tend to pull a married couple apart. The next section contains tales describing domestic strife. A complex web of family relationships sometimes brings about estrangement as a result of internal jealousies, rivalries, and quarrels. The tales in this section, by contrast, often begin with the separation of husband

and wife through no fault of their own and then confront the
probabilities of eventual reunion.

   The forces which separate loving couples are often the result
of natural causes. All but three tales involve the death of a
spouse, and there is a common underlying pattern. In tale 9 it is
the wife who is fated to die; she does, and the story is over. The
husband can do nothing to prevent it. Similarly, in tale 10 the
husband unknowingly marries a woman who is already dead, a
ghost. When he finds this out he rids himself of her. It is quite
a different matter, however, in the four tales in which the
husband dies. In tale 11 the wife dutifully remains with her
husband's parents until it is discovered that the deceased husband is about to conclude a new marriage to a spirit-woman.
Reminded of the past, he obligingly releases his earthly bride
from her solemn commitments. All this, and the couple had
only been betrothed, not fully married. Even more telling, in
tales 12, 13, and 16, the widowed bride is able to reach beyond
death and actually revives her dead husband.

   What these tales seem to suggest is that marriage to a particular spouse is more important for women than for men. Thus
women are endowed with special capacities to ensure that their
marriage will last. One of the tales in this section speaks of an
annual ritual called "Pitcher's Fourth" in which women fast to
ensure the continued good health of their husbands. We know
that widows are treated more severely than widowers. Throughout India many widows are not allowed to remarry at all. The
same proscription does not apply to men. In earlier times it was
even appropriate for the widow to place herself on her husband's
funeral pyre and thus follow her husband in death. Such a
woman—a *sati* or *mahasati*—was honored and even worshiped.
There was never such a custom for men. Therefore, the underlying message in all of these tales, customs, rituals, and practices
is that a woman should be devoted to her husband. She should
protect his life and welfare by all means available to her—
without him she is nothing, or worse, an inauspicious thing.

   There are also the cases of separation by causes other than
death. In two instances the husband is involved in a relationship
with another woman. In tale 15 the husband is involved with a
prostitute, and in tale 17 the young bride has six co-wives to

deal with. The means by which the two women dispose of their
competition are parallel. Their rivals admire them and the
clever young wives trick them into some ludicrous task, which,
of course, turns out disastrously and leads to their rival's down-
fall. Once this is accomplished, their husbands return to them.
It is noteworthy that the young bride does not reproach her
husband directly, but patiently and cleverly deals directly only
with that which distracts him.

In the final instance it is an envious male companion of the
groom who blinds him to her good qualities. Despite his lowly
nature, the young bride does not confront this male detractor
directly. Instead, she takes advantage of his absence to present
her true self to her husband. Again, she does not confront him
directly with his wrong—for he still does not know she is his
wife. Instead her clever perseverance wins him back.

Thus, most of the stories in this section are about women.
They tell how the ideal wife wins and keeps the husband her
elders have allotted to her. She must overcome competitors and
detractors to win his heart. She must overcome the forces of fate
and magic to defeat death itself and keep him. On the whole,
she relies on her own strength and character to do this. She is
patient, virtuous, and clever.

However, the immediate troubles confronting the young
bride—her husband's death or various rivals for his affection—
are not the whole story. In real life the young bride must leave
the protective custody of her natal kin when she joins her husband in marriage. If her separation from her natal kin is not
complete, her devotion to her husband's interests are thought to
be compromised. Well-meaning as they may be, the continued
attachment and interference of a woman's kinsmen often nega-
tively affects her relationship with her husband. Tale 16 is a
good example. The bride's brothers feel she is too frail to complete an important fast meant to ensure her husband's continued
health. They thus trick her into breaking it before the appoint-
ed hour. The result is that her husband dies.

Not all affinal interference, however, is so well-meaning. In
tale 13 a forgotten aunt (really an ogress) of the bride shows up
and poisons her husband. Tale 17 is even more complex. Here a
young heroine is forced to run away from home because her own

brother actually wants to marry her. Later, in the forest she is
adopted and raised by a crow. Still later, it is with the help of
her "crowfather"—a surrogate for her real family which
wronged her terribly—she is able to successfully overcome her
co-wife rivals and curry favor with her husband.

Not all of the interference is on the wife's side of the family.
In the next section we will encounter a beautiful tale (no. 41) in
which a husband's sister effects the separation of husband and
wife. But usually it is in the best interest of the husband's
family to insure that a new bride establishes a good relationship
with her spouse. In tale 15 the bride's mother-in-law suggests
ways in which she might force such a young groom to pay
attention to his wife. It is significant that none of these work.
Only after the bride herself devises a way to rid herself of her
husband's lover, so that he notices how attractive his own wife
really is, does their marriage get launched on the right track.

This group of tales, then, is not lacking in adventure and
romance. It is rich with typically Indian symbolism of sexuality
and desire. Often its focus is on the heroine. No prince comes
riding in to save these women from a life of cruelty and drudg-
ery. Instead, it is the woman herself who finds a way to tenderly
awaken her husband to the joys they will have together. Furthermore, only she can save him from the grip of death.

· 9 · The Girl Fated to Die by Snakebite (Nagaland)

Many Indian folktales are about the nature of a new bride. Marriages are generally arranged, and often a couple knows little about one another. This situation finds expression in stories that recount the strange character of one of the marriage partners. Some unexpected destiny unfolds soon after the match is finalized.

This story is from Nagaland. It describes a new bride who is fatally bitten by a snake. In this case the groom was warned that this would happen. Thus, while the story addresses common anxieties associated with newlyweds, it also depicts a common South Asian attitude toward fate. What has been predicted by a soothsayer will come true, no matter how a person struggles to prevent it. The bite at the center of the bride's forehead is of interest, furthermore, since that is the spot where the fate or destiny of a body is concentrated. References to the jungle and to specific magical plants give this tale some local Naga color. A waking vision as the means of learning one's future, however, is a theme found in oral traditions throughout India.

AT ONE TIME there was a husband whose wife was very pregnant. She was expecting a child within a few days. At this important time the husband went into the jungle to collect some special vegetables for cooking. He went so far in search of these vegetables that he could not return home on the same day. So he slept that night under a great *siris* tree.

While he slept under the tree, the husband saw a wonderful vision. He saw three different plants, led by witch-broom grass, approaching him as a group. [1] The plants announced they were on the way to see a soothsayer. They called out to the tree under which the man slept, "Oh please accompany us." The plants also explained that they were about to learn their future fate. The host tree replied that it could not follow, as it was protecting a guest. So the three other plants departed and went alone to the soothsayer. As they spoke with one another they rustled a bit as if to suggest a gentle breeze. The husband wondered what all this might mean.

After a time the three plants passed again beside the host tree. The tree inquired about what the soothsayer had predicted. One traveler shouted, "Fated to die by snakebite," and then all three plants left quickly. Hearing this voice, the man woke up with a start. It was dawn but he could see nothing unusual. So he returned home, thinking about the vision he had had. On his arrival, the man discovered that his wife had just delivered a baby daughter. Her birth had occurred at exactly the same time as his vision in the jungle. The husband soon realized, therefore, that the prediction made by the soothsayer had really been about his own daughter. So he turned to his wife and said, "Our daughter is fated to die by snakebite, for I had a vision last night in the jungle stating this fact." He then narrated the whole experience to his wife.

The couple soon began to nurse their young daughter inside their home, taking great care not to allow her outside. The child grew into a beautiful girl, and when she attained a marriageable age many young men came to court her. Her parents, however, refused all requests for their daughter's hand. They explained to each suitor the fate predicted for her and thus the need for the strict protection from all possibility of attack. But at last a determined bachelor came to ask for her hand. He promised her parents that he would always keep the girl inside, feed her the very best foods, ones he would cultivate himself, and that he would protect her with great care. The girl's parents were finally convinced. They agreed to give the hand of their daughter to this man.

On the wedding day all the appropriate ceremonies were performed at the house of the girl's parents. After the ceremonies, however, she had to travel a short distance to reach her husband's place. She was not allowed to walk. Instead she was carried inside a big basket made especially for this purpose. On the way, the girl asked to take a little rest and the wedding party stopped at her request. She then got out of the basket and began to breathe some fresh air. She also enjoyed looking around for the first time at the beauty of nature. Unfortunately, no one noticed that a snake had followed the girl after dropping to the ground from a nearby tree. Just as the girl began to talk to her new husband for

the first time, the snake approached and bit her at the very center
of her forehead. She died instantly from the poison.

· 10 ·   *The Yakshi's Descendants*
         (Kerala)

Ghost stories are prevalent throughout India, and this one tells
of one as a marriage partner. Strictly speaking, it is not about a
ghost (usually called *pishaci* or *preta*) but about a type of roaming
spirit called a *yakshi*. Yet the form and tone of the tale closely
resembles other known examples. The most common type concerns the ghost of a beautiful woman who waylays young men
traveling alone during the dead of night. In some parts of
southern India the same type of ghost is called a *masti*. She is a
woman who lost her life before getting married or having children, that is, before having fulfilled her feminine desires.
Stopping a young man, she will ask for some small article, such
as a matchstick. Their victims are found dead the next morning
with no apparent cause. Perhaps the reason why a similar fate
does not befall the man in this story is that he unwittingly
satisfies the spirit's desires.

THIS IS SOMETHING that happened near Murnad. There once was
a man who owned a bullock cart. He didn't have any close relatives and lived alone in his house. He used to go every day with a
cart full of firewood and come back home again late at night.
    This man was on his way home as usual one night. It was
nearly two in the morning. Suddenly he saw a beautiful woman
by the side of the road, crying. He stopped the cart, went over to
her, and asked what the matter was. But the woman kept on
weeping without giving a reply. After he persisted, she finally
told him that she had been going somewhere and had lost her
way. When it became dark she hadn't known what to do. He felt
sorry for her and told her to get in his cart and come home with
him. When they got to his house, she prepared some food and

they ate together. The next day the woman told him that she
didn't want to return home. She hoped he would have her, and
that she could stay and cook for him. He thought he was getting
a beautiful wife, so he agreed. This man and woman lived together for a long time. After a while they had a child. This boy
was unusually large for his age.

One night as the man was eating his dinner he decided that it
needed more salt. So he asked his wife to get some. Now the salt
was kept high on a shelf and as the man watched the woman reach
for it he was horrified to see her fingers grow longer and longer.
He trembled with fear. Once she had grasped the salt pot, however, her fingers returned to normal. Then she turned around and
saw her husband shivering with fright. At last the man managed
to ask, "You are a yakshi, aren't you?" The woman couldn't lie.
It was too late for that. She confessed that she was a yakshi who
had come home with him that night. "I am in need of human
love," she explained. "It was my desire to live with you. I will
leave you, but I have one request. You must take me at midnight
and leave me at the same place where you found me."

The man was terribly afraid to go with the yakshi in the middle of the night. He thought she would kill him on the way. He
thought that was why she wanted to go at midnight. Otherwise
why couldn't she go back alone? The poor man was expecting the
worst. He took the yakshi into the forest to the place where they
had first met. She told him to stop the cart. When she got down
and said goodbye, he sped away with a sigh of relief. He drove
home as fast as he could. Their child grew up. He turned out to
be of huge stature. It was the heritage of his yakshi mother.
Everyone in that family has a gigantic body.

· 11 ·   *A Marriage in the World of the Dead*
         (Nagaland)

This story justifies the marriage of a "widow" to a new groom.
She is only betrothed, not actually married, when her groom
dies, and because she is still young there is no shame attached to
her ongoing desire for a sexual partner and for a family of her

own. The parents-in-law are therefore being somewhat unreasonable by wanting to hold onto her. There is not so much a rivalry over their son as there is a desire on their part that she serve as a surrogate for the lost boy. This particular tale gains regional color through reference to a necromancer who is called in to commune with the dead son, a local Naga tradition. Though possession of the dead by spirits also occurs elsewhere in India, usually the spirit of the deceased is depicted as dissatisfied. An exorcist must be called in to persuade such spirits to return to their own world. The Ao Naga custom described here thus provides a distinct variant of wider South Asian traditions.

ONCE, LONG AGO, there were two lovers who were engaged to be married. They had gained the consent of both sets of parents. Now they were waiting for the great day of the wedding celebration. This was to be in a few weeks' time. The boy's parents loved the girl as if she were their own daughter. They were extremely pleased to have such a beautiful woman engaged to be their daughter-in-law. This girl used to help them with the housework even before her marriage. In the same way the young man used to help the girl's parents with their rice cultivation and also used to aid them in many other activities. Both the betrothed couple and their parents were enjoying a very fine relationship. Everyone was satisfied with the arrangements.

At the very time when the love of this couple was at its zenith, the young man died suddenly of an illness. Thus an unexpected gloom descended to replace a previous state of joy. However, the young man's parents comforted themselves in focusing their thoughts on their beloved daughter-in-law to be. She became their only solace from sorrow, and they wished her to be in their presence continuously. She began to help them daily, and it almost seemed that she was already living with them. As time passed, however, new suitors came to court this girl. She was beautiful and had a rare and fine character. She and her parents both agreed that she should get married, but the young man's parents now objected. They wanted her to remain as their daughter-in-law and not marry anyone else.

The girl's parents then decided to consult a man who could talk with the spirits of the dead. One day the parents of the girl and the parents of the dead man were both summoned by a special magician hired for this occasion. The young girl was then asked to sing a song which would be conveyed to her dead lover by the necromancer. The song contained a question about what he wished his former fiancée to do. This was the song:

> A new suitor I wish to choose
> So we can do life's work as a pair,
> But your parents are at a loss
> And prevent me from this with tears.
>
> If you were to come back again,
> I would wait and wait for you,
> But now is a new season with new leaves and new rain
> And a new man has a need for me.
>
> Like the hornbill that flew away,
> You have left us all in doubt.
> Send us a message today
> So that the tears may cease.

After a certain number of chants the magician fell on the floor in a trance. His body became rigid and stiff, as if he were himself dead. He seemed to be unconscious. The necromancer was no longer with this living world but was now communicating with the world of the dead. He had traveled to an invisible place. There he met the young girl's husband-to-be carrying a bundle of bamboo on his shoulders. He was walking along the road when the magician called to him and he stopped. The young man placed his load on the ground and began to chat with the stranger. The visitor then sang the song given him by the former sweetheart.

Tears rose to the eyes of the young man as he remembered his beloved. But then his mood changed and he told the visitor calmly that he was about to marry another lady from a new land. Indeed, he was currently collecting building materials for his new home with her. The man then asked the magician to convey to his former girlfriend his approval of her being married to someone still in the world of the living. He sang a song containing this message and asked that this be carried back, by the visitor, to his old sweetheart. The song was as follows:

An instant love in a new land,
And a happy wedding there,
I am now courting a new lady,
And building a new house,
In which to stay with her.

I have been careless to keep you in doubt.
Address the fairest lady of the living world;
Tell her to seek a marriage with a new groom.
I too have found a new bride and a new home.

The necromancer then returned to the world of the living. He awoke, sat up, and his consciousness returned. Then he spoke of his travels to the world of the dead and sang the song sent by the young man. The boy's parents now came to understand their son's wishes. They agreed to the girl's marriage with a new groom. The faithful daughter was very pleased. She married a new suitor and lived happily from then on.

· 12 · *A Dead Husband*
   (Assam)

Often Indian tales seem to be built around riddles. Such stories provide complex solutions to problems that contain an impossible set of conditions. In this tale, it is fate—personified as the god Bidhata—who sets the conditions. Just as fate cannot be evaded through conscious effort (see tale 76), so no escape can be found by running away. In some Indian tales, however, a clever and devoted spouse can thwart the inevitable.

BIDHATA (DESTINY) determines the fate of all creatures. When his sister gave birth to a girl, Bidhata calculated the fortunes of his niece and said, "Everything is all right with her. She won't have to think of food and shelter. But she will have to marry a dead husband." This prophecy so saddened Bidhata's sister that she took her child and left home. After wandering about hither and thither for a time, she managed to reach a village. After taking shelter there for one night, however, she again moved on. This time she lost her way and found herself in a forest. Her daughter quickly became tired of walking and cried out for a drink of water. But her mother insisted, and they went on and on. There was no sign of habitation anywhere. At last they came to a large palace. They stood at the gate there and called out to the inmates. Nobody answered. The girl wanted water badly and began to push on the gate. Suddenly it opened and the girl was carried inside by her own force. Then it immediately closed again and the mother could not get in. Then the girl began to cry. Her mother, too, became frenzied at losing sight of her daughter. At last the girl tired of crying and fell asleep. Her mother went away.

Toward evening the girl woke up and found a handsome youth standing beside her. The man treated her kindly and gave her food and drink. They began to talk and he said, "I will lose my life as soon as it is morning. I will come to life again only in the evening. Do not let this make you afraid. There is nothing to fear and there is plenty of food to eat." As soon as it was morning the handsome youth became unconscious, but the girl decided to stay. Months passed and she grew up into a young woman. Later the couple married and lived as husband and wife.

One day the girl asked her husband why it was that he had to die every morning. Then he told her his story: "I was born a prince. However, because my birth portended some evil or mishap, my mother used to put a necklace on me. When my mother died, my father took another wife. My stepmother could not stand me. She noticed the necklace around my neck, and one day while I was asleep, she stole it. I lost my life immediately. This created an uproar in the palace, but I could not be revived. So my father, not wishing to lose me altogether, had this building constructed and placed me here. He gave me all that I would require, just as if I had been alive. He comes to visit once a year just to have a look at me. My stepmother puts the necklace on during daytime, but as soon as it is evening, she keeps it in a pitcher full of water. When the necklace comes off her neck, I sit up. I die again every morning when she puts it back on. Even though I get back my life during the night, I cannot return to my father through this dense forest. So I remain here. If only someone could recover the necklace!"

After she had heard the story, the prince's wife thought out a plan. One morning she took her child—for they had one now—in her arms and started for the king's palace. When she reached it she asked if anyone wanted a servant. She was taken to the queen, who liked the attractive woman and the comely child in her arms. So the girl was given a job and asked to wash the kitchen utensils and the clothes of the queen. She worked her very best and tried to please her mistress. However, she always kept her eye on the magic necklace. One day the queen asked her to kill some lice that were in her hair. While lousing the queen, the girl pinched her child. It cried out. The queen then asked why the child was crying. The mother answered, "My child has noticed your sparkling necklace and wants to have it." The queen made an attempt to satisfy the child by giving him some other attractive things. The girl pinched the child again. Again it cried out. The queen did not want the lousing to stop, so she gave the necklace to the baby to hold. When it became evening the girl left with her child, but she first returned the necklace. In this way some days passed and the queen came to trust the girl entirely. Soon the child was given the necklace to play with regularly. One day while the child was playing, the queen went into her palace for a while. Finding the right moment, the girl picked up her child and the necklace and ran off into the forest. The queen sent out servants to find the girl, but she had disappeared.

The wife reached her own house and put the necklace in a pitcher filled with water. Her husband immediately sat up, took out the necklace, and put it on. Now both husband and wife could live without any worries. They cleared the jungle and made their home more attractive. Soon the prince's father came that way and when he saw how things had changed he was surprised beyond measure. He was very happy to find his son alive and married. When he came to know of everything his queen had done, he determined to have her punished by impaling her on a sharp stake. He then took his son and daughter-in-law back to his palace. Everything ended happily.

· 13 · *Four Friends*
    (Uttar Pradesh)

Folktales are often peopled by characters with wondrous talents who soon get enmeshed in a fantastic set of events. We expect this rather than question it. These talents and actions, however, may be related to subtle expectations inherent in real relationships. Such is the case in the next tale. The princess's faith in her husband's instructions, even in the face of danger to his life, reflects ideals all Indian women are asked to approximate.

The story of four friends resembles tales 7 and 8 in this collection because it, too, is built around a set of cooperative males. In each case all of the men concerned become involved in a courtship or rescue operation that revolves around a young, attractive woman. Significantly, none of the tales include an outright quarrel between these men over the final possession of the female. Instead, her loyalties get decided on the basis of very formal criteria. Yet this subtle evasion of conflict seems almost to be the point of these tales. Note, too, that in the present account the sought after woman is linked to the serpent kingdom and to deep pools of water, both common motifs in Indian folklore more generally.

THERE ONCE WERE FOUR FRIENDS—a shepherd, a carpenter, a Brahman, and a king. The four of them were very close friends. One time they went together to a foreign country. On their way, they came to the bank of a river where they found a second Brahman searching for his water buffalo. The shepherd asked him, "Why are you wandering about here?" The man replied, "Because I am searching for my buffalo." The shepherd then said, "Oh please, teach me how to search for things." And so the shepherd stayed and took up the study of how to track lost objects. Then there were only three friends. They continued to travel and

soon arrived in a city where the son of a noble family had died. A
great crowd of people were gathered around him at the time.
When the Brahman asked why there was such a crowd a by-
stander replied, "Our son has died and we wish to revive him."
The Brahman then said, "I also wish to know how to give life to
the dead. If you are kind enough to let me learn, I will stay here."
And so he stayed in that place. Now there remained only two
friends. After a time, these two came to a village where some men
were making flying cots. The carpenter asked them what they
were making and later requested that he be allowed to stay and
learn how to build these special beds.

Now the king was alone. He walked on and on until he
reached an isolated forest. There he climbed a mango tree. Near
that tree lived a serpent who possessed a beautiful jeweled ring
but who left home daily to feed. First setting his jewel under the
tree, the serpent would travel as far as one hundred sixty miles
and still see by its light. So the king decided to visit a craftsman
and have his weapons converted into a tub and an iron chain.
Taking these objects he then climbed the tree near the serpent's
hole. Soon the snake arrived and left his jewel there as usual.
Then it went into the forest to search for food. When the serpent
had gone, the king slowly slipped his newly made tub over the
jewel. That made the world grow dark and the serpent could no
longer see by its glow. So he returned home. Suspecting the jewel
was covered by the tub, he beat his head against it again and
again until he finally died.

At this point, the king climbed down from the tree, lifted the
tub, and put the magic ring on his finger. Soon afterwards he
dove into a nearby river. There he could see a splendid palace,
and in it sat the beautiful daughter of its king. This girl was very
charming and she wore sixteen kinds of beautiful ornaments. The
king immediately fell in love with her. But the girl quickly told
him, "My father will soon come and he will bite you. You will
die." To this, the king replied, "I have already killed your father." Then one day he said to the girl, "Let us go to a park and
play dice." The princess agreed and they left for the park at once.
While engrossed in their game, a prince on a hunting expedition
passed by. He, too, saw this beautiful girl. The couple quickly
jumped in the river to hide, but one of the princess's slippers fell

off in her haste. The prince picked up that shoe thinking, "This slipper is very beautiful. Its owner must be even more beautiful."

After this, the prince returned home where his father noticed that he was upset and sought the reason. The prince told him that he wished for the second slipper and for its owner. So his father sent for two ogresses. He asked the first one what she could do and she replied, "I can punch holes in the clouds." The second one was then asked the same thing. She said, "I can make holes in the clouds and also cover them with thatch." So the prince's father asked the second ogress to find the owner of the slipper. The ogress left immediately. She went straight to the river palace. There she knocked on the door saying, "Oh dear daughter, please open the door. Your *mausi* [mother's sister] is standing here." But the princess replied, "I have no mausi. Where are you from?" To this the ogress replied, "You are mistaken, dear daughter. You were very young when I left. I have been searching for you for a long time and only today have I found you." So the ogress was let in and she stayed for awhile.

The king then came to know that she was a fake and soon told the princess, "This woman is not your mausi. She has come to kill me. Please remember this: If I die, do not burn my dead body. Instead, please oil it, and then store it safely." A few days later the mausi said, "I have four *laddus* [sweets]." She then gave two to the king and the others to the princess. These were filled with poison and as soon as the king ate them, he died. Then the ogress told the princess, "Burn his body: otherwise it will rot." To this the princess replied, "I have obeyed each and every order you have given, but this I cannot do. I cannot burn the body of my dear husband." So she took off the ring that had the splendid jewel, and then put him in a box which she carefully locked.

Next the ogress told the princess to bathe in the river Ganges. The ogress took the princess to the middle of the swift current and after diving down very deeply she said to her, "Take your ring off and throw it into the river. If not, I will kill you." So the princess took off the ring and threw it into the water. Then the ogress took the princess to the palace of the prince. But the princess insisted that for twelve years she would have to distribute alms and do meritorious work.[1] Only after that would she agree to marry a new man. The prince agreed and soon had a separate palace built for the girl. He also provided servants to care for her. She then began to distribute alms to the poor each day.

Twelve years passed. Then the original Brahman friend, who had learned by now how to give life to the dead, arrived in the city where the princess was distributing alms. The shepherd, who had now learned how to trace lost objects, also found his way there. And so did the carpenter, who had learned to build flying cots. The three men met and decided to search for their fourth friend, the king. The shepherd tried to trace his friend as one would trace a lost object. But the king could not be found. Evening soon came and the three men decided to have their supper before searching further. When they went to buy some food they were advised that there was a Brahman princess in the city who distributed alms to the poor each day. If they went to her they could obtain their supper free.

So the shepherd went to the palace and asked for alms. However, the guard said he could supply food to only one person. The shepherd insisted that he had come with friends and that he wished alms for all four of them. So the guard sent a message to the princess. She then asked to see the man. When the shepherd arrived she asked why he sought alms for four instead of for one. He replied, "We are three foreigners. Our fourth friend is missing and we are searching for him. We three shall eat our portions and the fourth portion we shall save inside the earth." Then the shepherd returned to his friends with four food portions. They ate three shares, but buried the fourth. The next day the friends continued their search with no success. That evening the Brahman went to obtain alms again. He, too, was called before the princess because he asked for four portions. Giving the same reply as the shepherd, this man also obtained four shares. After the three men had eaten, they again buried the fourth share.

On the third day, the carpenter went for alms. He, too, was called before the princess. On that day she finally came to realize that the three men were looking for her dead husband, the king. So she asked to see all of them. When they arrived she told them the whole story about how he had been killed by an ogress. The three friends next asked the princess to wait while they went to search for the magic ring. When they found it in the Ganges, they proceeded to the door of the palace under the river. There

they unlocked the box of the king and restored him to life by
calling to him with the magic words, "Ram, Ram." The king
awoke and complained that he had slept too long. His friends
explained that they already knew his story and then told him
what had happened.

Finally the men took a flying cot and went that very night to
fetch the princess. They flew with her on it to the river palace.
There they filled the cot with precious goods before returning to
their separate homes. The four men remained lifelong friends.

· 14 ·   *The Farmer and the Barber
(Uttar Pradesh)*

Indian newlyweds are often mutually suspicious, but they must
soon adjust the idealistic expectations they have about each
other to ordinary reality. Because of a tradition of arranged
marriages, this initial adjustment can be very difficult on both
partners. A man is said to be particularly critical of his wife
during the early months, a period often lasting up to the time of
her first pregnancy. These next two stories depict extreme reac-
tions on the part of a groom. The first is from Uttar Pradesh
and involves two friends who undergo the rigors of marriage in
parallel, a situation not that uncommon in real life. The story
also involves social rank, as the farmer is a high-caste man and
the barber a lowly friend. This explains why the barber's prospective wife, probably of a poor family, only offered spinach,
while the fiancée of his farmer friend served him prestigious
foods. It also explains why the barber was so sensitive about this
difference that he was motivated to invert the facts and en-
danger his friend's marriage. The farmer's angry response,
directed at his own bride, causes him to blindfold himself at the
nuptial ceremonies. This motif occurs in many Indian wedding
stories. The significant point is that the new wife soon finds a
clever way around these difficulties. She manages to win her
husband's affections in a new context where he assumes she is a
different and more exotic woman. The same motif is found in a
well-known myth about a marital dispute Lord Siva has with his

own wife. In both stories the woman is a guileful victor, one that her husband eventually learns to admire.

THERE ONCE LIVED A FARMER and a barber who were very good friends. One day it became time for both of them to marry. It was customary in this area to go through a betrothal ceremony. Afterwards the prospective bridegroom would pay a special visit to his fiancée's home. When both weddings had been arranged, the farmer thus said to his friend, "Why don't you go to the home of your bride-to-be and see what the girl is like." (Now the barber's fiancée was rather homely, while the farmer's fiancée was very beautiful.) So the barber set off. When he arrived at his bride's home he found his betrothed standing at the door buying spinach from a passing merchant. Some hours later the barber was offered this spinach as the main dish of a ceremonial meal. Needless to say, he was disappointed with the lack of more prestigious and festive foods.

The next day the barber decided to visit his farmer friend's new in-laws. When he arrived he found that fiancée standing on the doorstep as well. This girl, however, retreated into her house and hid as soon as she saw a friend of the groom approaching. Furthermore, in this second house the barber was served delicious festival foods. He kept quiet, but secretly he thought to himself, "My bride is a bad woman because she fed me tasteless spinach. But my friend's bride is good. She gave me delicious foods like *puris* and *kacauris*." The barber was disturbed at his discovery and wished to hide these things from his farmer friend. So he said to his friend, "Listen! My bride is a fine woman. In my own in-laws' house I ate *puris* and *kacauris*. But your new bride is bad—at her place I was offered only spinach." The farmer responded by thinking, "My wife must be very bad!" When it came time for the wedding, the farmer decided to cover his eyes. He asked his mother and father to buy him four kinds of cloth and he blindfolded himself with these just before the consummation of the wedding was celebrated. Indeed, he made this a condition of going through the ceremonies at all. The farmer remained blindfolded through all the rituals. He also refused to eat anything but bread.

Now this farmer and the barber had established a habit of

playing a gambling game in the farmer's garden. One day, soon
after their weddings, they began to play again as usual. But the
farmer's new bride soon said to her mother-in-law, "Today,
mother-in-law, I wish to see the garden!" So the new bride hired
a special palanquin and with much ceremony and pomp she was
taken to see the garden. When she found the two friends gambling she said to them, "Oh! I wish to play this game too." At
this very moment the barber had to leave in order to urinate.
Meanwhile, the farmer was, of course, not blindfolded. So upon
seeing the face of such a lovely woman he was enchanted, and he
invited her to come and sit beside him. She then said, "If you can
find a way to send this barber off, I will agree to play a gambling
game with you." So the farmer found a way to send the barber on
a four-day trip. He then wagered his ring in a gambling game
with the girl. After a while she won the game and got up to go.
The farmer invited her to return for another game the next morning. The young girl replied, "Either I or my sister will come."
The farmer insisted on her presence, however, saying, "No, you
must come." After she had left, the farmer rebound his eyes and
went home to eat.

On the second day the young bride again arrived in order to
play a gambling game with her husband. On arriving she said,
"Let's play again." The farmer agreed and this time he wagered
his bracelet. The young girl also won the second game, and when
she left she took the bracelet with her. In the same way the couple
met again in the garden on the third day. This time the farmer
wagered a garland. The girl won this as well and left the garden
carrying it with her. On the fourth day the same events were
repeated. This time the farmer wagered his necklace, and again
the girl won and took this away. The farmer continued to invite
her to join him and the young girl began to go daily to the
garden. Finally she had won everything the farmer owned. When
he had nothing left, he went home and said to his mother,
"Mother! Please prepare food for several days. I am going on a
trip in order to look for something." The mother then took various things which her daughter-in-law had won from the farmer
and put them inside a special sweet. She made several of these
sweets, called "laddus," and told her son, "The little laddus are
for the barber and the bigger ones are for you."

The barber and the farmer then left on their trip. Soon, however, the farmer turned to the barber and asked him "Where is the village named Here and There?" The barber replied, "Brother, don't be silly. There is no village called Here and There." Then the two sat down to eat and the farmer broke open his laddus. In one he found the ring he had gambled. In the second he found his necklace. In the third he found the garland, and in the fourth his bracelet. The farmer was very astonished and he quickly ran back home. The barber begged him to stop but the farmer would not stop. When he arrived home he found his wife dressed in torn clothes, baking bread. He at once began to laugh and said to her, "You have deceived me very successfully." She replied, "You made me very sad. You bound your eyes and ate only bread, refusing to even look at my face." In this way the farmer learned that his barber friend had lied to him. Now he began to live happily with his wife.

· 15 · *The Story of a King (Tamilnadu)*

The previous story about newlyweds was from Uttar Pradesh. This tale is from Tamilnadu and is similar to the last in that this groom also insists on blindfolding himself at his own wedding because he thinks his wife is defective. Instead of a low-caste friend, however, this time the deceptive rogue who creates the problem is a prostitute and the husband's mistress. Her reasons for jealousy are obvious. Again, the new wife finds a clever way around her husband's apparently irrational rejection of her. Just as in the last account, the new bride soon arranges to meet her husband in a different context where he is impressed with her skills and her beauty. In this story, however, this man does not return to his wife easily. She must first devise a way to end her scheming rival's life. The wife's plan soon shows up the prostitute's stupidity and allows this woman to die of a head infection caused by her own silly behavior. A possible connection with venereal disease surfaces here, since both venereal disease and illicit sexual desire in Indian symbolic tradition are

usually thought to cause problems to the head and head hair. In
neither of these stories, furthermore, does the wife resort to a
physical disguise. Instead, it is her husband who has never
"seen" her because of his own inner psychological problems.
Her winning his affection is again linked to a man's eventual
recognition of beauty in his own wife.

A TOWN. A king. A son. That son once went to school, but his
course of studies was now finished. So this young man began
visiting the house of a prostitute. However, his father and mother
began to notice his comings and goings. So they said to each
other, "We must arrange our son's wedding right away." But as
the matter progressed their son spoke up. He said, "I must marry
a girl who resembles me exactly. Otherwise I will not marry at
all." The boy repeated these words over and over. So the mother
and father called their seven ministers together saying, "Oh, you
seven! Here is a photo of our son. Find a girl who looks just like
him and we will arrange a marriage!"

The ministers took the photo and set out. They traveled far
and wide, circling round and round. Then one day, the very last
day of their search, they stopped on a river bank, prepared a
freshly cooked meal, and began to eat. Soon the youngest minister said, "I must smoke." So he stood up and began looking for a
small cigarette (beedie). Then he noticed a cooking fire lit on the
opposite bank of the river. So he said to the others, "I'll cross over
there and ask if anyone has a beedie."

When the minister arrived on the opposite bank he began to
question the group of people standing at the fire saying, "Where
are you from? What business do you have here?" "We come from
a raja whose daughter demands a bridegroom who looks just like
herself," they said. "She has given us a photo but we cannot find
such a groom anywhere! Today we stopped at this river to cook
and to eat. The first minister replied, "My goodness! There is an
equivalence here. We have been wandering around for the same
reason. The minister then asked to see the girl's photo. The men
showed it to him. It looked just like the one his own group had
been carrying. So the two groups exchanged photos. "All right,
we'll recommend the marriage," each side said to the other.

The first group of ministers then returned home. They first

stopped at the prostitute's house, as they were looking for the king's son. But the prostitute herself opened the door and said she would take the picture to the prince. Then she slipped out a back door and ran to the local Ganesh temple. There she grabbed some lime paste and stealthily put some on both eyes in the photograph. Then she hurried back home. The king's son soon asked to see the picture and the prostitute showed it to him. As he looked at it, the prostitute said, "My goodness! They want you to marry a blind girl!" The son asked his parents about this, but they answered, "Everything has been arranged already."

So the king's son decided to go through with the wedding, but he insisted on one condition. He would never look at the bride's face. The marriage took place and the girl eventually came to stay with her husband. From the very first day he refused to speak to her or even look at her. Finally the new bride complained to her mother-in-law. This lady answered, "You must cook half a measure of pebbles in with the rice today." The girl agreed, but her husband found the stones and patiently plucked them out one by one. Still he would not speak to his bride. So the girl went back to her mother-in-law and complained again. The woman now suggested that the girl stand in the doorway and refuse to allow her husband in. She tried the idea that very evening, but the king's son ducked under her arms and forced his wife aside. Then he left for the prostitute's house and vowed never to return.

The young bride next asked her mother-in-law for a buffalo. She said, "I'll live by grazing this buffalo and selling its milk." Her mother-in-law agreed and gave her such an animal. The girl then walked around the village selling the milk. One day she saw the raja's son brushing his teeth at the prostitute's house. At the same time, the son saw a vision of a beautiful girl selling milk. Since he had never seen the face of his own bride he of course did not realize that the two women were one. He asked the girl how much her milk was worth. She answered, "It's worth its weight in gold." The young man paid her for a half a seer [one pound] of this valuable liquid and took it inside.

The next day the young girl passed near the house again, this time with buttermilk. Again the raja's son asked the price and the girl answered, "It is the same price as pearls." The young man agreed to buy some. Thus, the girl sold milk to her husband

daily. At last she obtained all his money. One day, he had only
one small ring left. On that day she managed to obtain this from
him as well. Later the girl who sold the milk gave birth to a son.
After a time she began to walk around, cradling the child in her
arms. Then one day the prostitute, out of interest, came to visit
her. She asked how a milk seller managed to maintain such a
lovely head of hair. The girl answered, "I rub my hair each day
with rocks. Then I tie bark from the cotton tree onto each strand
with rags. If you do this you too will have a beautiful head of
hair." So the prostitute tried this. She soon developed many sores
on her head and these quickly became infected. After a while she
died. It was at that time that the raja's son finally returned home.
He then noticed for the first time how beautiful his own wife
really was. They lived happily together from then on.

· 16 ·   The King's Daughter
(Uttar Pradesh)

In this story a woman's brothers nearly jeopardize her husband's
life. Ostensibly the brothers want to help their married sister
save her health by showing her a "fake" moon. They thereby
entice her to break a ritual fast early (without her suspecting her
error). But the purpose of this ritual fast, common throughout
North India, is to insure a husband's long life. By halting
before the true moon has appeared, this wife unwittingly breaks
short the required period. By implication then, her brothers are
responsible for their brother-in-law's sudden illness. The situation can be righted only by a set of wise priests who counsel this
woman's strict adherence to ritual procedure the following year.
Such consultations with learned pundits often are used, in real
life, to sort out various family tensions that can underlie physical complaints. Ritual vows are one of the most common ways
of dealing with these and similar psychological situations. The
festival of "Pitcher's Fourth," or Kalasi Chaturthi, mentioned in
this story is a festival popular throughout North India. All
married Hindu women fast for the welfare of their husbands for
the day, with the fast ending only after the woman has seen the
moon. Observing this fast is a very special way for a wife to

NEW BRIDES AND GROOMS 49

express her profound concern for her husband (see tales 42 and 57). The story also demonstrates, of course, how efficacious such selfless behavior can be.

ONCE THERE WAS A KING who had seven sons and only one daughter. The daughter was the youngest and very dear to everyone. She grew up and got married. When the day of "Pitcher's Fourth" arrived, she kept a fast like all married women. But she was very delicate and soon she became pale. Her seven brothers could not bear to see their sister so weak, so they thought of a plan. One brother climbed up high on a tamarind tree, and there held a lit lamp behind a large, round flour-sifter. The other brothers went and told the sister, "Come and look; the moon is rising. See the light behind the tamarind tree! You can give the offering to the moon and end your fast." The princess believed her brothers. She prayed and gave the customary water offerings to the gods. She then ate her dinner. But from the very next day, her husband fell ill. His disease grew worse, and no medication was effective. He simply got sicker and sicker. In the end, the princess called the priests and asked them what could be done to cure her husband. The pundits said that she had ended her fast on the "Pitcher's Fourth" before the moon had arisen, and that was why her husband was waning. The princess was very upset and begged the pundits to tell her how to correct her folly. The wise men said that the only way was to wait until the next year's "Pitcher's Fourth," and then to carry out the very same fast with renewed meticulousness. The princess waited and waited. When the next "Pitcher's Fourth" came, she kept the fast until she was sure that the moon was up. She offered water to the moon, gave gifts of fruits, sweets, and clothing to the elders, and offered money to Brahman women. After all that, her husband began to get better. He and the princess then lived happily forever.

· 17 · *Sanykisar the Crow-Girl (Kashmir)*

As is true of many Indian tales, this one is a compilation of several nearly discrete stories about the adventures of a single character. While Sanykisar is a popular folk figure throughout

Kashmir, some versions of her story lack the entire sequence of
episodes contained in this one. Conversely, the several subplot
themes found here form separate tales in other places, both in
India and around the world. The initial episode of this tale, for
example, in which a brother vows to marry his own sister, is
often omitted in other versions. But the same theme recurs in a
tale told among the speakers of Tulu in southern India. There, a
sister attempts to avoid an incestuous relationship by throwing
herself in a well. Her brother, seeing her image in the water,
throws himself in too, and they both become fish. Afterwards
they forever gurgle, making the sound, "tage-tangadi," meaning "older brother-younger sister."

ONCE UPON A TIME there lived an old couple and their two children—a son and a daughter. It was a happy family. The boy was
going to school and the girl helped her mother with the household chores. All was going well until one day when the boy returned from school. That day when he was served his meal he
found one hair entangled in his food. Pulling the hair from his
rice bowl, he said, "Whosoever belongs to this hair, she is my
wife." His mother then scolded him saying, "You can't say that.
Maybe it is mine." Ignoring what his mother said the boy went
on repeating, "Whosoever belongs to this hair, she is my wife."
"You cannot say that," repeated the mother, "Maybe it is your
sister's."

The mother knew the hair belonged to no other than her own
daughter, who had served the meal. Surprisingly, however, the
boy would not stop speaking. He kept on repeating, "Whosoever
belongs to this hair, she is my wife." The mother tried her hard-
est to explain to the boy that the hair he had found in his meal
was his sister's, and for obvious reasons, he could not marry her.
She therefore told him to simply shut up and to finish eating in
silence. Well, the boy was stubborn and wouldn't listen to anyone. Instead he kept repeating, "Whosoever belongs to this hair,
she is my wife."

The poor sister, Sanykisar, was listening to all that was said
between mother and son with tears in her eyes. She could no
longer stand to hear her brother's words. Tell me, how could she?

She therefore ran out of the house. The sister ran and ran, until she was out of the village. Panting, she finally sat down to catch her breath. Meanwhile it was getting dark and Sanykisar was getting scared. Now she started crying. Tears rolled down her beautiful cheeks. At that time a holy man (fakir) passed that way. He saw the beautiful girl, crying and alone in this deserted place. So he stopped and asked her what the matter was. She then told him about the sequence of events that had led her to leave home. She concluded by saying, "Here I am in this dreadful night. I don't know what to do or where to go." The fakir after having listened to her story attentively gave her seven seeds, saying, "Sow these seeds. Seven trees will grow out of them within a second. If you then climb one of those trees no harm shall come to you."

Sanykisar sowed the seeds as directed, and lo, seven tall and strong trees shot up. She climbed one and rested on the top. Back at home, Sanykisar's parents, not finding her around, began searching for her. The search led them to the spot where Sanykisar was resting. They asked her to climb down and to return home, but she refused. Again they asked and again she said no. This continued for a time until finally the brother and the father decided to cut the tree down. This would cause her to fall and they would then carry her home. Soon they started striking the tree with axes. While they were cutting the first tree, however, Sanykisar crossed over to a second before the first one fell to the ground. The father and the brother then turned their axes to the second tree, and she crossed over to a third. In this manner the father and brothers finally fell six trees. Then Sanykisar crossed over to the seventh and last tree. Undeterred, the father and the brother started chopping at the seventh tree as well. Now the poor girl got quite frightened and began to cry. What would she do? Where would she go? She at once prayed to Mother Moon.[1] "Mother moon, mother moon, open the door for me. I will climb up to you." Mother moon heard her prayer, looked down at the young girl with arms outstretched, and was moved to drop a ray of her light. Holding the ray, Sanykisar climbed up and joined mother moon. For a time she lived with her happily.

One day mother moon asked Sanykisar to comb her hair but warned her to be careful not to touch the center of her scalp. If she combed there it would cause pain and sudden hair loss, and this would make mother moon unhappy and angry. Sanykisar followed her instructions carefully and for many days she gently combed the hair of mother moon. But one day her luck failed her and she accidentally touched the forbidden point on mother moon's scalp. Mother moon then cried with pain and immediately her hair began falling out. She was furious, and she threw Sanykisar back toward the earth. Luckily Sanykisar fell into the nest of an old crow on another treetop. There was no one in the nest, however, as the crow had gone out in search of food. By sunset he returned and to his utter surprise, he found a beautiful girl in his nest. He asked her who she was and from where she had come. The girl then told her sad story. The crow was moved and, being childless, quickly adopted the girl as his own. He would fetch food, fruits, and other nice things for her, and she would keep the nest in order. Both spent the time quite happily.

One day Sanykisar's mother happened to pass that way and, seeing the girl on the tree top, recognized the girl as her daughter. Then she said, "Come down, Sanykisar. All your dolls and toys are waiting for you at home." Sanykisar refused. When all of her efforts at persuasion failed, the mother returned home alone. Soon after sunset the 'crow-father' again returned to his nest. This time he found Sanykisar crying. "Why are you crying, my child? he asked. "I have no dolls or toys to play with. I am bored being alone all day," said Sanykisar. "Don't cry, my child! I will get you all the dolls and toys you want," answered the crow-father. And saying this he went and brought the best dolls and toys he could. The girl was again all smiles.

Next day the girl's human father came to the tree and implored her saying, "Come down, Sanykisar. The colorful spinning wheel is waiting for you at home." Sanykisar refused. After all of her father's efforts at persuasion failed, he too returned home alone.

After sunset the 'crow-father' again returned to his nest and found Sanykisar crying. "Why are you weeping, my child?" he asked. "I have no colorful spinning wheel. I want a fine wheel to spin on," Sanykisar replied. "Don't you cry, my child! I will get you the most colorful spinning wheel in the world." Having said this the 'crow-father' went away and returned with a beautiful spinning wheel and some cotton. And she was again all smiles.

The next day the girl's brother came and said, "Come down, Sanykisar. Your bridal dress and ornaments are waiting for you at home." Sanykisar refused. After all of her brother's efforts at persuasion failed, he too returned home alone. After sunset the 'Crow-father' returned to his nest as usual and found Sanykisar crying again. "Why are you crying, my child?" he asked. "I have no bridal dress nor ornaments to wear," she replied. "Don't you cry, my child! I will get you the most beautiful bridal dress and the best ornaments in the world," said the crow, and he quickly flew away. After some time he returned with a beautiful bridal dress and many precious ornaments. And Sanykisar was all smiles again.

The next day after the 'crow-father' went out, Sanykisar put on the new bridal dress and glittering ornaments, sat at the spinning wheel, and started to spin. At that time the king of the country and his chief wazir [minister] were on a hunting trip together. They happened to pass that way. Upon hearing the sound of a spinning wheel both looked up and they saw Sanykisar spinning comfortably in the crow's nest. The king was fascinated by her charming beauty. "For God's sake, who created you?" he asked. "Tell me, are you a fairy or a human?" "I swear by God who created you, me, and the rest of the world, oh king, that I am a human and my name is Sanykisar," replied the girl. "If you are a human, your abode should be a king's palace, not a crow's nest. Come down, my dear, and be my queen," said the king. "I won't come down, nor shall I go with you, oh king, unless my 'crow-father' permits me to," said Sanykisar. "In that case, my dear, I will wait for your 'crow-father'. I shall not return to my palace without you," announced the king.

Having decided this, the king put down his arms and decided to wait for sunset and the return of the 'crow-father'. Meanwhile, his wazir interrupted: "Forgive me, your excellency, for advising you. The sunset is a long time off. By then it will get dark. We still have a long way to go; it could be dangerous to wander in the woods. Moreover, it does not befit you, a great king, to wait for a crow." "I appreciate your concern, my wazir, but I cannot go back to my palace without Sanykisar. I cannot live without her," replied the king.

At this point both the king and the wazir again requested Sanykisar to come down, but again she refused. This made the wazir angry, and he decided to cut down the tree and take Sanykisar away by force. So he said to the king, "Permit me, lord, to cut down this tree. Then we can take the young lady by force." "Do anything you like, but I must take Sanykisar with me, for I cannot live without her even for a second," replied the king. No sooner had the king agreed than the wazir ordered the tree chopped down. The entire hunting party of the king quickly brandished their gleaming axes and started striking at the tree where Sanykisar sat. She protested by crying and hurling abuses at the cutters. But nothing seemed to stop them. The tree was soon cut down and the king took Sanykisar with him to his palace.

The king, God bless his soul, already had six wives. Sanykisar was to be the seventh. One day the king summoned all his other wives, and gave them each an equal quantity of paddy. Then he said, "The one who husks this paddy quickest will be my chief queen." The six queens started on their job in earnest. Sanykisar had no experience at all at such tasks. She sat near the window of her room crying and sobbing over her helplessness. "If only my 'crow-father' knew where I was!" she thought, and tears rolled down her beautiful cheeks. At that moment the 'crow-father', who had been searching all this time, suddenly found the girl. He flew in her window and no sooner had he done this than she told her problem to him.

"Don't worry, my child. Everything will happen as you wish it." Saying this the 'crow-father' flew away. He soon returned with thousands of birds who very neatly and quickly husked the paddy with their beaks. After cleaning Sanykisar's room, they quickly left again. Sanykisar was happy and she hurried to report her progress to the king. On her way, she met other queens still struggling with their tasks. They asked her how she had finished so quickly. "It was very simple," she replied. "I put the paddy, the mortar, and the pestle into the river Jehlum. After a few minutes the paddy floated up all husked and cleaned," said she. All the other foolish queens went to the river bank and did exactly what Sanykisar said she had done. They spent many anxious hours waiting for their rice to emerge husked and cleaned. When nothing emerged, they realized their mistake. They returned to their rooms wailing. Soon the king visited their seven rooms to see who had won the contest. To his utter surprise he found that only Sanykisar, the crow-girl, had succeeded. All the others had lost their paddy.

The next morning the king summoned all his queens again. This time he told them to decorate their respective rooms. The one who did the best job would be made his chief queen. The six queens started on their job in earnest. They used the finest perfumes to wash the walls and all kinds of royal things as decorations. But Sanykisar had no experience at all at such tasks. She sat near the window of her room, crying and sobbing over her helplessness. At that time her 'crow-father' flew in again to inquire about her welfare. No sooner had he done this than she began narrating her problems. "Today the king asked us to decorate our rooms," she said. "I know nothing of that sort of thing. Oh, my crow-father, what do I do now?"

The crow answered, "Don't you worry, my child. Everything will happen as you wish." Saying this the 'crow-father' flew away. He soon ordered thousands of his fellow birds to get the best things available on earth to decorate Sanykisar's room. Then thousands and thousands of birds of all varieties brought the juices of beautiful and scented herbs and smeared the walls with them. They further decorated the room with all the finest things one might imagine to exist. It looked wonderful. Sanykisar was happy and hurried to invite the king to visit the room. On the way she again met the other queens, who were still busy decorating. They asked her how she had done this splendid job so quickly. Sanykisar replied, "It was simple! I mixed some cow dung, some human shit, and some cow piss. I smeared all the walls with these. Now the walls are as beautiful as can be."

The other queens, forgetting their previous mistake, brought huge quantities of cow dung, human shit and cow piss to the palace, mixed them, and then smeared the walls of their rooms. Oh! what a bad stench it was! Their rooms stank while Sanykisar's room shone. When the king visited the rooms of these six foolish queens, he was disgusted. He held his nose tight and

took a long fresh breath only upon entering the room of Sanykisar. Needless to say, Sanykisar won this contest, too.

Then, the next day, the king asked his queens to prepare some
delicious dishes. He promised that whosoever prepared the finest
dish would be his chief queen. The six women all started collecting fine ingredients for cooking, but poor Sanykisar had never
had any experience in this. So, sad as she was, she sat near the
window of her room sobbing and crying. At that time the 'crow-
father' flew in once more. No sooner had he done this than
Sanykisar told him about the newest task proposed by the king.
Hearing about this the 'crow-father' said, "Don't you worry, my
child. Everything will happen as you wish it to." The 'crow-
father' then flew away. Soon he came back with the same retinue
of birds. This time they were loaded with the choicest foods and
flavors, and they prepared the most delicious dishes the world
had ever known. Then they quickly flew away. Sanykisar was
pleased and she soon hurried to invite the king to taste the dishes
she had cooked for him. On the way to the king's chamber, she as
usual met the other six wives of the king. Naturally they asked
her how she had prepared so many delicacies within such a short
time. And, as usual, she replied, "It was simple! I brought some
trombi [an inedible herb], added cow dung to it for spice, and
then cooked it in cow urine. And that is all; the best dish in the
world is ready!"

The stupid queens did exactly what Sanykisar had described.
When the king started tasting the delicacies of the six queens, he
rushed out of their rooms vomiting and spitting. He was very
angry with these women. When he had recovered, he came to
Sanykisar's room. There he was delighted to taste dishes he had
never enjoyed before. He was very pleased and quickly made
Sanykisar his chief queen. He then divorced the other six women.
The couple lived happily thereafter, and they ruled for a long,
long time.

Part III
Parents and Children

---

*I*N THE EYES of most Indians, the bonds between parent and child are the most sacred of all human ties. A time of crisis can threaten sibling loyalties, or even dissolve a partnership between husband and wife; but for parents, little can rival the concern with protecting and nurturing a child. Similarly, people feel that nothing should detract from a person's willingness to care for aging relatives. Perhaps this is why so few Indian folktales focus directly on the bond between parent and child. This attachment is too firm, and too universally accepted, to be interesting. Hence stories about these issues, when they are found, go to great extremes. Exile, murder, and even cannibalism, for example, are common themes. Though these are shocking events, nothing less than gross violence can challenge such solid ties. The day-to-day dynamics of parent-child relationships, by contrast, remain largely unexamined in these tales.

The following section includes four types of stories about parents and children. They are: (1) male challenges to parental authority, (2) female challenges to the same authority, (3) desperate bargains made by childless couples, and (4) status claims made by reference to mythic parental acts. Not all the stories classed under these headings, however, have to do strictly with ties between parents and children. Other relationships such as bonds with father-in-laws and grandfathers are also included. In our view, this broad perspective adds to, rather than detracts from, an evaluation of the intergenerational attitudes found in our collection as a whole. Initiatives challenging parental authority come mainly from male children in these Indian tales. Significantly, too, the father usually (perhaps always) wins such contests. In fact, this is the case with each of the first three tales in this section. Notice, furthermore, that the son's challenge always relies on some kind of magic theme. A more direct rebellion would be crude.

The first story is from Nagaland and concerns a son who disobeys his father's injunction to help with the fieldwork. Instead, this boy wants to listen to prophecies about the weather provided by a bird. The father responds angrily to this little rival and eventually has the bird killed. As a result the son quickly loses his extrahuman communication skills. Following the first tale is a story from Kashmir. There a father's thoughtless behavior, as an uninvited guest at others' weddings, becomes a great embarrassment to his sons. They are already married men, and they now try to reeducate this aging parent, taking great pains and expending considerable resources to do so. But the senior male resists all efforts at reform and eventually lapses back into his old habits due to the force of certain eating rituals. His role as family master is thus regained. His sons have no choice but to submit. A third story, from West Bengal, shifts matters to a mythical plane. There we see Lord Dharma "testing" his three divine sons, Brahma, Vishnu, and Siva. The two elder ones ignore their father's putrid corpse, a clear act of filial impiety. But the youngest son is more compliant, or at least more shrewd. He welcomes and honors his "aged" father. That son is well-rewarded for his pains. All three tales suggest, then, that a son's deference to his parents (especially to his father) is very important. Male rebellion is shown to be costly and also to be very likely to fail.

The next group of stories deals with females, and here we find more upbeat themes. Two examples are provided. Both deal with magical figures whose initial place lies inside an ordinary human family. Gradually, the women's rejection of that milieu is merged with revelations of their more exotic status. Such differences illustrate how females, in contrast to males, generally respond to family confrontation. The first story is about a "truth daughter" who runs away to establish her own home. There her parents are turned back from the door and are not allowed to visit. This girl now reveals her status as a goddess, soon forcing members of several different groups to worship her. Eventually she becomes a "mother" whom new devotees, including her parents, begin to serve. Her link to the fertility of local fields furthers this redefinition of her role and enhances her shift in status. With this girl's successful rebellion from subordination, however, goes the development of a typically strong, volatile, and fearful personality.

The second story in this group has some similarities in form but concerns a gradual move toward independence made by a mistreated daughter-in-law. She also escapes by finding a way to link herself to the gods. Though called a mother's sister, this goddess is somewhat like a substitute for the mother, much as the little bird became a surrogate father in the first story. The two outcomes, however, are substantially different. The girl gradually becomes a leader in human terms and a founder of a local cult. Her parents-in-law eventually recognize her independent status. A parallel role for the boy never develops. He never becomes a magician or soothsayer.

The third group of stories in this section helps in further pinpointing the difference between sons and daughters. The next two tales both concern childless couples. More accurately, the first describes a king who has seven childless queens, the second a Brahman with seven daughters. Both these men suffer from an excess of dependent women. Neither has the son he needs. Thus each man finally strikes a bargain with an unknown outsider. Significantly, as in so many Indian stories, that stranger-mendicant has some special power over human fertility. The implication is that both strangers are forms of Lord Siva, the erotic ascetic of Hindu mythology, par excellence. Both beggars demand a hard bargain for their gift of life. In each case, a son, yet unborn, must be returned to the stranger at the point of adolescence. The desperate parents agree to this condition. Only when the boy matures does the full horror of this hasty bargain surface: now the child's own life must be given as the return gift. The implications are sacrificial and religious in tone. These parents are asked to choose between loyalty to god, a parentlike superior, and protection for their only son. This is a common tale scenario. In the end, the parents agree to this harsh divine will. But the audience can already predict that divine grace will influence the final outcome. In the first story the son saves himself by an act of bravery at the last minute (remember he is the son of a king). In the second tale the son submits (he is the son of a Brahman) but moments later is revived by the gods through acts of faith by his family. The parents thus pass their religious test. But the price is high: they must first sever the most sacred of all kin ties. Submission to god here takes clear precedence over all human bonds.

The final group of stories in this section concerns mythic parental figures. Here is the one context where the normal separation between secular family persons and sacred, other-worldly figures is allowed to soften. In the first story, from Gujarat, a farming community asserts their right to local lands, to divine blessings, to prosperity, and also to the use of cunning in the conduct of group affairs. Their claim is that Lord Siva is their personal father-in-law. If status and property rights are generally inherited from fathers, so are the more magical and cosmic parameters of being seen to flow from a marriage with the right woman. A caste origin story that refers to divine in-laws thus serves to merge paternal and divine roles. The final story of this set has a similar purpose. Again it concerns the mythical origins of a group of cultivators, achieving a contrast between their own farming role with that of hunters or fish-ermen (the first story depicted warriors). This time the family ancestor is a grandfather, another kind of pseudoparent. In both stories then, one can see how the bond between father and child plays an important role in the definition of social identity and the mapping of communal social status more generally.

· 18 · *The Boy Who Could Speak with Birds (Nagaland)*

This story has to do with the sacrifice of a dove. The scene is one of small rice fields bordered by thick jungle, and the focus on understanding bird language conveys a sense of animal and human closeness. The tale ending links it to local tradition, explaining why young people in the area should not eat the meat of the dove. This dietary restriction may be linked to local totemic beliefs since a secret sympathy between the boy and his pet bird also enables him to understand its language. Like the stories about the goddess Manasa (see tale 22), who appears to her devotee in the form of a fish and then as a snake, so the bird here also has some divine qualities. This dove is like a magical parent that serves to counter the harsh words of an actual guardian. The boy being forced to eat the bird's flesh provides a parallel with the parents of Akanundan in tale 24 being forced to eat their son. The two stories, however, have significantly different outcomes. The young Akanundan is brought back to life, but the dove is not revived. Instead the bird's death comes to form the basis of a lasting dietary taboo. These differences poignantly contrast mainstream Hindu attitudes, captured by the Kashmiri story, and the more tribelike worldview illustrated by the following tale.

ONCE THERE LIVED a village farmer who had a very smart son. The family paddy field was located on a gentle slope of a hill and at the edge of a jungle. A hill stream in the jungle flowed close to the edge of the field. This stream, however, was usually dry during the winter months. Water could only be found in a few small pockets of rocks that lay scattered along the bed of the stream. The father and son went to their fields each day to work while the mother stayed home to look after the house. The father worked long hours and would send his son to the stream to draw water. The boy often lingered a long time on his trips and would return to the house with his bamboo vessels only at the end of the day. In the course of his trips the boy loved to wander in the jungle. He found many birds there and he loved to listen to their cries. He grew to understand the birds' language, and he took a great interest in listening to their conversations. He heard the birds discuss their daily needs, the way that humans mistreated them, and learned how they constructed their nests and shelters. But the most important topic that the birds discussed was the weather. They were always concerned about the weather and the boy found that his friends were experts in forecasting what was in store.

Finally the boy told his father that he had become an expert in understanding the conversations of birds, but his father refused to believe him. Instead the man chastised his son for speaking incredulously. He suspected his son of lying and of wanting to spend extra time in the jungle so as to escape the hard work required in the paddy field. Indeed, the father was very worried about his son's total disinterest in farmwork. On the other hand, the boy was very worried about his father's disinterest in the secret knowledge of the birds.

One day the boy came running out of the jungle searching for his father who was again working in their field. The son was covered with sweat and as soon as he came within earshot of his father he cried, "Father, we must go home quickly. Hurry up! The birds are saying that a fierce hailstorm is going to descend on us this evening. We must go home now or be trapped until late at night." But the father did not believe his son's words and dismissed this warning as a form of madness. A few hours later a big storm arrived. It was accompanied by a cyclone, hailstones, thunder and lightning. The downpour and heavy winds continued for several hours. The father and son were trapped in a small shelter at the side of their field until late at night.

In the months that followed the young boy continued to draw water each day from the jungle stream, but it was winter now and there was little rain. Each evening he found the birds clustered around a few pockets of water hidden in the stream bed. Indeed he found great flocks of these creatures and he loved to watch them. He could see racket-tailed drongos, wrens, sunbirds, goldcrests, scarlet minivets, pheasants, curlews, emerald doves, choughs, bulbuls, owls, and many other kinds of birds. The boy always sat silently behind a large rock or tree, and from there he would listen to their conversations with great care.

At last spring was approaching and the people were beginning to sow seeds in their fields for the coming harvest. One day when the boy's father was sowing, the son ran up to him again. It was late in the evening after sunset, and the boy approached his father more cautiously than before. "Father, please listen to me this time. Don't consider me mad and don't dismiss my warnings as nonsense. This is very important. The birds are saying there will be a severe drought this year. They say the rains will be very late. Indeed, the birds are so concerned about a future scarcity of drinking water that they fear even for themselves. So, let us not sow our seeds now. It would be better to wait. If we sow them now they will dry and die before the rains arrive." This time, though, the father did not rebuke his son. Indeed he did not even think about what his son had said. Instead, he merely concentrated that much harder on his unending farmwork. The father was determined to continue sowing and to do as the other villagers were doing. He entirely dismissed the birds' prediction of drought.

That evening as the father and son began walking home they passed two doves sitting on a tree cooing loudly. Then the father turned to his son and said in a jesting manner, "Son, what are those doves saying to one another?" The boy replied in a serious tone, "Father they are speaking joyfully about all the seeds we have just sowed in the fields. They are saying all this will be theirs. The ground will remain dry and the seeds will not germinate. They are looking forward to a feast on our seed grain." The father replied only, "What foolish doves! How can those birds eat up all our seed grains?" The father and son continued walking and when they reached home the father narrated all these events to his wife. He spoke about his son's negligence of duty in the paddy fields and about how he had spent all day in the jungle. He also mentioned the boy's translation of the bird's conversation, saying that her son claimed to understand the bird's language.

The mother at once believed in her son's secret knowledge. She imagined that he might, in the course of time, become a soothsayer. This was not a favorable profession in his parents' eyes. The father also feared that his son would become lazy and continue to avoid work in the fields. If the son became well known for his supernatural power he might, instead, begin traveling around the countryside answering questions for others. Both parents finally

became convinced that their son really did have a knowledge of
the birds' language. But they decided to conceal this discovery
and hoped this would force him to abandon his secret. Indeed, his
parents went to greater lengths than this. The next day the father
left his son at home and went alone to the fields. There he laid
traps and managed to kill the two doves that had been speaking
to one another the previous evening. He brought these dead
doves home in a bag but kept them hidden from his son.

The following morning the parents cooked the two doves
while their son was still asleep. When the boy woke up his parents gave him some curry soup to drink in a big bamboo cup.
They told him that it was chicken soup. The boy gladly accepted
the drink but as he raised it to his lips he suddenly shouted, "No,
no father and mother! This is not chicken soup. I see two doves
inside my mug. Look here! They are the same doves who were
speaking last night near our fields. I will not drink this soup."
But the boy's parents forced him to drink, threatening him with
punishment if he refused. The boy closed his eyes and swallowed
the liquid with great reluctance. His parents also forced him to
eat the meat, saying that it was from a chicken. The boy suspected that the doves had been cooked. Nevertheless, he ate out
of fear of his parents' punishment.

A number of days passed and the boy began to lose his secret
powers. He could no longer understand the bird's language when
he listened to them in the family field or in the jungle. In addition to losing his knowledge of the bird's language he also became dull. The boy lost his common sense and he would not work
either on the farm or at home. He did not even remember to eat
unless told to do so by his parents. Sometimes he behaved like a
mad man, just standing or sitting without moving for many
hours. He was useless to his father in the fields.

The boy's parents then came to realize that the dove's soup
they had prepared had affected their son's brain. They regretted
their past actions and they regretted having forced him to eat this
special preparation. The drought then arrived as predicted. All
the rice plants dried in the fields. Only those few seeds which had
been sown late in the season grew well. The rains that year were
very late. As a result, a severe famine followed. The harvest was

very small. The boy's parents were further saddened because of
the loss of their son's secret powers.

To this day, therefore, elders advise their youngsters not to eat
the meat of the dove. They warn that this food will make a person
dull and will cause him to go mad. However, there is no restriction on the elderly. It is said that the old are not in danger
since they will die soon in any case.

· 19 · *The Uninvited Guest* *(Kashmir)*

The next story describes another kind of sacrifice, this time one
of family honor. The key figure is again a father who acts
against others' wishes and, particularly, against a request made
by his own sons. The theme is respectability, and when lost,
this is difficult for future generations of a family to regain. The
imagery again focuses on tabooed food as instrument for breaking key bonds between kin. The father of this story violates a
strong social norm by joining in feasts at neighbors' homes,
even when he has not been invited. The story turns on an
interesting psychological trait. This man cannot resist the appeal of eating whatever is served in ritual or ceremonial vessels.
Though told in Kashmiri, this lovely tale is again full of mainstream Hindu attitudes. It highly values wedding receptions
and family honor, and elaborate procedures govern the interaction of hosts and guests. It is interesting that such details here
take on an independent force. The rituals become so powerful
that they completely overpower an individual's better judge-
ment. In a sense, then, the heart of this tale is psychological. It
illustrates how strongly human behavior can be controlled by
culturally defined compulsions.

ONE TIME, not long ago, there lived an old man whose children
were already grown. They were all married and they all held respectable positions in society. The old man had everything an
average man his age might aspire to. But he did have one bad

habit. This man could not resist the temptation of attending a wedding feast. He would slip into the wedding party whether he had been invited or not, whenever he saw one. When he noticed a marriage in his neighborhood this man would dress himself cleanly and merge into the crowd. He would sit down in the midst of the other guests, smiling and happy. Usually, in such situations, no one knew whether he had been invited or not. The bride's side would think that he was a guest of the groom, the groom's side would think he was a guest of the bride. So for a time this man enjoyed a string of excellent wedding feasts and no one ever accused him of coming when not invited. Those people who did have doubts never expressed them for fear of being wrong.

But how long can such things remain undetected? Soon there were whispers among the feasting guests about the uninvited person who was always present. Tongues started wagging and now this news spread like wildfire across the village. Soon this gossip reached several neighbors of the old man's family. Finally it reached the ears of his own respected sons. No one mentioned the father directly to his sons. Yet, everyone came to know that people in the village were talking about him behind their backs. The sons felt insulted and hurt. They wanted to do something to stop their father's bad habit. So they went to their father and asked him to please be sensitive to the prestige of the family. They asked him to give up his habit of attending wedding feasts when he was not invited. But nothing seemed to help. The old man was like an experienced street dog. He could smell feasts no matter how far away they were and he would move toward one almost automatically.

Each time the man's sons asked him to reform he would politely listen. He would then assure them that he would do what they asked. Yet the moment the man heard of another feast he would be there, cleanly dressed. He would still sit among the guests, smiling and happy as before. Then one day a wedding was to be held in the very next house. For some unknown reason, too, the old man was not invited. This time the sons took extra care to see that their father did not repeat his old trick. Obviously, the family in the next house knew every member of the old man's household. He could not pass himself off this time unless he was formally invited. His sons saw this as the crucial test of their family's honor, and they wanted to safeguard it at any cost. The sons therefore asked their wandering father to stay home on this day. They then promised him they would cook the same special foods and sweets being cooked in the house the wedding guests were visiting. They thus planned an identical feast for their father to enjoy in their own home. There he would not have to suffer from whispered insults. The father agreed to their suggestion.

On the day of the feast the sons called their wives and instructed them to cook all the varieties of foods that were being cooked in the house next door. These obedient women did exactly what they had been asked to do. And when all the foods were ready the old man was made to sit near the window, in a side room, that directly faced the dining room next door. This way he could see for himself that each variety of food served to the guests at the true wedding was also being served to him in his own house. Even the schedule of serving the dishes was going to be the same. For example, when the sheets were spread in front of the guests next door, a sheet was spread for the old man in his own house. When a house guest next door was served water for washing his hands, the devoted daughters-in-law offered their father-in-law a hand wash as well. in the same manner, whenever a particularly delicious item was presented to the guests next door, the same item was served to the old man in his own house. Meanwhile the sons kept guard at the door. They wanted to make sure that their father did not leave and become captured by a temptation to join the party nearby. For a time the old man seemed happy with these arrangements. Everything seemed to be working well.

But then something surprising happened. The cook in the house next door entered the room where the guests were seated with a special earthen vessel and ladle. These implements were intended for serving the main course. The old man was watching with nostalgia. In his own house his daughters-in-law were serving him a similar course. But, alas, they did not use the traditional ritual vessel and ladle. The old man's head began moving sideways, like the hands of a clock. Something unexplainable began happening inside him. He suddenly got up, jumped out the window, and ran into the house next door. There he joined the other wedding guests who were being fed. Oh my, what a beautiful smile could now be seen on his face! The sons and daughters-in-law were stunned at this unexpected turn of events. Their prestige and respect were now in the gutter. No one was able to look their neighbor in the eye, and they all retreated from the windows. Indeed, they shut the shutters and hid in the interior rooms of the house. Meanwhile the old man sat happily among the neighbor's guests and enjoyed their feast, uninvited. Nobody refused him food for that would have been counter to custom. How could one refuse a close neighbor?

After eating his fill at the feast next door, the father returned home smiling and happy. But his sons were very angry and refused to talk to him. In the evening, however, they finally surrounded their father to demand an explanation. "Father, why are you so bent upon bringing disgrace to our family? We prepared every single dish that the house next door prepared. We took great care to see that our foods were equally well cooked. Everything, including the serving order of the foods was exactly like the one next door. What made you run over there, even though you were not invited?" The old man began scratching his head, and after a little pause he answered with a smile. He said, "It is true, my children! You prepared every variety of food served next door with the same great care. You are correct in saying that each dish prepared here was as tasty as that which I received there. It is also true that the items you served were offered in the same order as they were next door. But no special vessel was used, and no special ladle. When I saw those serving implements I could not control myself, even though I had no intention of disgracing you. Please believe me." The sons were speechless. They kept quiet and then slowly dispersed. But people say that they did not open the windows of their house for a very long time.

· 20 ·   *The Birth and Marriage of Siva (West Bengal)*

This account is one of several myths in this collection. It is about the origin of the great gods of Hinduism and about how procreation on earth began. As in most such stories, autochthonous reproduction and incestuous mating are both involved. Indeed, these irregular processes seem to be a logical necessity if one tries to imagine how a primeval state of oneness might have evolved into our current, bisexual human condition. Here an original male being called Dharma, a figure associated with cosmic necessity, creates his own daughter Sakti. Fourteen years later, at her maturity, Dharma impregnates this girl via a poison which he prepares and she surreptitiously drinks. Sakti then becomes a world-mother who in turn gives birth to the great divine triad: Brahma, Vishnu, and Siva. A second incestuous union occurs when Sakti herself marries the youngest of her own sons. And finally, the birth of creatures as we know it begins. This story is similar to many other Hindu myths about creation, both in the names and characters of the gods it describes and in the very prominent place it gives to a cosmic female principle. As in similar variants told in South India, Sakti here serves as womb-mother for the three great gods. The use of sweat, spittle, and poison for creative purposes are also widespread Hindu myth motifs. The concern with corpses and the linking of birth, death, and powerful eyesight are also significant Hindu themes. Finally, this account clearly represents a Saivite sectarian perspective. It makes Siva the cleverest of the three brothers, and Siva and Sakti the world's primeval couple.

LONG AGO, the primeval goddess Adi-Sakti was born from the sweat of Lord Dharma. But soon after creating this daughter, Dharma went to the riverbank to practice his meditation exercises. He remained absorbed in his own thoughts for fourteen long years. Finally, he was disturbed by his airborne vehicle, the owl [*uluk*]. This owl reminded him of his daughter and persuaded him to abandon his meditations and return home to check on her. But in fourteen years this daughter had become a young woman. When Dharma saw this he went in search of a groom for her. He left behind one pot of honey and one pot of poison. During his absence the daughter became more and more desirous. Finally, when she could not bear the feeling any longer, she drank the poison. This made her pregnant. In due course she gave birth to the three great gods: Brahma, Vishnu, and Siva. All three of these sons were born blind. They were also very religious. They soon went to the bank of a river to give themselves up to divine contemplation.

Seeing these three men absorbed thus in meditation, Dharma now determined to test them. So he floated down the river in the form of a putrid-smelling corpse. As Dharma's transformed body approached Brahma, he began to notice a terrible smell. So the sage took three palmfuls of water and ceremoniously sent the corpse on down the river. Next, the great Lord Dharma floated in front of Vishnu. The mighty Vishnu also noticed a foul smell and soon did the same, sending the corpse on down the river using three palmfuls of water. Finally, the corpse arrived in front of Siva. When Siva noticed the bad smell, however, he thought to himself, "How could there already be a smell of death when there has been no birth?" Siva, being a famous master of mysteries, thus came to realize that this smell could be nothing more than an illusion created by the great Lord himself. So instead of sending the body on down the river, Siva grabbed a hold of it with his two hands and began to dance. He also realized that he had been the only one of the brothers to have recognized Lord Dharma in his concealed form. Dharma was very pleased with Siva and responded by bestowing him with the gift of eyesight. Dharma's words were, "You were blind in both eyes. In recompense I now grant sight in those, plus one additional eye that can also see." Siva was very pleased. He bowed down at the Lord's feet and began to sing his praise. He then prayed to Dharma, asking him to bless his two brothers with eyesight as well. Dharma then explained to Siva that his spittle would be enough to bring sight to both his brothers. Siva then used his spittle and blessed both his brothers with divine vision.

The three brothers next went together to visit Adi-Sakti. Dharma then commanded Brahma to create the world. He charged Vishnu with protecting it and asked the three-eyed Siva to assume the task of destroying it. Then Dharma turned to Adi-Sakti and asked her to take on the work of giving birth to all creatures. But Sakti responded in puzzlement asking, "How am I to bring forth creatures in this world? I was born without parents and I do not possess the power of conception. Oh, master, what shall I do to carry out your orders?" Lord Dharma then asked her to follow his advice. She was to marry Lord Siva once in each of her many births to come. Adi-Sakti agreed. The fruit of her union with Siva was the birth of the many creatures in this world.

· 21 · *Chokanamma (Kerala)*

The heroine of this tale is referred to as a *satya kanni*. This is an awkward term to translate, but it appears again and again in reference to heroines in the folk mythology of many parts of India. Literally the phrase means "truth-girl," but its connotations are far broader than what the reader might associate with these words in English. It usually refers to a teenage girl or young woman of divine origin, who is sexually innocent and incapable of wrongdoing. Sita, heroine of the famous *Ramayana*, is such a woman. Folk literature stresses the persecution of such "truth-girls" which leads to a revelation of their supernatural powers and to their ability to cause strange events. It is not uncommon to find these heroines worshipped in local cults, as is the case with Chokanamma.

THERE WERE NO CHILDREN for the Brahman family of Mathila-kattu. The father's name was Chokanna Arakil Chitrar and the mother was called Edattandi Peruvala. Both were deeply grieved that they had no offspring. So Edattandi Peruvala went to Madhuvana to ask a boon from the saint, Irishiyavu. She gathered seven baskets of *camata* flowers as an offering and did forty days of penance. Irishiyavu then appeared before the woman and asked, "What boon would you desire from me?" Edattandi asked for a child. Irishiyavu received her offering of camata flowers, blessed them with a *mantra* [sacred words], and returned them. A doe soon smelt the fragrance of those lovely flowers and came from the forest to eat them. The deer thus became pregnant. After ten months she made a hollow under an *eccil* tree and delivered a

human girl as her fawn-child. The doe then abandoned the
human baby.

A man and a woman of the Kuruva tribe came along hunting
for deer and searching for honey. They saw the child in the hollow of the tree. "We cannot look after this child ourselves," said
the Kuruva woman. "The Mathilakattu family of our village has
no children." So they brought the child to the home of the local
Brahman family, and as is the custom, received a small present
from them in return. The Brahmans named the child Chokanamma. As she grew up they found that she liked to play in the shrine
room. As this made the room impure, her father warned her not
to play there. But Chokanamma continued to play in the shrine,
until her parents finally beat her.

After a time the girl told the Brahmans, "I don't want to stay
with you anymore." Then she collected up her toys and left the
house. Chokanamma wandered until she came to a place where
three roads crossed. There, as she swung on some vines, seven
carpenters passed by. She asked that they build her a house. They
refused to listen and continued on their way. Soon they became
lost. It was then that they realized that the girl was no ordinary
girl. She was what is known as a "girl of truth." Then the carpenters went back and asked her what kind of house she wanted. She
told them it must have seven doors. So they cut a tree and made a
house with seven doors. Chokanamma stayed there.

When she attained puberty her Brahman father said, "Our
daughter has reached puberty. We must prepare rice with milk
and present it to her." So Chokanamma's mother prepared the
rice dish and both parents brought this offering to her. But
Chokanamma saw her parents coming. So she closed the seven
doors and hid within the house. "Open the doors, daughter,"
they called to her. But call as they might, she refused to open
them. So the parents left the dish and returned home. After they
left, she opened the door and in a fit of anger threw the rice into a
nearby field. Thereafter the rice from that field was red rice and
the place became famous for its cultivation.

Chokanamma then decided to leave her house and go to
Ezhavanattu Lanka. There she saw a palm tree. She commanded
it to bow down at her feet and it did. She then became a spirit
and entered that tree. A Nayar general soon came along with a

company of Tiyyar warriors. They were searching for material with which to make a fine bow. The Nayar pointed to the palm tree and said that it would do nicely. He sent one of the Tiyyars with an axe to cut it down. "You must not touch me," the palm tree said. "You must not allow an untouchable to touch me," it told the Nayar.

So the Nayar cut the tree himself. When the tree fell, the goddess sat on the stump, while the Nayar had twelve bows made. Then the goddess entered the largest bow and thus she was carried to the house of the Nayar. There she caused such trouble that the Nayar called for a diviner to find out what the matter could be. The diviner soon realized that a goddess was involved. "It is Chokanamma," he told the Nayar. "You must make arrangements for a proper propitiation. A shrine must be constructed and every year a ceremony must be conducted."

This is the story of Chokanamma and of her worship.

· 22 ·   *The Youngest Daughter-in-law*
          (West Bengal)

The next story is about the interaction of a young girl with a powerful goddess. It also serves as an origin story for this deity's local worship. Divine and human characters often exhibit parent-child bonds, particularly in folk legends. Though in a larger perspective local deities are generally viewed as specific forms of great gods (Siva, Vishnu, Parvati), as localized figures they often have a family style of interaction with devotees. Female deities, for example, often take the form of magical daughters raised by favored human beings. In this tale the formidable Bengali goddess Manasa first manifests herself as a school of fish in a pond and later as eight snakes that become pets of a family's youngest daughter-in-law. She nurses these serpents, as if they were her own children. Afterwards this girl finds herself in heaven where she is treated like a daughter by the goddess. Tale 38, in the next section, provides an interesting male variant of these same parent-child and human-divine ties.

This paradoxical sometimes mother, sometimes daughter relationship is typical of the interactions of local gods with people. Most devotees bathe and feed symbols of divinity, as a loving parent would a child. Yet these same persons also submit to the authority of a deity and use parental terms of address (mother, father) in worship. This particular story describes the snakes through which Manasa manifests herself. Usually a goddess is guarded by several males, and it is in this sense that these snakes are addressed as young brothers. Snakes and water are strongly associated with the mythology of Manasa and nicely fit her fearful underside, which she shares with many other local goddesses. Many of these divine women reflect Parvati's own darker aspect as Kali. Generally, in Indian folktales, the youngest child is the one seen to have magical qualities. Yet the youngest also stands in danger of losing such qualities if a breach of taboo takes place. Here it is the youngest daughter-in-law who forms a relationship with a divine being. An alliance between herself, the youngest of seven wives, and Manasa balances out an otherwise underdog position. In her human family she is disliked by her mother-in-law and by her elder sisters-in-law, while in Manasa she finds an ally and protector.

THERE ONCE LIVED a merchant who had seven daughters-in-law. According to custom, he regularly received presents from the homes of all these girls, except from the very youngest. For this reason the wife of the merchant was very displeased. One rainy day all of the girls expressed a wish to eat something they considered very special. The youngest daughter-in-law was pregnant at the time and her desire was for boiled rice. She wanted the rice to be prepared by steeping it in cold water and to be served with a special sour preparation made of fish.

That same evening all of the daughters-in-law went to bathe in a nearby pond. The pond was inhabited by fish which had been hiding there since the time of a great forest fire. These fish were really serpents who had previously lived in the woods nearby. But as the fire had raced through their forest they had changed into fish, saving themselves by jumping into water. The youngest daughter-in-law now leaned over the edge of the pond and seized these fish in a cloth that she had with her. Her husband's brothers' wives noticed her catching something. Jealous of her luck they turned and said to each other, "Her wish for a tasty meal will soon be fulfilled."

The youngest daughter-in-law went home with the fish and the next day she began her preparations for cooking them. But to her great surprise she noticed that each one had taken a snake form. The girl then decided to nurse these snakes with a special preparation of milk and bananas.[1] The snakes were fed well by the girl, and they soon were invigorated and left her for Manasa's home in heaven.[2] There they told this deity how the youngest daughter-in-law had fed them so well. The goddess Manasa was pleased and went to fetch this new devotee. She dressed in a suitable way and presented herself at the house of the merchant. The goddess then addressed the wife, pretending to be a forgotten aunt. She spoke about her desire to take her youngest daughter-in-law away for a few days for a visit with her family.

The wife of the merchant agreed and the goddess Manasa set out with her daughter-in-law. The aunt helped the young girl into her chariot and told her to keep her eyes shut. She was to reopen them only when asked. After the goddess Manasa reached her home in heaven she asked the daughter-in-law to open her eyes. The young girl now saw that she was in a big mansion. She also found the eight snakes she had nursed waiting inside. Manasa then said, "You are to worship me everyday and to prepare warm milk for these eight snake brothers of yours. But be careful! Never look to the south."

The youngest daughter-in-law thought to herself, "Why am I forbidden to look to the south? What might I see there? So one day the young girl turned her eyes in the forbidden direction and there she saw the goddess Manasa dancing. As she watched she became enraptured. Thus the girl totally forgot to feed her serpent brothers. But when the goddess Manasa stopped her dancing the daughter-in-law remembered. She quickly warmed the milk. The eight snakes came at that moment for their drink. But the milk had not had time to cool. So when the serpents put their mouths to the saucer they were scorched by the hot liquid. The snakes now became very angry and tried to bite the young girl. But Manasa intervened saying, "You should not bite in my house. I want to send this girl back to her own home on earth. Follow her, if you wish, and bite her there."

Soon afterwards Manasa left for the earth with the young girl. She now warned the daughter-in-law that her snake brothers were angry with her. The goddess told her to praise these creatures as soon as she got home. Before Manasa left the house, however, she decorated one side of her daughter-in-law's body with ornaments. She then turned and laughed at the girl, saying in a deprecating voice, "What sort of fashion is this? I see half of a person decorated with ornaments while the other half is plain."

The youngest daughter-in-law replied to this unkind comment by saying, "I have taken care of my eight serpent brothers, fed them, and assured them life. Will they allow me to go half adorned? My eight brothers will decorate the other side of my body." The eight serpents listened from the cracks and corners of the house. Hearing the youngest daughter-in-law's praise they became very pleased and gave up their desire to bite her. The snakes then returned to Manasa in heaven. The goddess listened to the newly-returned serpents and deferred to their wishes. In compliance with their request, Manasa embellished the other half of the girl's body with ornaments. Later she also revealed herself before the youngest daughter-in-law in order to clarify her true identity. She said to the girl, "I am not really your aunt. I am the goddess Manasa. I am the queen of the serpents and my home can be found in the *sij* plant.[3] Your job is to perpetuate my worship on earth. For this purpose you are to gather specimens of this plant each year on the day of the Dussera festival, when the river Ganges is especially worshiped. You are also to gather the same plant on all days when serpents are worshipped. You must bathe before you make offerings to me and you are to prepare boiled rice steeped in cold water for your gifts. If you do these things you will never have to fear snakes."

Saying these things the goddess Manasa disappeared. The youngest daughter-in-law then told the rest of her family what had happened. From then on the whole family, and everyone in the region, began to worship Manasa with the rites they had been told to use.

· 23 · *The Wicked Mendicant*
(West Bengal)

This fascinating tale exhibits a host of clear images expressing fears that are widespread in village India. Childlessness or barrenness is a woman's greatest dread. The condition is inherently inauspicious and implies an act of misconduct or a curse in one's past. Attitudes toward the mendicant—called a *sannyasi*—are often negative, too. Such persons are believed to possess awesome supernatural powers. But, being wanderers, they are strangers wherever they go. Sannyasis are beyond the control of social norms and beyond economic coercion; they are outside all laws. This tale goes on to give voice to other fears: the unenviable position of the youngest bride, the fear of bearing deformed children, of giving birth to a nonhuman being, of losing one's child to some unhappy fate, and so on. The young prince of this story manages to keep his aristocratic courage throughout such a barrage of psychological onslaughts. He eventually conquers his fears.

ONCE UPON A TIME there was a king who had seven queens. But still he had no peace of mind because he had no children.

One morning the sweeper did not show up, and the king sent a policeman to fetch him. The policeman found the sweeper at home eating his meal and asked why he was taking his meal at such an unusual hour instead of being at work. The sweeper replied that since the king was childless it was inauspicious to see his face in the morning. When he did, he had to fast for the rest of the day. So, to avoid that discomfort, he was finishing his main meal before going to the palace to work. The policeman returned to the palace and informed the king of what the sweeper had told him. The king was mortified. He shut himself up in his chamber and resolved to put an end to his own life.

Soon a mendicant came to the palace and asked to see the king. The king came out of his chamber and received the holy ascetic with great respect. The mendicant knew the reason for the king's seclusion. He gave the king the root of a particular plant and told him to grind it into a powder and distribute the powder to each of his queens. If this was done, he assured the king, his queens

would conceive. However, he made it a condition of the conception that the best of the king's children must later be given to
him. The king agreed. The root was ground into a powder and
given to the seven queens. But the six older queens took all of the
powder for themselves and wouldn't let the youngest have any.
So, the youngest queen took some water and washed the stone on
which the root was ground. She then drank the water.

In due course, the queens all gave birth. The sons of the six
elder queens were born with defective limbs, while the youngest
gave birth to a conch shell. Seeing this, the king drove this queen
away from the palace. She was forced to take shelter in the forest,
where, with her conch shell, she built a straw hut and passed her
days in misery. At night the youngest queen began to dream that
a beautiful baby had come out of the conch shell each evening and
suckled at her breast. One night she only pretended to be asleep
in order to see whether this was really happening. Indeed, as she
lay there, a baby emerged from the conch shell and began to suck
at her breast. The queen then caught the child before it could
retreat into its shell, and took it into her arms, giving it tender
affection and holding it to her side. The young child then spoke
to her, saying, "You have done me great harm, mother. The
mendicant is sure now to come and take me away. It was for fear
of that that I concealed myself in the conch shell." The mother
assured the child that this would not happen. Together they returned to the palace and appeared before the king. Seeing the
beautiful male child in the queen's lap, he realized his mistake
and received the queen back to the palace with great respect.
When this prince reached the age of twelve, the mendicant returned and demanded that the king give up his best son. The
king could not refuse. The misery of the youngest queen knew no
bounds. Seeing her plight, some neighboring women advised her
to worship the goddess Sankata Mangal Chandi. This was her
only chance of getting her son back. The queen, in her misery,
devoted herself to the worship of that deity.

The mendicant, accompanied by the young prince, now entered a dense forest. At a certain place the mendicant stopped and
said to the prince, "There are two ways to my house. One is a
shortcut, but it is infested with wild beasts. The other is a round-
about way, but it is safe. Which would you like to take?" "I am
the son of a king! I am not afraid of anything. I wish to take the

shortcut," the prince replied. Following this path, the two reached a Kali temple. The mendicant was a devotee of this fierce goddess and worshiped her at this shrine. The mendicant next asked the prince to take his daily bath in the temple tank but forbade him to look toward the south. As the young prince was bathing, his curiosity got the better of him. He turned to see what lay to the south. He was horrified to find a huge heap of human skulls which laughed horribly as he stared.

"What are you laughing at?" the boy asked. The skulls replied, "We laugh at the thought that one more skull will be added to our pile today." "What do you mean by that?" asked the boy. "We were all brought here by the mendicant in the same way you have been. All of us have been sacrificed to the goddess. Today it is your turn. There is only one way you can avoid this fate, but it is a difficult way, indeed." "Tell me what it is and I shall do my best," said the prince. The skulls told him that at the end of his worship the mendicant would ask the boy to bow down in front of the idol of the goddess. They advised him to ask the mendicant to show him the proper way to bow at that moment since, as the son of a king, he had never had to bow before. When the mendicant demonstrated how to bow, the prince was told to take the sword from the hand of the idol and behead the mendicant with a single stroke. He should then sprinkle the man's blood on the heads of all the skulls. In this way they would all be brought back to life.

The prince carried out the plan and ended the life of the wicked mendicant. The skulls were revived and they, as well as the young prince, then returned to their respective countries. The parents of each missing child were delighted.

· 24 ·   *Akanandun the Only Son*
         (Kashmir)

Childlessness is a common theme in many Indian stories, and it could be considered as one of several popular formulaic devices for beginning a story which then allows the gods to intervene. On the one hand, barrenness leads to vows and to various kinds of religious penances. These are seen as compensation for a couple's previous misdeeds. A record of penance becomes a strong bargaining card which can eventually force the gods to bless a couple with fertility. On the other hand, divine figures can bargain back. They often use barrenness to test a devotee's faith and a person's willingness to submit to higher authority. One extreme example is a demand that one sacrifice one's own son. The theme of child sacrifice demonstrates a willing submission to the demands of more senior (and parentlike) divine figures. But such horrific actions are ultimately life-producing, just as ritual sacrifice is universally regenerative. The outcome of such stories, therefore, is always positive. Sacrificed children magically return to life with the help of the gods and thereby overcome early death—a fate that is often part of the earlier bargain their parents struck in order to lift a curse of barrenness. These classic themes are all nicely illustrated in the following story. Collected in Kashmir, this tale cuts across religious barriers and is popular among Moslems as well as Hindus. It has also been adapted by prominent Kashmiri writers and been used in highly successful theatre productions. Versions have been noted in classical and folk South Indian literature, too (Roghair, 1982:297–307; Hart 1980:217–36).

THERE ONCE LIVED a poor Brahman and his wife. They had seven daughters but no sons. The couple prayed and prayed and so did their daughters. But still there was no son for the parents and no brother for the seven girls. The Brahman visited all of the famous holy places. He met with many saints and religious men. He also gave alms to the poor, hoping that their blessings would earn him a son. But the gods did not seem to favor this outcome. The poor Brahman soon began to reason that his bad luck was the result of many sins committed in a previous life.

One day a beggar came to the Brahman's house seeking alms. The Brahman invited him in and showed him extensive hospitality. He first asked his wife to bring water to wash the beggar's feet. Then the guest was offered good food and rest. The visitor was pleased and soon asked if he could do anything in return. So the Brahman and his wife related their story and their woes. They cursed their fate for not having a son to continue the family line. Hearing of all this sadness the beggar was moved with pity. He soon said, "Oh Brahman! Do not grieve! You will have a son, but it will be on one condition." The Brahman was overwhelmed with emotion and interrupted at this point with the words, "I will agree to any condition whatever, oh holy man! Only let me have a son! I promise you I will do anything you want."

The saintly beggar then looked into the eyes of the Brahman and into those of his wife and proceeded with great seriousness, "You will have to return the boy when he is twelve years old." Then without waiting for the Brahman's answer the beggar suddenly disappeared. The household couple was saddened by the harsh condition the stranger had outlined. They were also puzzled by the manner in which he disappeared, but they did not have much time to worry as the Brahman's wife soon conceived. After nine months a son was born. This event filled the couple with hope and joy. Their great sense of happiness drowned the earlier sadness, at least for a few years. Indeed, the two almost forgot about the harsh condition the saintly beggar had set.

The young Brahman was soon given the name Akanandun, meaning "only son." He quickly grew to be a beautiful and very intelligent young boy. His mother and father showered much love and affection on him. And his sisters loved him even more. They would not let him out of their sight, even for a short while. When Akanandun reached the age of five he was sent to school. There he proved to be very clever in his studies, and he was admired by friends and teachers alike. At the age of ten the family celebrated his sacred thread ceremony with great pomp. This ritual entitled him to a second, or spiritual birth. But finally the day arrived when Akanandun was twelve years old.

One fine morning, while Akanandun was getting ready for school, the saintly beggar suddenly appeared at the door once again. At the sight of this man a dreadful chill went through the Brahman's spine. Nonetheless, he contained himself. What else could he do? A man's word cannot be given and then taken back. The mother and the sisters had also feared the reappearance of this man. It was the same fear that a lost lamb feels upon seeing a lion. As soon as the saintly beggar entered the house he asked for the young boy. "Where is Akanandun? Return him to me. Have you forgotten your promise?" he said. The Brahman answered, "Oh holy man! I stand by my word," but he was in tears. The drops rolled down this man's sunken cheeks. Nonetheless he soon brought Akanandun before the guest. The saint then said, "Give

the boy a ritual bath and wrap him in new clothes." The couple
gave Akanandun a bath. It was a bath of tears. They also clothed
him in new clothes and brought him to the stranger.

The saintly beggar then asked for a knife. When this was provided, the beggar swiftly cut off Akanandun's head. Then slowly
and carefully, like an expert butcher, he also cut off the limbs and
the other body parts. Seeing her only son torn to bits in this way,
the mother soon fainted. The sisters wept and beat their breasts.
They tore out their hair. Indeed the whole village came to know
of something which they had never heard of or seen in their lives
before. Soon after cutting Akanandun into many pieces, the beggar asked the couple to wash and purify the kitchen. He then
asked them to cook the little bits that had been Akanandun's
body. Amidst sounds of wailing so intense that they could have
melted stones, the butchered Akanandun was boiled.

Next the half dead mother was asked by the beggar to taste
this preparation, to see if it had enough salt. She did this. And as
if that was not enough, the beggar then ordered that the cooked
meat be served to both parents and also the the sisters and to any
other kinsmen who were present. But he also asked that one share
of the preparation be set aside in the name of Akanandun. Once
this had been done the beggar gave the order for everyone to
begin eating. My god! That was cannibalism! And no less than a
saintly beggar was ordering these actions! Everyone present heard
the sound of a roar in their hearts and in the sky. It was as if the
earth and the oceans had opened up. They felt day turn into
night. The animals and birds stopped breathing. Every star
which once shone in the sky disappeared.

Suddenly the saintly beggar asked the couple to call Akanandun's name and to ask him to come and take his food. This made
things even worse. No one could understand or even began to
question the purpose of such a joke. So they ignored the request.
But the beggar, true to his plan, was serious. He repeated his
order. "Call Akanandun. Call him and ask him to take his food.
Do what I say," he said. One of the sisters, fearing the wrath of
the beggar, finally obeyed. After mustering all her strength, she
cried out in a small voice, "Akanandana, Akanandana." And lo!
Akanandun suddenly appeared before his family, dressed neatly,
smiling, and holding his bag of books. No one present could
believe their eyes. Was this a dream or some kind of nightmare?

The mother, the father, and all the sisters broke into smiles. They began to kiss and to hug Akanandun. While this unexpected turn of events was being celebrated the saintly beggar disappeared. And so did all the cooked food. The birds started to fly again and animals began to move and to breathe. Daylight reappeared on the horizon and everything returned to normal. After this, Akanandun lived a long life with his parents.

· 25 · *Lord Siva and the Satwaras (Gujarat)*

Like tale 20, this is another short myth about Lord Siva. Instead of Bengal, however, this one comes from the opposite side of the subcontinent. It is a tale from the Saurastra area of Gujarat. The story provides a justification for the presence of a dominant landowning community there called the Satwara, who control much of the agriculture of this region. Furthermore, this tale describes the origins of a particular caste community rather than of the gods themselves. The account makes the ancestors of these men sons-in-law of Siva and their wives the god's own daughters. Siva grants them land in Saurastra in reward for their military prowess, but only on the promise that they serve as loyal farmers and return half of each crop to him. These clever men later trick Siva with a traditional ruse (tale type AT1030, Crop Division; see also tale 32) which promises him the useless half of the crop: roots in the case of millet, leaves and stalk in the case of sweet potatoes. Finally Siva agrees to let these men reap the full benefit of their labors. A similar myth, popular among agriculturalists in South India, makes a link between military prowess, land ownership, agricultural skills, and general cleverness. Hence, this story seems to be representative of agricultural caste origin stories throughout India. A mention of Parasuram also links the following account to Vishnu through one of his best known incarnations. It provides a bridge between this story and the great myths of Hinduism.

ONCE LONG AGO, in a period called the Satyuga, Parasuram wanted to exterminate the Kshatriyas, a class of warriors. Parasuram wandered all over the earth carrying an axe in the hopes of killing these fearsome men. Once he pursued sixteen young Kshatriyas who were frightened and who sought refuge in a temple dedicated to Lord Siva. The Kshatriyas began to pray saying, "Oh Siva, ocean of compassion and mercy, save us from the sharpened edge of Parasuram's axe." Lord Siva, in his mercy, heeded these prayers and created sixteen maidens out of the perspiration and dust of his own body. Siva then asked the warriors to marry these maidens and they agreed.

When Parasuram saw the sixteen warriors he raised his axe to kill them. But Lord Siva intervened at once and told him not to kill the men as they were all farmers and his sons-in-law. As a result Parasuram did not kill the Kshatriyas, and they lived on to claim their status as farmers. But this created a problem for Lord Siva. The Kshatriyas were sitting around with nothing to do. So they asked Siva to give them land. Siva agreed but only on certain specific terms. The great Lord insisted that each farmer give back to him half the produce on all lands that he would grant to them. The farmers agreed to comply with this request. Then the men asked, "Lord, what part of the crop would you like to share, the upper or the lower?" Sive answered, "The lower!" The farmers agreed, saying, "Well and good, Lord!"

Soon afterwards Lord Siva left for the Himalayas, and the sixteen farmers began to cultivate the land they had been given. These sons-in-law planted millet. After some months Lord Siva returned for another visit, at the farmers' request. But when he arrived he saw that all the grain had already been harvested and that only stalks remained behind in the fields to be shared. Lord Siva now realized that he had been cheated. But he did not utter a word. Instead he resolved not to be cheated again the following year. So he devised a plan to this effect. Next Siva returned to his home in the Himalayas.

When the rainy season arrived all sixteen Satwaras farmers called on Lord Siva again. They prayed to him and turned to his mountain abode saying, "Oh, Lord Siva, you are the greatest amongst all the gods." On hearing these prayers, Lord Siva opened his eyes and interrupted his meditations. He asked the farmers the reason for their visitation. The Satwaras replied, "Oh Lord Siva, we wanted to ask what part of the new crop you would prefer, the upper or the lower?" Lord Siva replied at once, "Only the upper part!" So the farmers agreed. They all bowed at the feet of the Lord and requested his blessings. Siva wished them well and they returned to their farms. The men plowed the fields with care and worked very hard. When it was time to sow they now planted sweet potatoes.

The farms were properly tilled, manured and watered, and the crop of sweet potatoes was abundant. The men were all delighted and they were in a jovial mood. They had never imagined that they would harvest such a prosperous crop. They were also gloomy, however, at the thought that half of this harvest would have to go to Lord Siva. Then one of the men realized that, "We will have to leave only the leaves of sweet potatoes for Siva. That is the upper part of the crop!" A second answered, "Yes, yes! You are correct. Siva demanded only the upper half." Then all the men agreed and they began to dance around in happiness. Later one of them traveled to Lord Siva's abode in the Himalayas. When he reached Mount Kailasa he asked Siva to descend to the farm to collect his share of the harvest. As in the agreement, Lord Siva's portion had been kept to one side. But it was obviously nothing but leaves and creepers. Lord Siva saw this but could say nothing as this was the bargain that had been struck beforehand. Henceforth, Siva agreed to give the entire harvest to his sons-in-law, saying, "You are the best and the most industrious agriculturalists in the world."

It is how the Kshatriyas became Satwara agriculturists, and how they became famous for their prosperity throughout Saurashtra and Gujarat.

· 26 · An Old Man's Wisdom (Nagaland)

This didactic tale, told among the Ao Nagas, needs little introduction. Its message is straightforward and readily understood in terms of a Western work ethic. What sets this story apart from others that are also popular among the tribal peoples of Eastern India is its pragmatic character. Here we see no animal helpers (see tale 18), nor do we have an intervention from the spiritual realm (see tale 22). Perhaps this tale is the product of Ao contact with outsiders, either Christian missionaries or Hindu peasants of the Brahmaputra plains.

ONCE UPON A TIME, in a certain village, an old man advised other men to spend their time cultivating rice. But those others went right along hunting wild animals and fishing in the streams. They gathered wild yams and wild fruits, not heeding the old man in the least. The work in the fields was entrusted to women, while the men kept on roaming the forest in search of wild foods. Soon the crops were overgrown with weeds, because the work of women alone was not enough to keep back the jungle.

The old man had a grandson who was very smart. Indeed the two lived together in the same house. The boy wanted to follow his friends hunting and fishing in the forest. He asked his grandfather's permission to go, but the senior man always refused. Grandfather was still strong and healthy, and he worked diligently in his fields. Still he insisted that his grandson come with him, and that they work together the whole day, every day, from planting right up to harvest time.

One day the grandson asked his grandfather if he might go with the other boys to hunt and fish in the forest. The old man gently denied his request. Instead, he asked that his grandson's friend bring back a small fish, alive. The friend agreed. Later that day he returned with such a fish. The old man then told his grandson to put the fish into the wooden trough often used for feeding pigs.

"Now, boy," said the old man, "catch this fish and give it to me." At first the boy thought it would be easy, so he used only one hand. Not being able to catch it with one, he soon tried with both hands. Still he couldn't catch the fish. Indeed he tried and tried, but he still couldn't succeed. The grandfather, watching him, then said, "Dear grandson, if you cannot catch a fish in a wooden trough at home, how do you expect to catch one in the running water of a stream?" The boy remained silent. The wise old man then told his grandson, "Let us tend to our rice cultivation with full attention. If we have enough rain we will have everything we need. Fish, venison, and meats of all kind will come to us for the asking. You will know more about this magic at harvest time."

Finally the harvest came and the old man and his grandson had an abundance of rice. Two large granaries were filled. But in the fields of others weeds had choked out the rice and the harvest was poor. Most people had barely enough to last for a few months after harvest. The days passed. The other villagers, after finishing their little stock of rice, came to the old man and his grandson to borrow some. They brought with them the fish and game they had hunted in forests. They carried loads of yams and wild fruit they had gathered. All these they gave in exchange for rice, for rice was their staple food and without it they couldn't live.

"I once spoke of the magic by which fish and meat and fruit would come to us at our command. Do you see my reasoning now?" the grandfather asked. When we have an abundance of rice everything else follows naturally. The boy soon realized the truth of the old man's advice and gave his complete attention to rice cultivation. The other villagers, after several years of famine, followed suit. Thereafter, with hard work, there was always abundance.

Part IV
Sisters and Brothers

*T*HIS NEXT GROUP of stories looks at sibling groups, both from the outside and from the inside. When the sibling group is viewed in relationship with another entity it is seen as a unitary body, a corporate group sharing a common identity and a singleness of purpose. The unity and strength of the group is often expressed in the number seven: "seven brothers," "seven sisters," or "seven brothers had a younger sister."

Interestingly, in the two tales concerning more than two siblings of the same sex—tales 27 and 28—this group is seen in a bad light. In each such case the potential contribution daughters or sons might make to the family becomes exaggerated and offset by a severe deficiency. Seeking husbands for daughters is never an easy task. Add to this a female speech defect and multiply it by seven and you have a perfect cast for comedy. In the first tale, the foolish sisters provide the script for this with their own self-destructive bickering and quarrelling, topped off by the eldest's public display of stupidity. The seven sons in the next tale are similar. Sons are generally desired for their strength and hard work in the fields, but these boys go awry, applying their strength to thieving and bullying their neighbors instead. Furthermore, their collective dull-wittedness is no match for one clever old man who eventually manages to set them straight.

Two further tales entail a cross-sex sibling group: seven brothers plus a younger sister. In these stories the set is por-

trayed in more positive terms. Now the seven brothers protect
and support their sister, even when they are separated from her.
In virtually all parts of India a girl leaves her natal home at
marriage to live the rest of her life among her husband's kin. A
woman's well-being in this new social setting depends heavily
on her husband's attitude toward her and also on the nature of
relationships he already has with his own kin (see the commentary for the next group of tales). If life is hard in their husband's
household, most women have only brothers to turn to. In these
two tales, seven brothers act as a single entity on their sister's
behalf. In one case they go off seeking a fortune in which she
will share, and in the other they avenge a cruelty committed by
the girl's husband. This bond, which links brother and sister, is
made especially vivid in tale 30. There this tie not only tran-
scends physical separation, but even death itself. Tale 16, in a
previous section, also describes seven brothers and a sister. In
that story, the seven are overprotective and nearly cause the
death of their sister's innocent husband. The imagery of this
latter account nicely captures these tensions inherent in the
transitional period, the time soon after marriage during which a
woman is expected to transfer her loyalties from her natal home
to that of her husband.

The collective identity associated with siblings in Indian
folklore is no doubt related to two very important Indian kin
groups: the lineage and the joint family. The strongest bonds in
both are those between siblings, persons who form the core of
every effective local lineage. To the degree that siblings are able
to maintain their corporate identity even after they grow up and
produce their own children, they form an alliance to be reck-
oned with in the community. Such sets offer a degree of mutual
support and protection the individual can never attain on his
own.

In India, as is true in many traditional societies, the strongest
of all social ties are those based on common birth. Siblings thus
have very strong claims on one another. But such claims are not
always acknowledged automatically. When a folktale takes us
inside the sibling group and shows us how brothers and sisters
treat one another, we see a different picture. A frequent theme
concerns the different fortunes life has provided for two people,

both born to the same parents, such as an elder brother and younger brother, elder sister and younger sister or a brother and a sister. One sibling may have many children, while the other has none; one sibling may have grown wealthy, the other poor. Each one of these tales has a clear moral to it. In each of the tales that follow, it is always the sibling whose life was more favored who treats his or her less fortunate sibling wickedly. This wickedness is more than simply the product of an evil character, furthermore. It is always due to foolheartedness and self-destructiveness as well. Another closely-related feature of the seamy side of sibling relations is that such rivalries are often displaced by a generation. Let us look more closely at several stories to see how these features interplay. Tale 31 begins by establishing a contrast between two sisters. The elder has everything—beauty, marriage, many children, and good health. The younger has none of these things which define fulfillment. Now, in accordance with the prevailing matrilineal morality of Kerala, an elder sister should share her bounty with less fortunate junior ones. And at the start of the story this is what the situation is. But soon the children of the first selfishly resent the presence of their useless aunt and plot to get rid of her. Their mother passively assents to their scheme. Hence the children tie up their aunt and abandon her in the woods. At this point, however, the aunt falls (literally) into a fortune, which she then generously shares with her younger sister as per the rule above. When she upholds this lineal ideal by providing the family with desired goods, the greedy children are not satisifed. They now hatch the idea of doing the same thing to their mother that they did to their aunt, but succeed only in getting rid of her instead. The lesson to be learned is that these girls tried to obtain a fortune independently of their larger lineal family—they saw both their mother and aunt as sources of wealth they hoped not to have to share.

In matrilineal ideology the welfare of the next generation is provided through the mother. Indeed, the very life itself of the next generation of the lineage is through the mother. Lineage unity is provided by the bond between sisters. Thus a child's link to mother is a source not only of life but also of the hereditary benefits which their lineage provides. To view this as

a one-way flow is selfish, placing an overemphasis on independent, individual benefits. The mother's passive encouragement
of this is wrong. More than sinful, selfish children are down-
right stupid. The girls' greed so befuddles their minds that they
terminate the very link—their mother—which provided them
with all that they had.

Tales 32 and 33 have a structure and a moral remarkably
similar to the account just discussed above. Collected from an
area in which patriliny prevails, the issue now revolves around
brothers and brothers' children. And in this, incidentally, we
see how folktales are generally responsive to local variations in
Indian social organization. At the start of these tales, too, the
elder sibling has everything, the younger, nothing. Then,
through unexpected events, and through no help of the elder,
the younger sibling suddenly acquires something of worth. He
then shares this for the benefit of all. The elder sibling, by
contrast, attempts to utilize his unexpected gain for his personal
good and again ends up the loser.

There are some points of difference between the above tales
that provide us with additional insights into kin relations.
While the story about sisters does not explicitly mention any
male characters, those about males do mention females. In each
case women—the wives of brothers—goad their husbands into
action and instigate a rivalry between them. The monkey-son,
for example (tale 32), presents the whole situation from the
perspective of the child of the younger sibling. From this position—that of the underdog—insight, quick wit, and cleverness
are characteristics which get highlighted. The monkey-son
easily perceives his uncle's greed and uses devices common to
many other folktales to allow this avarice to play itself out. The
father's elder brother meanwhile loses sight of the real source of
bounty (crops, cows, wealth) to be shared by the kin group.

The only tale in this section that concerns a pair of siblings of
the opposite sex has a relatively simple message. A sister is
justly shamed for snubbing her brother when he was poor and
destitute. We have seen how important a brother is to a woman
when she is in trouble. The least she could have done when the
situation was reversed would have been to honor him in her own
house as if he were a king. Tale 34 does not quite fit this same

pattern. Here two girls are cast as stepsisters, rather than real or immediate ones. The elder girl is the child of her father's previous marriage and is the underdog. Her sibling bond to the others is only partial. The mother is the one at fault here, spoiling her real daughter and thus emphasizing the difference when she might have treated the two equally.

While the foregoing tales minimize a real sibling bond, the last three in this section attempt to approximate the same where none in fact exists. The four species of animals in tale 36 are undifferentiated at the start: "All four were females and worked well together. . . ." Although it is said only that they are friends, the imagery which describes their collective unity could just as well be applied to a sibling group. Then the tale goes on to establish differentiation, based initially on a voluntary division of labor and the appreciation of the special skills of one group member. That bond of unity is first weakened through self-sacrifice and finally broken down completely due to the ridicule of others. In the end a denial of a bond of cooperative unity produces the physical characteristics which distinguish the four animals. As is true with the remaining tales, bonds not based on true kinship is shown to be superficial, temporary, and unstable.

Only in cases where a bond of kinship is formed with a deity, as in tale 38, is the tie a lasting one. There, too, it cannot be forced. Humans cannot place themselves in a position of authority over deities by assuming the role of an elder kinsman. Tale 38 ends with the human couple honoring as their mother a deity they had initially regarded as a younger brother. While the final kinship terms may sound incongruous to the Western ear, the structural relationship, which is more important to an Indian listener, is entirely appropriate.

· 27 · *Seven Dumb Daughters (Kashmir)*

This is a humorous tale about seven sisters who all have a severe speech impairment. It encapsulates, in exaggerated form, the anxiety many Indian parents feel about the marriageability of their daughters. Weddings are normally arranged through matchmakers, and it is necessary to impress upon go-betweens that the girl under discussion is beautiful and full of admirable qualities (see tale 63 for a parallel with a prospective groom). A daughter who is stupid or who cannot speak properly would be anyone's nightmare. The parents in this story try to conceal such handicaps. An important comic or ironic twist is central to the account, in that the eldest daughter is responsible for botching their plan. By insisting on her own correct behavior she gives away the very secret her parents wished to hide. Thus this story illustrates the common antagonism felt toward older siblings, making them out to be self-centered and stupid. Instead of protecting her juniors, this eldest girl's behavior endangers the future well-being of all seven sisters.

THERE WAS ONCE a poor family made up of a husband and his wife and their seven dumb daughters. All the daughters had reached a marriageable age. Both the father and the mother were worried, for it was difficult to find matches for dumb daughters. They tried their best, contacting many matchmakers, but their efforts were of no avail.

One day, after hectic activity, they finally engaged a matchmaker from another village. This man would soon visit their house to see the girls. The matchmaker was new to this village and did not know that the girls were dumb. On the day of his visit, the man arrived at the time agreed upon. As he neared the house he was welcomed warmly at the entrance, and offered a comfortable seat in the living room. Meanwhile all seven daughters were taken to an adjacent area, and told not to enter the living room. They were also not to misbehave in any way as long as the matchmaker was in the house lest he get a bad impression. Strict instructions were given to the girls not to say anything while the matchmaker was there, lest their dumbness be dis-

covered. The seven sisters agreed to abide by these instructions
and to wait in a room adjacent to the one where the matchmaker
was sitting. Having instructed her dumb daughters the mother
went to join her husband who was engaged in conversation with
the matchmaker. Soon the mother began praising her "nice
daughters." She tried to impress upon the matchmaker how mod-
est and virtuous her daughters were. She described how they
would not talk to nonrelatives, not enter a room where strangers
were present.

At that very moment, however, one of the dumb daughter's
feet accidentally stamped on the toe of another one in the adjacent
room. Thinking that she had been hit deliberately, the second
dumb girl grumbled and retaliated by hitting back. A quarrel
began. Several other girls also joined in. Voices—dumb voices—
could be heard. Realizing the gravity of the situation, and in an
effort to bring it under control, one of the elder girls tried to
pacify the others by shouting: *"Maji ka bobuy, maji ka bobuy"*?
[What did mother hay? What did mother hay?][1]

The seven sisters, undaunted, did not stop quarreling. Instead
all of them except the very eldest, joined the chorus: *"Maji ka
bobuy, maji ka bobuy?"* The dumb voices grew louder and louder
and could be clearly detected in the next room. Hearing those
unusual sounds the matchmaker raised his eyebrows and looked
in that direction a couple of times. The mother was alarmed and
hurriedly excused herself. She stepped into the other room to
pacify her quarrelling daughters, scolding them and trying to
calm them as best as she could. At that moment, however, the
eldest daughter, who had thus far been quiet, stepped forward
and said to her mother with a glorious smile, *"Me ma bobuy
kihiny"* [I didn't hay anything].

The matchmaker who was silently listening to this whole
drama quickly understood the situation. He collected his bag and
left the house. No amount of requests or pleadings would stop
him.

· 28 ·   *The Clever Old Man*
   (Assam)

As mentioned in reference to an earlier tale, the image of seven
brothers and a younger sister conveys the devotion with which
brothers support and protect their female counterparts. This
time there is no sister, and the brothers' actions are now
nefarious. What is emphasized by this new seven-brother image, then, is an old man's cleverness. Seven tough and rowdy
brothers—a gang—are no match for his wit. Structurally, repetition carries somewhat the same message: time and time again
they are outwitted.

The use of fictive kinship terms throughout the tale establish
a convention of politeness, deference, and paternalistic kind-
liness, all of which conceal the real intentions of each party. The
relationship quickly becomes a more generalized one of youth
versus maturity. Interpreting the message in this way, we see
several impatient, avaricious youths again and again bested by a
wise, insightful elder. This competition between the strong and
the weak can also be seen in tales about husbands and wives (see
tale 48). Deception and the avoidance of direct confrontation are
necessary if the weak are to hold their own in this world.

IN A CERTAIN VILLAGE there lived seven brothers. They all lived
by thieving and burgling. They lived separately but always
worked as a team. One day the eldest said, "Brothers, that old
man there has plenty of money. Let us burgle his place tomorrow." The others agreed.

The old man then had a dream that these men would pay a
visit to his house the next day. When he woke up he said to his
wife, "Old woman, I'll tell you what! Have we got a fair quantity
of rice-beer?" When she said that they had, he said, "Well then,
tomorrow at noon you must cook for seven people and keep your
dishes of meat and rice ready. Cook *matimah* [pulse] too. When
the visitors arrive, ask them to sit down so that you can serve
them a meal. I will go out in the morning to the field and take
our pet paddy-bird with me. But I will be back by noon."

Next morning the old man was plowing his field. The pet
paddy-bird sat close by looking for frogs. Soon the seven thieves

came along and, seeing the old man, they accosted him thús:
"Grandfather, what are you doing?" The old man answered, "My
sons, I have got to feed my old lady, hence I am driving this
plow. But which way are you bound?" They said, "We plan to
visit your house." "That's very well," replied the old man. He
then addressed his pet, saying "Paddy-bird, go home and tell
grandmother to kill the fowl and prepare food for seven guests."
He then drove his bird off with a stick and it flew back home.

After a time the old man and his guests reached home. The old
lady had kept everything ready. The thieves were surprised to
find such a good meal, and they thought that she had prepared all
these things because she had received the bird's message. After
the meal was over they thought that they could also use the services of such a bird. Then they too could have timely and fine
meals. When the old man asked them, "My boys, what made you
come to my place?" they answered, "Grandfather, we want this
bird." The old man then said, "No, I can't give up my bird. It is
our mainstay. It's because of it that we two are still alive." But
the thieves were keen on the bird and would not leave without it.
In fact, they took it away by force.

Soon the time came to try out the bird. So the eldest thief took
it to a field. When it was about noon he raised a stick over the
head of the paddy-bird and said, "Go, tell my wife to cook a fowl
and to keep some rice-beer ready." But when he returned home
he found that his wife had not cooked anything. There was only
leftover rice from the last night's meal. However, the thief was
hungry and ate whatever he was given. Then he took the bird to
his next younger brother. The latter then asked him, "How did
you find our new bird?" "Oh, it was all right," he replied. "I
gave it a message and my wife prepared rice, meat, and rice-beer
for me. I had a hearty meal." The younger brother then sent the
bird from his field with the message: "Go, and tell my wife to
prepare some rice, meat, and rice-beer." However, instead of a
warm and rich meal he too had only left-over rice to eat. This
man then passed the bird on to his younger brother. In this way
each of the brothers tried the bird and each found himself cheated. The youngest brother, in fact, soon blurted out, "Why, we
have been had by this old fellow." The others agreed.

One evening they planned something new: "We will go to-

morrow and tie up the old man and take all his money and gold."
That night the old man had another dream. Again he came to
know of their plans. He said to his wife, "Old woman, those men
are coming again. Please keep a meal ready as before. Prepare
some rice-beer, too. Strip a piece of banana tree bark and put it in
the room where we pray to the goddess of wealth. And please
place a stick of mature bamboo by my seat. Then go and borrow
our neighbor's daughter saying that she is needed to help you.
Keep her hidden in the room belonging to the Goddess Mainao
[the goddess of wealth]. But you have to do more. While serving
our guests rice you must pretend to slip on the floor because you
accidentally trod on one of their leaf-plates. Leave the rest to
me."

After giving all these instructions, the man went out with his
plow early in the morning. After a time the thieves came along
and the old man now addressed them saying, "My sons, which
way are you going?" They answered, "We are going to your
house, grandfather." The old man then replied, "Very well. But
please wait while I finish my plowing." So after a while they
followed the old man to his house. The old woman then brought
out the rice-beer. After all of them had sat down to eat, the old
lady pretended to let her foot slip on the leaf-plate of one of the
guests. The old man then immediately took the stick and waving
it at his wife he began to roar, "You old woman, don't you see
with your eyes! Though you are old you don't know how to behave! Let me turn you into a young girl!" So saying, he began to
strike the piece of bark from the banana tree. After a while a
young girl came to serve rice and curry. The thieves were impressed beyond measure with the magic virtues of the old man's
stick. How wonderful! It could change even an old lady into a
comely girl! They then forgot the mission with which they had
come and asked the old man for his stick. But he would not agree
to part with it, so they took it by force.

Then the eldest thief thought, "My wife is already old, let me
turn her into a young woman." He thus began to beat her, saying, "Be young, be young." The heavy stick was too much for
the woman, however, and she lost her life. The thief then hid her
body and passed the stick to his next younger brother, saying,
"My wife has turned into a young woman." The second brother's

wife also lost her life in the same way. Indeed, soon all their wives had died, but when the youngest one's wife lost her life, he began to cry aloud. The other brothers then admitted sorrowfully that their wives, too, were dead. They now worried constantly about how to manage their children and run their homes. They hadn't the means to marry again and now became more determined than ever to rob the old man of his wealth. They decided they would not be dissuaded again from their purpose.

Again the old man had a dream and came to know of their plan. So he instructed his wife, saying, "Old woman, do you see that nest of hornets in the banana tree? Detach it from the tree carefully and keep it in a corner on the veranda. When I say to you: 'Old woman where have you kept our money? I seem to have forgotten where it is,' you must answer, 'Why, it is there in the pitcher in the corner of the verandah'." The thieves arrived that very evening. The old man started drinking rice-beer when he saw them, and as if intoxicated, he soon cried out, "Old woman, I seem to have forgotten where the money is kept. Where is it?" She responded, "You old fellow, you have forgotten everything by drinking so much rice-beer. Why, it's there in the pitcher in the corner." The thieves overheard this and were happy that they were at last going to have the old man's money. So the eldest thief went up to the hornet's nest. As he put in his hand the hornets stung him on his hands and face. He stepped back quickly and the next brother then went up and put his hand in, with the same result. None cried out, each appearing as if he had pulled out money from the pitcher. In this way, one after another, all the men were severely stung by these ferocious hornets. As they left, however, the youngest brother cried out, "Ah, how severely was I stung! Oh brothers, I am half dead with pain!" The older brothers than admitted how much they had suffered too.

After a few days, when their pain had subsided, the thieves again planned to pay a visit to the old man's house. But he came to know of their plans as before. So he now said to his wife, "Old woman, make a small hole in the wall. I will lie by that hole with a razor in my hand. Prepare a paste of some rotten fish and rub me with it so that I stink. Keep some hot chili paste by the granary as well. When they arrive, start wailing. Say that I am dead, and when they question you, ask them to smell me through the hole to see if I am dead or not."

When the thieves arrived the old woman began to wail. When they asked her why she was wailing she said, "Ah, my sons, the old man is no more. These seven days he has been rotting in the house because there's no one to carry him away. I am passing my mornings and evenings by wailing." They then asked, "Where's the body lying?" She answered, "Why, in there! You can smell him through that hole." So the eldest thief tried to peep inside. His nose was then quickly cut off. So he stepped away, covered his nose, and said, "Ah, what a disgusting stench!" Then the next brother peeped in. His nose was cut off too. He also stepped back, saying, "What a disgusting stench!" In this way, one after another, all the men lost their noses. But when it came the youngest he cried out, "Alas, my nose is no more!" The other brothers then admitted that their noses were gone also. In the meantime the old man cried but from inside the house, "Old woman, that fine salve I've put there don't give it to those rogues; don't let them have it!" The men then went directly up to the chili paste and rubbed it on their wounds. They could now hardly stand the burning and smarting this paste gave them. Roaring in pain, they left for home and promised that they would no longer depend on thieving and burgling for a living but would try to lead an honest life.

· 29 · *Thabaton*
(Manipur)

The extreme importance placed on brothers supporting their sisters is often indicated in Indian folklore by a story where seven brothers share one younger sister. This image is found in innumerable tales all over India, from the Tibeto-Burmese cultures of Northeastern India to the Dravidian cultures of the South (see the next tale). In some of these tales brothers support a sister against in-laws and even favor her over their own wives. In this one, however, they save her from a demon. These events are reminiscent of Sita's famous abduction by the demon, Ravana. Nonetheless, many specific details found here are native to the Manipuri area. The crow or sparrow as trickster is another common Indian motif. It is a surprise, however, to find a demon husband who jumps into his wife's funeral pyre. This reverses a common story pattern: the wife who decides to join her husband in death by entering the flames of his cremation pyre.

LONG AGO, there were seven brothers who had a younger sister. She was named Thabaton and was known far and wide for her chastity, beauty, loyalty, and obedience to her brothers. The brothers were poor and lived from hand to mouth. They decided among themselves that they must do something to better their condition. So they resolved to go away in search of treasure.

The men called out to their younger sister, Thabaton, and told her, "Look, dear sister, we are very poor. We have decided to go in search of treasure and leave you alone in the house. Keep the place locked up until we return. Don't open the door to anyone whosoever. Answer only when you hear the particular refrain 'Sona O, Naril O.'[1] Then you will know that we seven brothers have come back and you may open the door." With this secret injunction, the seven brothers went away in search of a fortune.

Soon a demon called Keibu Keioiba or "tiger man" heard of the beauty of Thabaton and wanted to abduct her. He was a local terror. One day he went to the house of an old woman, a neighbor of Thabaton's, and told her in his hoarse and terrible voice, "Ha, Ha! I feel like eating human flesh today and I smell human flesh. Old woman, open the door of your house. I will eat you up today." The old woman was terrified, but she did not lose her wits. Within seconds, she had thought of a way to save herself from Keibu Keioiba and answered him, "Look, Keibu Keioiba, I am old and my wrinkled flesh will not be tasty. I will tell you of a young and beautiful girl who lives alone in my neighborhood. Her name is Thabaton. Go to her and eat her young flesh." Keibu Keioiba felt happy and went to the house of Thabaton. He knocked at her door and told her to open, using his hoarse and terrible voice. Thabaton replied from within, "Who are you? Your voice does not resemble the voice of my brothers and so I will not open the door." Keibu Keioiba felt defeated and in great anger he returned to the house of the old woman. There he said, "Look, you old hag. Your Thabaton did not open the door when I told her to. She said that my voice did not resemble the voice of her brothers. In her place, I shall have to eat you."

The old woman was very resourceful and she now said to Keibu Keioiba, "If you behave that way, Thabaton will never open the door. You have to be very clever to deal with her. Come along with me. When she opens the door, pounce on her as you like." She then led Keibu Keioiba to the house of Thabaton, and at the door she said, "Sona O, Naril O, we seven brothers have come, open the door." Thabaton knew the refrain but she knew there was a difference in the voice. So she answered from within, "Your voice does not resemble the voice of my brothers. I cannot open the door." The old woman knew that Thabaton would not open the door for her and therefore she said, "Look Thabaton, I am the old woman in your neighborhood. I want to borrow a needle for my work. Can you open the door and lend me a needle?" Thabaton Replied, "Yes, grandmother. I will not open the door, but I can pass a needle out to you." So saying, she passed the needle through a small hole in the wall. The old woman then said, "Thabaton, dear, you are so kind, but in the dark I cannot see the needle. Will you kindly open your door a little bit so that I can take the needle from your hand?" Thabaton opened the door a little bit to hand over the needle. Just then Keibu Keioiba, who was hiding behind the old woman, forced the door fully open and pounced on Thabaton and carried her away.

Thabaton regretted her folly. She could find no way to escape from the clutches of Keibu Keioiba. While she was being carried into the thick jungle, she tore away small pieces of her clothing and dropped them so that in case her brothers came in search of her they might know where she had been taken. After a lapse of some years the seven brothers did return home with great treasures. When they arrived, they found the house empty and the door wide open. At first they could not imagine who might have taken their dear sister. Finally, they decided that she must have been carried away by Keibu Keioiba and set out in search of her.

In the thick jungle, the brothers found pieces of their sister's clothing. They followed the path carefully until they saw a hut in the jungle and their sister inside. They watched and tried to meet her alone. They wanted to know what had happened. One day they found their chance and the sister told them the whole story. She said, "I want to take revenge against this Keibu Keioiba and punish him. All of you wait here. Hide yourselves and watch what I do." The brothers did as Thabaton told them. They found

that Keibu Keioiba had been happy with Thabaton and had not
eaten her. Instead, he had kept her as his wife. Indeed, he did
whatever Thabaton told him to do. All day he would go out in
search of things she wanted. One day Thabaton told him, "Look
Keibu Keioiba, I want the skin of an old woman. Can you bring
one for me?" Keibu Keioiba was only too happy to do so and went
away in search of an old woman. He found one, sheared her skin
off, and brought it home for Thabaton.

The next day Thabaton said, "Keubu Keioiba, I feel thirsty!
Please bring me some water from yonder stream." She gave him a
bamboo pole that was hollow on both ends and commented:
"You can carry it in this." Keibu Keioiba went off happily. He
reached the stream and tried to fill the hollow bamboo pole with
water. But when he attempted to cover the hollow on one end
with his long and wrinkled fingers the water inside would run
out the other. He tried time and again but was never successful.
Meanwhile, Thabaton set fire to his jungle hut and hurled the
skin of the old woman into the flames. As the fire blazed, she ran
away with her seven brothers who had been trying for days to
rescue her.

While Keibu Keioiba was struggling with the hollow post, a
crow sat on a branch of a tree nearby. He had watched all these
events and now said, "Oh! You damn fool. While you were
struggling here your hut caught fire and your dear wife has been
lost." The crow repeated this several times and each time the
Keibu Keioiba tried to drive him away by hurling pebbles. The
crow flew away when the pebble was thrown, but came back
quickly to sit on the same branch. Thus he continued his cries for
sometime. Keibu Keioiba finally looked toward his hut and saw
it in flames. He then ran toward the house in great haste. There
he found the skin of the old woman burning inside. He mistook
this for Thabaton, jumped in the blazing fire himself and quickly
died.

· 30 · *Kini Mulki*
(Karnataka)

This is a Tulu tale told about a hunting caste called the Mugerlu. These people, like many others in Southern India, practice cross-cousin marriage. Among the members of this community, a man is given first rights to marry the daughter of his mother's brother (a maternal cross-cousin). But the man in this story is an only child, spoiled by a mother who selfishly dotes her attentions on him to the exclusion of his bride. The only recourse for a woman ill-treated by her husband and mother-in-law is the support she can get from brothers. Even with marriages taking place within such close kin circles, the quarreling and vengeance taken can be very severe.

KINI MULKI was the only child of his mother. By contrast, Bale Ermal was a younger sister to seven brothers. One morning Kini Mulki woke up early, washed his face and hands, and then went to visit his seven male cousins. "My cousins," he said, "You must give me your sister, Bale Ermal, in marriage." "We have only one sister, and you are the only child of your mother. It is said that an only child is ruthless," they replied. "That may be, but still you must give me your sister," said Kini Mulki. So they sat and ate betel nut together and the seven brothers agreed to give their sister away in marriage. As they poured the ritual waters that accompany the wedding ceremony, Bale Ermal asked her brothers, "Have I become such a burden to you that you will give me to Kini Mulki, the only son of a mother? He will be a ruthless person. My life has come to a sad end." In sorrow she followed Kini Mulki and left her brothers. The two went to Kini Mulki's house as husband and wife.

After a few months passed Kini Mulki heard news of war. "Oh mother, there is a war and I shall have to go. I shall be away for more than a year: six months fighting, plus six months on the road moving to and fro. Bring me my weapons, dear mother." At the time Kini Mulki left for war, Bale Ermal was already pregnant. When he left, Kini Mulki's parting words were, "Mother, my bride is now three months advanced with child. You must care for her and watch over her." Bale Ermal watched him go down the road until the top of his head disappeared beyond the horizon. The mother-in-law, Orti Ermal, then said to her, "So, child, you are three months pregnant! If you have cravings for toddy (palm beer) and fish, you should go to Ermal where your brothers live and get these things there." So saying, the mother-in-law put some polished rice in one bag and unhusked rice in another. She finally sent her daughter-in-law away. Carrying her two bags, Bale Ermal walked along the road towards her natal home. From a distance her seven brothers could see her approaching. The youngest said, "Oh brothers, do you see her! Look! Our sister, Bale Ermal is coming along the path." Her brothers expressed their joy and talked about the beauty of seeing their sister. Meanwhile, she came close to them. "Where are you going child?" they asked. "They sent me here to get toddy and fish," she replied.

The brothers brought large pots of toddy and liquor for their sister to drink. They put out a mat for her to sit on and they all gathered around her. "Pour toddy and liquor for our sister who is with us again," they said. They also brought puffed rice and beaten rice for her to snack on. They gave her golden bangles, so that her arms would be beautiful, and fetched flowers to beautify her hair. Then they said, "Sister, your husband, our brother-in-law, went to war. But he will be returning soon. You must go now." So they filled a pot with toddy and put fish in a bag to send away with her. Together they planned to set out to see her new home. "Sister, sit in the shade of that grove during the heat of the day. Eat some beaten rice before you start walking," they continually advised her.

Just at that time Kini Mulki had returned from the war. "Mother, where has my Bale Ermal gone?" he asked. "You ask about your wife! As soon as you left, she went away and hasn't returned," his mother replied. In surprise and anger Kini Mulki took up his quiver and bow and went to Ermal. There he climbed a tree and hid in the bushes a short distance from the house. He drew an arrow from his quiver and shot it. That first arrow fell to the right of Ermal. The second fell to the left. The third he shot above her. The fourth fell between the legs of Bale Ermal. The fifth pierced her breast and she collapsed, dead. Then Bale Ermal took the form of a bird and perched in a serpent grove.

Meanwhile the seven brothers had started walking ahead along the path. There the youngest heard their sister's voice and pleaded with the others to turn toward home at once. They soon found the corpse. The youngest asked, "Whose corpse is this, brothers? Whose corpse is this?" The others replied, "It is the body of some child who fell along the path. What concern is it of ours. Let us be on our way." But as they passed the serpent grove the youngest brother heard a bird sing as follows: "I have seven brothers. A mother had seven sons and a single daughter. Bale Ermal was born in back of seven brothers. They tied me in marriage to Kini Mulki, the only son of that mother. Today my husband took my life." Hearing all this the youngest brother called to the others and said, "Listen to how beautiful the words of the bird are."

Standing before the serpent grove, the seven brothers now heard the bird say, "I am your sister, Bale Ermal. You tied my hand to the only son of a mother. He is a violent man. Today one arrow went to the right of Ermal, and one to the left. One went over my head, one fell between my legs. The last fell into my breast." The brothers rushed back to examine the corpse they had seen. They picked up the body and put it on their laps. "Alas, it is true," they said. "If you are our sister then let that bird touch the feet of this corpse and give new life to the body." Then the bird flew out of the serpent grove and settled at the foot of the corpse. Bale Ermal came back to life. As she lay in her brothers' laps she gasped for breath. The brothers put their arms around her and kissed her. They gave her seven balls of rice and brought her home.

"You stay here; we shall return," they told her, and they went off to Mulki's house. From a distance Orti Ermal saw them coming. She got a woven mat, rolled Kinni Mulki up in it, and hid him in the attic. When the seven brothers arrived they asked, "Mother-in-law, where did your son go?" "He who went to war has not yet returned," she replied. "Don't lie to us, mother-in-law," they told her. The youngest son went inside and took down the mat. "Brother-in-law! Why are you in this mat? We must leave now, together. We saw an animal in the forest. We will catch it now and make a curry of it. We will get toddy and have a feast."

They took Mulki along and went after the animal they had

spoken of. They showed Mulki an earthen mound made by a porcupine and made him get down and dig it up. When he had dug himself into the hole, the top collapsed and Mulki was killed. The seven brothers then cut flesh from the right thigh of his body and returned to their mother-in-law's place. "Oh mother-in-law! Your son killed that animal. Look we have brought meat!" they told her. She cut the meat into pieces and put the preparation on the hearth fire. She ground spices and pepper to make curry. "Where did Mulki go?" she asked. "We sent him to the toddy shop to get puffed rice and toddy," they replied. "Mother-in-law, taste the curry and see if it is salty enough," they urged. "Wait until the toddy comes, then we will taste it," she replied. "Don't ask us to wait until then. When we pour the toddy we will be too eager to eat. You taste it now," they insisted. So she tasted the meat.

"Mother-in-law, you bore a single son," the brothers said. "We killed your son and you have eaten his flesh. You have sinned. You tried to destroy our sister by putting thorns inside our house. That did not succeed. Now you must take those same thorns into your own house." So saying, the seven brothers returned to their own home for good. They then fed and cared for their younger sister, giving her one portion from each of their own seven shares.

· 31 ·   *Greed Can Be Perilous*
          (Kerala)

This is a tale from the southern state of Kerala. It is about tensions between sisters. A younger sister is often resented because she is thought to be more beautiful, more protected, and luckier in marriage than her elders. In this story, however, the youngest daughter has the opposite problem. Here she is ugly and never marries at all. Through a combination of luck, fast thinking, and unselfish generosity, this heroine escapes what seems certain death and instead acquires a bundle of wealth.

Similarities and contrasts can be seen between this tale and a number of others in the collection. A parallel can be drawn

between the sisters in this tale, found in matrilineal Kerala, and
the next two tales about brothers, collected in the neighboring
patrilineal region of Tamilnad. The tale also recalls the two
sisters-in-law in tale number 42. There, too, the better off, self-
centered elder woman greedily imitates the younger, with similarly disasterous results. Contrasts can be seen in the treatment
of the elder and younger co-wives in tale 43. There it is the
younger who is the aggressor. Structurally, this tale is almost
identical to tales 39 and 40, although the sets of kinsmen
involved are quite different. All of these tales (and number 34 as
well) are very similar, indicating a very widespread popularity
for this thematic configuration throughout India.

ONCE, LONG AGO, there lived two sisters. The eldest one was
married and had many children. But the younger sister was not
very beautiful. Thus no one came forward to ask for her hand. So
this woman remained a spinster and finally became old. After a
while the two sisters decided to live together, but the youngest
one was not in very good health. She was unable to help with the
work of the household, and her nieces thought that she had become a burden. Finally her children conspired to kill their aunt,
determining to burn her alive. The very night this decision was
made, the old woman's hands and legs were tied and she was
gagged to prevent her from shouting. She was then carried to the
cremation ground, and there her body was covered with firewood. When these preparations were finished, however, the children remembered that they had not brought any matches to light
the fire. They returned to their home to find something suitable.

While the children were gone the woman managed to free her
hands and legs from the bonds that held them. She then re-
arranged the firewood so that it would not be obvious that her
body was missing. After this she climbed up on the branches of a
nearby tree to watch what would happen. Sometime later the
children returned. The pyre was lit and the firewood began to
burn. The children were happy that they were finally rid of their
sickly aunt. They left the fire burning and returned home. Meanwhile the old lady continued to watch from her perch on the
nearby tree. She was shivering with fear and had to grasp a branch
with both hands. She didn't want to fall. Time passed and soon it

was midnight. Then she heard the sound of footsteps. Someone was running toward the tree. After a while she also heard murmurings. Slowly she opened her eyes. She then saw three persons sitting under her tree opening a knapsack. The three were robbers. The old lady was so frightened that she lost her balance and, 'ptho', she fell down. Fortunately, however, she fell right on top of the knapsack.

The robbers thought that a ghost or devil had appeared among them and ran away in fright. But the woman was unhurt. After a while she recovered from the impact and began to open the bag. She was surprised to find it full of gold and coins. When dawn appeared she put these valuables back in the sack and set off for home. When she reached the front door everyone was surprised to see her. They thought that a ghost had returned to haunt them. But the woman called out to her elder sister and to all the children. "Do not worry, I am alive. How lucky I am, as well! Look at the riches I have brought," she said. Then she showed the family all the gold and coins she had found. Seeing the fat knapsack they were all very happy. From then onwards the family treated this woman well.

The children of the family thought about all this and reasoned that the new wealth stemmed from their decision to cremate their elderly aunt. Then one of them suggested cremating their mother as well. Perhaps this would bring more wealth! The children discussed the plan among themselves and their mother also agreed to it. It was decided that she would be cremated that very night. The children then proceeded to tie the legs and hands of their mother in the same way that they had done for their aunt. They also stuffed a cloth in her mouth in the same way and carried her quickly to the cremation ground. There they stacked firewood on her body and lit the pyre. Their mother squirmed and wriggled but was soon burnt to death. The children witnessed this happily, thinking that she would reappear the following morning with a new sack of gold. But the next morning their mother did not reappear. The children waited and waited but she did not return. They had lost their mother forever.

· 32 · *The Monkey-Son*
(Tamilnadu)

The next two stories present descriptions of male (as opposed to
female) sibling groups. This one depicts a competition between
two families, headed by two brothers. The elder brother has an
ordinary child, the younger (presumably suffering from a barren
marriage) adopts a monkey. In the end, however, this strange
youth triumphs and his father's brother is killed. Traditional
inheritance customs favor naturally born sons, while adopted
ones must vigorously press their claims. This story illustrates
the triumph of a sibling underdog in such contests and depicts a
common problem with lineage-based rivalries. The fact that the
child is a monkey seems to symbolize his double disadvantage as
an adopted son of a younger brother. He finally enjoys success as
a trickster. The uncle repeatedly tries to imitate the successful
actions of this monkeylike nephew, but without similar re-
wards. The story is a version of tale type 1535, except that it
substitutes a rivalry between brothers for the more common rich
peasant versus poor peasant theme. The trick concerning upper
and lower parts of a plant (tale type 1030) can also be found in
tale 25.

THERE ONCE WERE two brothers. The younger brother had no
children. One day a man came to the village with a monkey tied
in a bag. He kept it in the bag and pretended it was a child. The
younger brother asked the price and the man answered, "It is
worth one measure of maize plus one quarter of a rupee." So the
younger brother bought the bag without even opening it. Afterwards, when he looked inside, he discovered a monkey. The
monkey jumped up on a rafter and began to cry. The young may
was very sad. His wife was sad as well.

The monkey turned to the couple and asked them why they
were sad. The younger brother answered, "Can you operate an
irrigation device at our well?" The monkey said "Of course I
can." He then went and assisted both brothers at their family
well. For every single bag of water that the two men could lift the
monkey managed to lift two more. After a time the monkey began to call the younger brother his father. He then asked the

elder brother what types of grain grew best in his field. The elder
brother answered, "Tobacco grows well." The monkey continued
and asked, "Do you want the upper or the lower part?" The elder
brother asked for the lower part. The monkey boy agreed that he
and his father would take what was left.

The monkey then began to harvest tobacco leaves and to take
them home. Keeping to the bargain, he carried all the tobacco
stalks to the elder brother's house, and all of the fine upper leaves
to his own home. This started an argument between the elder
brother and his wife. Finally this man said, "Wait until the next
harvest and we'll see what happens then." So after the harvest the
monkey asked again, "What crop grows well in your field?" The
elder brother now answered, "Onions grow best." So the monkey
planted onions and when they were well grown he returned to the
elder brother and asked, "Do you want the upper or lower part?"
The elder brother remembered his previous experience and now
said, "This time I'll take the upper part." So when the harvest
came, the monkey took all the onions for himself and carried only
the upper leaves and stems to his father's brother's home. Again
this started an argument.

The elder brother was so angry at his monkey-nephew that he
now killed the two cows that operated the irrigation device for his
younger brother. But the monkey boy called two leather workers
and asked them to cure the hides of these dead animals. The
leather workers did their work. Then the monkey took the hides,
went to a nearby field, and climbed a tree. He knew of a spot
there where a group of thieves always met. Monkey-boy was
ready. The thieves soon brought some money to that spot and
began to divide it. One thief was blind. As the men were dividing their money, the blind man said to the others, "Divide it
fairly, otherwise the sky will fall in." At that moment, monkey-
boy let go of the hides that had been prepared. They fell on the
thieves who quickly became frightened and ran away. The
monkey then came down and picked up the money that they had
left behind. He took it home and gave it to his father.

The next day the monkey's mother asked her husband to go to
his elder brother's house to fetch a measuring basket. She wanted
to count just how much money the boy had brought home. But
the elder brother was puzzled as to why they suddenly needed to

measure so much wealth. So the monkey explained that he had
cut the tanned skins into pieces, and that he had sold these in the
market for cash. When the elder brother learned about this he
killed all four of his cows, had the leather cured, and then took
the skins to market. But no one was willing to buy them. The
elder brother returned home. Next he decided to burn down his
younger brother's house. One day he did this and his younger
brother's house was reduced to ashes. The monkey-boy however
had already left it empty, having carried all of the family's be-
longings outside. Then the monkey-boy tied all the ashes left
from the fire in a large sack. He put that sack in a place where he
knew that thieves habitually met. When the thieves arrived the
monkey-boy said to them, "Look at all the cash and jewels I have
stolen. Let us sleep awhile. Then we can divide up the proceeds."
When the thieves fell asleep, the monkey exchanged his bag for
one the thieves had been carrying. After that he crept off and
returned home.

When the monkey boy arrived with the big bag full of jewels
his mother again asked him to fetch a measuring basket from his
father's brother's house. Once more the father's brother wondered, "Where is all their money coming from?" So this time he
took a little tamarind and stuck it to the bottom of his basket to
make sure some trace of the measured contents would remain
inside. Monkey-boy explained that he had sold the ashes from his
burnt house and obtained some money. The elder brother
thought he would try this too. So he burned down his own house.
He then filled a huge sack with the ashes and took it to market.
No one would buy it. This caused another fight in his house. He
and his wife now decided that one way or another the monkey-
boy would have to be killed.

The elder brother soon caught the monkey and tied him in a
sack. He took the sack to a river and threw it in. But a young boy
was grazing goats nearby, and he heard the monkey crying out,
"They brought me here to the river because I refused to marry my
father's sister's daughter."[1] The shepherd ran into the water and
grabbed the sack. He let the monkey out and pulled him from
the river. Meanwhile, the elder brother had returned home. He
had gone to get a stick to beat the sack with. But by the time he
returned to the river the monkey had tied the shepherd boy inside

it instead. When The elder brother began to beat this sack the boy cried out and tried to explain what had happened. But the elder brother did not believe him. Meanwhile the monkey-boy took all of the shepherd's goats home. When the elder brother returned, he found the monkey and asked how he had escaped. He replied, "I have lots of relatives in this area. They gave me all these goats. Indeed, they have invited me to come back and get some more. Therefore, why don't you tie me in a sack again?" But the elder brother said, "Put me in the sack instead. I would like to have some goats too." So the monkey took his father's brother to the river in that sack and drowned him.

· 33 ·   *Monkey-Boy's Story*
         (Tamilnadu)

This story, like the previous one, highlights the theme of a young boy as monkey. Instead of complex uncle and nephew interactions, however, this tale concerns the more direct jealousies between siblings. As before, it is the younger boy who is disadvantaged, both by a low-status marriage and by his monkey label. Just as with the theme of sisterly rivalry discussed above, there is a principle of mirrored behavior here. The elder imitates the younger, at first without success. But this time the ending is a happy one, as the elder finally achieves equality with the younger in the last few lines. The two stories make a nice pair in that two similarly constructed tales can have rather different endings.

THREE BROTHERS lived in a village. The elder two were fine men and were married to respectable women. But the youngest was called monkey-boy and he was married to an outcaste girl. The first two had their marriages arranged, but the last boy had made a love match.

One day the youngest boy left the field where he was working and jumped in a nearby river to swim. Once in the water he began to shout and cry out loudly. Two gods, Siva and Parvati, happened to be passing by. They heard the boy shout, so they came to see what the matter was. "Why are you shouting?" they asked. When the boy saw these gods appear before him he answered, "I haven't a single coin to spend. Give me some money." Siva took pity on the boy and handed him half a rupee saying, "Go to the store, buy three coconuts, and return here quickly." When monkey-boy returned Siva said, "Now take these three coconuts home. Sweep the house and break each coconut in front of the sacred spot in your central wall. If you make a wish at that time, what you wish for will come true." After this Siva and Parvati disappeared.

Monkey-boy took the three coconuts. He went home and swept thoroughly. Then he broke the first fruit and wished for lots of pearls. As he did this, a heap of pearls appeared on the floor. Then, as he broke the second coconut, he wished for gold. A heap of gold appeared before him. Then he broke the third fruit and wished for a house that was two stories tall. Suddenly his house grew into a fine building with an upstairs apartment. Realizing that they were now rich, monkey-boy and his wife slept until ten o'clock the next morning. At that moment the wife of one of the elder brothers arrived. "What are you doing," she asked, "sleeping so late?" The monkey-boy then told her all about what had happened the day before.

The elder brother's wife returned home and told her husband the story. She found him in a field plowing. The man listened intently to his wife's account of how the monkey-brother had jumped in the river and become rich. So he decided to try this for himself. Now the elder brother leapt in the water, thrashed about, and began to shout. Again, Siva and Parvati overheard him. They came to the river and asked "What is the matter? Why are you shouting?" The elder brother answered with a sob, "I haven't a single coin to spend." So Siva handed him half a rupee and told him to go buy three coconuts. He then advised him to take these home, sweep his house, break the coconuts in front of the sacred wall spot, make a wish, and told him that what he wished for would come true.

So the elder brother went home, carrying his three coconuts with him. When he found his wife he asked her to sweep the house. Then he broke the first coconut. But as he broke it his wife asked him, "What did Siva say to you?" "Hair," he replied.

And so a large pile of [fibrus coconut] hair appeared. Then he broke the second fruit. But as he broke it, his wife asked again, "What did Siva say to you?" "Your head," he replied. And so a large pile of [headlike] coconuts appeared. The elder brother then began to break the third coconut. This time his wife said nothing. Now lots of pearls and lots of gold filled the house. After this the two elder brothers and the youngest one all lived happily together.

· 34 ·   *Tolerance and Jealousy*
         (Tamilnadu)

This short story from Tamilnadu is typical of a whole subgenre where rival women, in this case stepsisters, are compared through a set of parallel adventures. In these, the first actor is always the underdog. In time, kindheartedness, modesty and selfless behavior win this girl a handsome prince. Then the next girl, jealous of this success, tries to mirror her opponent's behavior. But the second fails to distinguish certain parallels in external events from a marked difference in internal attitudes (as is true in tale 42). Focusing on the former, the imitator fails to achieve the desired outcome (another handsome prince). The moral of the tale focuses on selfless intent, and it has been deeply imbedded in the very structure of this tale. The account stands alone in our collection, however, by also providing an overt statement of this theme in a concluding line. That particular element of story style may be due to European influence. Furthermore, the reader will certainly want to ask: who is most to blame for the disastrous second set of results, the stepmother or the young daughter? That sociological dilemma saves the story from being flat and raises interesting issues for philosophical debate.

THERE ONCE LIVED a woman who had both a daughter and a stepdaughter. Of the two, the stepdaughter was the older, and she was maltreated by her stepmother. One day the stepmother drove this girl out of the house. Then the stepdaughter began to wander about, crying all the way. After some time she found herself in a forest. There she discovered a lovely little stone which said to her, "Little girl, the sun is so hot that I am soon going to break in two. Will you please pour some water on me?" The girl, being kind by nature, fetched some water from a nearby river and poured it on the stone. As she walked further she found a small plant which told her, "Little girl, I am not able to stand erect. The wind blew too violently yesterday. Will you kindly help me to stand up straight?" The girl did as the plant asked. A little further on the girl came to an elephant which said to her, "Little girl, a thorn pricked me and has lodged in my foot. Will you please help me pull it out?" The girl helped the elephant and it soon walked away.

After a while the girl felt very tired and hungry; soon she found a solitary house and sat down in the front yard. Then an old woman came out and on seeing the girl she asked, "Who are you?" The girl explained and the woman said, "If you help me do the household chores I will give you food and protect you." The girl agreed and was very happy. The grandmother then gave her all sorts of hard work to do, such as making dried cow dung cakes and sweeping. But the girl was very patient and soon finished all these tasks. The old woman was pleased and next asked whether she wanted hot, fresh rice or old, warmed-over rice to eat. The girl told her that old rice would be fine. The grandmother then asked her to remove her torn clothes and gave her new ones instead. But the girl did not accept this gift. Instead she said that her old clothes were enough for her needs. That night, when it was time to retire to bed, the grandmother asked the girl whether she wanted an ordinary mat or a soft mattress. The girl chose the ordinary mat.

As time passed the stepdaughter became very beautiful. One day a prince who had come to hunt saw her and liked her very much. He went to the old woman straightaway and asked for permission to marry the girl. The grandmother gave the girl some family jewels and blessed them both. Soon the prince and his wife were ready to leave. The elephant was waiting in the front yard to carry them both on its back. As the two went merrily through the forest, they saw the plant that had received help from the girl. It had become a large tree, and it showered beautiful fragrant flowers on the couple. The stone that the girl had helped now paved the way for the couple as well. The two enjoyed their journey very much. Indeed, the elephant carried the couple all the way to the house of the girl's stepmother. But that woman was very jealous of her stepdaughter and the handsome new husband. So she asked her stepdaughter about what had happened. The girl narrated her whole story. Then the stepmother called her own daughter and demanded that she imitate everything her stepsister had done, and that she should be sure to come back home with a similar husband.

The daughter left home quickly. As she started through the forest the rock asked her to pour some water on it. The girl replied, "Do you think I am as foolish as my stepsister? I haven't come here to pour water on you," she replied, and she walked off. Next the elephant asked her to remove a thorn from its foot. The girl answered it in the same way. Soon the daughter arrived at the front yard of the forest house. Then the old woman came out and asked, "Who are you?" The girl explained and the woman said, "If you help me with my household duties I will give you food and shelter." The girl reluctantly agreed. When the old woman asked her to do any hard work, however, she would comment at once, "Don't think I am as foolish as my stepsister." When the old woman asked her whether she wanted hot rice or old rice soaked in water, the daughter replied that she wanted only hot rice. Likewise she demanded new clothes when the woman asked what garments she needed. When she went to bed she also asked for a soft mattress instead of an ordinary mat.

Soon the old woman got angry and thought that this girl should be taught a lesson. So when a shepherd came by her house with his sheep the grandmother called him in. She gave him nice clothes and asked him to marry the girl. The young daughter, however, was not aware that this man was only a shepherd. "Give me jewels like the ones you gave my stepsister," demanded the girl. But the grandmother beat her with a broom instead. She told her that that was the only jewel she deserved. Then she drove her out of the house. So the girl left with her new husband. This time an elephant was waiting to chase and scare them. Both of them had to run like devils. The stones along the way made their path painfully rocky. And when they stood under a tree to have some rest, it showered thorns on them. They had to struggle to get the thorns out. At long last, they managed to find the girl's natal home. Her mother then came out and saw the awful sight. Her daughter's face and body were swollen because of all the rough travel she had undergone. Next the mother saw her new son-in-law, the shepherd. Then she said to her daughter, "Don't come into my house again, you foolish girl," and she shut the door.

Tolerance always wins. Those who are jealous will suffer a lot in the end.

· 35 · *The Story of a Brother and a Sister (Uttar Pradesh)*

This tale concerns the important bond between brother and sister, including the continuing obligation for each sibling to help the other through hard times, even after both are married. Siblings should always remain equals in terms of their access to economic goods. A woman's dowry at marriage, for example, is sometimes expressly intended to balance out her brothers' future inheritance of fixed goods, usually land and living quarters. But when hard times befall one or the other sibling after marriage, the second is supposed to help out. A brother should offer shelter to his abused, abandoned, or impoverished sister, while a well-heeled woman should always honor her brothers with festival foods and magical blessings. In North India a particular day, "Brother's Second," is ritually set aside especially for this purpose. The following story, however, shows how a careless and pampered woman can forget to help her brother. He has his moment of revenge, however, when a gift he brings his sister becomes a constant reminder of her cruel and selfish behavior. The bond between brother and sister thus contains some magical reciprocity: whatever blessing or curse be initiated by one can later be returned, in similar spirit, by the other.

ONCE THERE WAS a brother and a sister. The sister was married into a rich family and lived a very luxurious life. But the brother lived in poverty. One year, on "Brother's Second,"[1] he decided to pay a visit to his sister to celebrate this festive day. The servants went and told the sister, "Your brother has come." "How has he come?" the sister asked. "His clothes are hanging in tatters. The dogs are barking at him," answered the servants. "Let him stay in the potter's kiln," said the sister. She busied herself with her activities and did not bother at all about her brother. At night, when she got ready for bed, she remembered that she had not sent any food to her brother the whole day. So she went to the kitchen, but there was nothing left except some stale greens and a piece of dry corn bread. She sent these to her brother. The brother put the dry bread in his pocket and left without saying a word.

After a long time, the same man came to visit again on the next festival of "Brother's Second." He had earned a lot of money in the meantime, so he now arrived with great pomp and show. There were elephants, horses, and musicians in his procession. He brought anklets for his sister. The servants went to the sister and said, "Your brother has come." The sister asked, "How has he come?" "The elephants are swaying, the horses are neighing, the music is playing; there is a large entourage of servants and followers with him," the servants answered.

The sister asked the brother to stay inside. She received him with warmth and affection. The sister then rushed to her neighbor and asked, "My brother has come; what should I cook for him?" "Give him rice cooked in butter," the neighbor said. The sister went back and began to cook rice in clarified butter. She cooked and cooked, but the rice wouldn't soften. She went back to the neighbor and asked, "I've been cooking for a long time, but the rice is not done yet." The neighbor asked, "How are you cooking the rice?" "I've put rice and ghee in the pot and have put it on the fire," she replied. The neighbor laughed and told her to add water to it, too.

The sister went back. This time she cooked the rice with butter and water. It turned out well. She served the food to her brother. The brother gave her some lovely anklets. She put them on very happily. When she walked around, the anklet tinkled. She wondered what the sounds meant. When she asked her brother about this jingle, he replied, "When I came the last time, you gave me stale greens and dry bread. I don't know how the family goldsmith heard, but he must know about it because that's what the sound in your anklets says, too. The jingle goes: 'Here comes darling little brother! Bring out the stale greens and the dry bread'."

The sister was much shamed and she apologized to her brother, profusely.

· 36 · *The Origin of Different Water Animals (Nagaland)*

This story, told by the Naga tribesmen of Northeastern India, may be looked at as a simple origin tale or as a tale with a deeper moral. Certainly, a degree of self-sacrifice is necessary for cooperative endeavors, and the Ao Nagas, like other peoples, place a high value on such service. Arrogantly ridiculing one who has sacrificed his or her life for others has permanent consequences. It is tempting to view this tale as a metaphoric commentary on the Hindu caste system, with its artificial differentiation of humanity into ranked groups. Naga society, like that of the cooperative group of water animals at the beginning of this tale, is relatively egalitarian. Yet these people have been familiar with the idea of caste organization in varying degrees for some time. One could argue that, in their view, caste demeans the value of individual contribution and upsets a society of equals. An alternative, also plausible, would be to simply classify this next story as a tall tale!

ONCE UPON A TIME a crab, a frog, a shrimp, and a minnow were friends. All four were females and they worked together very well. Each helped the others by doing what she could do best. Each day at dinner time they arranged a fine meal and ate together. Like humans, these animals grew rice. They worked as a group (*aluzunga*) in one another's fields, thus making the work more enjoyable, due to the company. The four took turns cooking. The one whose turn it was to cook would leave the field early and go home to prepare a dinner. When it was ready she would call her friends from the fields, asking them to join her.

After a while it was agreed that the crab's cooking was the best. So, they asked the crab if she would cook every day. She would be delighted to, she said, and thereafter this was her job. One day, there was no meat available to make a decent meal. So the crab took off one of its own legs and added it to the vegetables. When the meal was ready she called her friends as usual. They thought the meal was especially good that day and helped themselves to extra portions. They praised the crab for sacrificing its leg and making such a good meal, even in time of want.

The crab was so pleased with the praise she received from her friends that she continued to remove one after another of her legs each day. She put each leg into the curry until only the stump of her body remained. Each day the group praised her again for her cooking and urged her to continue in her role as chef. She gladly accepted, because their praise warmed her heart.

One day, while the group of three friends was working in the field they realized it was already past time for their midday meal. Still they waited patiently for the crab to call them to dinner. But there was no call. Eventually they decided to go home anyway. But the crab was not at the house. The friends called for her but there was no answer. They decided that she must have returned to the river to bathe or perhaps to grow new legs. They were hungry and so they decided to eat without waiting for her. It was already quite late. As they opened the curry pot to serve their food, there was the crab's body right in the middle of the curry, flavoring the whole dish with her tasty meat.

Seeing the sacrifice the crab had made of herself, the other three animals all started to laugh. They laughed and laughed until they couldn't stand up straight. They laughed until they rolled around on the floor. They laughed until evening, when they finally stopped from sheer exhaustion. When the frog tried to get up, however, she could no longer stand erect. Her back had become permanently bent at the base of the spine from laughing so hard. The fish's neck had become so swollen that it no longer had the graceful curves it used to have. Now it was stiff and straight. The shrimp could no longer walk forward, but only backward as she had been doing during her fit of laughter. Unable to continue their work in the fields, all these animals took to the water. And that is where we find them today.

· 37 · *The Man Named Unige Mada*
(Nilgiri Hills, Tamilnadu)

This next tale preserves some of the oral storytelling style of a
folk bard and thus has a special grammatical flavor worthy of
note. It comes from the Nilgiri Hills and was told by a Badaga.
These people represent one of several important communities
who have long resided in this anthropologically well-known
district of Tamilnadu. These, plus a few other groups, together
form a relatively isolated caste-like system. However, this whole
population is so small and distinctive that it is generally called
tribal. The Todu group stands at the top of this hierarchy and
are the priests and buffalo keepers. Next come the Badaga who
are farmers, and under them are the Kurumba who are sorcerers,
and then the Kota, who are known as artisans and musicians.

The following story depicts a Kurumba who came to a
Badaga in a time of need, and eventually became his dependent.
In this sense it serves as a kind of origin tale for traditional
Badaga-Kurumba social relations. It also portrays the Badaga as
keepers of fine buffalo herds. Buffalo ownership is often linked
to the status claims of the Todas, even though many Badaga
own such animals too. In this sense the present tale also asserts
the wealth of the Badaga community vis-à-vis the ritual importance of buffalo for the Todas. However, since no reference is
made to the highly important Kota group, it is clear that the
tale of Unige Mada stops short of providing a general charter for
Nilgiri society. This Badaga tale would normally be told in the
form of a narrative song. It would be sung before a group of
Badagas during a lull in some ritual event.

On quite another level, this tale is also interesting for what it
says about hospitality. The Badaga invites an exhausted Kurumba into his house and nurses him lovingly back to health. For
this act of generosity his family can expect to enjoy much future
prosperity. Such actions help counteract diaster and starvation,
not only in an immediate sense, but also in the long run. The
images of prosperity used are especially important. The teller
speaks of many children under the Badaga's arm, grandchildren
on his lap and great grandchildren under his widespread shawl.
A similar formulaic phrase, used by bards on the plains just

below these hills, likens the family of a man blessed by the gods
to a great, spreading clump of bamboo. Hospitality, furthermore, is an expression of brotherhood. This Badaga treats his
needy guest as he should a true brother. That is why this tale
has been placed alongside several others in this collection that
depict support between actual brothers.

THERE ONCE WAS a man called Unige Mada who lived in a place
called Bani.[1] He had eight sons. Here is his story. At one time
Bani became very dry[2] and there was no rain at all. Mada first
dug up some earth near a plantain tree and found it was very dry.
He then dug up earth near a toddy palm and found it, too, was
dry. Mada could find no food to eat and no water to drink. What
could he do? He had eight sons. But with no rain, what could
such a man do? After a time all of Mada's sons died. He wife died
too. Now Mada wondered and wondered what to do. He no longer had clothes to wear. He was forced to pick fern leaves. He tied
these around his head to serve in place of a cloth turban. He also
took a jungle creeper and wound it around his waist as a lower
cloth.

Finally, Mada thought of a friend who lived in a nearby place
called Malladu. So Mada made some vessels out of bamboo and
tied three on each end of a bamboo rod. He placed the rod on his
shoulder and set off for Malladu. Mada set off from Bani. He
traveled and traveled. Along the way Mada dug up some tubers.
He also searched for fern roots. Mada further collected wild honey
from the biggest bees' nests. But soon Mada barely had the
strength to drag himself along. He did not have enough for his
stomach. What was Mada, the man from Bani, to do? He worried
and worried. Finally Mada approached a place called Kinil Hada,
near the settlement of Kinnakore. Mada was unable to walk any
further. His right leg refused to move and his left leg would not
step forward. This was the state that Mada found himself in.
What could the man from Bani do? Mada soon fell down exhausted. He had lost all his energy. Then Mada found a jagged
jujube bush[3] and rested his feet on its stump. He placed his head
on a senna plant. Mada collapsed in the place called Kinilhada,
not far from Kinnakore.

In Kinnakore lived a man called Jogi who also had eight sons and many grandchildren. He had grandchildren in his lap, children under his arms, and great grandchildren under the ends of his shawl. Jogi was sitting on the council podium in Kinnakore. Soon he noticed that the buffaloes that should have been grazing on the village green had all gathered together in a tight circle. He saw this and was worried. So Jogi looked towards his home and called out to his wife, "Are you in the house? There may be some danger to you or to me or to our property. All the buffalo, all the cattle, have formed a tight circle. There may be a tiger[4] close at hand! Oh little wife, please come and get these many sons, daughters, grandsons, and granddaughters." His wife Kade appeared and asked, "Oh husband! Are you not the little Jogi, a father of eight sons?" But Jogi was already hurrying to get all of the young children inside. Then Jogi went and grabbed his well-kept gun from a top shelf. As he came out of the house he could see the buffaloes still gathered together. He went closer and counted them. He could see that not a single buffalo had been lost. So he drove all these animals toward the village.

Then Jogi saw the man called Mada, fallen and almost unconscious at the side of the road. He could see his legs on a stump of a jagged jujube bush and his head resting on a senna plant. "Oh what a shameful thing I see," said Jogi. "Perhaps this exhaustion is due to starvation. Perhaps this man has had no food and no water." And so Jogi lifted Mada into his arms and carried him into his own house. He then called out to his wife, "Oh wife, you will get holy blessings if you can help this man! He is exhausted six times over for want of food and three times more for lack of water. Please give him some curds." So the wife of Jogi, father of eight sons, took some curds from the milk pot. She gave these to her husband and he poured them with a spoon into Mada's mouth. Thus he slowly wetted the man's throat. Then little by little Jogi poured in more curds. He began to think about how much merit would descend on his many children. The man named Jogi, father of eight sons, continued to pour curds gently down Mada's throat. Finally, all the curds had reached Mada's stomach. Then Mada opened his eyes and took in his surroundings. He spoke saying, "O Sir, father of eight sons! O man named Jogi! Merit from heaven will descend on you and your many children. I suffered six times over for lack of food, and three times more for lack of water. When you poured curds into my mouth my eyes opened again. You will surely be blessed. Now, please, it would be good of you to give me some food." Upon hearing this Jogi replied, "Wife! Your children will receive holy blessings. Please give this man some food." And so Jogi fed Mada day after day.

The stranger took these meals and time began to pass. Then one day Mada spoke up saying, "Man called Jogi! Little Jogi of Kinnakore! My sons, too, were eight in number. But Bani was dry. There was not even a drop of rain. And so in the end there was no food to eat and no water to drink. I dug up bulbs and I searched for fern roots. I collected honey from wild bee nests. Indeed, I tried and I tried. But there was never enough food for me and my family. So all my eight sons and even my wife Hirige Madi passed away. After that I thought of leaving Bani to look for some permanent source of support. I thougnt of begging. I started out with empty milk containers made of bamboo. I thought of going to some friends in Malladu, to the place inhabited by Toda dairymen. I thought that if I gave them these milk vessels they might give me some coins in return.[5]

I came all this way with such thoughts in my mind. But when I reached the village green at Kinnakore, O my master, I was unable to walk further. I had no strength below the waist. I could not even crawl. I was exhausted for want of food. I collapsed and my feet lay on the stump of the jagged jujube bush and my head on the senna plant. That is how I fell down. Then you found me and gave me food. You thought of the divine blessings that would fall upon you and your children. You gave me some of your own curd from the milk pot and after that curd reached my stomach my eyes opened once more. Now I have had many meals and strength has returned. Let me serve you henceforth by looking after your buffaloes."

This then was the way Jogi came to support Mada. He found this way to give him food and clothing and keep him there in the village. What would the man called Jogi, the father of eight sons, do next? Now Jogi turned and addressed the stranger saying, "O Kurumba, as long as you live you may tend my buffaloes." In this way Mada was properly cared for. He began looking after Jogi's buffalo, and soon he began to thrive. Soon the

man named Jogi began to sing. He had his children in his arms
and his grandchildren on his lap. He sang a happy song and felt
contented. Things were going well. Such is the story that is told.

· 38 · Mamo Jalwalo
         (Gujarat)

This story from the Saurastra area of Gujarat is about a local
male deity who takes the disguise of a youthful, handsome
farmhand. He appears at a moment when a local couple is
unable to cope with the work of cultivating a distant field.
Acting like a faithful young brother, the stranger helps these
peasants to the point where they become dependent on him.
Later he reveals his true identity as a god and retires to live in a
large tree. The couple then bows down before him in worship.
This behavior provides a kind of male equivalent for the goddess
Manasa, who similarly appears first as a fish and then as a snake
in tale 22. In both cases a local deity enters the family circle and
is treated as a junior relative. Soon this growing dependency
relationship is reversed, however, and the true divinity and
parentlike status of the peculiar character is revealed. In this
respect the present story parallels those of many other local
deities where a god first presents himself in something small
and unthreatening but later unveils larger powers. These developments suggestively parallel that of a true child, who
eventually takes over the family from aging parents, who in
turn, become dependent on their juniors. In many such stories
an important link is provided to some striking aspect of the
local landscape, such as a rock crevasse or a stony hillock. In this
tale, the neighborhood landmark is a large and lonely tree. The
god's magical lock of hair furthermore matches other Indian
folktales where a key character is controlled through the con-
cealment of some part of his body in a distant container. In this
case the hair tuft reminds one of a common Hindu ritual
custom. A lock of hair growing from the top of the head is often
said to be the means by which the dead are lifted to heaven.
    Mamo Jalwalo's association with rain and with crop fertility

is noteworthy. But a still more remarkable custom has grown around this tale and its characters. When villagers come down with mumps they go to the children of the farmer in this tale to have the story related. While doing so, the teller rubs the patient's cheek with his palm and blesses him, relieving the pain.

MANY YEARS AGO in the village of Chandarva there lived a tailor who used to stitch clothes. This tailor was very poor, and although he did own a field he had no money to hire a farmhand. As a result he was extremely busy and his life became a burden to him. He had barely enough money to feed himself and his wife, despite his long hours of labor.

One evening the tailor and his wife were returning from their field completely exhausted. They had been working from morning to night. The couple were grateful when they saw a tree along the road and decided to sit down in its shade for a while and rest. It was the beginning of the rainy season, and big black clouds were moving slowly across the sky. Lightning could be seen now and again toward the east, and there was thunder to be heard in all ten directions. The poor man sighed. He then turned to his wife and said, "Tomorrow it will definitely rain."

The wife answered her husband saying, "It seems it will be so." But the husband continued to express his worries. "We shall not be able to cope with our work of sowing the seeds," he said. His wife concurred. Then the husband said, "We shall lose our entire crop." The wife echoed his words by adding, "We both will die without any corn or any grain to eat." Her husband said, "Nothing will be left to eat." Then the wife continued, "We are barren and poor. We have only four hands between us, two of yours and two of mine. A farmer needs at least six hands for field work if he is to harvest a good crop." The husband sighed again. With broken hearts he and his wife both stood up and started to walk towards home. Darkness quickly descended and lightning continued to flash around them in all directions. It thundered and began to rain. The way became difficult, and the couple worried that they would not reach their humble dwelling. So they turned around and went back to the tree where they had found shelter some moments earlier. This time, to their surprise, they found a young and sturdy man standing under its branches. The two joined the man and sat down.

For awhile it rained so hard the threesome were unable to hear each other speak. But as the storm let up the farmer turned and asked, "Young man, where were you going?" The man replied, "I wasn't going anywhere in particular. I don't know anyone here!" Then the farmer continued saying, "If you don't have any place in particular to go, why don't you join us?" The man replied, "Well, I would be pleased to!" The farmer explained, "Tomorrow morning, early, we shall return to our field to sow seeds in the furrows." The stranger then spoke up saying, "I will accompany you and help you with your work." On hearing this the wife of the poor man became extremely happy. She felt that God himself must have sent this young man to them to help them. It was now her moral duty to welcome him and to offer him the best of their humble hospitality.

The stranger joined the poor farmer and his wife and was accepted into their home with love, respect, and honor. The man was pleased with the comforts offered, and in the morning he joined them on their trip to the field. The stranger worked very hard. But he had not worked long when the couple discovered that they had an insufficient quantity of seeds to sow the entire field. So they asked the stranger to return to their house to fetch some more seed from an earthen pot that sat in the darkest corner of their single room abode. The stranger left and returned with these grains in no time. The farmer and his wife both noticed how quickly the stranger had made the trip. They also commented to each other about how fast he worked and about how he seemed to have superhuman skills and abilities. The wife began to reason to herself, "It is not possible that he is a mere human. He must be some kind of supernatural being." She also noticed that the farmers in the surrounding fields were still laboring hard to finish the work of sowing. She then thought to herself, "This very special man should not be allowed to leave us."

By noon the work of sowing was finished and the poor farmer and his wife sat down to rest. A neighbor now approached and asked, "How is it that you were so swift? We must be very slow and lethargic workers by comparison!" The farmer felt as proud as a peacock. But he was quick to give credit to his stranger-guest saying, "My young friend has helped us a lot. He is very smart, and he is strong and swift. He is an expert assistant." His neighbors then commented, "Oh, what a fine man. You must not allow him to leave." The farmer thus made up his mind that this young stranger should not be allowed to part company with the family.

The poor farmer now turned to his wife saying, "Have you noticed the efficiency of this young man's work?" "Yes," she replied. The farmer added, "He cannot be an ordinary young man." The wife interrupted commenting, "You have judged him as I have. He must be some kind of superhuman." The farmer continued by saying, "I would like to keep him here with us permanently." "Why?" asked the wife. "To help relieve our poverty and to reduce the amount of hard work with which we are burdened from morning to night," he answered. "But how can we possibly convince him to stay with us?" The wife laughed at her husband's words and replied, "That is something that you must leave to me, my dear!"

"What?" said the farmer. The wife remained silent. She was thoughtful for a while and then she spoke saying, "This stranger is a superhuman. Therefore we must take a lock of hair from his hair bun and preserve it carefully. The husband then replied, "If this is the case, it will not be difficult," The wife continued, "Oh my sweetheart, just listen to me!" "I will do that," said the husband. "If you listen everything will be all right," replied the wife.

A little later, when the new seeds had begun to sprout, the couple and the stranger returned to the field. They were weeding and furrowing between the young sprouts. While the stranger was working, the cunning farmer soon managed to cut off a small piece of hair from his hair bun by carefully following the directions given by his wife. The stranger tried his best not to allow the couple to do this, but they succeeded anyway. So he submitted to them. Once they had a piece of his hair, he became a kind of slave of the poor man's family. The couple now took the lock of hair home and thought of hiding it. The wife asked, "Where shall we keep this lock of hair, O husband?" The husband replied, "I think we should store it with the grain. That is the safest place." "Yes, I agree," said the wife. The lock was then hidden in a big earthen vessel underneath the seeds that were being stored in the darkest corner of the house. The hair was concealed in such a way that the young stranger would certainly be unable to discover its location. The wife then turned to her husband saying, "Let us guard the secret of this lock of hair very carefully. If the young man finds it we shall become helpless. If he gets his hair back we shall lose him, and we shall never enjoy his energetic and skillful assistance again. Our prosperity lies in his continuing presence in our home." "Yes, yes! I understand very well what you are saying!" replied the husband.

But although the rainy season had already begun, the rain now suddenly stopped. The seeds that had been sown in the field did not grow properly. Several fields turned brown and many young sprouts died. As a response to this, a number of farmers began sowing a second time. The poor couple worried about their own crop, and they too determined to sow a second time. Dawn came and they again carried seed grains with them from the house. By noon, however, these had been exhausted and the farmer again asked the young stranger to go back and fetch an additional bag. This time the man returned to the house with the farmer's wife. Then, while she was busy cooking, he went to the pot in the darkest corner to take out some more seed. As he opened the lowest part of the container, however, he found a lock of his own hiar lying there. The man silently took this hair. He then approached the farmer's wife, saying, "My kind lady! Please grant me leave to return to my own place." The woman was startled. She turned and asked the stranger, "Where do you live?" The stranger replied "I live in the Piludi tree, that large tree over there on the wasteland beside your field." The wife replied saying, "Oh! I understand! But didn't you come to fetch some seeds?" The stranger answered, "Now I will not fetch more seed. Now I have found my hair lock. I am taking it and leaving you for my own place. I am Mamo Jalwalo."

On hearing this news the wife stood up at once. She then bowed down in front of the man. Standing before him with folded hands she said, "Please favor us. You must be like a mother to us children. You must bring us happiness and guard us as you would your own family." Then the young man disappeared. The people of the region believe that even today Mamo still lives in the Piludi tree on the outskirts of Chandarva village.

Part V
Domestic Strife

STRIFE, CONFLICT, competition, jealousy, and greed all make this a rather harsh group of tales. Co-wives vie with one another for their husband's attention. Wives disobey and cheat on their husbands. Sisters-in-law react jealously to one another's successes. Daughters-in-law plot the destruction of their mothers-in-law. At times these rivalries even express themselves in violent acts: murder, burning someone alive, crippling a rival, or changing an enemy into a snake by means of magic.

But the focus of these tales is not violence itself. Instead, it is merely that relationships between kin are here expressed in extreme and vivid terms. This is most often the case when a tale contains a strong moral message. There is no question about who in these stories is the wicked aggressor and who is the innocent victim. In the end the wicked person is justly punished and the innocent vindicated or rewarded. That is the point.

What is somewhat unexpected is that most of the hostility occurs among women in this group of tales. A look at the interpersonal structure of the Indian household helps one to understand why this should be. In most of India, a woman leaves her natal house at marriage to move into her husband's home. There she enters a world of women, all having a position more privileged than her own. As a new bride she is supposed to respect her mother-in-law, who is already in charge of household affairs. A woman's husband's sisters are the darlings of the house, and at least until they go off in marriage, they are favored by their mother over the young bride. Even a woman's husband is apt to continue to pay more attention to his sister than to his wife and to express his affection to her more openly. If the husband has elder brothers who are already married, their wives have a position senior to her, and they will jealously guard whatever privileges and attention they have gained through the years. Only gradually, as her mother-in-law grows older, and as her husband's sisters leave to live with their husbands, does a woman gain command of her own life and the privilege of running her own house. The cycle is slow, taking a lifetime to revolve one full turn. A woman must be patient.

These folktales identify points of tension in such large, complex families. Seen from the male perspective, it is the nagging wife who goads one brother to cheat another. But from the female perspective the source of tension is different. Indian social custom brings together in the tightly hierarchical structure of a family women who were once strangers to one another. Men of the family are kin from birth. These males are also the focus of household activities and the source of the household's wealth. Women, it is often remarked, are their dependents, first as daughters, then as wives, and finally as mothers. It is no wonder then, that many of the rivalries and jealousies among women involve their different ties to men. Competition among women often takes the form of insidious attacks on the bonds other women have with the men in their own family. A new wife sees that she might hasten her own rise to power, for example, by weakening the bond between her husband and his mother. A sister will be jealous of the attention her brother pays to his new wife. A mother's privileged position is threatened by the attraction her son feels toward his new bride. Co-wives vie for the affection of a common husband by attacking each others' children.

It might be surprising to see Indian women cast in such aggressive roles as we see them in this group of tales. Men, when they do figure at all in these stories, are shown as manipulated for desired ends, unwitting accomplices used by a woman as a tool in her animosity toward some other female. But often, too, it is the absence of a male figure which provides the opportunity for one woman to attack another.

It must be remembered that most tales such as these contain an important and blatant message. Good and evil conduct are strongly contrasted. All this seems to point to the fact that strong moral norms regulate the structural relations between women. The legal codes found in Indian literature give little recognition to this complex network of intrafamilial social ties. They merely emphasize that women, like children, are always subject to the authority of adult males. It is quite remarkable, therefore, to find a rich and significant source of commentary on codes of honor and propriety in female social relations in folktales. If one can generalize from this collection, this function of folktales may prove to be a valuable resource for future research into women's issues.

The women in the tales in this section are not stereotypically passive or submissive in their relations with their husbands. However, they are not openly aggressive either. Tales about husbands and wives are mostly lighthearted and humorous, in contrast to the moralistic and confrontational tales that concern interpersonal relations among women. In stories about rivalries between husbands and wives, women are successful competitors for food and sex. Yet various features of these tales remove them from serious real-life implications. Several, for example, are jokes. In others the action takes place among deities. In still others, persons are cast in animal roles. Indeed, there is a consistent message here that in competition with men women can obtain satisfaction only when they resort to clever, indirect and circumspect means. Parvati only angers her husband when she beats him at the game of *cenne;* but obtains complete satisfaction when she disguises herself as another person. Mrs. Mouse tries to conceal the fact that she ate both her husband's and her own share of the dinner by repeatedly misdirecting him in his hunt for food. She is nearly killed when her husband, tired of searching, confronts her directly. In tale 49, a wife is killed after mocking her husband publicly, but she comes back to haunt him, taking one ghostly form after another. This provides a parallel to the "wild-goose chase" Mrs. Mouse led her husband on.

In sum, the psychic strength of women is portrayed well in both oral and literary Indian story materials, but the emphasis is different. In the folk milieu women succeed by virtue of their cleverness, their guile, and their magical powers. In more learned texts, however, they are honored most for their religious merit and wifely devotion.

· 39 · *The Fish Head*
(Assam)

There are many kinds of domestic tensions, of course, but one of
the common ones depicted by Indian as well as by European
tales concerns the interaction of mother-in-law and daughter-in-
law. This tale is from Assam and concerns a widowed woman
who is mistreated by the wife of her only son. First, the mother
is denied the tasty morsels of fish that her daughter-in-law
should respectfully save for her, and second, she is accused
behind her back of wanting to remarry. This is particularly
vicious gossip, since older women and widows are expected to
lead ascetic lives. This is the time of life for women to renounce
family concerns. Circulating an innuendo that a woman's sexual
needs are instead on the increase would be highly disrespectful
behavior. As for the setting, a forest with clouds and impending
rain is often associated in Indian poetry with emotional tension,
confession, self-discovery, and personal intimacy.

THERE WAS ONCE an old woman who had both a son and a
daughter-in-law. She loved her son very much and the latter re-
ciprocated by taking good care of his mother. One day the old
lady had a sudden urge to eat the head of a carp fish. She mentioned her desire to her daughter-in-law but the latter was un-
obliging. She would eat all the cooked fish heads herself, or else
she would give them to her husband. The old lady would then
quietly dip her fingers into her own bowl of curry and ask cryp-
tically, "Did you forget, my dear?" The daughter-in-law's reply
would be short but sweet. She would say, "Indeed, I did."
     Several days passed in this way until one day the son overheard
his mother and wife talking. He became curious and asked his
mother, "What is it that you say has been forgotten?" "Forget
it," she would answer. "It is nothing my son," she would say.
But the son was not satisfied with this reply. So one day he asked
his wife what had been forgotten. His wife then turned and whispered in her husband's ear, "Your mother wants a husband!" This
news was a great shock for the young man. The very next morning he said to his mother "Mother, let's go out together. I will
find you whatever you want." The simple woman followed her

son without asking any questions. After a while the two reached a forest. There the son left his mother's side abruptly and soon hid behind a tree. The old lady was now left alone. The weather was cloudy and it was about to rain. Soon, therefore, she began to cry out loud saying, "Oh thunder! Don't rumble, don't roar. I have been left in the forest because I desired a fish head. Please let my son return home safely." The son heard all this from behind the tree. He was mystified and asked his mother to explain her words. The old lady then sorrowfully recounted how she had developed a desire to eat the head of a carp and how her daughter-in-law had behaved. The young man now realized how wicked his wife had been. He took his mother back home. He then gave his wife a good beating and drove her out of the house.

· 40 · The Cruel Daughter-in-law (Kerala)

This tale and the one before it are clearly versions of one another (see also tale 31). It would seem they are representatives of a tale structure popular in India, but not noted elsewhere in the world. As in the previous tale, the daughter-in-law in this story understands that she must weaken the bond between her husband and his mother if she is to gain the right to run her own household. Although her simple desire is certainly shared by many young women of India, the impatient greed, vicious lies, and cruel treatment of a mother-in-law depicted here deserve proper punishment. Note how this girl's impetuous character contrasts with the uncomplaining, self-sacrificing character of the older woman. Yet other stories reverse this pattern and depict the daughter-in-law as a kind and gentle soul persecuted by her villainous mother-in-law. In the tale of "Kini Mulki" in the previous section, for example, the mother-in-law easily deceives her son into believing that his wife is guilty of misconduct. It is probably the case for all mother-in-law and daughter-in-law tensions that some rivalry over the sons' affections is involved. Indian sons are particularly dedicated to their mothers, and the fact that in all of these tales the sons eventually take their mothers' side over and against their wife's seems natural and correct to an Indian audience. There may well be regional variation in the extent to which the senior or the junior woman is cast as the stereotypical aggressor in this situation. Praphalludatta Goswami reports a lack of the persecuting mother-in-law figure in Assamese folktales, but we do not yet know if such a generalization may apply to other areas of India.

ONCE UPON A TIME there lived a mother and her son. When the mother became old and weak she found her son a wife. But the son continued to love and care for his mother so deeply that his wife could not stand it. In all matters of running the household the son used to consult his mother instead of his wife. The daughter-in-law tried her best to make son and mother quarrel with one another, but all of her attempts were in vain. Then she began to serve her mother-in-law smaller and smaller portions of food. Gradually the old woman became lean and weak.

The mother did not tell her son of this cruel treatment for fear that it would cause a disagreement between husband and wife. The old woman merely kept quiet, weeping only when she was alone. Her sadness went unnoticed for a long time. One day, however, her son saw her tears and asked why she was crying. The mother did not reply. So he finally asked his wife. "Your mother wants to remarry," she told him. At this the son's anger was aroused. His wife had soon set her husband against his mother. "There is only one way left to us," she continued. "We must put mother in a sack, take her to the forest and set her on fire."

Following his wife's plan, the son put his mother in a sack, tied it up, and carried it into the forest. He could not, however, bring himself to burn his mother alive. Returning home again, he falsely reported to his wife that the job had been done as planned. After a short while, some boys came to that same part of the forest to herd their cattle. They heard the old woman's feeble cries and let her out of the sack. The mother then began to wander and by evening she had reached an abandoned temple where she lay down. Late in the night she awoke to hear a band of thieves offering their daily prayers to the deity of that temple. In their worship they called out in a loud voice, "Half of the stolen goods will be presented to you! May we be blessed with an in-

crease in our loot tomorrow!" The old woman heard this and kept
very still. Then the gang set out on their nightly mischief.

In the morning, sincere to their promise, the returning thieves
placed half of their night's earnings before the deity. This consisted of a large heap of gold jewelry and lots of money. Seeing these
offerings, the old woman was filled with joy. She gathered them
all up and set off quickly to find her way back home. When she
finally arrived at the house, the daughter-in-law could hardly
believe her eyes. How could the old woman be alive? The mother
joyfully gave all of the money and jewelry to her son. There was
not a trace of reproach for what he had done. Seeing the gold, the
daughter-in-law became senseless with greed. She begged her
husband to put her in a sack too, and then to leave her in the
forest. By this time the husband had seen through his wife's cruel
games. So he put her in a sack, tied it tightly, and carried it to
the forest. There he set fire to the sack and burned her alive.

· 41 ·   *A Flowering Tree*
         (Karnataka)

A man's wife and sister are often at odds for his attention. A
beautiful young bride, who has a very special ability to turn
herself at will into a flowering tree, is here envied by her husband's unmarried younger sister. The latter's scheming and
sheer callousness combine to convert this young bride into a
terrible cripple. It hardly seems an accident that the unfortunate
woman is then given shelter by the groom's elder sister, even
though she does this being quite unaware of the important kin
bond between them. Later this same sibling is also instrumental
in helping the wife recover her original lovely form. The underlying principle seems clear enough: married sisters have little
reason to compete for a brother's attention, unlike younger ones
still living at home who experience a new wife's direct intru-
sion. This Kannada story contains a number of special motifs.
The equation of a young girl with a flowering tree is important,
as is mention of a ritual where water is poured (or sprinkled)
over something in order to transform it. The reference to wom-

en playing on swings is also a common image. As one of the
longest stories in the collection, this tale is a good example of
how rich with detail a simple folktale can be. Other links between persons and trees can be found in tales 2, 38, and 44.

A CERTAIN TOWN. A certain King. He had two daughters and a
son. The first daughter was married.

In the same town there lived an old woman with her two
daughters. She did menial jobs to feed and clothe and bring up
her children. When the girls reached puberty, the younger sister
said one day, "Look here, sister. It's hard on mother to work all
day to bring us up. I will turn myself into a flowering tree. You
can take the flowers and sell them for good money." The older
sister was amazed. She asked, "How will you turn into a flowering tree?"

"I'll tell you about it later. You first sweep and wash the entire
house. Then take a bath, go to the well and bring two pitchers
full of water," said the younger sister. The older sister listened to
her carefully, swept and wiped and cleaned, took a bath, and
brought two pitchers of water without touching them with her
fingernails.

Right in front of their house stood a tall tree. The sister swept
and wiped the ground under it too. Both girls then went there,
and the younger one said, "Look here, sister: I'll sit under this
tree and meditate on the Lord. Then you pour the water from this
pitcher all over my body. I'll turn into a flowering tree. Then you
pluck as many flowers as you want, but do it without breaking a
sprout or tearing a leaf. When you've done, pour the water from
the other pitcher over me, and I'll become a person again."

The younger sister sat down and thought of the Lord. The
older one poured water from the first pitcher all over her sister.
At once, her sister turned into a great big tree that stretched from
earth to heaven. The older sister plucked the flowers carefully,
without hurting a stalk, or sprout, or leaf. After she had had
enough, she emptied the second pitcher of water over the tree and
the tree became a human being again, just like before. The
younger sister shook the water from her hair, and stood up. They
both gathered the flowers in baskets and brought them home.
The flowers had a wonderful fragrance. They wove them into

garlands. "Where shall I sell them?" asked the elder sister. "Sister, take all of them to the king's palace, they will pay well. Mother is always doing such awful jobs for our sake. Let's save some money and surprise her," said the younger one.

So the older sister took the basketful of garlands to the king's house and stood before it, crying, "Flowers, flowers, who wants flowers?" The princess said, "Mother, mother, the flowers smell wonderful. Buy me some." "All right, call the flower girl," said the queen. They both looked at the flowers; they were lovely. The queen asked, "How much do you want for these?" "We are poor people, give us whatever you wish," said the older sister. They gave her a handful of coins and bought all the garlands.

When the older sister came home with the money, the younger one said, "Sister, sister, don't tell mother. Hide it. Don't tell anyone." They sold flowers like this for five days, and they had five handfuls of coins. "Shall we show this to mother?" asked one. "No, no, she'll get angry and beat us," said the other. The two girls were eager to make money.

One day the king's son saw the flowers. They smelled wonderful. He had never seen such flowers anywhere. "What flowers are these? Where do they grow, on what kind of tree? Who brings them to the palace?" he wondered. He watched the girl who brought the flowers: one day he followed her home to the old woman's house, but he couldn't find a single flowering tree anywhere. He was quite intrigued. On his way home he tired himself out thinking, "Where on earth do they get such flowers?"

Early the next morning, while it was still dark, the king's son went and hid himself in the tall tree in front of the old woman's house. That day too, the girls swept and washed under the tree. As usual, the younger girl became the flowering tree, and after the older one had gently plucked all the flowers, the tree became a young woman again. The prince saw all this happen before his very eyes. He came straight home and lay on his bed, face down. His father and mother came to find out what the matter was. He didn't speak a word. The minister's son, his friend, came and asked him, "What happened? Did anyone say anything that hurt you? What do you want? You can tell me." Then the prince told him, bit by bit, about the girl turning into a flowering tree. "Is that all?" said the minister's son, and reported it all to the king.

The king called the minister, and sent for the old woman. She arrived, shaking with fear. She was dressed in old clothes and stood near the door. Finally she sat down. The king calmed her, and softly asked her, "You have two girls at your place. Will you give us one?" The old woman's fear increased: "How does this king know about my daughters?" she thought. Still, she managed to stammer, "All right, master. My giving is not as great a thing is it, as your asking for my daughter?" The king at once offered her betel leaf and betal nut (tambula) on a silver platter. She was afraid to touch it. But the king forced these on her and sent her home.

As soon as the old woman reached home, she picked up a broom and beat her daughters. She scolded them saying, "You bitches, where have you been? The king is asking after you, where did you go?" The poor girls didn't understand what was happening. They stood there crying, "Amma, why are you beating us? Why are you scolding us?" "Who else can I beat? Where did you go? How did the king hear about you?" The old woman raged on. The terrified girls slowly confessed to what they had been doing—the girl turning into a flowering tree, selling the flowers, and hoarding the money. They showed her their five handfuls of coins.

"How can you do such things, with an elder like me sitting in the house? What's all this talk about human beings becoming trees? Who's ever heard of it? Telling lies, too. Show me how you become a tree." She screamed and beat them some more. Finally, to pacify her the younger sister had to demonstrate it all. She became a tree and then returned to her normal human self, right before her mother's eyes.

Next day, the king's men came to the old woman's house and asked her to appear before the king. The old woman went and said, "Your Highness, what do you want of me?" The king answered, "Tell me when we should set the date for the wedding." "What can I say, your Highness? We'll do as you wish," the old woman said.

The wedding arrangements began. The family made ritual designs as large as the sky, and built a canopied ceremonial tent as large as the earth. All the relatives arrived. At an auspicious moment, the girl who knew how to become a flowering tree was given in marriage to the prince. After the nuptial ceremony, the families left them alone together in a separate house. But he was aloof, and so was she. Two nights passed. Let him talk to me, thought she. Let her begin, thought he. So both groom and bride were silent. On the third night, the girl wondered, "He hasn't uttered a word, why did he marry me?" She asked him aloud, "It is for this bliss you married me?" He answered roughly, "I'll talk to you only if you do whatever I ask." "Will I not do as my husband bids me? Tell me what you want." "You know how to turn into a flowering tree don't you? Let's see you do it. We can then sleep on flowers, and cover ourselves with them. That would be lovely," he said. "My lord, I'm not a demon, I'm not a goddess. I'm an ordinary mortal like everyone else. Can a human being ever become a tree?" she said very humbly. "I don't like all this lying and cheating. I saw you the other day becoming a beautiful tree—I saw you with my own eyes. If you don't become a tree for me, for who else will you do that?" he chided her.

The bride wiped a tear from her eyes with the end of her sari, and said, "Don't be angry with me. If you insist so much, "I'll do as you say. Now first bring two pitchers of water." He brought them. She uttered chants over them. Meanwhile, he shut all the doors and all the windows. She said, "Remember, pluck all the flowers you want, but take care not to break a twig or tear a leaf." Then she instructed him on how and when to pour water, while she sat in the middle of the room, meditating on God. The prince poured one pitcherful of water over her. She turned into a flowering tree. The fragrance of the flowers filled the house. He plucked all the flowers he wanted, and then sprinkled water from the second pitcher all over the tree. It became his bride again. She shook her tresses and stood up smiling. They spread the flowers, covered themselves with them, and went to bed. They did this for several days. Every morning the couple threw out all the withered flowers from their window. The heap of flowers lay there like a hill.

The king's younger daughter saw the heap of withered flowers one day and said, "Look mother, Brother and Sister-in-law wear and throw away a whole lot of flowers—the flowers they've thrown away are piled up like a hill. And they haven't given me even one. The queen consoled her, "Don't be upset. We'll get them to give you some."

One day the prince had gone out somewhere. Then the king's daughter (who had spied and discovered the secret of the flowers) called all her friends and said, "Let's go to the swings in the *surahonne* orchard. We'll take my sister-in-law; she'll turn into a flowering tree. If you all come, I'll give you each flowers that smell wonderful." Then she asked her mother's permission. The queen said, "Of course, do go. Who will say no to such things?" The daughter then said, "But I can't go alone. Send sister-in-law." "Then get your brother's permission and take her." The prince came there just then and his siser asked him, "Brother, brother! We're all going to the surahonne orchard to play on the swings. Send sister-in-law." "It's not my wish that's important. Everything depends on mother," he answered. So she went back to the queen and complained, "Mother, if I ask brother, he sends me to you. But you don't really want to send her. So you are giving me excuses. Is your daughter-in-law more important than your daughter?" The queen rebuked her, "Don't talk so rudely. It's not good. All right, take your sister-in-law with you. Take care of her and bring her back safely by evening." Reluctantly, the queen sent her daughter-in-law forth.

Everyone went to the surahonne orchard. They tied their swings to a big tree. Everyone was playing on the swings merrily; suddenly the king's daughter stopped all games, brought everyone down from the swings, and accosted her brother's wife. "Sister-in-law, you can become a flowering tree, can't you? Look, no one here has any flowers on their hair." The sister-in-law replied angrily, "Who told you such nonsense? Am I not another human being like you? Don't talk about such crazy stuff." The king's daughter ranted at her cruelly, "Oh, I know all about you. My friends have no flowers to wear. I ask my sister-in-law to become a tree and give us some flowers, and look how coy she acts. If you don't become a tree for us, will you do that for your lovers?"

"*Che,* you're awful. My coming here was a mistake," said the sister-in-law sadly. Then she agreed to become a tree. She sent for two pitchers of water, uttered chants over them, instructed the girls on how and when to pour it, and sat down meditating on God. But the silly girls didn't listen carefully. They poured the water on her indifferently, here and there. She turned into a tree, but only half a tree. It was already evening, and it began to rain with thunder and lightening. In their greed to get at the flowers, they tore up the sprouts and broke the branches. They were in a hurry to get home, so they poured the second pitcher of water at random and ran away. When the princess became a person again, she had no hands and feet. Indeed, she had only half a body. She was a wounded carcass. Somehow in that flurry of rainwater, she crawled and floated into a gutter. There she got stuck in a turning, a long way off from home.

Next morning, seven or eight cotton wagons were coming that way. This half-human thing was groaning in the gutter. The first cart driver said, "Let us see what that noise is about." The second one said, "Hey, let's get going. It may be the wind, or it may be some ghost, who knows?" But the last cart driver stopped his cart and took a look. There was a shapeless mass of body, only the face was a beautiful woman's face. She wasn't wearing a thing. "*Ayyo,* some poor woman," he said in sorrow. He threw his turban cloth over her, and put her on his cart, paying no heed to the dirty talk of his fellows. Soon they came to a town. Outside it was a ruined public shelter. They stopped their carts there and lowered this 'thing' on to its floor, saying "Somebody may feed you. You may survive." Then they drove on.

When the king's daughter came home alone, the queen asked her, "Where's your sister-in-law? What will your brother say?" She answered casually, "Who knows? Didn't we all find our own way home? Who knows where she went?" The queen panicked and tried to get the facts out of the girl. "*Ayyo!* You can't say such things. Your brother will be angry. Tell me what happened." The girl answered with anything that came to her head. The queen found out nothing. She had a suspicion that her daughter had done something foolish. After waiting a couple of days, the prince talked to his mother. "Mother, mother." "What is it, son?" "What has happened to my wife? She went to the orchard to play on the swings, and never came back." "O Rama, I thought she was in your bedroom all this time. Now you're asking me!"

"Oh, something has happened to her," thought the prince. He went and lay down in grief. Five days passed, six days passed, fifteen days passed, but there was no news of his wife. "Did they push her into a tank? Did they throw her into a well?" He asked his parents. What could they say? They, too, were worried and full of fear. He got disgusted, changed into an ascetic's long robe and went out into the world. He just walked and walked; he just didn't seem to care where he went.

Meanwhile, this thing somehow reached the town into which her husband's elder sister had been married. Everytime the palace servants and maids passed that way to fetch water they used to see her. They said to each other, "She glows like a king's daughter." Then one of them couldn't stand it any longer and decided to tell the queen. "Oh queen, she looks very much like your younger brother's wife. Look out the window and see for yourself." The queen looked and the face did seem strangely familiar. One of the maids suggested, "Queen, it would be nice if we could bring her to the palace. Shall I?" The queen pooh-poohed it, "We'll have to serve her and feed her. Forget it." So the next day the maids again mumbled and moaned, "She's very lovely. She'll be like a lamp in the palace. Can't we bring her here?" "All right, all right, bring her if you wish. But you'll have to take care of her yourselves," ordered the queen. They agreed and brought the thing to the palace. They bathed her in oils, dressed her well and sat her down at the palace door. Every day they applied medicines to her wounds and finally the sores got better.

Now the prince wandered through many lands. He ended up outside the gate of his sister's palace, looking like a crazy man, his beard and whiskers unkempt. When the maids fetching and carrying water saw him, they went back to the queen in the palace and said, "Oh Queen! Someone is sitting outside the gate, and he looks very much like your brother. Look through the window for yourself." Grumbling indifferently, the queen went to the terrace and looked through the window. She was surprised. "Yes, he does look remarkably like my brother. What's happened to him? Has he become a wandering ascetic? Impossible," she thought. But she sent her maids down to bring him in. When they said to him, "The queen wants to see you," he brushed them aside. "Why would she want to see me?" he growled. "No, sir, she really wants to see you, please come," they insisted. Finally they persuaded him to come in. The queen took a good look at him and knew he was really her brother.

She ordered the palace servants to heat up whole vats of oil and great vessels of steaming water for his baths. She served him and nursed him, knowing he was her brother. She served new kinds of dinner each day and brought him new styles of clothing. But whatever she did, he didn't speak a word to his elder sister. He didn't even ask, "Who are you? Who am I?" By this time, they both knew they were brother and sister.

The queen wondered, "Why doesn't he talk to me though I treat him so royally? What could be the reason? Could it be some witch's or demon's magic?" After thinking for days, the queen started sending one or another of her beautiful maids into his bedroom every night. She sent seven maids in seven days. The maids held his hand and carressed his body and tried to rouse him from his stupor. But he didn't say a word or do a thing. Finally the servant maids got together and dressed up the thing that sat at the palace door. With the permission of the disgusted queen, they left it on his bed. He neither looked up nor said anything. But this night, it pressed and massaged his legs with its stump of an arm. It moaned strangely. He got up once and looked at it. It was sitting at his feet. He stared at it for a few moments and then realized it was really his lost wife. Then he asked her what had happened. She who had no language all these months suddenly broke into words. She told him whose daughter she was, whose wife, and what had happened to her. "What shall we do now?" he asked. "Nothing much. Bring two pitchers of water, without touching them with your fingernails," she replied.

That night he brought her two pitchers of water without anyone's knowledge. She uttered chants over them and instructed him, "Pour the water from this pitcher over me, I'll become a tree. Wherever there is a broken branch, set it right; wherever a leaf is torn, put it together. Then pour the water of the second pitcher." Meanwhile she sat and meditated on God. Well, he poured the water on her from the first pitcher. She became a tree. But the branches had been broken, the leaves had been torn. He carefully set each one right. Then he gently poured water from the second pitcher all over the tree. Now she became a human being again. She stood up shaking the water off her hair and fell at her husband's feet.

Then she went and woke up the queen, her sister-in-law and touched her feet also. She told the queen the whole story. The queen wept over her sister-in-law's hardships and embraced her.

Then she treated the couple to all kinds of food and services. She had them sit in the hall like bride and bridegroom and undergo a ritual, called *hase*. She kept them in her palace for several weeks and then sent them to her father's palace with cartloads of gifts.

There too, the king was overjoyed at the return of his long lost son and daughter-in-law. He took them home on an elephant-howdah, in a grand ceremonial procession through the city streets. Once at the palace, they told the king and the queen everything that had happened. Then the king had a great pit dug, and seven barrels of burning lime were poured into it. He then threw his youngest daughter into this pit. All the people who saw this said to themselves, "After all, every wrong has its punishment."

· 42 · Two Sisters-in-law (Uttar Pradesh)

Folktales of a region share many common features, even though each one may be regarded as a unique composition. Rivalry between kin is commonly expressed in a relatively small number of different forms and themes, even when quite different kin relationships are involved. This tale, for example, shares with tale 57 the theme that a performance of duty with good conscience may result in a reward for the poorer or the younger of two protagonists. Like tales 31, 32, and 33, an older kinsperson here imitates the behavior of the younger. Since greed rather than sincerity motivates her actions, however, the results are negative. This mirror action technique was also used in tale 40, which is about a cruel daughter-in-law, but there it was the junior woman who suffered the cruel fate she had contrived for her elder relative. Finally, like tales 16 and 57, this story is generally told at the time of an annual festival and conveys a clear moral about the performance of worship. Stories of this kind, called *vrat katha,* are usually told by women, and most examples utilize the different forms of tale type 750B, "Hospitality Rewarded," or 750J, which we propose as a new type, "Devotion Rewarded."

THERE ONCE WERE two sisters-in-law. The elder one was very rich and the younger one was very poor. The younger sister-in-law worked at the house of the elder sister-in-law all day. She was always given a little grain in return. This woman tried to sustain her own family by grinding and making bread with that grain. One day the festival of *sakat* came. The elder sister-in-law then ordered a feast prepared for lord Sakat. The younger sister-in-law worked hard on this all day. She didn't even get time to swallow a simple morsel. That evening the elder sister-in-law gave her nothing but a bunch of weeds. The younger one brought these weeds home. Then she bathed and dressed herself, and afterwards she boiled the weeds. Then she rolled them into a ball, having only a small drink of water for herself. That night, lord Sakat came to her disguised as an old man. He asked her for something to eat. She answered: "Grandfather! I have nothing except a weed ball. It is stored in a wire basket hanging from the ceiling. Please take that." The old man ate the weed ball and then said, "I feel like going to the toilet. Where can I find it?" The woman said, "Grandfather! You may have my whole hovel. Please use whatever place you wish."

Early the next morning the old man departed. When the younger sister-in-law finally got up she found heaps of gold lying all over her hut. She busied herself picking them up and storing them safely. As a result, that day she could not go to her elder sister-in-law's home to work. The elder sister-in-law soon came to find out what was the matter. When she found the house of her younger sister-in-law filled with gold, she was dumbfounded. The younger sister-in-law then explained how she had gotten this gold. The elder sister-in-law commented: "I would now like to work at your house as a servant. Please treat me just as I have treated you." In this way a whole year passed. When the day for the sakat festival came, the elder sister-in-law did exactly what the younger one had done a year earlier. She first put a weed ball in a wire basket and then went to bed. That night an old man came and asked for food, and the elder sister-in-law directed him to the weed ball. After a while, the old man said, "I need to go to the toilet." So the elder sister-in-law said, "The whole house is yours, Grandfather!"

When the elder woman got up in the morning, however, she

could barely breathe. The whole house was full of feces and the smell was intolerable. She now rushed to her younger sister-in-law and began to quarrel. But the younger sister-in-law said, "Don't pick a quarrel with me. I had nothing but a weed ball to offer, and you had everything. Yet you tried to imitate me because of your greed and envy. So you got your just desert."

· 43 · *Kecha Nahar*
(Assam)

This Assamese tale, and the Manipuri tale which follows, give full expression to the jealousy and hostility co-wives often feel toward one another. The motif of co-wife rivalry can also be seen in tales 17 and 57, but the level of hostile oppression never reaches the intensity it does in these tales. In this story a husband is absent and the younger co-wife wickedly attempts to eliminate her competitor.

ONCE THERE LIVED a merchant named Paniya Danr. He had two wives, the senior being called Kecha Nahar and the junior Mukuta.[1] Kecha Nahar was pregnant, but before she could give birth to her child her husband, Paniya Danr, was called away on business. Now Mukuta, the younger wife, was jealous of Kecha Nahar because she was not expecting a child of her own. At the time of delivery, Mukuta persuaded Kecha Nahar to have her eyes bound. As soon as she delivered the child the jealous co-wife, through some magic means, turned this new mother into a snake. Soon the snake slid out of the house, but before it left it entrusted the baby to a maid, saying, "Tend my child, and whenever it cries out, take it to the back of the house. I will come and nurse it." Having said this, Kecha Nahar left the dwelling.

Mukuta let the maid bring up the young son, but she warned her, "If you report this matter to the merchant, I'll kill you and kill the child too. So, beware!" The boy was named Ban Kowar [forest prince], and he was well looked after by the faithful maid. Whenever the baby cried out this maid sought an opportunity to

go outside. Without the knowledge of Mukuta, she would exit
from the back of the house and sing:

> "Come out, come out, O Kecha Nahar,
> The child is dying of hunger.
> The merchant will come, he will come,
> And Mukuta's bones will be crushed."

After singing thrice in that manner the snake would come out of
a hole, throw off its covering, and become human again. It would
nurse the child, and after the feeding, it would put on its snake
covering and enter the hole again.

This went on for some days. Finally the merchant returned
and, of course, inquired about Kecha Nahar. Mukuta then said,
"Oh, after her delivery she disappeared somewhere. She's not to
be found." But Paniya Danr found the answer strange and asked
about the child. Mukuta answered, "We have her child. I have
looked after the boy myself. There's the maid, too. She has also
helped." Paniya Danr soon took the maid aside and asked her
about his missing wife. But she was afraid to tell the truth because of Mukuta. She was afraid of the merchant, too. However
she did say, "My lord, would you first question Mukuta? She
knows about it." Paniya Danr then questioned his junior wife,
but she denied all knowledge of Kecha Nahar. So he threatened
her saying, "If I find you telling a lie, see what I do to you."
Mukuta answered, "You can do whatever you like."

The merchant turned again to the maid. She assured the merchant saying, "Kecha Nahar will be found, but the problem is
how to get her back into human shape. She has been changed into
a snake. Let me ask Kecha Nahar herself what can be done." So
the maid took the child, went behind the house and sang:

> "Come out, come out, O Kecha Nahar,
> The child is dying of hunger.
> The merchant will come, he will come,
> And Mukuta's bones will be crushed."

The snake came out and the maid reported that the merchant had
returned and wanted her back. The snake then said, "You must
tell my husband that I do not want Mukuta punished. She is,

after all, my co-wife. After he promises that he won't punish her, then I will tell you how to get me back into human shape." The maid reported to the merchant what she was told, and he promised not to punish the guilty woman. The maid then went back to the snake. It then told her, "Keep a fire of ricehusks ready and get some curds. When I slip out of my covering, in order to give suck to my child, take that covering and quickly throw it into the fire. Then immediately fall flat on the ground with your face downwards. As soon as the snakeskin is in the fire, I will lose my temper and hit you hard on your head. You will fall unconscious. Ignore the pain in your head, get up directly, feed me curds, and take some of them yourself. We will then live together. Also, see that the merchant is somewhere close by. Have him throw a stone into my hole and thus block it."

The maid went and told all this to the merchant. She asked him to stand close by and to do everything Kecha Nahar had outlined. Kecha Nahar then regained her normal shape for good. But the merchant kept her hidden while he questioned Mukuta. Even though he threatened Mukuta with her life, this obstinate woman went on denying all knowledge of her senior co-wife. Finally Kecha Nahar herself was asked to appear. Now Mukuta could no longer bluff and had to confess her guilt. In fear of her life, she fell at the feet of Kecha Nahar and pleaded for forgiveness. The merchant then kept his promise not to punish her, but he said, "You are an evil woman, and though I am not going to take your life, you cannot escape some sort of punishment. Henceforth you will have to serve Kecha Nahar as a servant and do all the household chores." He was thus reconciled with his good wife. He also rewarded the maid in appreciation of her loyal services.

· 44 · *Lord Krishna's Wives*
          (Karnataka)

With this tale we move to a more lighthearted portrayal of co-wife rivalry and sexual competition. Krishna, most familiar of the incarnations of the great Hindu god Vishnu, is often given mischievous qualities in classical literature, art, and dance. Stories of jealousy between Krishna's two wives, Satyabhama and Rukmini, are common to the folklore of many regions of India. The Tulu version presented here is sung by women as they plant rice seedlings in the paddy fields. A single woman leads the group, singing one line at a time, which others then repeat. Though their work is tedious and their backs ache, these women's thoughts are filled with stories, artfully woven and playfully elaborated with picturesque imagery. The language and style of these fieldsongs is next to impossible to convey in written form, but the basic events in a given story cycle are sometimes captured in prose narrative, and it is in this mode that we present them here. The playful criticisms of Lord Krishna are understood as covert praise by these female devotees.

THE GOD BRAHMA lives in a heaven called Brahmaloka. Old grandfather Brahma! He woke up early one morning and created the flowering tree called *parijata*.[1] Its flowers have silver petals on a golden stalk. Brahma called a girl of the flower seller caste and instructed her to plant this flowering tree. Then he called a servant girl and instructed her to water that tree with a thousand buckets of water. She cared for it morning and evening. Every day there were new flower buds, and every day Brahma picked these and took them with him to Brahmaloka. Next he called his servant girls and told them to make a thousand garlands by plaiting the flowers together without using thread. Then he called a flower seller and said to him, "I have a grandchild who lives in the temple (*matta*) in Udipi. She is called Rukmini Devi.[2] I want you to take these to her."

So the flower seller bundled up all the garlands, put the bundle on his head, and carried it from Brahmaloka to the Udipi temple. There he stood outside the gate and called to Rukmini. Rukmini soon appeared to see who was calling. The flower seller told her he was sent from Brahmaloka to bring her garlands of flowers. Rukmini took the blossoms and sent the flower seller on his way. She then brought the lovely garlands into her garden, where she oiled and combed her hair. She then plaited as many garlands into her braids as they could hold. Next she put oil on her Lord's head and combed his locks. She put flowers in his hair, too. She even placed *ettayi* flowers[3] on the *tulsi* shrine, and then she went into the bedroom.

Just about this time, Satyabhama's servant went to get water. She came across the parijata flowers with their silver petals and golden stalks. "What lovely flowers," she thought, and she went racing to tell her mistress. When she reached home, the maid told Satyabhama the whole story about how Rukmini had been given these beautiful flowers and about how she had tied so many in her hair. She then described how Rukmini had also placed some on her Lord's head. Finally she told how Rukmini had placed ettayi flowers on the tulsi shrine and had gone into the bedroom.

"Why has he never brought so many flowers to me?" asked Satyabhama, filled with jealousy. All this time Sri Krishna was out walking around the village. The maid servant saw him in the distance as he was coming home. She warned her mistress of his return. Satyabhama locked the great wooden door and threw herself down on the bed. "What is this, wife! Open the door! I'm tired and thirsty. Give me something to drink," cried Krishna. But Satyabhama would not listen to his pleas. "Here I am, a childless mother! I won't open the door and quench your thirst. You have brought beautiful new flowers to another. You put them in her hair, and she put them in yours! She placed ettayi flowers on the tulsi shrine and then you went to bed! For this childless mother you don't even bring a twig!"

"Listen, my dear," said Lord Krishna, "Rukmini may be more beautiful, but there is no finer woman than you. Now open the door and give me some water." "No, I'll never open the door and give you water," Satyabhama vowed. "All right, it's true that you are childless. If you want, I'll create children for you. If you want, I'll tie flowers in your hair. I'll even create a flowering plant and give it to you," Lord Krishna promised.

Satyabhama jumped up and got water and milk and brought it to her lord. After quenching his thirst Krishna went and created a flowering bush. He made a platform and planted his bush upon it. Satyabhama had water brought and poured it on the plant. "Now for the childless mother, I will make children," said Krishna, and he created 1001 parrots. "You may feed in all the

courtyards and eat whatever you wish," Lord Krishna told the
parrots. And to Satyabhama he said, "In the morning put milk
out for these birds and in the evening give them water." In this
way she began to raise her "children." There, in the courtyard,
the 1001 parrots scratched and nibbled everything. They dirtied
the place and flew all around.

The next day when she got up, Satyabhama went out to give
her "children" milk. "Alas!," she said. "My lord created children
for this childless mother. And now what a pile of manure I have!"
Hearing these words, the 1001 parrots drew up their legs, beat
their wings and leapt up into the air. They put their faces to the
west and flew away. When Krishna came home he asked how the
"children" were. Satyabhama answered, "I am tired of the heaps
of manure! There is so much! When I was bringing them milk I
told them so, and they flew away in anger." "I will go and fetch
the children," said Lord Krishna, "Give me your sari, though. I
shall need it." So he put on the sari and wove his hair into a
braid.

The parrots flew and flew, chirping and screeching as they
went, until they reached the seaside. There they rested, pecking
in the grains of sand. Just at that time a servant girl from Sri
Gangamma's palace came along carrying water. Seeing how beautiful they all looked, the girl dropped her pitcher of water and
went running to tell her mistress. When Sri Gangamma Devi
heard about these beautiful birds she got a small pitcher of milk
and a bunch of bananas and went to see the parrots. She offered
them the milk and bananas. But the parrots leapt into the air and
flew to the highest branches of the trees. "Ah! You! You must be
the children of that dung-toting cowherd, Krishna. You pimply,
runny-nosed kids! You're the children of that thief who sneaks
around from house to house stealing curds, aren't you? That's
whose kids you are! That flat-nosed, potbellied rascal! His children!" Gangamma Devi cursed and scolded them until they flew
away.

All the while, Krishna was walking along searching this way
and that. When he finally saw the parrots he asked them where
they had been. "When our mother insulted us we left in anger.
We went to the seaside and Gangamma Devi brought us milk
and bananas. Then she taunted us," they replied. "What did she

say to you," Krishna asked. "She said we were the children of a
dung-toting cowherd. She said you had a flat nose and a potbelly.
She called us pimply, runny-nosed brats. She called you a curd-
stealing rascal," they told him.

Lord Krishna asked the "children" to leave and said that he
would follow. Then, still dressed as a woman, he went and sat on
the low stone wall that surrounded Gangamma Devi's well. Soon
a maid servant came to fetch water. There, at the well, she saw
the most beautiful woman she had ever seen in her life. When she
returned to the house she told her mistress, "I had thought you
the finest lady in the world, but just now I saw one yet more
beautiful than you sitting at the well." Gangamma Devi went
out to the well to see for herself. There she saw the woman.
"Where are you from? Where are you going?" she asked the lovely lady. "I'm just traveling," was the reply, "and I have come
this far." "It is getting late. Already it is evening," answered
Gangamma. "Please come to my palace, sister."

"But you must not touch me," replied the beautiful woman.
Gangamma promised not to touch her and again invited her to
her house. Even so, the beautiful stranger refused. "You are my
sister, girl, and I am yours. I, too, am a woman, isn't it so?"
Gangamma coaxed her. "I won't touch you and grab you. Come,
sister." So the beautiful stranger went with Gangamma to her
palace. Gangamma Devi heated water and invited her to take a
bath before dinner. The beautiful woman refused saying that she
mustn't bathe before going to the Udipi Matta temple. She said,
"I must go to Udipi to eat. I am one of those who cooks for Lord
Krishna." So Gangamma bathed alone and ate alone.

When it was time to lay down, Gangamma Devi invited the
woman to sleep on the same mat with her. But the woman refused. So Gangamma had a separate mat put down for her and
they both lay down to sleep. Krishna, in the disguise of a beautiful woman, looked at Gangamma and saw how beautiful she
was. But he hid these thoughts and said to her, "The insults you
flung at my children have now returned to you. You are all of the
things you said of me."

The next day Krishna got up and told Gangamma Devi he was
going. Gangamma Devi begged him not to leave, and that if he
must go, that she would go with him. "How can you come with

me?" he asked. "I will become a lime fruit and come in your shirt
pocket," she said. "You can't do that. If I bring limes with me
when I return people will want to cut them up to make juice to
drink," said Krishna. "Then I will become a garland of flowers
and hang on your neck," she said. "You can't do that either," he
replied, "because flowers get squeezed and pinched and thrown
away." "Then I shall become a golden fly and ride along on your
thigh," she said, and so she turned herself into a golden fly and
returned home with Krishna.

When Krishna arrived at the house Satyabhama brought him
two glasses of water and two cups of milk. She set these down in
front of him. Krishna drank one glass of water and one cup of
milk and then asked whom the others were for. "Why, for her
who came with you," said Satyabhama. "Who has come along
with me?" protested Krishna. "Gangamma Devi has come with
you," Satyabhama insisted. "Then where is she?" asked Krishna.
"Why, she is sitting on your right thigh," replied Satyabhama.

So Krishna decided to go to the Matta in Udipi. Rukmini had
just begun to wonder where her lord had gone and why he had
not yet returned. When she saw him coming she got two glasses
of water and two cups of milk and placed them before him.
Krishna drank one of each, as before, and asked who the other
was for. "Why, for her who came with you," said Rukmini.
"Who has come along with me?" "Gangamma Devi has come
with you," replied Rukmini. "Where is she, then?" "Why, she
is sitting on your right thigh!" replied Rukmini. This is why in
Udipi, Rukmini now sits in the East Matta and Gangamma Devi
sits in the West Matta.

· 45 · *Sandrembi and Chaishra (Manipur)*

This long and beautiful tale is so popular among the Meiteis of
Manipur that it is frequently performed as a folk drama. In it
the main characters embody several contrasting characteristics of
good and evil. The jealousy and cruelty exhibited by the younger co-wife and her daughter remind one of the wicked

stepmother character in European Cinderella tales. Many of the
peculiarities of the story, such as transformation from human to
animal form, the belief in multiple souls, and multiple communication channels between the living and the dead in dreams,
are distinctive features in stories of the Tibeto-Burmese
peoples.

ONCE UPON A TIME two women were co-wives. The elder had a
daughter named Sandrembi, and the younger had one named
Chaishra. When their husband died, they had a very hard time.
The younger wife and her daughter always planned to bring ruin
to the elder wife and her daughter, Sandrembi. One day both
wives went to catch fish in Lake Shilempat with a *long*.[1] The
mother of Sandrembi caught many fish and filled her *tungon*[2] to
the brim. But the mother of Chaishra, instead of catching fish,
caught only small adders. She also kept these inside her tungon.
When evening came, both women returned home. On the way
they stopped to rest under a big fig tree. Chaishra's mother suggested they eat some figs and so she climbed the tree to pick its
fruit. Then she asked Sandrembi's mother to open her mouth to
taste one of the fruits. The latter stood under the fig tree with her
jaw wide open and waited for the fruit to drop. One fig fell into
her mouth and it was very tasty. When the younger wife asked
how she liked it, she answered that it was very fine. "Then open
your mouth again as wide as you can," Chaishra's mother said,
"for I am dropping a bigger and tastier one this time." She
opened her mouth again and waited. But Chaishra's mother, instead of dropping her fruit, dropped the adders she had kept in
her tungon. Sandrembi's mother was bitten by the adders and
died. Chaishra's mother then concealed her dead body under a
nearby pond. Taking her tungon containing fishes, she returned
home alone.
    When Sandrembi found Chaishra's mother returning alone
without her own mother she asked what had happened. "Your
stubborn mother insisted on staying to catch fish until sunset.
When I asked her to return, she turned a deaf ear," answered the
younger mother. Sandrembi wept bitterly and waited for the return of her own mother without taking any food. When
Chaishra's mother heard her weeping in the middle of the night,

she admonished her and asked her to stop disturbing her sleep. Finally, in the wee hours of the morning Sandrembi managed to fall asleep. Her mother than appeared to her in a dream and said, "Look, my dear daughter, I have been killed by your stepmother. She poured adders into my mouth, and my five souls changed into a tortoise which has settled at Shilempat. As soon as day breaks, come with a long and catch me. After that, keep me for seven days in a pitcher with water. I will see if I can transform myself into human form again." With this the spirit of Sandrembi's mother vanished.

The next morning Sandrembi set out toward the lake with a long in her hand. She tried to catch the tortoise, but she was crying and sobbing. First she caught a Ngamu fish. Looking at it, she quickly said, "Oh, Ngamu, I don't want to catch you, what I want is my dear mother." So she set the fish free. Indeed, she set free all the fish she caught until she finally secured the tortoise. She came back home with this and hid it in her lap. When Chaishra's mother asked her how many fish she had, she answered that she had not caught any. She said she had no experience and showed the woman her empty container. But the girl was afraid lest Chaishra's mother would demand to see what was in her lap. Next Sandrembi was asked to prepare some food for the family. As she entered the house, she slipped the tortoise into a pitcher. But this act was seen by Chaishra, who was carefully spying on her. Chaishra then reported what she had seen to her mother. Her mother told her to demand a drink of water from the pitcher containing the tortoise. The next morning Chaishra's mother asked Sandrembi to give Chaishra water to drink from the pitcher. Chaishra then said, "No, I do not want the water she brings. I will take water from the pitcher myself and drink." Sandrembi did not know what to do. Finally she gave in, and Chaishra discovered the tortoise in the pitcher. She took it out and gave it to her mother. Chaishra's mother asked Sandrembi to cook the tortoise and poor Sandrembi was dumbfounded. Finding no other escape, she put the tortoise in a pot and started to boil it.

"Sandrembi, my dear daughter! My feet are boiling," the tortoise cried from inside the pot. Hearing this, Sandrembi took the burning firewood out from under the pot and wept bitterly. Chaishra reported this to her mother too, and her mother then told Chaishra to slap Sandrembi on the face. Being afraid of her stepmother, Sandrembi again started the cooking fire. The tortoise cried, "My dear daughter! I have been cooked up to my waist, up to my neck, and now my whole body has been consumed." Sandrembi wept bitterly in the kitchen and refused even to touch the curry prepared from the tortoise. Chaishra and her mother ate up all the flesh and threw away the bones. That night Sandrembi's mother appeared in her dream again and said, "My daughter! Pick up all the bones that were thrown away. Keep them concealed for seven days in your *phiruk*³ by covering it with cloth. On the seventh day I shall appear in human form." Sandrembi did as she was advised. But she was too curious. On the sixth day she opened the covering to see what was happening. The bones, instead of changing into human form, had transformed into a sparrow and it now flew away.

Sandrembi and Chaishra soon grew up into full girlhood. One day both of them went out to fetch water, each one carrying a pitcher. Sandrembi was clad in rags, and Chaishra had on brand-new clothing. On their way they were met by Tukaoba, a king, who was returning with his servants from a hunting expedition. Even though Sandrembi was in rags, she was beautiful and shining. Like gold in dirt, her beauty soon attracted the king. He approached Sandrembi and begged her to give him water to drink from her pitcher. Sandrembi was apprehensive of what her stepmother would say. She therefore requested that the king drink water from her sister's pitcher instead. Disappointed, the king went away without drinking at all.

When she reached home, Chaishra reported this incident to her mother. The next day, the two girls were again sent away by Chaishra's mother to fetch water. Chaishra wore Sandrembi's dress, which her mother thought might attract the king, and Sandrembi wore Chaishra's dress. This time king Tukaoba was waiting on his horse without any servants nearby. He could not take his eyes off Sandrembi, whose beauty was doubly increased in that beautiful dress. Putting aside his shame, he came near her and, as on the previous day, begged her to give him some water to quench his thirst. Seeing this Chaishra was red with anger. Sandrembi, as before, asked the king to take water from her younger sister.

The king then said, "I want to drink water only from you and not from anybody else. Will you kindly quench my thirst?" He persisted and Sandrembi, finding it difficult to refuse, finally held the pitcher up to the king who was on horseback. Instead of taking the pitcher, however, the king took hold of Sandrembi's hands. Lifting her on his horse he now ran off with her. After Sandrembi had been carried away, Chaishra threw down her pitcher and returned home. She then narrated the whole incident to her mother. Both of them were very disappointed. But at the house of the king, Sandrembi was very happy. She led a free and contented life. Chaishra and her mother, however, continued scheming about a way to bring ruin to Sandrembi once again.

After a while Sandrembi gave birth to a son. The following year Chaishra and her mother invited her to a lunch at their home. Sandrembi came, leaving her son behind in the house of the king. But when she was ready to leave, she found her clothes had been taken by Chaishra. She then said, "Dear sister, let me go. It is getting late, Please give me my clothes. My son may be weeping." Chaishra grew furious at this. Taking off the clothes, she threw them under a cot. When Sandrembi knelt down to take them back, Chaishra's mother poured boiling hot water over her. Sandrembi died instantly and her five souls were transformed into a forest bird. Then Chaishra put on Sandrembi's fine clothes and left for the house of the king. But she was hesitant to go near him. The king soon noticed Chaishra's coarseness and was suspicious. He said, "My dear Sandrembi, how is it that you come back home today after a visit to your mother's house with these pores on your feet, long eyelashes, and eyes that look so ugly?" Chaishra answered these suspicious questions saying, "My dear love, I ran home in haste, lest my son might be weeping, and my feet developed ugly pores. My eyelashes have become long weeping for my parents. My eyes are shrunken from my crying." The king was not satisfied with these answers, but he could not do anything.

After some time, Sandrembi came and settled on a branch of a tree in her new form as a forest bird. Under that tree, the king's Moslem gardener was cutting grass. Looking at this man the forest bird said,

"Kukhru Ku Khangmeitat[4]
Look you, grass cutter,
Tell your lady,
Who has long eyelashes,
To take proper care
Not to destroy and hurt
My son, the crown prince,
Who has been properly born
As a cloth woven with the necessary warp and woof.
If you fail to tell her,
Your sickle will be lost,
Your horses will die,
And you will not have anything to ride.
Chaishra is on the throne
O king Tukaoba!
Do you forget my crown prince?
Kukru Ku Khangmeitat."

Hearing this human voice coming from the bird, the grass
cutter was struck with wonder and he went running to the king.
While he was reporting his experience to the king, the forest bird
came and sat on a wooden beam of the veranda. Seeing the bird,
the king now said, "Oh, you with flowing feathers and tail, if
you are really a transformation of my dear Sandrembi, come down
and pick up these grains from my palm." At this, the bird came
down and took some grain from the king's hand. At that moment, the king caught hold of the bird and managed to put it in a
cage. In a dream, Sandrembi now appeared to the king and said,
"My dear king, please keep this forest bird for seven days. Do not
tell anybody where I am. I shall try to assume human form again
on the seventh day and help raise my son."
     The king's son soon became curious about the bird. He would
often come near the cage to look at it. Sometimes the little bird
took dirt from the eyes of the son with its beak. This loving
gesture was very much resented by Chaishra. One day the king
went out hunting with his servants. Chaishra then killed the forest bird and prepared a curry out of it. The king returned and,
finding the bird nowhere, asked about it. Chaishra then replied,
"The bird played mischief with my son, so I killed it to prepare a

curry." The king was furious, but he could not express his feelings outwardly. Still, he did refuse to taste the curry. The king's
portion was thrown away and after a time a mango tree grew out
of the bones that had been tossed out. Then a mango fruit appeared on the tree. The grass cutter was fond of eating fruits. So
one day, with permission from Chaishra, he plucked that mango
and brought it home. As soon as he reached the veranda he was
called by the king. But first he put the mango inside a grain bin
so he could eat it after he came back from meeting with the king.

On the next day the grass cutter remembered the mango. He
went searching for a knife to cut it, but he could not find a knife
anywhere in the house. Finally he found a knife, but now the
mango could not be located. In this way the grass cutter found
the knife one day, but on that day the mango could not be located. On days when the mango was located, the knife could not
be traced. Seven days passed, and on the seventh day the mango
changed into a beautiful woman. On the eighth day, after the
grass cutter went to do his work, the woman who had come out of
the mango prepared some food. She kept everything ready for
him and then hid herself in a corner of the house. This happened
three days in a row. The grass cutter enjoyed the food but could
not figure this out, so he asked his neighbors. They told him they
knew nothing about these strange events. The cutter now became
apprehensive lest some demon had an evil design on him.

Finally, one day, pretending to go cut grass, the cutter hid
himself in his own house to see what was happening in his absence. Thinking that he had gone, the woman came again, as
usual, to prepare some food. Seeing this, the grass cutter rushed
toward her and was about to catch her sari when she said, "Look,
grandfather grass cutter, I am Sandrembi." Then she narrated her
story and described her transformation from mango into a woman. The cutter ran to the house of the king and reported the
whole incident. The king sent his men to fetch Sandrembi from
the house of the gardner. When Sandrembi arrived, the king
announced, "I must settle this once and for all. I must know
which of you is my true Sandrembi. Both of you will be armed
with a sword and you must then strike each other. Whoever dies
is not Sandrembi." Accordingly, each of the women was given a

sword. Chaishra struck at Sandrembi first. Nothing happened. Sandrembi then struck Chaishra and cut her into pieces. Thus Chaishra finally died. The innocent Sandrembi survived and lived a long and happy life with the king and her son.

· 46 ·   *The Tale of the Mouse*
(Kashmir)

In addition to in-law problems, direct husband-wife rivalries are commonly depicted in Indian folktales. In this next story, this problem is nicely depicted through the use of animal surrogates. The tale describes a greedy wife, who tried to cover up her self-centered behavior with clever lies. Though her husband is clearly the wronged partner, he obtains no redress. Instead, his wife leaves the house when he tries to beat her, a typical female response in real life. The wife then survives quite successfully on her own, eventually ending up at her own parent's house, as many Indian women would. In a sense, one might call this an Indian variant of a feminist story. Perhaps this explains why this tale has been conveniently cast with animal characters, so that the parallels with human life have a somewhat covert quality. Interestingly, the tale was collected from a male domestic servant. Perhaps he had some special sympathy for female roles. In any case, this story could easily and realistically depict a household servant, since any cook could take the same actions, necessitating only minor changes in the simple cast of story characters.

THERE ONCE LIVED a male and a female mouse who were husband and wife. One day the husband said to his wife, "Let's have some fried rice and green gram for dinner today." "Not a bad idea," said the wife. "Go and fetch the ingredients, and I will make you an excellent dinner." The husband went away and returned shortly with some rice, green gram, salt, oil, turmeric powder, ginger, aniseed powder, and firewood. He handed all those things to his wife and said, "Here you are, I shall go out to amuse myself for a while. You cook the dinner, and by the time it is ready I will be back." Having said this the husband went out and joined one of his friends.

The female mouse then cleaned the rice and also the green gram. She lit the fire and started cooking. When these preparations were almost finished she tasted a little bit to see whether she had used the right amount of salt. She found that her food was very tasty indeed, so she tried a little more. "After all, what difference does it make if I eat a little bit here and there," she thought. Then she ate some more. And in this way, thinking she was tasting the salt, the wife discovered to her surprise that she had soon emptied the entire bowl that she had prepared. Nothing was left for her husband. "Oh, my goodness. What shall I do now?" she asked herself. With this the wife began to cry in despair. But soon her husband returned and asked, "Is the dinner ready?" He wet his dry lips with his tongue. "Yes, my dear. The dinner is there in the kitchen. Why don't you go and help yourself?" said the female mouse, pretending to be very busy.

"Where is the food? I cannot find a thing here," shouted the he-mouse. "It's there under the glass vessel," the wife replied. "It's not there," shouted the husband. "Then it must be underneath the mud pot," said the wife. "It's not there either," shouted the husband. He was becoming very angry. "Oh, then it must be under the lid of the pot," said the wife. "It's not there either," answered the husband. "Try under the bowl." "No, it's not there." "Well then it must be under the big brass vessel," suggested the wife. "No, nothing is there." "Oh! I forgot, It's under the container where we heat the gram." "No. It's not there either." "Well, try under the measuring vessel for the gram." "It's not there either," the husband shouted. His eyes were now red with anger. "All right, try the grinding stone," said the female mouse with a treacherous smile on her lips.

By now the poor male mouse had searched the entire kitchen. He had looked under all the utensils, all the lids, all the measures and in all the corners, yet he couldn't find the dish of his dreams anywhere. He now began shivering in anger. There was anger in his eyes, all over his face, in his ears, and even in his anus. He became more and more agitated, and he suddenly picked up the mortar used for grinding and threw it at his wicked wife. The female mouse ducked and escaped certain death. However, she did receive a small cut. Blood started oozing down from a torn ear and she became frightened.

The she-mouse then ran out of the house crying and shouting. The wife ran and ran and finally reached the shop of a cotton carder. There she went in and called saying, "Oh, brother carder, brother carder! Give me some cotton to dress my torn ear." When the carder saw the bleeding he felt sorry for the she-mouse and immediately gave her some cotton. Then this woman went on to the house of the weaver. There she said, "Brother weaver, brother weaver! Give me a little thread to stitch my torn ear. I want to wear gold and return to my father's house." The weaver gave her some thread and she left satisfied. Next the she-mouse went to the house of the tailor and said to him, "Brother, tailor, brother tailor. Please help me to stitch my torn ear. I want to wear gold and return to my father's house." The tailor agreed and immediately helped her to stitch her ear.

After her bleeding ear had been dressed and stitched, the female mouse went to the goldsmith. She said to him, "Brother goldsmith, brother goldsmith! Please give me some gold. I want to wear it for my return to my father's house." The goldsmith gave her a small piece of gold. She wore it and went to seek refuge in her father's house. Meanwhile the he-mouse was still sitting at the door of his own kitchen. He was sulking and upset. He had not enjoyed the dinner of his dreams, nor did he have his wife.

· 47 · As Long as You Keep Your Legs Up (Bihar)

The previous story depicted a husband and wife in a dispute over food. This next tale, also from northern India, concerns anger over illicit or adulterous sexual favors. Again the wife is shown to be the indulgent one, and the husband ends up jilted. The story is meant to have a comic tone and apparently circulates only in male circles. A rough and lusty description provides much of the fun. The teller, a folklore lover and teacher of Hindi, claims that similar accounts are widespread in

western Uttar Pradesh. Certainly the tale fits with a whole
genre of such stories, found both in the north and the south,
that depict adulterous wives. They reflect a very old, traditional
motif. An account similar to this modern one can be found in
the early, Buddhist, *Panchatantra* story collection. In Indian
folk tradition, women are generally thought to be the more
lustful of the two sexes. Also, of course, their chastity is more
highly valued. This makes for great relish in describing their
presumed, forbidden, transgressions. The occurrence of the reverse tale type, the unfaithful husband motif, is most
uncommon. It is also significant that the wife in this tale is
young and beautiful, while her spouse is quite old. This provides a sterotypical occasion for such a sexual escapade. The
reference to a wild boar is interesting, too. This animal has
some general link with wildness, with reversals of normal behavior, and with sexual lust, at least in the oral traditions of
southern India.

THERE ONCE WAS an old man and his young beautiful wife. This
woman had many male friends, and they used to visit her regularly after her husband had left for work. The husband realized that
his wife was unfaithful, but he could never succeed in catching
her in the act. As a result, the poor man used to get restless and
worried. He would always hurry back home at the end of the day
in the hope of keeping these lustful visitors away.

One day after finishing the morning meal, this old man surprised his young wife by saying, "Dear! I'm leaving for town on
an important task. It may be late at night before I return. So
please take care of everything." "Don't you worry, my dear. Everything will be fine. Please take care of yourself on your trip,"
replied the young woman. But the husband only pretended to be
going away. After crossing the village street he cleverly managed
to double back to the house unnoticed. He then entered by using
the backdoor.

The young wife was happy about the long absence of her aging
husband. She lost no time in calling her lover, who soon arrived
with a present. When the two of them entered the bedroom, the
old husband was waiting. He had crawled under the bed and now
hid himself there, motionless. The two lovers soon began their

love play. The present the man had brought was a pair of leather slippers. He gave them to the young woman, and she was very pleased. She immediately put the slippers on. "What nice slippers these are!" she said and the lover answered, "If you are nice to me today, I will bring you something even nicer tomorrow." Both lovers then removed their clothes and they jumped into the bed. The old man hiding underneath could hear giggles, creaking sounds, and even exclamations such as "Ah!" and "Eh!" His heart began to beat like a drum. But the young woman had forgotten to remove the slippers she had just been given. While they were engaged in lovemaking, the young lady stretched her legs up. She wanted to enable her lover to batter her while pretending that he was a wild boar. At that time her eyes fell on the lovely slippers. So she asked her lover, "How long do you think these will last?" The reply, surprisingly, came from under the bed. It was, "Only as long as you keep your legs up."

· 48 · *Siva and Parvati*
  (Karnataka)

This Tulu tale is one in a series told about the adventures of Siva and Parvati. Like this one, the others in this set all picture this divine couple in very ordinary human terms. There is a competitive spirit in all of these tales—a playful war of the sexes. Parvati always wins. The story imagery suggests several levels of interpretation. Starting with the game of *cenne,* which in this context suggests legitimate and leisurely sexual activity, the scene soon shifts, using a delightfully symmetrical structure, to other "games people play." Similar lover's quarrels can be found in some of India's devotional poetry.

SIVA AND PARVATI once decided to play a game of *cenne.*[1] So Parvati went up to the seventh floor and brought down a golden board and silver playing pieces. The two then set up the board and began to play. Siva lost the first "house" in the first round of play, and when they played a second round, he also lost the second "house." When they played the third round, he soon lost a third "house." And so it went until he had lost them all. Siva then said, "I am hungry and thirsty. My head is spinning and I feel giddy. Quick, Parvati, go inside and bring me some milk and water."

Parvati then got up to get milk and water for her husband. As she crossed the threshold of the room, however, she tripped and banged her head on the top of the door frame. "Alas! Why did the threshold obstruct me and the door frame hit me?" she cried. Then she thought to herself, "These problems may be a sign of some inauspicious things about to befall me!" Parvati then returned to the cenne table bringing some milk and water with her. But as soon as she sat down, she noticed that the cenne board had been turned around so that the winning side now faced Siva. Parvati was now furious and she kicked the board over. Seeing what she had done, Siva became angry too. He grabbed her by her braid and slapped her. Then in anger Siva said, "I'm going to the forest to shoot birds." As he left he cursed Parvati with the words, "I hope your silk sari is eaten by white ants!" He stormed out of the house, remembering to take with him his golden knife, silver snuff box, and silver lime box.

As soon as Siva left the house, Parvati began her menstrual period. For three days she remained outside, and on the fourth day she made preparations for her bath by crushing soapnuts to wash with and calling for clean clothes from the washerman. Then she brought water for the washerman to wash his hands and gave him a large rice meal. When he was through eating, Parvati said, "Please take as much betel leaf and arecanut as you want." He chewed these and then she brought him a cup of oil with a spoon. She also poured spoonfuls of oil onto his head. Then she took a measuring pot, filled it with rupees, and gave it to him. When the washerman left, Parvati thought to herself, "Now I think I'll have a look at my good silk sari. When she opened the trunk, she was shocked to find that it had been ruined by ants! "Oh, alas! What is this?" she cried, and she laid the sari back into the trunk. Parvati quickly pounded some charcoal and added water to it to prepare a paste. Then she smeared the paste on her face to make herself black. Next she changed her sari, dressed as a woman of a forest tribe, and took out a curved knife.

Then Parvati left for the forest and sat down at the base of a tree. Using her curved knife like a comb, she began to pick the lice from her hair. While she was doing this, along came Lord Siva. He stopped by her and said, "What are you doing here, Korpalu?"[2] "Oh, nothing, my Lord! I'm just sitting her picking lice from my hair!" replied the Korpalu. "Don't stop what you are doing because of me," said Siva. "I've got some fine arecanut, so sweet that the bats have even chewed its outer husk. I also have the choicest of betal leaves. Let's chew together!" "Oh, no, I don't want to, my Lord!" said the Korpalu shyly. "I have my own arecanut that I collected, and I have some wilted leaves that have already turned yellow. I will chew what is mine!"

But Siva was insistent. "What you have, you can keep for later. Let's chew the tender leaves that I have while I hold your hand!" "Oh my! What kind of a way is that to speak to a Korpalu?" she answered. "What difference does it make if you are a Korpalu? You are a human being, aren't you? I'm a human being too. Our blood is the same is it not?" argued Siva. "What you are saying is not right," answered the woman. "You are a god. I am a Korpalu." Then Siva and the girl remained in the forest together for two days and three nights.

On the third day, Siva said, "I'm going now, Korpalu." "If you are going, go," she replied, "but just one thing. If I get pregnant, who will pay for my expenses?" "I will provide for your needs. Here is a golden knife, a silver case for lime, and a silver snuff box. I also have a golden ring with my seal on it. Take these things. Use them for your expenses if you get pregnant!" said Siva. "Now I am going back to my palace, Korpalu." Siva ran back home by one path, while Parvati ran home by another path.

When she reached her house, Parvati quickly took a bath, put on *kumkum*, (a kind of decorative powder) and a red dot, and combed her hair. Before she even had a chance to put on her sari, however, Siva arrived home. He sat down on the swinging cot, and Parvati brought him milk in a dish and water in a bowl. As she gave him the water she said, "I have the feeling that you had a good time with a forest woman." "No, I didn't," said Siva. "Didn't you have sex with a Korpalu?" asked Parvati. "When you left here you took your golden knife, your silver box for lime, and the silver snuff box. Didn't you give those things to the Korpalu?" "I didn't give them to her," said Siva. "Don't say

things like that about me. I didn't do it!" "Don't lie to me!" said
Parvati. "A Korpalu came here and gave those things to me!"
"Where did you see her?" asked Siva. "She came here and gave
them to me," repeated Parvati. "Didn't white ants eat your silk
sari?" asked Siva. "No, even though you cursed as you were leaving, nothing happened," answered Parvati. "While I was gone,
what did you do? What happened here?" "Nothing happened
here!" said Parvati. "I didn't hold the hand of a washerman nor
did I share the food of a washerman." Then Siva drank the water
and the milk she had offered him and said, "You have no defects.
You were born from truth. Let us be on good terms together."

· 49 · *The Story of a Man Who Had Awful Lips (Tamilnadu)*

The next story is a clever psychological commentary couched in
terms of a classic case of domestic strife. A man cannot stand his
wife's mockery and disrespect (the two are mixed), especially
when she does this publicly in front of friends. After this, the
husband kills the poor woman, yet reminders of those domestic
interactions continue to haunt him. The wife's critique has been
internalized and is projected onto every sound he hears. Tale 35
has a similar theme. This tale is from the far south. The parallel
comes from the northern state of Uttar Pradesh. It differs by
depicting a sister's memory of mistreating her brother.

THERE ONCE LIVED a man whose lips protruded and were an
awful sight to see. He was known as *utatan* which means "one
who has conspicuous lips." Even his wife used to call him utatan.
One day utatan told his wife "Hey, one of my friends is coming
to our house for dinner. So please don't call me utatan today."
His wife agreed. The friend came for dinner. The wife controlled
herself until the guest had finished eating. After dinner the husband called to his wife and asked her to bring him and his friend
some betel leaves and arecanut.[1] She answered him at once saying
"Yes, utata." The friend just stared at him. After some time he
left their house. Then the husband began to yell at his wife for

having called him "utatan" in front of his friend. Not only that, he went so far as to kill her and bury her in the backyard. But after a few days a small plant grew at that spot which said "utata, utata" whenever there was a little breeze. Utatan was furious on hearing this. So he cut down the whole plant, plucked the leaves, and boiled them. But as it boiled, the water too said "tala tala utata, tala tala utata."

The man's anger now became greater and greater. Soon he threw the water to a dog. But after licking it all up the dog barked at him with the sound "val val utata, val val utata." The husband then said to his dead wife, "You wretched woman! You still have the courage to call me "utatan." So next he called a scavenger and asked him to kill the dog. The scavenger obeyed and made a drum out of the dog's skin. But when he later began to beat the drum its sound was "dum dum utata, dum dum utata." Utatan's anger now found no bounds; he burned the drum, but it still made the sound "buus utata" before it disappeared!

· 50 · *Vayanatu Kulavan (Kerala)*

Divyan (the divine one) is said to be the procreator of the Tiyyar caste of Kerala. This is the story of his own creation, as told by people of the Vannan caste during certain dramatic possession rituals celebrated each year for this deity. Readers who are familiar with the Sanskritic *purana* tradition will perhaps be surprised to see the great gods of Hinduism characterized in such base images as they are in this folk narrative. Some of the themes of this tale, such as Siva and Parvati as hunters (see tale 48), are found in other folk traditions. And some specifically associate the couple with the Tiyyar caste, whose traditional occupation is to make alcoholic toddy from palm sap. (Tale 25 however, links Siva to a farming caste of Gujarat). But some aspects of both the narrative style and the imagery contained in this myth resemble Brahmanical traditions, such as the opening lines. This brief invocation indicates that the myth is sacred and

powerful. Furthermore, Siva's behavior as a wild, "drunken"
man, his dancing, and his creation of beings from his own anger
are important in ancient literary traditions all around India.
These are meant to contrast with his wife's tender touch of the
palm's roots and her concern to foster a more passive, vegetal
kind of beauty.

OH, LORD GANAPATHI and goddess Saraswathi, you must help
me. Lord Krishna, and my great teacher, stand by me! I haven't
the wisdom to tell about the great creator alone.

Siva, the Lord of Kailasa, once entered the forest in the form of
a hunter. He found toddy in the base of the life-giving palm. He
saw toddy flow there like the rays of the sun! He approached and
drank. Drunk, he danced like a madman. Parvati, daughter of
the mountain, ran away in fear upon seeing him. She went into
the forest in the form of a huntress. Parvati went to the palm and,
rubbing its base, made the sap flow up to the flowers. Then Siva
came again to drink toddy. But it no longer exuded from the base
of the palm. He became angry with the daughter of the mountain, and he slapped his sacred thigh. From that slap a son was
created.

The Lord of Kailasa was pleased. He gave his son the name
Divyan. Parvati, daughter of the mountain, was pleased too. Divyan now awaited Siva's words. Siva then told him to drive away
the evils and the hardships of the world.

· 51 · *The Enchanted Water Hole*
(*Manipur*)

In the worldview of the tribal people of Manipur, the dividing
line between humans and nature is not always very clear. Plants,
animals, and features of the landscape are often endowed with
humanlike characteristics. This Paite story shows that the reverse can be true, too. That is, humans can assume the traits of
animals. In this case, the transformation is a tragic result of a
woman ignoring her husband's warnings not to drink water

from a certain pool. It is interesting that it is the duties of a woman toward her family—a trait shared between humans and tigers—which keeps her in both worlds.

ONCE UPON A TIME a couple lived happily in a village situated on a lofty mountain. Together they cleared the bushes and weeds from a patch of hillside. Then they planted their garden. In their labors the couple encountered many hardships, not least of which was lack of good streams or wells in the immediate area. Soon the wife was thirsty, and she pleaded with her husband to let her go in search of water. Although he loved her very much and sympathized with her, the husband would not let her go.

The husband knew of a water hole on the southern side of their property, but it was enchanted. "We cannot drink the water from the water hole to the south of our land," he told her. "Whoever drinks from this place will be turned into a tiger. No matter how thirsty you are, you must not drink that water," he said. His wife listened patiently as her husband talked, but still she pleaded with him to let her go looking for water. Finally he relented and allowed her to depart. He remained alone in the field. The wife searched and searched but nowhere could she find water, except in that forbidden water hole. Unable to bear her thirst any longer, she finally drank the enchanted water. After satisfying her thirst she returned to the field. She then lied to her husband, telling him that she had been careful not to drink from the forbidden pond but found water elsewhere.

The couple then went back to work together, but soon the wife began showing some tigerlike traits. When flies buzzed in front of her she caught them with her mouth! She also scratched at herself like a tiger! She still looked like a person, but from her behavior her husband knew she must have drunk water from the enchanted pond. He was sad, for he knew that nothing could be done for her now. She, too, was sad. She loved and honored her husband deeply, but she had lied to him. When evening came the two returned home. The wife now fed the children and put them to sleep. Then her husband ate and he, too, went to sleep. After everyone had bedded down, the woman left for the forest. She prowled here and there, just as a tiger might prowl in search of prey.

Although the water from the pond had affected her, this woman's love for her family was still strong. Each night she assumed the form of a tiger, but by day she was a wife and a mother as usual. When she made a kill during the night she ate what she could and brought the remainder back for her family. One day she killed a man and brought the uneaten portion back to the house and left it on the verandah. Her husband was shocked. What could he do? Although his wife had drunk the water of the tiger pond and became a tiger at night, her love for him and their children still kept her human during the day. He returned to the enchanted water hole and sealed it with a bison horn. Then he placed three big rocks around it so that no one else could drink water and turn into a tiger in this way.

Part VI:
Moral Virtue or its Lack

*I*NDIAN FOLKTALES often do not end with a pithy exhortation on moral virtue as European ones frequently do. Yet a concern with ethical issues comes through very clearly in most South Asian stories. Loyalty, honesty, hospitality, and selfless generosity are key issues that appear again and again. For great rulers, the virtues of tolerance and fairness are important in matters of state policy, too. The other values just named each have another primary context or milieu. Loyalty, for example, is a central issue for close friends and work associates. Where it is found violated we see the influence of economic or political stratification. The bond between a king and his minister, similarly, requires a diffuse sense of trust. Yet such mutuality can be easily threatened by differences in perspective due to their unequal social rank. Honesty and generosity also have great importance in contexts where superiors interact with subordinates. Hospitality provides the reverse side of this coin. It is rigorously enjoined on persons when receiving equals or superiors. These same norms also extend to the interaction of men with gods. For example, a devotee is expected to treat a symbol of divinity (such as an icon) as a host would an honored guest. A god, in return, is expected to be honest, compassionate, and generous. He is to reciprocate for human favors with divine blessings (tale 57).

These moral principles find expression in Indian folktales through certain conventional narrative structures. Six such pat-

terns are nicely illustrated in the following section: (1) a tale
with two halves, where the main character fails to act correctly
in a first setting but then recognizes the mistake and rectifies
the initial error when confronted with a parallel event (tale 57),
(2) a tale where the main character and a rival reverse positions
or statuses and where this experience of reversed roles then
provides insight into the initial mistake (tales 53, 58, and 65),
(3) a tale with two halves where the mistake of the main protagonist is imitated or mirrored by a rival in part two, thus
revealing the root of the problem through repetition (tales 55
and 56), (4) a tale with another tale inside it that takes the form
of a mirror, quickly revealing the problem posed by the larger
account (tale 52), (5) a tale whose key idea undergoes accor-
dionlike expansion, so that the initial mistake of the protagonist
gets gradually magnified until its underlying character is made
obvious (tales 59, 61, 62, 64) and (6) a tale dominated by a
trickster figure who takes advantage of some initial point of
moral weakness and then rides this through to a triumphant
conclusion which then mocks that small and innocent faux pas
found near the beginning (tales 54, 60, 63, 66 and 67). Looking at these six patterns, one can readily see that most Indian
tales about virtue depend on a clever logical structure, and/or
on surprise reversals for their inner message. This presentational
technique relies on revelation through rearrangement and the
use of metaphorical echo devices. It shies away from the blunt,
direct moralizing common to many (though not all) European
counterparts.

Some of the main issues in tales in this section involve behavioral details that are especially characteristic of Indian cultural
attitudes. Eating habits, for example, are a key issue in several
accounts that follow. Consuming meat, eating feces, or devour-
ing babies particularly touch on Hindu sensibilities, as does
alcohol consumption. Therefore, such images get used frequently in tales about moral weakness. Pollution by slime, by
not washing, and (more metaphorically) by having the black
color of a crow, are similarly salient in a world where ritual
cleanliness is given a very high value. Brahmans, similarly, are
particularly prominent in stories about virtue. They always seen
to bear the brunt of the joke, revealing an underside to what is

supposedly high and pure. Men of social stature are brought low
in such tales, and a disjunction between outward respectability
and inner moral weakness is asserted by others but never by
Brahmans themselves. The theme is universal. Still its particular manifestation in these Indian stories relies on local
stereotypes and value hierarchies. More generally, the small and
the weak triumph repeatedly. In a society where hierarchy is so
pervasive, imaginative folk themes relating to status inversion
also run deep.

One of the most interesting features of this section involves
three accounts of extreme immorality. These stories involve in-
tentional and severe injury to a friend (tale 54) or a plan to eat
the babies of a host (tales 56 and 66). All three tales rely on
animal protagonists. Each such story, furthermore, is paired
with a less extreme version that features human characters. Thus
animals are commonly chosen for radical messages and events,
extreme situations where using humans might bring the matter
too close to the listener's bone. In tale 53, for example, a poor
but hard working friend of a rich girl eventually succeeds in
outdistancing her, both in material terms and in moral sen-
sitivity. In the following story, however, the smaller and weaker
partner to a friendship breaks this bond entirely and nearly kills
his rival. This time the two are a fox and a squirrel. Similarly, a
lack of initial hospitality sets the scene for tales 55 and 56. But
in the first instance guests merely force their host to come across
with tasty foods by using a clever ruse, while in the second the
visitor retaliates with the radical action of eating the family's
infant children! Needless to say, it is the second tale which is
cast with animal characters.

A third example of animals breaking through normal moral
barriers can be found in tales 65 and 66. In tale 65 a man
surrepticiously steals some eggplants but is finally made to re-
pent. In tale 66, however, a guest surreptitiously steals his
host's youngest child, hoping to eat it. The mother of the infant
then uses her own tricks to prevent this outcome. The guest is
now a cat (disguised as a human ascetic), while the host is a
female bird. The collector further mentions that this cat story is
used politically, providing a metaphor for the Hindus who tried
to colonize the Meiteis of Manipur during the early eighteenth

century. Feelings about this domination by outsiders remains
strong today. It is easy to imagine how the other animal tales
cited above could also be used in politically inspired ways.

These tales about virtue come from all corners of the Indian
subcontinent. The first, from Bihar, is followed by a second
from Assam, and a third from Kerala. The fourth in the series
was collected in Kashmir. The oscillation of locales continues.
Similarly, in the three pairings of human and animal tales just
discussed, we have juxtaposed: (1) Assam with Kerala, (2)
Kashmir with Kerala, and (3) Gujarat with Manipur. In general, the continuities are strong in these stories, and the various
regional forms are significant more for their political content
(the references to Brahmans, and ambivalence about eating
meat, for example) than for their differences on more basic
moral issues.

The final account in this section has a special status, as it is
more a legend than a true folktale. It represents the one example
of its kind in our collection and therefore deserves special attention. Legends constitute an important Indian story genre and
have been severely undercollected to date. Babar is an outlaw, a
thief, and a murderer. Yet he is also a character with considerable political and moral appeal. The story itself cites important
parallels with Gandhi's leadership of the pre-Independence re-
sistence movement, centered in this same area (Gujarat). As a
folk hero, Babar Deva epitomizes many of the moral strengths
mentioned by the other tales in this section. Babar is extremely
loyal to his gang and demands unflinching support from his
followers, for example. He is also generous to friends and relatives in moments of need, even at points when his own life may
be at stake. Finally, Babar is a kind of trickster. If this final
story stands apart in terms of its genre character, then it also
unifies in one legend many of the themes and principles found
scattered throughout this section. The description of Babar's life
provides a novel way to treat these together as multiple dimensions of a single account.

· 52 · The Prince and the Shepherd
   (West Bengal)

This tale is almost two stories in one, and the two are not
serially related. Neither is this merely a tale told within a tale, a
type of account for which India is famous. Instead this is a
moralistic story about friendship—or rather the neglect of such
a bond between a king and his childhood shepherd companion.
The first story is suspended (alas, for the king!), while another
tale about the queen and her imposter, the maidservant, is
worked out. Afterwards the first tale is concluded. What is the
connection between the two? The embedded story becomes a
parable played out among women in place of men. It also serves
as the device that brings about a restoration of the earlier bond
between the king and the shepherd.

ONCE UPON A TIME there lived a prince and a shepherd. They
were great friends. The prince promised the shepherd that he
would make his friend a minister after he, himself, became king.
In the course of time the prince did become king. He married a
lady named Kanchanmala and made her his queen. In the days of
happiness and fulfillment which followed, the king forgot all
about his friend, the shepherd.
    One day, the shepherd appeared before the palace gate saying
he wanted to see the king and queen. The guard drove him away.
The very next morning the entire body of the king—his face,
mouth, eyes, right up to the hair of his head—became covered
with needles. He couldn't eat or sleep. He couldn't even move.
Queen Kanchanmala herself was able to carry on her daily activities only with great difficulty. One day, the queen went to the
tank to take her bath. There a beautiful girl came before the
queen and asked whether she needed a maidservant. The queen
answered that she did, indeed. She purchased the service of the
girl by giving her gold bangles. The new servant was thenceforth
known as Kankanmala.
    "Queen mother," said Kankanmala, "it seems you are so dis-
tressed that you have not even had the heart to bathe. Come, let
me anoint your body all over with *khar* and *khail*." The queen
agreed. So Kankanmala removed the queen's ornaments and

rubbed the queen's body with khar and khail. "Go and dip yourself in the tank now, mother," she said as she finished. The queen
stepped out into the tank until the water was up to her neck.
Then, in the twinkling of an eye, Kankanmala put on the queen's
ornaments and dressed herself as the queen. When the true queen
came out of the tank, she was forced to dress as her own maidservant. On their return to the palace Kankanmala now became the
queen and the former queen became her maidservant. The king
knew nothing of this change.

One day, the new maid met a man walking past the public
bathing spot at the tank. He was carrying a huge quantity of
thread and was asking everyone he met for needles. Kanchanmala
told the man that she could give him all the needles he wanted if
he would follow her. She led him to the palace. There, he spoke
to the imposter queen saying, "O queen, today is the day to
worship the deity *Pit Kuduli.* Rice-powder cakes are to be distributed throughout the kingdom. The courtyard should be decorated with festive designs (*rangoli*). Let your maidservant help you
in these things." So the false maid Kanchanmala and the false
queen Kankanmala both prepared rice-powder cakes and drew
festive designs on the courtyard floor. Now, as everyone knows,
rice-powder cakes and elaborate festive drawings are skills which
require fine taste, a delicate touch, and years of practice. Achievement in such fine arts is a mark of a woman's upbringing and a
symbol of her family's status. The people of the kingdom were
able to see which of the two women was the queen once they
tasted the rice-powder cakes and saw the designs each of them
had made. But only the man with the thread dared to ask the
queen's imposter how it could be that she had such a poor knowledge of these feminine arts.

Furious at the man for trying to expose her, the queen quickly
ordered the executioner to kill him. But the thread merchant
quickly recited a magical formula and caused all of the needles to
drop from the king's body. The king then opened his eyes and
recognized his old friend, the shepherd, standing in front of him.
The needles which had dropped from the king now suddenly flew
to the body of Kankanmala, the imposter queen, and drove themselves so deeply into her flesh and eyes that she died. The king
then came down from his throne and embraced his long-lost

friend. Later he made a golden flute for this shepherd. He soon
became a minister of the king and played on his flute while the
king listened.

· 53 · *Rich Girl, Poor Girl*
(Nagaland)

The tribal groups of the Naga are not as distinctly separated
into hereditary subunits as castes are in the Hindu social system. Yet there are still important differences in family status
based on wealth and prestige. Depending on fortune, these
differences change from generation to generation, and even
within the lifetime of one person. A woman of good character
and a hardworking man can often establish a prosperous and
prominent household. The symbol of their success in life is their
granary. The moral teachings of one's parents and the school of
life's hardships ensure the welfare and good name of a family.
Such experiences can be symbolized by unpredictable harvests
that result from the shifting cultivation practices popular in this
area.

ONCE UPON A TIME, in a certain village, there were two girls.
One was from a rich family and the other from a poor one. They
were neighbors and the closest of friends during their early years.
They used to play together all day in the village lanes and mead-
ows while their parents were at work in the fields. Each day these
girls would have their lunch together. One girl would bring her
share to the other's house in turn. The rich girl's rice was always
of the finest quality and the curry she brought consisted of several
different vegetables. The poor girl's rice was of inferior quality
and the curry was simple, but since they were both children these
differences were not noticed.

As the years went by and the two girls entered their teens, each
one grew both beautiful and smart. Their childhood play dimin-
ished and they began to help their parents in the fields more and
more. Although they still remained friends, they had less and less
time to be together. And most importantly, the poor family often

had to borrow rice from the rich family. Since the daughters were good friends, the parents of the poor girl would send her to ask for food. The rich girl's parents would then ask their daughter to take the poor girl to the granary and give her the amount of rice she needed.

One particular year the harvest was terrible. By the end of that year, and right up to the next harvest, the poorer families of the village were faced with unprecedented scarcity. Some people died of starvation, and others pulled through only by gathering wild roots and leaves in the forest. The poor begged daily from the rich and the latter were able to extract a promise of two measures of grain from the next harvest for every measure lent. Thus the poor girl was forced to beg rice from the rich girl, on the promise of two for one. Not only was the poor girl in want of food, but her clothes had turned to rags, as had those of her mother, father, sisters, and brothers. The family was truly destitute.

As the famine grew worse, and with the harvest yet weeks away, the rich girl finally grew tired of the poor girl's constant begging. She began to resent the poor girl's visits because her clothes were so shoddy. She did not understand the difficulties faced by the poor in the village because she, herself, was still able to live a life of plenty. One day, she teased her friend, saying, "Were your clothes eaten by a wolf as it tried to bite at your body?" The poor girl replied, "No, they have been eaten by famine which is much worse than a wolf." After that, the rich girl let it be known that the poor girl was not welcome in such rags anymore. The poor girl was thus in a fix: she had no other clothes, yet her family needed the rice she was able to borrow.

One morning, the poor girl's family had no food for breakfast. The father put on his loin cloth and went into the jungle to gather wild yams and fruits. The mother went to another rich man's house to work in return for a small quantity of grain. The girl knew her parent's attempts would be futile, yet they had told her not to beg from her friend. Missing one day's meal was not such a serious thing. Still the poor girl could picture her parents returning from their work exhausted from hunger. She looked at her brothers and sisters. They were weak with starvation. Unable to bear it, she decided once again to go to her rich friend and ask for more rice. Having reached the house, she said, "*Atong* [dear friend], I have to ask for rice again today. I have no alternative but to come to you." The rich girl frowned and said, "I am tired of your constant visits to borrow grain. Why must you always come empty-handed? I get nothing from you. All I do is give!"

The poor girl stood silently, not uttering a word. The rich girl finally led her friend to the granary, her face showing her usual disdain. "Friend, stay outside at the gate. I will bring the grain from inside myself and put it in your basket. I am afraid threads from your rags will fall and contaminate my grain. The very smell will pollute the air. Next time, if you wear better clothes, you can come in. This time I'll get the grain for you. Tears welled up in the poor girl's eyes. She had said nothing; but her heart had been broken by her old friend's words. She brought the basket of grain home but hid her tears from her parents. The poor family had a hearty meal that night, the first in many weeks. The mother had earned a basket of rice for her wages; the father had gathered a basket full of yams. While they ate, the girl related the events of the day, telling of the cruel insults her friend had made. The wise father made no comment but comforted his daughter, telling her not to let such things disturb her mind. He talked of how to conquer life's trials and how to remain cheerful in the midst of grave troubles.

Within a few days, before their stores had once again run out, the grain began to ripen in the fields. Soon the harvest was in full swing. The famine came to an end; starvation faded like a bad dream. This year the weather had been ideal—just the right amount of sunshine and rain. There was a bumper harvest. Even the poor, who had borrowed on the promise doubling the amount returned, had plenty in their granary for the coming year. During the next several years, the rich girl and the poor girl were married to men of the village and began to raise their own families. After many years their parents passed away and the girls—now mothers of large families—had only themselves to depend on. They had to work hard to feed their families.

The daughter of the poor man worked hard. She had learned to do so in childhood. Her husband was pleased with her. Together they raised industrious and obedient children who later helped them in the fields. They lived happily and their farm prospered. In time, they became quite wealthy. The rich girl, though, was

not used to the burdens of being a housewife and raising a family.
She was lazy and arrogant and inexperienced in farmwork. There
was no harmony in the family. The husband and wife could not
cooperate in these day-to-day tasks. They lost all of the wealth
her parents had left them. Without any outside support, they
soon became poor. Every year, several months before the harvest,
they ran short of stores and had to borrow grain from wealthier
families.

One morning, just a few days before harvest time, the former
rich girl came to borrow grain from the former poor girl who was
now the rich one. The rich girl gladly took her friend to the
granary and gave her as much grain as she could carry. As she was
about to leave with her load, the girl who was now rich said in a
gentle voice, "Friend, please look carefully to see that there are
no filthy rags or bits of thread in my grain. Such dirt may be in
my rice; so before you eat it make sure to check it carefully, lest it
be contaminated." Now the girl who used to be rich remembered
the words she herself had spoken years ago. She felt ashamed but
could do nothing. Her family needed the borrowed grain. She
realized her mistake and became wiser in her poverty.

· 54 ·   *The Dexterity of a Squirrel*
           (Kerala)

Here, as in many tales, we see human characteristics projected
onto the animal world. Usually it is the fox who is cunning and
succeeds in getting his way with both larger and more able
adversaries. But here the fox meets his match in the still smaller, quick-witted squirrel. The fox himself now becomes a
helpless victim due to the squirrel's not-so-charitable offer to
"take care of" his property. In the end, all his foxy friends are
also humbled by this alliance of small creatures. It is not uncommon to find that a clever opportunist wins out in Indian
animals tales. In fact, maybe the fox had it coming to him!

ONCE UPON A TIME a fox and a squirrel were friends. Farming
was their livelihood. The squirrel was jealous of the fox because

his crop always turned out so much better. This time the fox was cultivating pumpkins. He happily watered them twice a day and tended them carefully. Sometime later, when the little seedlings were coming up, the fox took ill with fever and started vomiting. He gave charge of the garden to the squirrel and went to the hospital. While the fox was gone the squirrel looked after the garden. As the pumpkins ripened he picked them one by one and took them to a distant coconut tree for safekeeping. After a time the fox returned, his illness cured. When he found no pumpkins in his garden, he set out in search of the squirrel. He walked and walked but couldn't find the squirrel. At last, exhausted, the fox fell asleep under a coconut tree. As he slept, something fell on him. He woke up with a start and looked around. It was the skin of a pumpkin. Then he looked up and saw his friend the squirrel gnawing on several nice fruits. This he couldn't tolerate. He went off thinking of ways to teach the squirrel a lesson.

After a while the fox returned with a whole pack of foxes. They tried to reach the squirrel by standing on one another's backs. In this manner they reached nearly three-fourths of the way up the tree. The squirrel panicked. There were no trees nearby to which he could leap. But then he saw an ant on his way down the trunk. He called to the ant for help, promising to give him a pumpkin in return. The ant agreed. The foxes had nearly reached the top of the tree by the time the ant reached the ground. But then the ant bit the back of the fox at the bottom of the pile, the one on which all the others rested. The fox couldn't stand the pain of that bite. It fell to the ground and began to roll in the dirt. All the other foxes came crashing down too. Meanwhile, the squirrel was able to escape.

· 55 · *The Mincemeat Spirit*
          (Kashmir)

Hospitality is a very important virtue in Indian cultural tradition. One should never refuse a guest, even if it means personal hardship. Gods often test their devotees precisely in this fashion, by appearing before them and asking for shelter and food.

Persons who give generously, particularly to wandering saints and other religious figures, are therefore much admired. It is believed they are assured of a lasting divine blessing. The present story, from Kashmir, plays on this important ethic. But it has a certain poignancy and humor too. Meat is extremely expensive, and serving it is reserved for special occasions, such as the arrival of guests. Meat is also considered a stimulant and for many is either a forbidden food or an occasional indulgence that one would not laud before neighbors. This makes the strong smell of the mincemeat curry especially funny and also especially embarrassing for the wife in question. Meat eating, furthermore, is often associated with spirit possession and avaricious behavior generally. The ruse the guests in this story use to procure some of the hidden curry is thus quite in keeping with the setting described. But the storyteller implicitly mocks all the participants, implying that the spirit possession is a sham. The tale is one of a general North Indian story type that desctibes greedy guests who grab chicken legs or other foods when not directly offered them by miserly hosts.

THERE ONCE LIVED a husband and his wife and their two children. One day, the husband bought some mincemeat and handed it to his wife saying, "Here is some meat. Please cook it for dinner. Let us have a good meal with rice and mincement curry today." Having said this the husband left for work. The wife labored the whole day to prepare a delicious, spicy, meat curry. When she had finished her cooking, she sat on the front steps of the house waiting for her husband to return. As she waited, she noticed two uninvited guests who seemed to be coming toward her house. Suspecting that these people might wish to stay for a meal and to eat her mincemeat, the wife hurriedly hid the bowl with the curry in it. She hung it on a special ceiling hook with the hope that it might go unnoticed by any guests.

Soon, however, the people in question arrived at the door. They were welcomed by her and she exchanged pleasantries with her visitors. The guests were ushered into her living room where they sat down to chat. Soon it was dinnertime and the husband now returned home as well. The guests started talking to him. The wife served everyone tea and snacks. But there was no offering of mincemeat curry. Everyone, of course, had smelled this spicy dish the moment they entered the house. They were hoping for a taste of this delicious preparation, but none had yet been offered to them. And they knew they could not politely ask. Finally, therefore, the guests worked out a plan. One of them pretended to become possessed by a spirit. This spirit caused one visitor to shake and jump and to beat his hands on his breast. He also began to shout, "Mincemeat rose to the ceiling, rose to the ceiling." One of his companions then tried to hold the man back and calm him down. Speaking softly, he said, "You will be cured! We will bring you some mincemeat. Calm down, and we will bring it."

The possessed guest, however, continued to fret and to shout. The words "mincemeat curry, mincemeat curry," were heard again. His companion continued to try to calm him with the promise of tasty morsels. However, the shouting and agitation continued. The hosts both became worried about the condition of their demented guest. Soon they joined his companion in trying to calm him. But nothing seemed to help. The possessed visitor continued to shout and continued to beat himself. He even continued to use the words "mincemeat curry."

Finally the couple asked the man's companion the cause of this odd behavior. The companion answered, "Don't you know that he is possessed by a mincemeat spirit? It seems you have some mincemeat somewhere in this house and this is what has caused this condition. He's asking for it, and unless he gets some mincemeat he will not recover from this seizure." Hearing this, the hosts finally said to their guests, "We will feed you some mincemeat. Please calm down." Reluctantly, they then brought down the mincemeat from the ceiling hook where it had been kept and placed a large portion before the possessed guest. Seeing this delicious curry, he suddenly returned to his normal condition and the possession trance disappeared. He and his companion then ate the entire pot of curry. They emptied the bowl and left for home. As they took leave, of course, they did not forget to exchange a few pleasantries with their host.

· 56 ·   *The Crane and the Crow*
(Kerala)

The last story was about a mildly rude guest. It was collected in
Kashmir, the very northernmost part of India. The next tale is
about a much more aggressive visitor who ends up actually
murdering the host's children. It is from the extreme southern
state of Kerala. Because the behavior described breaks so many
taboos, it is not surprising that the characters used are birds.
However, their personalities and language clearly imply human
parallels. For one thing, clear status contrasts exist between the
two birds. The crow is black and its garments never look clean.
The crane is white and so are its clothes. Also, the crow's house
is rough-hewn and washes away in the rain. By contrast, the
crane's house is sturdy and beautifully smooth.

But as the story progresses, a more complex intermixture of
human and animal symbolism is involved: the color white and
the crane are symbols of birth and life, while the color black and
the crow are symbols of funerals and death. If in several images
the stork represents human life and the crow represents its opposite, what then can we make of the concluding scene, where
the stork, following the Hindu tradition of placing rice balls on
the roof for the deceased to be eaten by crows, places a stone in
the offering in order to kill the crow?

THERE ONCE LIVED a crane and a crow. When they went to wash
clothes the crane's washing came out very white, but the crow's
washing always looked black. Furthermore, the house of the
crane was tiled and very smooth while the house of the crow was
rough and made of cowdung. When the rains came the house of
the crane was undamaged, but the house of the crow was washed
away. After the crow lost his home, he flew to the house of the
crane and knocked on the door. Here is their conversation.

Crow: "Crane, crane, open the door."
Crane: "Just a moment, I'm giving my child an oil bath."
Crow: "Crane, crane, open the door."
Crane: "Just a moment, I am in the midst of bathing my
child."
Crow: "Crane, crane, open the door."

Crane: "I am still bathing my child."

Crow: "Crane, crane, open the door."

Crane: "Just a moment, I am now wiping my child."

Crow: "Crane, crane, open the door."

Crane: "Just a moment, I am powdering my child."

Crow: "Crane, crane, open the door."

Crane: "Just a moment, I am combing the hair of my child."

Crow: "Crane, crane, open the door."

Crane: "Just a moment, I am breastfeeding my child."

Crow: "Crane, crane, open the door."

Crane: "Just a moment, now I am singing a lullaby to my child."

Crow: "Crane, crane, open the door."

At last the crane opened the door and the crow entered the house. The crane then asked the crow, "Where would you like to sleep? Do you prefer the bed, the mat, the cowdung hut, or the ash hut?" The crow then replied, "I do not want to sleep in any of those places. I want to sleep directly beneath the cradle." The crane agreed, saying, "You may sleep there if you wish." Time passed and around midnight the sound kadum-mudum was heard. The crane woke up at this noise and asked, "Crow, crow, what is that?" The crow answered, "That is the sound of eating jackfruit seeds. I went to market this morning and bought ten jackfruit. The kadum-mudum sound is the noise I make while chewing them." After a time the sound kadum-mudum was heard again. The crane then called out and asked, "Crow, crow, what is that sound?" The crow answered, "That is the sound of the jackfruit seeds. I have now finished the second seed."

Then after a time the sound kadum-mudum was heard again and the crane cried, "Crow, crow, what is that sound?" The crow answered, "That is the sound of chewing on jackfruit seeds. I have now finished the third seed." After a time the sound was heard again, and the crane woke up and cried, "Crow, crow, what is that sound?" The crow answered, "That is the sound of chewing on jackfruit seeds. I have now finished the fourth seed." After a time the sound was heard again, and the crane cried again, "Crow, crow, what is that sound kadum-mudum?" The crow replied, "That is the noise of chewing on jackfruit seeds. I have now finished five seeds."

The cracking was repeated for a sixth time. So the crane asked, "Crow, crow, what is that sound?" The crow answered, "I am eating the jackfruit seeds that I got from the market. Out of ten seeds, I have now finished six." But then the sound was heard again, and the crane asked, "Ah, crow, what is that sound?" The crane answered, "That is the sound of eating jackfruit seeds. I have now finished seven of the ten seeds." When the sound occurred again the crane inquired, "Ah! crow, what is that sound kadum-mudum?" The crow answered, "That is the sound of chewing on jackfruit seeds. Of the ten seeds, eight are now finished." But the noise continued and the crane woke up and cried, "Crow, crow, what is that sound?" The crow replied, "I bought ten jackfruit when I went to market. I have now finished nine seeds." When the sound was heard for a tenth time, the crane inquired, "Crow, crow, what is that troublesome noise?" The crow then replied, "I recently bought ten jackfruit seeds at the market, and all of them are now finished."

By that time it was dawn. So the crane got up and opened the door. At that moment the crow swiftly slipped through the opening and flew away. The crane then went to see her children, but she couldn't find any of them. Instead, she found only skins and bones. Thus the crane came to realize that the crow had been sitting on the bar of her cradle and had been eating her children all night long. So the crane decided to take revenge. She found a stone, covered it with cooked rice, and placed it on the roof of her house. After a while the crow passed by and saw the rice. It swallowed the ball greedily and the stone as well. When the stone reached the crow's stomach, the bird became dizzy and it fell off the roof. Finally the crow's eyes popped out, and it died of pain.

· 57 ·   *The Tale of Bibgaraz Maj*
          (Kashmir)

The rivalry between co-wives is again and again the cause of much hardship (see tales 17, 43, and 45). In this story one woman's sincere devotion to the goddess prevails over the selfish machinations of her many detractors. Mrs. Lalita Handoo, who contributed this tale, informs us that it is invariably told in the Hindu homes of Kashmir on the occasion of the annual *pan* rituals celebrating the festival of Bibgraz Maj (see tales 16 and 42, also told in connection with religious observances). A large number of tales, from all parts of India, are perpetuated in this manner.

THERE ONCE LIVED a very poor woman and her unmarried daughter. They earned their livelihood by making cowdung cakes[1] or by selling the firewood that they collected in the nearby forest. One day it was *venayak tsoram*[2] and a Sunday. On that day, while on their way to the forest to collect firewood, both the mother and the daughter saw some smoke rising far away in a corner of the forest. Both wanted to know the cause of the smoke, therefore they walked to that spot. On reaching the place, they saw some people baking *roth* [sweet cakes]. When these people had finished baking their cakes, they all offered prayers to the Goddess Bibgaraz Maj. The mother and the daughter, more curious now, inquired as to what the whole thing was about. They were told, "Today is the day of Bibgaraz Maj, and whoever celebrates by baking roth and worshipping her gets rid of all troubles and miseries. Their wishes are fulfilled."

Hearing this, both the mother and the daughter joined in the prayers. After the prayers were over they ate the *roth* that was offered to them as *navid*[3] (a part of the offerings) and left the place. The daughter had been impressed by the celebrations and she now said, "Mother! Why don't we also worship Bibgaraz Maj and try our luck? Maybe we can get rid of this miserable poverty once and for all." Her mother agreed, but being so poor, they had no wheat flour, nor the money to buy any to bake roth to celebrate the day of the Goddess. Soon, however, they thought of a plan. The mother and daughter went to the king's stable, collected some horsedung, mixed it with water, and sieved a few grains of wheat out of it. Then they washed the grains, dried them, and ground them into flour. But with this small quantity to start with they could only make a small 'roth' [called *ka-nikivor*].[4] They also made a few cowdung cakes. They kept all these in a basket and covered them with a cloth. Soon they began the ritual of worshiping Bibgaraz Maj. They now prayed for hours. When they had finished praying, the two removed the cloth over the basket and what did they find? To their great surprise they discovered that the cowdung cakes had turned into cakes of gold. The mother and daughter could not believe their eyes. Their joy knew no bounds. Their wish had been granted. They were no longer poor but rich.

After a time, the king of that country came to the woods to hunt. On his way he happened to pass by the house in which the newly rich mother and daughter were living. He soon saw the beautiful girl, was charmed by her, and wanted to marry her. When he returned to his palace, he sent a messenger to the girl's mother. "Oh noble lady! My master seeks your permission to marry your beautiful daughter," announced the messenger. These words fell like nectar into the ears of the mother. She readily agreed, "We are honored," she said. "Please tell the king he has my consent." The messenger returned with the good news for the king. The king was pleased. His wish was fulfilled. Soon, an auspicious day for the marriage was fixed. Preparations were made, and the nuptial events were celebrated with great pomp and show.

For a time everything seemed well with the king and his new queen. One year passed. Finally the day of celebrating Bibgaraz Maj arrived. The queen sought the permission of the king to celebrate the day with special devotion. He consented and ordered bags of wheat flour, sugar, and cauldrons of ghee brought for the roth. Everything was made available. The queen took a bath, put on a new dress and baked as many roths as she could. She performed the usual rituals and made her offerings. Then she sent navid to the king. Now this king had other wives too, and they were very jealous of this youngest queen. Being young and beautiful, the king naturally showered all his love on her. So they wanted to get rid of her.

When the queen sent navid through a maid to the king, she found him sitting with his other queens. Noticing this good opportunity, these women tried to poison the king's ears against the new queen. "This is not navid, my lord. This is some magic to harm you. We beseech you not to eat this. Your new queen is a witch." Hearing this, the king was furious. He immediately threw the navid away. It fell on his shoes. Hardly had it touched his shoes than ominous drums were heard. Soon a group of rebels entered the king's chamber, and the king was dethroned and arrested. Everyone was stunned. The youngest queen was in tears. She had lost everything. She left the palace and joined her mother. Now she was as poor as before.

After some time, while sleeping in a dark cell, the king had a dream. He saw Bibgaraz Maj before him. Addressing the king, the goddess said, "You are in trouble because you insulted my navid. However, you can be forgiven, provided you celebrate my day with the same devotion that your queen once did." Saying this, Bibgaraz Maj disappeared and the King woke up. He repented his past doings and somehow managed to send a message secretly to his youngest queen. He apologized for his behavior and requested her to perform the Bibgaraz Maj celebrations he had seen in his dream. He also requested some navid.

The secret messenger went in search of the youngest queen. He found her in rags in a hut and delivered the king's message. Having received the message, the poor queen again went to the king's stable, collected wheat grains from horsedung, and again made kanitivor, just as she had done earlier. She then performed the rituals as usual and offered prayers to Bibgaraz Maj. She even managed to send navid to the king in the prison. The king touched his eyes with the navid and ate it. No sooner had he done this than he heard the victorious drumbeats of his loyal soldiers. Soon he was released and his kingdom was restored to him. The king then returned to his palace and immediately sent for his youngest queen. She was brought back to the palace with all the honor a queen deserves. The king and the queen happily ruled their subjects, thereafter. Just as their grief disappeared, let it disappear from the whole world and from our lives too.

· 58 · *The Children of the Crab*
(Karnataka)

This tale about generosity, hospitality, and helpfulness (or their lack) finds some resonance in the basic attitudes of villagers all over India. Here a childless king ignores a crab's instructions because he wants more children than he was promised. An elder sister drives away her dog-mother for fear her in-laws will mock her. And a greedy husband readily sets off on a wild-goose chase thinking his in-laws will bring him fortune. It is interesting to contrast the meanness of these human characters with the heroine's kindly animal helpers. Their miraculous gifts save her in her times of need.

ONCE UPON A TIME, in a certain village, there was a king who had no children. He was very sad. One day, as he was walking alongside a paddy field he saw a mother crab who had just hatched some babies. He stopped to look and thought of his own lack of children. He began to lament out loud, "Oh crab, you have so many beautiful children and I have none." The crab listened and felt pity for the king. "King, you take two of my children. Put one in a banana and give it to your wife. The other you can give to your dog. If you do this you, will have a child," she said.

So the king took two tiny crabs and on the way home he bought a banana. Then he thought, "Why should I give one to my dog? If I put them both in the banana, maybe I shall have many children." So he put them both in the banana and gave it to his wife to eat. He then went away. While his wife was eating the banana, the dog came to her and looked hungrily at the fruit. The wife broke off a piece and gave it to the dog. Not long afterwards it became obvious that the king's wife was pregnant. To the shock of the king, however, she gave birth to two dogs. On the same day, the dog gave birth to two baby girls. The king tried in vain to exchange the baby dogs for the human babies. Finally, he drove both the dog and her human babies out of the house. In the forest at the edge of town, the mother dog began to raise her children.

When the dog's two girls grew up, they were very beautiful. Soon they felt they should be married and went in search of husbands. Each found a mate in a different village. One day, alone and hungry, the mother dog went looking for her departed children. First she went to the house of her eldest daughter. This girl, fearing the other villagers would laugh at her if they knew that her mother was a dog, took a pot of rice which was cooking on the hearth and threw it at her, burning her badly. In mortal pain and hunger the mother dog then sought out her younger daughter. There she received a warm welcome, but alas, she died shortly afterward. The second girl then worried about how to dispose of the dead dog so that her husband (who was away the whole time) would not notice that anything had happened. "If I bury it, he'll see the fresh dirt. If I burn it, he will see the ash," she thought. In the end, seeing her husband coming, she put the body in a pot and hung it from a rafter.

Her husband arrived home and saw the pot. He soon wondered what was in it. So he took it down and looked inside. There he found a gold necklace and a silver belt. Astonished, he asked where these things had come from. His wife answered that while he was out her relatives had visited and had given them to her. The husband now decided that since his wife's people were so rich, they should both go and live with them. The couple set out immediately. The two walked all day and by evening they still had not found the wife's house which, after all, did not exist. Finally, the wife said that it was just over the next hill, but that they should first rest for the night and climb in the morning when they were fresh. The husband insisted on climbing the slope that very evening. He wanted to at least see the house. So he told his wife to wait under a banyan tree until he came back.

While the wife was waiting, a huge cobra came down from the tree. He had a large swelling in his neck. The cobra explained that he had been pierced by an animal bone he was eating and that his wound had become so swollen with pus he could no longer swallow. He pleaded with the woman to put her hand down his throat and burst the infection. The woman hesitated, thinking he might then bite and eat her. But the cobra promised that if she would help him, he would not eat her. Instead he said he would grant her any boon she wished. She finally agreed. So the wife reached into the cobra's mouth and burst the boil. In return she asked that he create a castle for her, complete with cattle, chickens, gardens, and all. A castle then appeared in the distance, just as she had wished.

The woman then saw her husband coming and called for him to hurry. Soon she explained that the house of her family lay in the opposite direction, but she had initially forgotten exactly where it was. Somehow she had not seen it when they had looked in that direction before. As they neared the house, the husband was so pleased he did not even notice the absence of his wife's family. Indeed, he already considered this fine house his own. Some days later, the elder sister and her husband arrived, destitute, hungry, and exhausted from their wanderings. Since her ill-treatment of the mother dog, her own fortunes had taken a terrible turn for the worse. She and her husband had been forced to wander. The younger sister soon recognized their common kinship but offered the two only a place in the cattle shed, tending the cattle. In the end, the second couple was forced to accept this, and they all lived thus until their end.

· 59 ·   *The Rupee Note*
         (Assam)

Just as there are many tales about hospitality, so too there are many like this next one which make fun of misers. Members of the Brahman community are a particularly popular choice as a subject for jokes. These people, as priests, are supposed to concentrate on their otherworldly religious concerns. For that reason, to imply that they have a fixation on money is particularly inappropriate and particularly funny. The story below is a typical one on this theme. The teller says it is based on a real incident. Some of the special pleasure the tale provides for listeners relates to a ready ability people would have to have to visualize the old man described as he tries to walk delicately through a swampy ooze of mud.

THERE ONCE LIVED a Brahman in a small village. He was fast becoming old, and his sons were already grown and were looking after him. Nonetheless, this greedy Brahman continued to keep up his work of conducting religious ceremonies for others. He would never refuse the chance to conduct some local ritual and thus earn a few annas as his rightful fee.

Once, during the rainy season, this Brahman was returning home in the evening from the performance of a small *puja* ceremony in a distant village. His return route took him through a swamp. Indeed, it was even necessary for him to wade through water for part of the way. As the tired old Brahman picked his way through the hyacinth plants that grew in this swamp, he suddenly slipped into a patch of deep mud. Once fallen, he sank in up to his waist, finding it impossible to get himself out. Then he remembered a brother-in-law who lived close by. So, in fear of his life, the Brahman cried out loudly, "Oh brother-in-law! I am deep in the mud. Please help me." It had already grown dark, but fortunately the brother-in-law heard his cry. He arrived with a lamp and found his relative stuck in the swamp. The brother-in-law pulled him out, took him home, and gave him a change of clothing. The rescuer also kindled a fire in order to help warm the old man. At this moment, however, the Brahman forgot himself and cried out, "Don't worry about me. There is a rupee note in my bag. Please warm the rupee, warm the rupee."

· 60 · *The Value of an American Thank You (Karnataka)*

In the following story, speaking English adds another dimension, beyond wealth, to a man's prestige in a local setting.

WELL! You know, they all like the sea beaches, swimming and canoeing. And Kerala has all that. So no wonder many foreign tourists come straight down to Kerala.

Well, there was this American. He was very tall, well built, red faced, wearing shorts and a big cap with a camera and binoculars around his thick neck. He arrived in a small seaside village and wanted to take a ride in a village canoe, in the backwater lakes. Kerala, as you know, is full of them. This tall American could not go unnoticed. A boatman guessed his intentions, approached him, and offered his canoe for the ride. The American agreed and said, "OK, OK. I'll take your canoe. What would you like to have in return? Money or a thank you?" The boatman only knew a few words of English. He recognized "Sir," "Yes, Sir," and "No, Sir," but not "thank you." But he thought a "thank you" must be far better than money. He had heard that

American tourists had dollars, tape recorders, cameras, and many other things. Certainly a "thank you" must be something like these things and far better than Indian money which could fetch little these days anyway. The boatman was pleased with this idea and agreed to accept a "thank you" instead of rupees.

The American smiled and boarded the canoe. He enjoyed a ride for more than two hours, and when the canoe returned he stepped back on to land. The boatman followed him. Then the American held out his hand for a handshake. The boatman was pleased and gladly offered his hand. Shaking his hand the American said, "Thank you! Thank you very much."

· 61 · *The Brahman's Lime*
(Assam)

This next story makes fun of the miserly character of Brahmans much as does "The Rupee Note" (tale 59). This time, however, it involves one-upmanship on the part of a male servant. Also involved are such themes as a youth triumphing over an elder, an employee triumphing over his master, the clever trickster making fun of a dumb rival, and a person of lower caste making fun of a high-caste Brahman. Generalized in this way, these themes are common in folklore throughout India. The miserliness in this particular story revolves around a master's unwillingness to share something nice to eat. Lying, another personal fault, is also important. It is used to poke fun at a social and (in principle) moral superior. Finally, the whole story turns on a strong, indisguisable food smell. In this sense, the tale is similar to the one from Kashmir about the mincemeat spirit (tale 55).

THERE WAS ONCE a Brahman priest who had a young servant boy. This lad seemed to be a simple chap, but as a matter of fact he was extremely clever. He used to spend his time thinking of ways to steal tasty morsels to eat. For example, when the Brahman brought home some tasty molasses, he would later find it had disappeared from the household pot. His servant would explain that the molasses had been found and eaten by the cat. At other times he would bring home a bunch of bananas and lay them on the shelf. When he next looked, the bananas would be gone. "Those bananas were eaten by mice," the servant would explain. All along, of course, the thief was really the servant boy, Sarukan.

One find day the Brahman was on his way home with a pot of thick curds. These curds were of excellent quality and the Brahman thought to himself, "If that rogue comes to know of the curds, then my chance of eating them would be lost. I will tell him, therefore, that all I have in my pot is lime." In thinking this way, the man was ignoring the old proverb which says, "A fear of tigers brings on the night." Soon Sarukan saw his master from a distance and hurried out to meet him. He greeted the Brahman respectfully and asked, "Well, sir, what are you bringing home today?" The Brahman replied, saying, "Only some lime from the shopkeeper, my boy! I use a little lime everyday so I thought I would buy it in quantity." The servant lad said, "You have made a wise decision. By the way, I couldn't find any lime to use with my betel leaf chew today. Could you let me have a little?" But the Brahman responded in anger, saying, "I did not buy this for you! Go quickly and bring the cows home. Stop bothering me."

Sarukan guessed what his master had really bought, for after all, lime did not smell like curds! Nonetheless, he left to tie up the cows for the night. The Brahman hung up his pot carefully. He then went to check on the garden to see if Sarukan had weeded it properly. At this moment, however, Sarukan returned stealthily to the house. He saw where his master had hung the curds. As he approached the pot, however, his master cried out, "Sarukan!" "Yes, sir?" the boy answered. "How much weeding did you do today?" he asked. "I had very little time to weed today, sir. The cows gave me so much trouble that I had to watch them constantly. When I tied one up, the others ran off. And if I tied another one, a third ran off." "Is that so, my little rogue!" said the Brahman. He now lost his temper, grabbed a switch, and began to beat the young boy. Then Sarukan began to wail and soon he said, "I would rather die than suffer this beating. At least let me die quickly by swallowing my master's lime." Announcing this, he grabbed the pot of thickened curds and began to gobble them up. The Brahman shouted at him, "That pot has lime in it! Don't eat it. Don't eat it!" The poor Brahman wondered why he was always so unlucky. But the servant boy enjoyed himself. He ate the curds with relish and thought quietly, "I manage to outsmart my master everytime!"

· 62 ·   *The Feast*
          (Assam)

Here a minister, traditionally a Brahman (see also tale 74), is cast in a pretentious role. The king's straightforward bluntness provides a delightful, humorous counterbalance.

PROVIDING FEASTS for Brahmans is a way of earning merit. A certain king once invited a large number of Brahmans to a Brahma-bhojan or ceremonial feast for Brahmans. Being a king, he was able to provide tasty and sumptuous dishes. He was satisfied that the arrangements made were good and that the poor Brahmans were likely to have a good time. His minister, however, told him, "Your Majesty, when the Brahmans arrive and sit at their meal, you are to bow to them and say, 'O respected guests, my means are limited. I have not been able to provide all the things that may be necessary. Please forgive me and be pleased with what little I have been able to offer you.'"

The Brahmans arrived and the king bowed to them and said, "O respected guests, my means are limited. I have not been able to provide all the things that may be necessary. Please forgive me and be pleased with what little I have been able to offer you." Then the guests cried out in one voice, "No, no, your Majesty, you have provided us with everything that is necessary. In fact, we had never seen such sumptuous dishes before."

The king then commented, "I thought so, too, but my minister does not seem to agree."

· 63 · *Borrowed Earrings*
(Andhra Pradesh)

This short Telugu tale, like the Assamese one which precedes it (tale 62), uses blunt candor as an antidote for pomp and pretense. Both tales exemplify a form of popular humor found everywhere in India in jokes, folk dramas, and stories.

ONCE A YOUNG MAN was going for a marriage interview (*pelli cupulu*). He took a friend along with him for company. He wanted to look his best in the eyes of the would-be bride and hoped to impress her father. So the man borrowed a pair of expensive gold earrings for the occasion. At the time of the interview, the bride's father asked, "Which one among the two of you is the groom?" The companion responded, "This friend of mine sitting next to me is the groom, but the gold earrings are not his." But the father refused to give his daughter to a man who wore borrowed earrings, and as a result, the match failed. The groom was now angry with his companion and asked him, "Why did you tell them that the earrings were not mine? You shouldn't have done so." The two friends then went for another marriage interview. This time the man's companion introduced the groom saying, "This friend of mine hopes to marry your daughter. The earrings he is wearing are his." But this match failed too. The young man was very frustrated. He now said to his friend, "Why do you have to say anything about the earrings?" Then they went for an interview for a third time. Again introducing his friend, the companion said, "This man is the bridegroom. Don't ask me about the earrings he's wearing."

· 64 · *Oh! Calcutta*
(West Bengal)

This example of urban folklore must have its counterparts in nearly every industrial nation. While it is doubtful that India can claim originality for the story, Calcutta can possibly make the best claim to being a place worse than hell!

ONCE THERE LIVED a rich man in Calcutta. Because he was rich, he naturally indulged in all sorts of dirty games: he used to drink a lot, gamble a lot, and do a lot of womanizing. Besides, he thrived on corruption, bribery, and dishonesty. In short, the man was rich but also sinful and dirty.

Now you know, rich people don't die young. So this man also enjoyed life till the end. He died at the ripe age of eighty. And as I said, the man was loaded with sin. Therefore, soon after his death, he was transferred to *Yamaloka,* the realm of the dead. There he could be seen in the long queue of dead people waiting for their turn to have an audience with Yamaraja, the god of death. All were waiting to find out their fate after death. Those who spent virtuous lives on earth would be sent to *Swarga* (paradise) and those who spent sinful lives would be sent to *Naraka* (hell).

Soon this sinful man had his turn. Yamaraja had his deeds on the earth assessed, and then declared, "Your place is in hell." This verdict did not disturb the man at all. He kept on smiling. Yamaraja was surprised. "I never saw anyone smile when being sent to hell!" said Yamaraja. "Sir, I have lived my whole life in Calcutta. Hell cannot be worse than that," replied the sinful, dirty man.

· 65 · *Dala Tarwadi*
(Gujarat)

This tale contains a classic folk image of the Brahman and his relationship to farming. Ancient Hindu codes say that a Brahman should devote himself to ritual activities and to scholarship. But folk traditions often make fun of this role as being one of thievery and deception. Here the Brahman's wit is no match for the protective alertness of a watchful farmer rival.

DALA TARWADI was a Brahman. One day his wife asked him to bring an eggplant so that she could make a curry out of it. So Dala Tarwadi went out to a farmer's field. In the field belonging to Vasaram Bhuvo, a very hardworking farmer, he found eggplants in abundance. Seeing no one around, Dala Tarwadi sneaked into the field to help himself. To ease his conscience he then asked out loud, "Field, field, may I pick one of your egg-plants?" To have a reply he then said, "Oh, well, dear Dala Tar-wadi, why not take ten or twelve?" So, indeed, Tarwadi did.

Dala Tarwadi's pilfering soon became routine. But Vasaram Bhuvo was a smart and watchful man. "Why are there always less eggplants than blossoms?" he thought to himself. "There must be something wrong. I take great care with these plants. Let me keep a good watch over them and see if I can discover the reason." One morning Bhuvo came earlier than usual to his field and quickly hid in the bushes. A little later Dala Tarwadi came along to pick eggplants, as usual. Again he used his own, original way of asking permission. Vasaram Bhuvo watched. Suddenly he jumped from his hiding place and rushed over to grab Dala Tar-wadi. The Brahman did his best to escape but he couldn't. Vas-aram Bhuvo caught him and tied him up. Then he took Tarwadi to the irrigation tank where there was a water lift that had a large leather bucket on one end for dipping out water. He tied Data Tarwadi inside that leather bucket and lowered him to the surface of the water. Then Vasaram Bhuvo asked the well, "Well, well, how many times shall I dip?" Tell me!" In reply, he answered himself saying, "Oh, my dear Vasaram Bhuvo, why should you give him only one or two? Be generous! Give him ten or twelve!" Drenched and near drowning, Dala Tarwadi now begged to be released. Vasaram Bhuvo finally relented and untied him on one condition: that he should never set foot in his fields again. Dala Tarwadi promised this and ran away as fast as he could.

· 66 · The Story of Pebet
   (Manipur)

This next story is about a cat who tries to deceive a mother bird into trusting it with her children. But the cat's real intention, of course, is to eat the tasty young fledglings that are growing in this mother's nest. Though collected in Manipur State, this tale lies within the general and well-known *Panchatantra* tale

framework. The keystone to the cat's deceptive strategy is its
pretense of being a holy man. It wears a chain of prayer beads,
makes familiar ritual sounds, pretends to be vegetarian, and
even wears saffron robes. This is a well-known Indian tale type
(AT113) of which at least sixteen other examples have been
recorded. The main joke, like in several preceeding tales, turns
on stereotyping the religious mendicant. Though orthodox on
the surface, these wandering holy men are often said to be
wolves in sheep's clothing. The clever mother bird in this story
sees through the cat's thin disguise and focuses on warning and
protecting her children. She also subtly tests the sincerity of this
"ascetic" by flattering him about his good looks. The cat's
obvious pleasure at the praise is out of keeping with its ascetic
pretenses. The story later uses another common deception device
(type 122G, and motif K562) when the youngest baby is caught
in the cat's claws. But the mother advises the cat to wash the
bird properly, as would be in keeping with any true ascetic's
concern with clean food. This, of course, gives the little fledg-
ling its chance to escape. The tale ends with the cat licking its
paw and enjoying a bit of excrement the bird leaves behind.
This is a particularly poignant jab at the mendicant's false ascetic status, since nothing could be more disgusting for a
devout man than eating excrement. That inventive twist adds a
distinctive Manipuri touch to a basically pan-Indian story. Anti-
Indian feelings are widespread in Manipur State and lend political overtones to the story, as well. Many folktales that depict a
contest between the large and the small, or the strong and the
weak, have a similar political potential, of course, when told in
the right setting.

THE PEBET is a small bird found in the jungles of Manipur. Once
a pebet lived in this area. It had seven small sons. The mother
pebet was very concerned to teach her little ones how to fly. She
wanted to insure that her sons could lead independent lives. In
the area where the pebet lived, there was also a cat who had
become a recluse. This cat pretended to avoid any kind of meat.
Nevertheless, he was very fond of the flesh of the pebet bird and
was always on the look out for an opportunity to catch one. This
cat paid daily visits to the home of the pebet with the hope of

catching one or more of her small sons. This was an unusual cat
with pretensions to sainthood. It carried a chain of devotional
beads and dressed itself in saffron robes. It also made a very special devotional sound, *kingkaramala, kingkaramala,* when it
moved.

One day this cat arrived at the home of the pebet and asked it,
"Do you find me beautiful?" The pebet replied with great humil-
ity and modesty, saying, "Oh, Sir! You are as beautiful as a
pitcher full of water, or a measure of paddy filled to the brim, or a
long garland of dry fish!" The cat was flattered by this answer and
expressed his satisfaction by a small trembling purr in his neck.
He then left the house and the mother pebet turned to her sons
saying, "My dear ones! You must be very careful of this man. He
is really interested in eating you. He is only looking for an opportunity to accuse me of some wrongdoing and hence to distract
me. The moment he has a chance he will pounce on you and
devour you all. You must learn to fly quickly. It is only then that
you will be able to escape his grasp. I will continue to flatter him
when he visits us until you all learn to fly. The moment you can
fly I will tell him the naked truth." Saying this, the mother pebet
coached her sons and urged them to try to fly every day.

The next time the cat visited this family he asked his usual
question, "Do you find me beautiful?" This time, however, the
pebet was more confident of her children's ability to escape. So
she now decided to tell the truth and said in answer to the cat,
"Why do you ask me this silly question again and again? How
can you be anymore beautiful than an ordinary cat?" With these
words she also gave a signal to her sons, indicating that they
should fly away. All of pebet's children did so except for the very
youngest. The cat quickly caught hold of this little bird and was
eager to eat him. Seeing this the pebet said, "Look, Sir! If you
want to eat the flesh of my son, first bathe him properly. Clean
all the dirt off his sticky feathers. Then seat him on the palm of
your foot and dry him carefully in the sun. You should turn him
carefully seven times until he is fully dry and only then set about
eating him." The cat followed the mother's instructions very
carefully. It gave the young bird a bath and then held it in the
palm of its foot. As the cat began to twirl it for the seventh time
the young bird somehow managed to fly. But before it left, it

defecated on the cat's paw. Then it flew up high, well beyond the reach of the cat.

The cat was very dejected at its loss of this tasty meal and did not know what to do next. So it turned to its paw and began to lick what the young bird had left on it. The cat found the leavings very tasty. So it consoled itself saying, "Oh! how much more tasty would the flesh of the bird itself have been when what it defecated was, itself, such a treat!"

· 67 · *The Outlaw Babar Deva (Gujarat)*

The next story is the only example in this collection of a very underreported Indian genre, the historical legend. As is the case with most tales of this type, this story describes a rather boisterous and unsavory character. Just as in the West, outlaws often become folk heroes in India. Many legends express admiration for men or women who successfully challenge the powers of their day and get away with it. Such outlaws embody combined qualities such as bravery, physical prowess, and nomadism. They live far from the concerns of normal family life, though they enjoy the excitement of great battles and love affairs. Often they are also associated with guerilla or revolutionary political movements that champion the ordinary person. Both male and female outlaws have been reported. They generally do not rob or murder innocent underdogs. Instead, their targets are the wealthy and powerful, or else those who live a life of dependence on establishment networks.

In this particular legend from Eastern Gujarat, the juxtaposition of a Gandhian social worker and an outlaw is artfully constructed. Even though the social worker is critical of the outlaw's use of violence and of his attacks against landed peasants instead of a foreign government, the outlaw is able to appreciate his parallel protest role. Also worthy of note is the fact that for the hero, personal loyalty is placed above all other values. Babar will always support his friends in time of need, and he expects the same from them. Babar's poignant murder of his own wife and sister point up his disdain for such conventional kin bonds, and his high regard for courageous action. These decisions bear witness to his personal commitment to a separate set of standards. Indeed, the outlaws of Saurashtra are said to have had a strict moral code of their own which gang members have continued to uphold for several generations. Similar patterns of outlaw life are also reported to have existed elsewhere in India.

This kind of story tends to grow with time, and with many retellings it can later become the source material for a popular epic. In its current state this material can be classified as an incipient legend, consisting of colorful snippets about a local character's adventuresome life. These vignettes provide raw material that may later undergo creative development by local poets or bards. Indeed, Babar's life has already been described in fixed stanzas sung by local women while they dance a particular festival step called garba.

Babar Deva is an actual historical figure. He was born at Goral, a small village near the Gulf of Cambay, in the Kaira District of Gujarat. Although Babar was killed as a young man, his junior brother, Rama Deva, was still alive in 1962. Both brothers belong to the Patanwadia Koli caste, a dominant peasant group in the region. This community is particularly numerous in the Borsad Taluk, the area where Mahatma Gandhi launched his Satyagraha Movement in protest against the payment of revenue taxes to the British government. Babar Deva is said to have been inspired by an earlier outlaw named Sayadu Minyano who once plundered and looted Cambay. The people of the area say that Babar, in turn, helped to inspire Gandhi's own resistance movement. The Kheda Satyagraha that began in the Borsad area in 1923 was in fact supported by the social worker mentioned in this tale. It had Sardar Vallabhabhai Patel, the so-called Iron Man of India, as its parallel leader.

THERE WAS ONCE a very dedicated social worker who lived in the Borsad Taluk of Gujarat. This man moved from village to village trying to strengthen the morale of local residents to resist taxes levied by the British government. He tried to persuade local peasants not to pay any revenue at all to British officials. As a result, many people refused to pay these duties in either cash or kind. In response, the British began seizing local lands, family cattle, and household goods. They auctioned these things, and many local farmers were becoming paupers. Still the peasants resisted. Their movement was headed by Sardar Vallabhabhai Patel, known as the Iron Man of India. In spite of many pressures from British officers, most local residents stood their ground and rose to the occasion.

During the same period there was a famous outlaw named Babar Deva who was also harassing the people of this area. He used to loot and rob them, and he even kidnapped people at times in order to extract their money. Local residents claim that this man was inspired by Sayadu Minyano, another outlaw who had once plundered and looted Cambay, a town close to the place where Babar Deva was born. That folk tradition inspired Babar Deva to try his fortune as an outlaw. One night, when passing through a small village, the famous social worker encountered Babar Deva himself. He was very much afraid. The two men met in the depth of the night. Babar Deva approached his rival and threatened him saying, "Who are you?" The social worker answered, "I am an outlaw too!" But Babar retorted, "An outlaw? How can it be? Babar Deva is the only outlaw known in this area." The social worker replied, "I am another one." Babar Deva shook his head and said, "Another one? I do not know of another outlaw anywhere in the region! Never . . . no . . . never!"

The social worker looked Babar in the face and questioned him saying, "Do you doubt my honesty?" Babar replied, "No, but you have created questions in my mind." The social worker then said, "Well, let us sit down and discuss this problem in all its many aspects." The outlaw was puzzled. He did not feel he could trust a stranger, and he also remembered that it was a dark night. But he could see the man had no weapons in his hands and no place to hide them either. Therefore, he thought, "There is no reason to fear this stranger." So the two sat down together at the side of the road and began to chat. "Babar Deva, I am an outlaw against the British Government," said the social worker. "But we outlaws never harass the poor, the meek, or the innocent. We fight against the British Government, but we never hide anything. We differ from you in that you oppress the poor. You hide from the government while we give the police information about our strategy and our movements." Babar mumbled, "How can that be?" Then the social worker replied, "Is this a matter to be doubted?" The outlaw became thoughtful.

Then the social worker began speaking again. "Babar, we are wedded to the cause of truth. Our gurus are Mahatma Gandhi and Vallabhbhai Patel!" Babar then asked, "Did those men ask you to practice truth and also to be outlaws?" "No," replied the social worker. "Our goals demand truth but no violence." Babar retorted, "These are double-edged swords that you use." The social worker replied, "But the British Government dislikes you too." "Me?" asked Babar. "Yes," replied the social worker. "It is not good to harass innocent merchants and other loyal peasants. "Oh, I see," said Babar. The social worker continued, "You harass the tillers of the soil!" "I understand you," replied Babar. "You are a good brother. I shall try my best to put your words of advice into practice." Then the social worker gave Babar his blessings, saying, "May the almighty lead you on the right path." Then he set off for the next village, leaving the outlaw in a serious and pensive mood.

A few days later, a letter arrived at the Taluk office in Borsad. It was addressed to Mahatma Gandhi and to Sadar Patel and written by Babar himself. In it Babar said he too would now become an outlaw against the British Government, but his methods would be his own. He claimed that he was incapable of practicing nonviolence. He also said that if any news was received about a tax officer in the district having been shot, that this would be the work of Babar Deva. In this way the outlaw promised to prove himself as a fighter against the British Government. However, Babar again affirmed that he would never be able to put nonviolence into practice. The letter was read by Sardar Patel and was sent on to Mahatma Gandhi. Gandhi forwarded the letter to the highest authorities of the state, warning them so that they could take security measures. They would now need special protection for the white, foreign tax officer in the district. But Gandhi insisted that Babar Deva himself should not be punished for the letter he had written.

Sometime later, Babar Deva agreed to attend a wedding party. The ceremonies would finalize the marriage of the daughter of an old friend. Her father was a Thakore who ruled several villages in the Goral area of Gujurat, the locale where Babar Deva had lived as a child. The Thakore was a friend of the outlaw and a very rich man. Hence the wedding was to be celebrated with pomp and grandeur. A huge feast was to be offered to all the guests, and the proud father had purchased sixty tins of clarified butter (*ghee*) to be used in cooking sweets for the occasion.

One night, just before the marriage took place, some robbers broke into the storehouse and stole all of the precious tins of butter. The next day the cooks were called to prepare sweets for the celebrations. But when they opened the storehouse there was not a single tin of clarified butter to be found. The bad news was reported at once to the Thakore, and he realized immediately that someone must have broken into his storehouse. But the Thakore had no time to investigate the robbery properly. The wedding party was to be held in only two days' time. So he hurriedly wrote a note to his friend Babar Deva and asked him to come to see him. The Thakore reasoned that only Babar Deva could help him in these difficult circumstances. Babar arrived riding a horse and arranged to see his friend in private. As soon as they met he asked, "Why have you called me with such urgency? What is the news?" The Thakore then narrated the whole set of events to his friend. On hearing the news Babar Deva tried to reassure him and promised that he would find the Thakore sixty tins of clarified butter by the following morning. The next day Babar Deva arrived with two carts each drawn by four bullocks. These were packed with tins of butter. He thus fulfilled the promise of the outlaw.

The Thakore then thanked his friend and made him promise to attend the wedding ceremonies. Babar agreed but said he would only come in disguise, as the Thakore had also invited several government servants, some police officers, the local Magistrate, and even the District Collector. Babar Deva would only be safe if he wore a disguise. Babar Deva kept his word and arrived at the wedding ceremony unnoticed. But when he left the ceremony, he arranged for a gun to be fired just to inform the government officials that he had, indeed, attended the rituals. On leaving his friend's home Babar crossed a river using a small country boat. Once he reached the opposite bank he felt sure that no one could pursue him.

At one point Babar Deva also decided to shoot his own wife, suspecting that she might not have been faithful to him. He was fearful that she might be smuggling information to various police officers about his activities or his hiding places. Somewhat later Babar Deva acquired a mistress. He had a daughter by her. When this young girl had grown to a marriageable age, however, Babar Deva was heavily involved in his outlaw activities. The British police force was now keeping a very careful watch over his activities. So he had to think carefully about how to invite his friends and relatives to the wedding ceremony. Babar Deva had promised that he himself would be present at this ritual where his daughter would be given away. The police, however, were equally vigilant. They were determined that they would catch Babar Deva the moment that he attended the wedding of his only issue.

On the marriage day the bridegroom arrived with a party of relatives and friends. But Babar Deva was nowhere to be seen. Instead, he had dressed himself as a woman and joined the ladies of the family on their trip to the potter's house. In this preparatory ritual women bring earthen vessels to the wedding home to be used in the marriage ceremony. Babar Deva had veiled his face and covered his head with the end of a sari. Then he had joined the group of women on their way to the potter's house. He also returned with this group to the wedding site. His arrival was known only to his mistress. When his daughter's hand was about to be given in marriage, however, Babar Deva stepped forward with his face veiled. Disguised as a woman, he ceremoniously performed these rituals in place of a normal father. He left the house immediately afterwards, and the police only later came to realize that Babar Deva had indeed given away his daughter while using a disguise.

This is the story of how Babar Deva shot his wife. One night when he arrived in his own village of Goral, he immediately ordered his wife to cook a fine dinner. In a short while she had prepared it according to his wishes and he was asked to sit down to be served. Babar Deva was eating the sweets she had cooked. His wife was serving him seconds when she began to speak, saying, "My good man, I have come to know that you are an expert in aiming guns." "You are correct," he replied. Then she asked, "Do you spare the life of the person you are aiming at?" "Not unless the person is favored by God," he answered. Then she said,

"May I ask you one more question husband." "Surely!" came the answer. "Can you show me how you aim a gun?" This question made Babar Deva suspicious. Why would a woman be so interested in asking about the use of a gun? Why would she want to learn the technique of aiming? This was not the proper role of a woman, he reasoned. Therefore, there must be something wrong. He decided that she must have some plan or scheme afoot in order to have asked such questions.

Then the wife spoke up again, "Do you hear what I said, my brave man?" Hearing this Babar Deva finished his meal, washed his hands, and went to the place where he kept his gunpowder. He kept it in a bag hanging from a peg on the wall. He also took his gun in hand. He brought both of these to the place where his wife was standing. Then he held the gun against her breast. He took aim and said, "This is the way in which one aims a gun." And then Babar pulled the trigger and took the life of his own partner. In just a few seconds his wife lay in a pool of blood. Babar Deva now left the house in a callous manner. The woman died on the spot and was gone forever.

Babar Deva also had several sisters. Their husbands, his brothers-in-law, were also members of his gang. The nephews of these marriages were strong supporters of his exploits. The whole group lived together in the fields and in the forests, changing their abode regularly. But the more distant relatives lived in Goral, along a street which is now named after Babar Deva. The family home was a very grand affair. The family had obtained a great deal of money from Babar's looting and built several splendid homes along this ancestral street. These were the residential quarters of all Babar Deva's family. But the outlaw himself, and his gang, preferred to live in the open fields. There they constructed small huts and lived off the farm lands.

Once Babar Deva appeared on the edge of a field that belonged to a member of the family. There he sat down in the midst of several sisters. His mother and father were also present. Then he asked whether any of them had been harassed by the police or by the village headman or by any other person from outside the region. His sister replied in a flattering and rather artificial manner saying, "My brother is Babar Deva. Even God would not dare to harass us, his relatives! Only God knows my brother's power and ability. With him to protect us, why should we be afraid of the police, or the village headman, or of anyone else?"

Babar Deva, however, had heard rumors that his own sister had been smuggling the news of his whereabouts to police informants. So Babar then said, "I know about your activities, and you should be the last person to flatter me." The sister replied, "Who would flatter the bravest of brothers except his own sister?" Babar now became angry and said, "Stop this false talk! I know how much love and respect my sister has shown for me." She retorted in anger asking, "What are you saying? Do you mean to imply that I do not love you?" But Babar persisted, saying, "I know about you. Please be gone. Get out of here!" The sister then turned and left. There was a dejected look on her face. Babar Deva was not pleased with this manner of departure. So he raised his gun to his shoulder and aimed at his sister. He shot once and she died in her tracks.

Part VII
Knowledge and the Fool

*T*HROUGHOUT history, and all around the civilized world, India has been renowned for its great wisdom. Two of the world's great religions—Hinduism and Buddhism—arose there. In ancient times, pilgrims from all over the Orient traveled to India in search of knowledge and learning. One of the forms in which this wisdom was conveyed was in collections of literary tales, such as the *Panchatantra* and the *Hitopadesha,* both written over one thousand years ago. These tales, and others from India, were carried to distant lands where they met with ready acceptance among people of all classes.

But where did these ancient Indian scholars turn for the insight into life these collections represent? Western scholarship has long distinguished two levels of literary form in Indian thought and civilization, sometimes referred to as the great tradition and the little (or folk) tradition. In some ways this is a convenient way to separate the legacy of Indian culture into two categories: that handed down by scholars in literary texts and that perpetuated by villagers in oral tradition. We must not go so far as to suppose, however, that these two forms belonged to widely different groups of people. While it is still unclear exactly what the relationship between these various traditions is, modern scholarship has shown that many of the great literary works had their origins in local stories. The *Mahabharata* and the *Ramayana,* for example, probably first existed in oral form, sharing many features with folktales and legends still heard today.

The *Panchatantra* relates how these early story traditions were collected. In the south of India there lived a king, named Amarasakti, and he had three sons. Each of these boys was such an utter dunce that he could learn nothing of what was necessary to manage the affairs of the country. The desperate king then asked his advisors, "By what means may their intelligence be awakened?" His advisors recommended a wise and aged Brahman named Visnusharman, who accepted the challenging task. He promised to teach these boys all they needed to know in a mere six months. The means by which he accomplished this task was to tell them the set of tales now known as the *Panchatantra*. Now Vishnusharman—scholar that he might have been—drew not from law books and religious treatises, but from a store of practical knowledge contained in the folklore which surrounded him and in which he, too, was steeped. Whatever else he might have been, he was a householder and a member of a community which started with the king and ended with the ordinary villager. Somewhere in that milieu we must place his family, his in-laws, his castemates, his friends, his servants, and all of their associates.

Literary traditions present us with a refined and polished form of a tale, universal in its message, but frozen in form. Oral traditions, we know, are more malleable. What are the tales of wisdom we find among Indian folk today? There is something distinctive about the portrayal of knowledge in folktales. Cleverness and cunning, rather than abstract knowledge gained from "book-learning" or meditation, are the character traits most frequently admired in Indian folk traditions. The setting of such tales, whether among animals in the jungle, or people in the village, generally involves the real world of power struggles. Thus the world of the folktale describes the big and powerful, as well as the small and vulnerable. The little guy must live by his wits. Folktales show us the "man in the world," rather than the ascetic who has removed himself to become a "forest dweller" (*vanaprastha*). The knowledge the folk hero displays is that gained from life experience not through penance (*tapas*), or through sheer devotion (*bhakta*).

Among animals, the clever hero is usually a tiny fellow. Mosquitoes (tale 69) and ants (tales 68 and 70) avenge their

victimized companions when others refuse to budge. In tale 68
the ant, alone of a group of animals which includes tigers and
leopards, is the one who offers to humble the mighty elephant
and upset the tyrannical rule other animals of the forest have
suffered. The ant has to put up with much ridicule for his
courageous claims, both from both his companions and his adversaries, yet he is finally able to demonstrate his true worth.
The same is true of the skinny little human warrior in tale 71.
His more powerfully built neighbor (the potter), lacks the
strength of valor inbred in the warrior's caste line. When the
village is attacked by a gang of thieves, the potter runs while
little guy drives off the intruders. Often animals fill set role
stereotypes in power struggles that are strikingly human. For
example, the mosquito, ant, sparrow, and parrot are usually
intelligent little guys, the fox and jackal tricksters, the crow
proud and greedy, and the crocodile indolent or dumb.
Monkeys are cast in fool's roles, but like court jesters, may have
much camouflaged intelligence.

In other tales wit is contrasted with bravado and pretense. In
tale 73 the "10,000 wit" tortoise, the "1,000 wit" cobra, the
"100 wit" mongoose, and all of their followers are stranded in a
burning haystack. Yet the "single-witted" but practical jackal is
the only one to escape. Tingali Ramalingadu, in tale 74, similarly uses a Brahman's greed and a king's wealth to point out
the foolishness of court life and avenge his mother's ghost.

Often wisdom is also addressed through its absence, by using
the character of the fool. The fool is one who has no understanding of the more practical aspects of life. In the tales in this
section he is an exaggerated character. The stupidity of fools is
still greater in tale 84 where three silly men compete to see
which of them is the "greatest fool of all." The standard fools of
Indian tales, furthermore, are often identified with particular
castes. The Brahman—whose knowledge comes from books—is
particularly singled out. In tale 81, animals even act foolishly.
Herdsmen, too, are sometimes attributed with a mentality no
better than that of the animals with which they must associate.

Another common image for a lack of good sense is revealed in
the fool's attempts to communicate with others. In tale 80,
misuse of language is shown in a bilingual setting (see also tale

60) and tale 79 involves the ambiguities of language use. Mis-
apprehension of the speech of others is involved in tale 81.
Choosing an inappropriate means of communication—use of the
hands when holding onto a limb high in a tree—imperils the
life of yet another fool. And the very act of communicating
causes a foolish crow to lose his meal to a clever fox.

We have encountered the clever and the foolish in tales in
previous sections. We have seen, for example, how a clever wife
restores her husband's life (tale 12) while another successfully
competes against her spouse (tale 48). We have seen clever
nephews drive their greedy uncles to distraction (tale 32). Most
of these tales use cleverness to convey a larger moral. Intelligence is an aid to the oppressed and victimized. The contrast
of good and evil is perhaps even more central to the focus of
these tales than is the theme of cleverness. Often these stories
assume a pattern of mirrored actions. Good and clever people
succeed while the bad and foolish fail. Both cleverness and
foolishness thus tend to take on a moral weight consistent with
some larger social framework.

In this section, cleverness and foolishness are both addressed
directly. They are shown to have a general adaptive, or mal-
adaptive, value both for the individual and for those around
him. The main function of many of these stories, however, is
humorous entertainment. Hence their structure tends to have a
linear quality rather than the dichotomous form of some earlier
accounts. In a number of examples fools reveal themselves
through a long series of three or more action clusters.

The ambiguous quality of many foolish characters is best seen
in the several stories containing transformations. In tale 78 we
see the Gujjar progressively change from fool to trickster. The
story of the Manipuri heroes, Chamden and Yuthung, reverses
this pattern, making an initial trickster into a fool. But most
remarkable is the sparrow in the final tale (no. 88) who manages
to churn the whole world of human categories away in a flood of
water loosed from his anus! If the tales in this section are filled
with both wisdom and humor, then, they also remain quite
different from more literary story collections for which India's
learned writers are well known.

· 68 · The Elephant and the Ant
(Gujarat)

This lovely story is about how a tiny but clever weakling manages to outmaneuver a giant. It belongs to the *Panchatantra* tale tradition. Unlike some of the other animal stories in that collection, no direct parallels to this tale are known. Aside from its generally pleasing construction, the story is interesting for two reasons. One, it makes an elephant rather than a lion the lord of the jungle. As in the *Panchatantra,* a bullock is given a key role. He is the noble advisor or seer. It is the bullock that advises the great elephant to respect his tiny persecutor, in keeping with the Hindu view of his gentle character and sacred status generally.

THERE ONCE LIVED a sturdy and powerful elephant. He roamed in a vast and dense jungle, and he ruled over all the animals within it. Indeed, this elephant was treated as the king of all beasts. Even the tigers, panthers, and leopards in the jungle were afraid of him. Being king made the elephant very proud, and he refused to heed anyone's advice. Indeed, he thought he was the wisest and strongest animal in the whole kingdom. Whenever there was a dispute in the jungle, all the other animals like to come to the elephant and ask his advice. But the elephant often made decisions that disregarded the happiness and well-being of others. As a result, there was widespread discontent among the residents of this jungle.

One day, all the animals decided to rise in revolt and throw off the rule of the elephant. Tigers, leopards, jackals, and foxes were all present at the forest meeting. But none of these animals dared to utter a single word against their king. None of them would come forward in public to challenge the elephant. At last a small, weak, and ugly little ant came to the front of the crowd and humbly said, "My friends, I desire to take on the challenge that has been put before us." The tiger roared with laughter and said, "You weakling!" A leopard also questioned the ant and doubted its courage. But at last a jackal that was dozing near the tiger requested that there be general agreement to allow the ant to take up this challenge.

The news of the meeting of the forest animals spread through the jungle like wild fire. When the elephant heard about it, he laughed as loudly as he could. Finally, he said with a certain egotism and pride, "Who needs to bother about that weakling. An ant deserves only mercy, not unkindness." Many days passed and nothing untold happened to the elephant. Meanwhile all the other animals began cracking jokes at the ant's expense. But the latter waited patiently. It was firm in its decision to challenge the elephant.

One day the elephant was lying quietly under a large banyan tree. It was very cold and he began to snore loudly. The other animals all realized that their leader was fast asleep. The ant, therefore, found a welcome opportunity to execute his plan. Slowly and steadily it crept closer and closer to the sleeping beast. Then it entered the trunk of the elephant and gentle crawled up into its head cavity. Finally the little ant reached the very upper reaches of its head. On finding the inner palate, the ant began to run so swiftly that it caused the elephant a severe pain. The strong and sturdy animal now lost its peace of mind and became agitated. Like a mad man it leapt up and screamed. Then it began to run back and forth helter-skelter. Meanwhile, the ant was enjoying its new surroundings. He was exploring the palate and tickling the marrow of the elephant's bones. When the elephant failed to find a way to end this constant pain, it finally stopped running, so as to consult a friend. Soon it was narrating its troubles to the bullock. The bullock thought seriously about the problem. Then it said, "I believe this difficulty is due to the work of an ant." The elephant said with a startled cry, "An ant? That insignificant little insect?" The bullock then answered, "My friend, don't utter such insults about ants! You would do better to pray for this little creature and to wish it a safe, long life. Watch the results that will come of your good thoughts." The elephant heeded the counsel of the bullock, and the ant agreed to come out of its trunk. The pain soon stopped and the elephant regained his peace and composure.

· 69 · *The Crow and the Sparrow (Uttar Pradesh)*

This tale, and "The Parrots and the Carpenter's Scales" which follows, are examples of cumulative tales. As these two tales from widely separated regions of India indicate, cumulative tales are popular all over India, among villagers and city dwellers alike. The characters vary, but the structure of the tale remains remarkably similar. In each, a helpless victim approaches a long chain of potential helpers, each of whom refuses to give his support. In the end, it is a tiny hero who sets the system in motion.

A CROW ONCE FOUND a pearl while a sparrow found a grain of rice. The sparrow immediately ate her rice, but the pearl remained with the crow. The sparrow then addressed the crow, saying, "Crow! Give me the pearl." But the crow simply flew away and sat on a *neem* tree. The sparrow then went to the tree and demanded, "Neem, neem, make the crow fly away!" But the tree answered: "Why should I make him fly away? What has he done to me?" The sparrow then lamented as follows, "The neem tree won't make the crow fly away, the crow won't give me the pearl, and therefore this bird is weeping."

The sparrow then went to the woodcutter and demanded, "Woodcutter! Woodcutter! Chop the neem tree down." But the woodcutter answered, "Why should I chop down the tree? What has it done to me?" The sparrow then lamented as follows, "The woodcutter won't cut down the neem tree. The tree won't make the crow fly away. The crow won't give me the pearl. And therefore this bird is crying."

The sparrow then went to the village chief and demanded, "Chief! Chief! scold the woodcutter!" But the village chief answered, "Why should I scold the woodcutter? What has he done to me?" The sparrow then lamented as follows, "The village chief won't scold the woodcutter. The crow won't give me the pearl. And therefore this bird is weeping."

The sparrow then went to the king and demanded, "King! King! Punish the village chief!" But the king answered, "Why should I punish the village chief? What has he done to me?" The sparrow then lamented as follows, "The king won't punish the village chief. The crow won't give me the pearl. And therefore this bird is weeping."

The sparrow then went to the queen and demanded, "Queen! Queen! Pout and sulk at the king!" But the queen answered, "Why should I pout at the king? What has the king done to me?" The sparrow then lamented, "The queen won't pout. The crow won't give me the pearl. And therefore this bird is weeping."

The sparrow then went to a mouse and demanded, "Mouse! Mouse! Chew up the queen's clothes!" But the mouse answered, "Why should I chew up her clothes? What has the queen done to me?" The sparrow then lamented, "The mouse won't chew up the queen's clothes. The crow won't give me the pearl. And therefore the bird is weeping."

The sparrow then went to the cat and demanded, "Cat! Cat! Eat up the mouse!" But the cat answered, "Why should I eat the mouse? What has the mouse done to me?" The sparrow then lamented, "The cat won't eat the mouse. The crow won't give me the pearl. And therefore this bird is weeping."

The sparrow then went to the dog and demanded, "Dog! Dog! Chase the cat!" But the dog answered, "Why should I chase the cat? What has the cat done to me?" The sparrow then lamented, "The dog won't chase the cat. The crow won't give me the pearl. And therefore this bird is weeping."

The sparrow then went to a stick and demanded, "Stick! Stick! Beat up the dog!" But the stick answered, "Why should I beat up the dog? What has the dog done to me?" The sparrow then lamented, "The stick won't beat up the dog. The crow won't give me the pearl. And therefore this bird is weeping."

The sparrow then went to the fire and demanded, "Fire! Fire! Burn up the stick!" But fire answered, "Why should I burn up the stick? What has the stick done to me?" The sparrow then lamented, "The fire won't burn the stick. The crow won't give me the pearl. And therefore this bird is weeping."

The sparrow then went to the sea and demanded, "Sea! Sea! Put out the fire!" But the sea answered, "Why should I put out the fire? What has the fire done to me?" The sparrow then lamented, "The sea won't put out the fire. The crow won't give me the pearl. And therefore this bird is weeping."

The sparrow then went to the elephant and demanded, "Elephant! Elephant! Drink up the sea." But the elephant answered, "Why should I drink up the sea? What has the sea done to me?" The sparrow then lamented, "The elephant won't drink up the sea. The crow won't give me the pearl. And therefore this bird is weeping."

The sparrow then went to a mosquito and demanded, "Mosquito! Mosquito! Fly into the elephant's ear!" And the mosquito answered, "Right away!" But the elephant asked, "Why fly into my ear? I will drink up the sea right away." The sea then asked, "Why drink me up? I will put out the fire right away." But the fire then asked, "Why put me out? I will burn up the stick right away." But the stick then asked, "Why burn me up? I will beat the dog right away." But the dog then asked, "Why beat me? I will chase the cat right away." But the cat then asked, "Why chase me? I will eat the mouse right away." But the mouse then asked, "Why eat me? I will chew up the queen's clothes right away." But the queen then asked, "Why chew up my clothes? I will sulk right away." But the king then asked, "Why sulk? I am going to punish the village chief right away." The village chief then asked, "Why punish me? I will scold the woodcutter right away." The woodcutter then asked, "Why scold me? I will chop down the neem tree right away." But the neem tree asked, "Why chop me down? I will make the crow fly off right away." But the crow then said, "Brother tree! Why pester me? Here's the pearl." And the crow gave the pearl to the sparrow.

· 70 · *The Parrots and the Carpenter's Scale* *(Kerala)*

This tale and the tale of "The Crow and the Sparrow" which preceeds it are examples of "cumulative" tales (see also tales 97, 98, and 99). This story about parrots was collected in a village, deep in southern India, where the story of the crow and the sparrow was collected in the city of Delhi. Though their characters vary, the two story structures remain remarkably consistent.

A PAIR OF PARROTS once sat in a banyan tree in front of a carpenter's house. They were very sad. Soon a rat came along and asked them why they were so sad. The parrots said, "We made a nest and laid our eggs in this banyan tree which stands in front of the carpenter's house, but the carpenter took our eggs. He fried them and ate them. So, rat, please go and gnaw the carpenter's scale." But the rat said no, he would not, and he went away.

Then a cat came by and asked the parrots why they were so sad. The parrots replied, "We made a nest and laid our eggs in this banyan tree which stands in front of the carpenter's house. The carpenter took our eggs. He fried them and ate them. The rat refused to gnaw the carpenter's scale. So, cat please go and chase the rat." But the cat said no, he wouldn't, and he went away.

Next, a dog came along and asked the parrots why they were so sad. The parrots replied, "We made a nest and laid our eggs in this banyan tree which stands in front of the carpenter's house. The carpenter took our eggs. He fried them and ate them. The rat refused to gnaw the carpenter's scale. The cat refused to chase the rat. So, dog, please go and bite the cat." But the dog said no, he would not, and he went away.

Then some schoolboys came along and asked the parrots why they were so sad. The parrots replied, "We made our nest and laid our eggs in this banyan tree which stands in front of the carpenter's house. The carpenter took our eggs. He fried them and ate them. The rat refused to gnaw the carpenter's scale. The cat refused to chase the rat. The dog refused to bite the cat. So, children please throw stones at the dog." But the schoolboys said no, they would not, and they went away.

Then a teacher came along and asked the parrots why they were so sad. The parrots replied, "We made a nest and laid our eggs in this banyan tree which stands in front of the carpenter's house. The carpenter took our eggs. He fried them and ate them. The rat refused to gnaw the carpenter's scale. The cat refused to chase the rat. The dog refused to bite the cat and the schoolboys refused to throw stones at the dog. So, teacher, please punish the schoolboys." The teacher said no, he would not, and he went away.

Then a fire came. It, too, asked the parrots why they were so sad. The parrots replied, "We made a nest and laid our eggs in this banyan tree which stands in front of the carpenter's house.

The carpenter took our eggs. He fried them and ate them. The rat refused to gnaw the carpenter's scale. The cat refused to chase the rat. The dog refused to bite the cat. The boys refused to stone the dog, and the teacher refused to punish the boys. So, fire, please burn the teacher's mustache." Fire said no, it would not, and it went away.

Then water came past the tree and asked the parrots why they were so sad. The parrots replied, "We made a nest and laid our eggs in this banyan tree which stands in front of the carpenter's house. The carpenter took our eggs. He fried them and ate them. The rat refused to gnaw the carpenter's scale. The cat refused to chase the rat. The dog refused to bite the cat. The boys refused to stone the dog. The teacher refused to punish the boys, and fire refused to burn the teacher's mustache. So, water, please go and douse the fire." Water, too, said no, it would not, and it went away.

Then came an elephant. The elephant saw the parrots and asked why they were so sad. The parrots replied, "We made our nest and laid our eggs in this banyan tree which stands in front of the carpenter's house. The carpenter took our eggs. He fried them and ate them. The rat refused to gnaw on the carpenter's scale. The cat refused to chase the rat. The dog refused to bite the cat. The boys refused to stone the dog. The teacher refused to punish the boys. Fire refused to burn the teacher's mustache and water refused to douse the fire. So, elephant, please muddy the water." The elephant said no, it would not, and it went on its way.

Next an ant came along and asked the parrots why they were so sad. The parrots replied, "We made our nest and laid our eggs in this banyan tree which stands in front of the carpenter's house. The carpenter took our eggs. He fried them and ate them. The rat refused to gnaw the carpenter's scale. The cat refused to chase the rat. The dog refused to bite the cat. The boys refused to stone the dog. The teacher refused to punish the boys. Fire refused to burn the teacher's mustache. Water refused to douse the fire and the elephant refused to muddy the water! So, ant, please enter the elephant's trunk." The ant said yes he would.

So the ant entered the elephant's trunk. The elephant muddied the water. Water doused the fire. Fire burned the teacher's mus-

tache. The teacher punished the boys. The boys stoned the dog.
The dog bit the cat. The cat chased the rat and the rat gnawed the
carpenter's scale. All this happened because the carpenter fried
and ate some parrot's eggs which lay in a nest in a banyan tree
that stood in front of his house.

· 71 ·   *The Potter and the Wagher*
         (Gujarat)

The word for caste in virtually all Indian languages is *jati* or
kula. The same word also means "kind, race, type, group, or
species." Jati is also related to the root, *jan-*, meaning, "to be
born." An individual is thus seen to be born with the characteristics of his caste. But, as this tale instructs us, caste
characteristics are not equivalent to physical traits. They are,
rather, attitudes and aptitudes which enable one group to do
certain things better than other groups.

ONCE UPON A TIME there were two friends, a potter and a
Wagher. The latter was a member of a caste of warriors. The men
were neighbors, and their wives were friends as well. These wom-
en used to sit and gossip together in their spare time. Now the
potter was strong, tall, and sturdy while the Wagher was very
thin. And the potter's wife used to chide the Wagherani, saying,
"How can such a thin man hold a spear and a sword? How can he
face a powerful foe?" The Wagherani felt badly, but she could say
nothing in reply. She knew her husband was a weakling.
    One day, the pot-drums thundered and a band of outlaws en-
tered the village to loot and plunder. In fear, the potter tried to
hide himself on the veranda of his house. The Wagher, however,
picked up his sword and came out of his house at the sound of the
warning drums. He saw the potter crouched in a corner, trembling with fear while a crowbar lay nearby. The Wagher thus
walked into the potter's house, picked up the crowbar and called
the potter's wife. When she came out of the room in which she
was hiding, he told her to watch and see if he was brave or not.
Then he took the crowbar and bent it in a circle around her neck
to form a collar. Afterwards he went outside to face the outlaws.
He fought bravely and soon drove them from the village.

Everything returned to normal in the village. The Wagher and his wife lived peacefully in their house. But the potter's wife was too ashamed to come to visit anymore. She wanted her husband to go to the Wagher and ask him to free her from the crowbar which still hung around her neck. He refused.

One day, full of shame, the potter's wife finally came to see her friend the Wagherani in person. She was received with courtesy, and the Wagherani soon asked, "Why have you not visited all these days?" "Because I have been busy with my work," replied the potter woman. "But could you please ask your husband to open out this crowbar and free me of my burden?" "Oh, my friend," replied the Wagherani, "that can't be done at this time. My husband is inspired with such strength and valor only when the drums thunder and danger is at hand. When that time returns you will be set free." "But such things happen once in a lifetime!" lamented the potter's wife.

· 72 · *The King of Delhi and the King of Turkey (Uttar Pradesh)*

If fools are a popular subject in Indian folktales, so are clever characters. Intelligence can be highlighted in several ways. Some tales, for example, describe a person's ability to answer an intricate riddle. Such is the case with this next story, which was collected in Uttar Pradesh. The person who succeeds is a wise man employed by a powerful ruler. Most suitable, too, is the fact that this riddle is posed to a foreign king by an Indian one. When the answer is found, the local ruler is pleased. Significantly, the foreign king never gains advantage over the Indian king except to win relief from the threat of military conquest. Three interesting motifs color this story. The first is the parallel suggested between a large melon and a man's head. The same equation is sometimes made in Hindu shrines. In temple rituals, a gourd, a coconut, or a piece of sugarcane may be sacrificed as a symbolic equivalent to the offering of the worshiper's own head. Second, a point is made concerning a wife's inability to keep a secret and of a woman's general lack of concern for her husband's reputation. Ironically, it is an honest prostitute who

comes to the hero's defense. Indian folktales, particularly ones
popular with men, often stereotype wives in this way. Third, a
critique is offered of an Indian king for not properly weighing
the evidence of a crime. In contrast to Brahman fools, who are
often shown to be miserly and greedy, here a ruler is shown to
be vulnerable where wisdom and justice are at issue. Instead of a
low-caste servant, a foreign wise man is used as a vehicle to
show him up.

AT ONE TIME there was a king of Delhi who sent a riddle to the
king of Turkey. The riddle was phrased as follows, "What is the
meaning of the phrase 'The false of the not false and the not false
of the false, the dog of the door and the ass of the court?'" The
king of Turkey was asked to explain this on the threat of losing
his kingdom. When this news arrived in Turkey, the king there
became very upset. So he went to consult with a Moslem wise
man. The wise man asked the king why he was dejected, and the
king explained about the riddle. The wise man said, "Give me
five hundred rupees, and I promise to find you an answer." The
king agreed and the wise man used the 500 rupees to travel with
his wife to Delhi. Upon reaching the city, the couple took a room
at an inn.

After looking around the city for a few days, the wise man
went to the court of the Delhi king. There the doorman stopped
him saying, "You cannot enter this court." But the wise man
tried a bribe and found that by offering a small sum of money to
the doorman he was able to gain access to the court. He began
making it a habit to visit the court daily.

One fine day the wise man encountered a melon merchant on
the way home from the court. He bought a melon, and when he
entered the house his wife asked him what he had with him. He
replied, "Today I cut off the head of a man. Please don't tell
anyone." As soon as her husband was out of earshot, however, the
wise man's wife began to spread the news that her husband had
cut off someone's head. Eventually the king of Delhi heard about
this. He then gave an order for his men to arrest the murderous
Turkish foreigner. But when an assistant came for the wise man,
a prostitute who lived nearby objected to his arrest. Her comment was, "Why has he been condemned? This man has committed no error."

Nonetheless, the wise man was arrested and brought to the court. There the king asked him about his behavior. The wise man replied, "I have been calling at your court daily. Yesterday I bought a melon on my way home and my wife asked what it was. So I told her that inside the melon was the severed head of a traveler. I ordered her not to tell anyone. Now you have called me here. I wish to answer the riddle you posed to the king of Turkey. I am his representative. Here is the answer: My wife spoke against my order and therefore was false, not true. The prostitute next door saved my life by asking your men not to beat me. Therefore she who was false is not false. Your doormen are dogs of the door because they have taken my bribes, and you are an ass because you condemned me before seeking the truth." The king of Delhi was very pleased with this answer from the wise man, and he sent news to that effect to the king of Turkey.

· 73 · *The Single-Wit*
        (Gujarat)

In northern India the quality of tea is sometimes measured as "10-mile tea," "20-mile tea," or "40-mile tea" depending on its strength. Similarly, to boast of having a "100,000 wit," "1,000 wit," etc. does not sound as peculiar to an Indian ear as it does to a North American one. When it comes to wisdom, both cultures seem to agree that quality, not quantity, is what counts. This tale may be viewed as a version of a *Panchatrantra* tale about two fish, one characterized as a "1,000 wit" (*sahasra-buddhi*) and the other as a "single-wit" (*eka-buddhi*). In that tale, the single-wit and his family escape a fisherman's net, while the much larger group following the lead of the 1000 wit are captured.

THERE ONCE WAS an enormous haystack near a village. Many insects and animals used to live in it. Chief among them were a tortoise, a cobra, a mongoose, and a jackal. Each of these believed himself to be the wisest member of the group. The tortoise called itself a "100,000 wit." The cobra believed itself to be a "1,000 wit," and the mongoose believed he was a "100 wit." Only the

jackal claimed to be a "single-wit." Then, one day, there was a
fire in the haystack. All the animals quickly went to consult the
three wisest among them, tortoise, cobra, and mongoose. The
jackal, too, joined the crowd. All these characters assembled in a
corner unscathed by the fire and asked what was to be done.

The tortoise replied first, saying, "I know more than one hundred thousand ways and means to save us from this fire." The
cobra raised its hood and proudly said, "I know at least one thousand ways." "And I, nearly one hundred," said the mongoose.
Somebody then asked the jackal, "And you, my friend?" "When
there is a fire in a haystack, there is only one solution," replied
the jackal, "and that is to run away." "Coward!" somebody
grunted.

And so, when the jackal saw that the fire was spreading he ran
away from the haystack, caring little what others would say. The
tortoise, the cobra, and the mongoose tried to hide themselves in
their holes, but before they could escape they were roasted by the
heat. Meanwhile, the jackal was resting under a nearby tree.
Seeing the sorrowful plight of the self-claimed wise ones, the
jackal reflected:

> "The 100,000 wit is confounded,
> The 1,000 wit is troubled;
> The 100 wit is burnt,
> And the single-wit is saved."

· 74 · *Tenali Ramalingadu*
(Andhra)

There is a series of folktales in Telugu satirizing courtly life.
These all revolve around the personage of one famous figure,
Tenali Ramalingadu (also called Tenali Ramakrishna). The sto-
ries are as popular among educated urbanites as they are among
illiterate peasants. Some of the characters, such as the king of
Vijayanagara, Krishnadevaraya (who ruled at the height of his
empire's glory, 1509–29), are real historic figures. Tenali
Ramalingadu and his infamous exploits are, however, probably

the products of a vivid folk imagination. He also shows up in Tamil folklore as Tenali Rama, a jester at the court of Irayur, king of Tondamandalam (Dorson 1975: 199–201).

WHEN KING KRISHNADEVARAYA'S mother died, she had a craving for mangoes. But they were out of season and therefore Krishnadevaraya was not able to give his mother the mangoes that she had wanted so badly. The king was later advised by the family priest, Tatacharyulu, to make up for this inability to satisfy her final wish by giving mangoes of solid gold to Brahmans on every anniversary of his mother's death. So the king had hundreds of gold mangoes made and announced that the Brahamans would get them on the prescribed day.

Tenali Ramalingadu heard this story and decided to do something about the greed of the Brahmans. On the next anniversary day, he had burning coals with iron rods heating in them set at the entrance to the king's palace. As the Brahmans entered the palace, he told each one of them that they would get as many gold mangoes as burns they agreed to receive on their bodies with these red-hot irons. Each Brahman eagerly asked for as many as he could suffer. Some took four, some took six, and some endured as many as ten.

When these men went in to ask for the mangoes, however, they were quickly disappointed. Each was given only one mango. They then went to the king and complained that while they had received many burns on their bodies, they had been awarded only one mango each. The king was completely dismayed and inquired about what was going on. He soon learned that Tenali Ramalingadu was cauterizing the body of each Brahman who entered the palace. He ordered this intruder brought at once to explain what he had been doing.

Ramalingadu appeared and humbly said, "Your highness, just as your mother died asking for mangoes which you could not give her, so my mother died of rheumatism for which the treatment was cauterization of the joints. I could not supply her with this cure. So I decided that these Brahmans should receive it for her. It just happened that my mother died on the same day as yours. I knew that the Brahmans would not be as eager to be cauterized as they would be to receive mangoes. But my mother deserves to be

happy too. So I devised a plan by which I could induce some
Brahmans to receive this treatment."

· 75 ·   *The Ghost of a Brahman*
         (West Bengal)

Another type of cleverness that is commonly seen in Indian
folktales concerns tricks designed to capture or defeat demons.
The next tale is well-known to Indian folklorists, and variants
have been reported from both the North and the South. At least
nine such accounts are currently known. As tale type 926A,
"The Clever Judge and the Demon in the Pot," this story
appears to be uniquely Indian. Its more general form, "the
Spirit in the Bottle" (type 331), however, is also known outside
South Asia. The idea that a ghost can return to the human
world and want to enjoy the pleasures of family life is a familiar
fear in many local Indian belief systems. In Tamilnadu, for
example, spirits of men who die at an unnaturally young age are
sometimes thought to return to trouble young girls as supernatural lovers. In the present story, such a look-alike simply
replaces a man and enjoys life with his wife. It is interesting
that a young boy finally solves this problem. As in so many
Indian stories, the clever person is very junior in status. His
mental skills, however, enable him to outwit kings, counselors
and Brahmans alike.

THERE ONCE LIVED a very poor farmer. By dint of great efforts he
managed to collect a small sum of money by begging from door
to door. He then used this money to marry a beautiful young
girl. But he was hard pressed to supply a livelihood for his new
family. So the young husband finally decided to go abroad to earn
money. The boy was a Brahman. He now approached his mother
and offered her whatever he had saved. He then said, "Mother, I
have decided to go abroad to earn some money. I will not return
home until I have earned a substantial amount." His mother was
sad, but she did not object to her son's departure. Instead she
bade him goodbye and gave him her blessings.

Next to the house of this Brahman family there was a large wood apple tree. In that tree there lived a ghost of another Brahman. The evening of the same day on which the young man left home, this ghost came down from the tree and took the departed boy's form. The ghost then entered the house. On seeing him everybody thought the young boy had returned. The boy's wife hurriedly asked, "How is it that you have returned so soon?" The ghost replied, "It was an inauspicious day today. I have returned in order to wait for a better moment of departure." Neither the mother nor the wife of the boy suspected foul play. The ghost therefore stayed on in the house and behaved as a master without encountering resistance. Several years passed this way. In the meantime the true husband earned a considerable amount of money in a foreign country. He now decided to return to his old home. When he entered his house, however, he found another person impersonating him and living there in his place. He became very angry. On seeing this intruder the ghost also became angry. It said to the returning boy, "It is unlawful for you to enter house without my permission."

The mother and the wife of the young man were shocked at these events. They did not know what to make of this domestic dispute. Not finding any solution, the true Brahman husband decided to lodge a complaint with the king of his country. The king then asked his court to solve the mystery. He required both men to appear before his counselors on the following day. The unhappy Brahman returned home, having cried from anxiety all the way. While crossing a field, however, he happened to see some boys playing in the shade of a tree. They were imitating a king presiding over a court of justice. On seeing the Brahman crying, the young boys asked him to explain his sorrow. The Brahman then narrated his story to the children.

One boy, the one who played the role of the king, was very clever. When he had heard the story, he decided to go to the true king of his country. There he said, "Your majesty, kindly let me offer a solution to the problem of the two Brahmans who lay claim to the same house." The king gladly agreed to let the boy try to solve the problem. The next day the trial began in the king's courtroom. The Brahman and the ghost were each asked to make a statement. The young boy was also present. After hearing

both sides, the boy stood up and pointed to a bottle. He then
asked each of the two men if they could enter this bottle. He
promised that whoever entered it first would become the master
of the house in question. The boy first asked the true Brahman,
"Can you enter this bottle?" But the man replied, "How can a
full grown man enter into a little bottle?" The boy next asked the
same question of the ghost. This second party replied confi-
dently, saying, "Certainly I can enter your bottle." He then became very small, and in front of the entire crowd, he squeezed
himself into the bottle. The clever boy immediately corked the
bottle and the ghost became trapped. With this the dilemma was
solved. The true Brahman returned home in a state of great
happiness.

· 76 ·   *The Daily Measure*
            (Assam)

Fate or *karma* plays an enormously important and complex role
in sophisticated Hindu thought. In India's oral traditions, however, fate is often seen in very simple terms. Usually fate is
personified as a man, as in this story, but in the South it may be
a woman. Sometimes fate is said to be written on one's forehead
at birth, and sometimes it can be determined by astrological
configurations. In folktales, a person's destiny is only rarely
determined by the morality of one's actions in past lives. Furthermore, Ravana is made a rather comic figure in this tale, in
contrast to the fierce and imposing character he displays in
Indian epic accounts.

RAVANA, KING OF LANKA, was once taking his morning stroll by
the seaside. As he walked, he noticed a person measuring sand
with a cup in the distance. The man was measuring and keeping
each cupful either on this side or on that. Curious, the king went
up to him and asked what he was doing. The man answered, "I
am Bidhata (Fate), and I am determining the daily measure of
food for each man."
    The proud king paused for a moment and then asked, "Does

every man have his measure?" "No, your Majesty, not every one." "Have I got my measure?" "Yes, you have." The king wondered how Bidhata could determine what his daily measure was; who was he to stop him from enjoying whatever he wanted? He therefore said, "Will you withhold my measure for the day?" "How can that be, your Majesty?" Bidhata said. "Whatever is allotted as one's measure cannot be altered. This is the rule of Fate." "No, you must withhold my measure. Do withhold my measure," said Ravana, wanting to test the power of fate.

When the king insisted, Bidhata agreed to withhold that day's measure of food. Ravana went away satisfied. On his way home he bought a large fish head at the local market. After sending the fish head to the kitchen, he sat in his court to conduct his royal business. When the king finally went in for lunch it was past midday. The large fish head was there waiting for him, cooked in a manner befitting such a great king. When he saw the head he burst out laughing, for how could such a creature as Bidhata prevent him from having what he wanted to have? Mandodari, the queen, was in her period, and therefore she was watching from a ways away. She wondered how the king would like his meal. When he laughed out loud, she thought that the meal must not be up to the normal standard. She spoke out, "What sort of man are you? This meal has been cooked by your sister-in-law, Bibhisan's wife, because I am not clean today. She may not have cooked well, but is it nice of you to act this way about it?"

The king had spent a busy morning, and now to withstand his wife's carping when he was about to eat was too much. He got up from his seat right away, out of disgust, and left the meal untouched. When his temper cooled a little, however, he realized the significance of what had occurred. He had missed his day's measure! In the afternoon when the king again went for a stroll by the seaside, he went up to Bidhata and said, "Bidhata, I acknowledge your power, for I missed my lunch today." Therefore, when someone misses something of which he was sure, the situation is described as *Ravanar bhog,* Ravana's measure or share.

· 77 ·   *Badsah the Great King*
   (Kashmir)

This story describes the ability of a saint to transfer his soul
from his own body to that of another person. Unlike some of the
other stories in this collection, many of which concern false
ascetics, this one depicts the powers that genuine ones are supposed to have. This set of ideas accords with a general Hindu
belief in hidden powers and in the ability of truly self-controlled
men to determine the course of much larger events. But this
same tale has a strong flavor of Hindu religious partisanship. It
paints a very dark picture of the reign of a particular Moslem
king and shows how his Hindu physician finally gained the
upper hand and arranged for the rule of a more just and tolerant
man. A Hindu saint thus serves as the supernatural rescuer of
the Kashmiri people and the instigator of a large scale transformation. Not only does the story credit this magician with
saving the original king from a dread disease, but it also credits
him with transforming that man's basic personality through
manipulating him from the inside. The physician of this story,
therefore, is a bit of a trickster. He figures out how to trap the
soul of the saint inside the king's body and thereby insures a
pro-Hindu shift in his style of rule. The tale thus reasons from a
Hindu perspective about how a Moslem king requires a Hindu
saint's help if he is to become a renowned and just ruler. As in
many stories, a description of cleverness becomes mixed with
ideas about religious power and an ability to see behind ordinary
things.

THERE IS AN OLD PROVERB in Kashmir which says that the Hindus of the region were once persecuted until only eleven families
were left. These were persons who survived the wrath of a cruel
and unjust Moslem ruler Zain-ul-Abedin. Most Hindus fled from
him and hid in hills. Shri Bahat, who was the royal physician at
that time, was the only Hindu who continued to live in the central valley. His life was spared because he had cured the local king
of a very serious disease when he was a young prince. Then one
day the same king fell ill again with another mysterious disease.
Doctors from all over the land failed to properly diagnose the

problem, and these men were helpless to recommend a cure. The king's condition grew worse each day. The royal physician, Shri Bahat, was worried. His own treatment was not working either. Bahat's own prestige was at stake and he knew very well that if the king was not cured he would lose both his job and his life.

At this time a wandering saint came to Kashmir. Only God knows why he chose to come at this time. This saint was surprised that he could not find a single Hindu home to stay in. After a long search, someone led him to the house of Shri Bahat. The physician welcomed this saint and gave him food and shelter. Then after dinner, Shri Bahat revealed to the visitor that the king was suffering from a mysterious disease. The physician spoke of his fear that the king would loose his life and that he, as court physician, would be sentenced to death. The doctor then asked for the saint's help. The visitor promised to try his best and asked if he could see the king in person.

This visiting saint was no ordinary wandering teacher, like the ones normally seen these days. Instead, this man had attained the highest level of spiritual power. Indeed, his soul could leave his body at his command. It could travel wherever he wanted it to. And he could do this without anything unusual being noticed. So the next morning, when Shri Bahat took the saint to visit the ailing king, the guest's invisible soul followed him to the palace. On examining the king, Shri Bahat found that he had already died. He was now overcome with despair. Indeed, this physician began to lose his mind. Soon he started beating on his forehead with his hand. Then he cried in front of the saint saying, "Alas! we are too late. The king is already dead. We are doomed my friend. You had better escape if you can. Leave me here to my fate." The saint tried to calm the physician down. He said, "Do not worry my friend. I have a plan. My soul will enter the body of the king. This will cause him to rise and appear cured. But you will have to preserve my body, which I will leave behind in your house. I will reenter this body at a later time, after we find some way of saving your king."

Having said this the saint's soul entered the king's body. The king then arose from his bed and was cured. Shri Bahat's eyes shone with relief. He thanked the saint for saving his life. He made sure the monarch was alive and well, and then he left the palace and announced the good news. Hearing this the king's followers rejoiced and showered blessings on Shri Bahat. The people of the town began to say, "He is a miracle man." "He is the greatest physician on earth. He has extraordinary powers. He saved our great king. Praise be to Allah." The king's miraculous escape from death was celebrated with enthusiasm by all his subjects.

During the next few days there were more surprises for the king's subjects. The king now ordered the release of all his prisoners. He personally gave alms to the poor, sent an appeal to all those who had left the country to return, and promised them help and personal safety. In addition, the king began openly preaching religious tolerance. People were very surprised at these changed attitudes. In their hearts they all praised God that their king had become so merciful.

Shri Bahat watched all these developments with interest. Of course, he was not surprised because he knew that it was the holy soul of his guest, the saint, who was acting in the king's body. Shri Bahat loved his country and his countrymen. He felt happy and satisfied when he saw the king change from a cruel to a compassionate man. He also saw a change from a vengeful style of rulership to one of forgiveness, and from an attitude of bigotry to one of tolerance. One evening, while sitting at home, Shri Bahat suddenly was filled with a strong desire. He thought to himself, "Why can't we have a good and just king like this forever?" He then pondered his question. He knew that in a few days the soul of the generous saint would have to leave the shell-like container of the old king in order to reenter its own body. He feared for the day when the kingdom would be plunged back into the abyss of relogous bigotry, cruelty, vengefulness, and unending tyranny.

Shri Bahat was becoming upset at these thoughts. Suddenly he got up, went into the room where the saint's body was lying and approached it. It looked as it was in some kind of sleeping trance. He paused in a fit of madness; he lifted that body in his arms. He carried it out, laid it on the cremation ground, and burnt it. With this act Shri Bahat closed the doors forever on the saint's soul. It could no longer leave the king's body and return to its old home. From then onward the saint's soul remained trapped in Zain-ul-Abedin's body. It stayed there until the end of the latter's natural life. This was the reason that he was able to rule for so many years as a just, honest, and tolerant king. Indeed, he enacted so many good deeds that the people eventually renamed him great King or Badsah.

· 78 ·   *The Foolish Gujjar*
          (Kashmir)

The Gujjars are a nomadic hill tribe whose religion is Islam. They are the targets of a whole series of humorous stories in which they are depicted as being more brawny than brainy. While this tale is a part of that series, it is unusual. Here the Gujjar is not as foolish as he might at first seem. Perhaps the story primarily serves as a commentary on the depth of many of their Islamic practices. It is paralleled by many folk stories which make similar fun of conventional Hindu religious behavior. In one Assammese tale, for example, a devotee is described as calling out to the goddess to catch and sacrifice the required pigeon offering herself. In another a humble propitiator is seen to gratefully offer up a louse!

ONCE A GUJJAR climbed a tree to cut firewood. He went on climbing and cutting off the branches which supported his climb, until he reached the top of the tree. Now he was very happy, as he had cut off enough firewood for the day's needs. So he thought of climbing down. To his great surprise, however, he soon discovered his stupidity. Having cut off all the lower branches, how would he come down? The Gujjar regretted his foolishness and cried for help. But nobody could hear his voice in the deep woods. Having failed to rescue himself, he finally turned to Allah. He began praying and promising gifts. He raised his head towards the heavens and prayed, "Allah! I will give you buffalo, goats, chickens, and eggs, indeed everything I have, if you will help me climb down from this tree safely." During this prayer, the Gujjar had slipped a little. He was no longer on the tree top. On discovering that his plea had been accepted and that he had begun the safe climb down, the Gujjar was quite happy. He now prayed again, with even more strength and conviction. "Allah! I will give you a buffalo if you help me climb down from this tree safely." After a while, the Gujjar discovered that he had slipped down a little more. Now he was almost halfway. So he raised his head again and prayed, "Allah! I will give you a goat if you help me climb down from this tree safely."

By now the Gujjar knew that he could slide down safely. After covering a little more footage, he again prayed, this time without raising his head, "Allah! I will give you a chicken if you help me climb down from this tree safely." Still further down he ended his prayer with reference to an egg, "Allah! I will give you an egg if you help me climb down from this tree safely." Now the Gujjar had safely climbed down from the tree. He was standing on solid ground, safe and sound. So he looked the tree over, from top to bottom, and with a feeling of victory, he said his final prayer, "Allah! Tell me what should I give you now? I climbed up the tree myself and came down myself. So why should I give you anything at all?" Saying this the Gujjar collected the firewood that had caused his problem, and with a self-assured smile, he left for home.

· 79 · *Our Wife*
(Andhra Pradesh)

This is one of a number of Telugu tales collectively called "The Stories of Paramanandayya." They narrate the events in the life of a wise teacher and his foolish students. It can be understood as a dig at polite, sophisticated conduct generally.

PARAMANANDAYYA was sitting on the front porch of his house one day when his disciples came to say, "Teacher, your cows are coming home." The teacher then gave his students a lesson in proper speaking. He told them that it was inappropriate to say "your cows" because a teacher and his students belong to one large family. Therefore, it was explained, a respectful student should say "our cows." The disciples learned their lesson well and left for the day. The next morning the same students saw their teacher's wife coming from the well carrying a pot of water on her head. So the disciples ran to the teacher and said, "Teacher, our wife is coming."

· 80 ·   *I'll Take Two*
          (Andhra Pradesh)

In every region of India there are popular "bilingual" jokes and stories that cleverly play on meanings of words in several languages. Most of these stories have a modern tone and utilize English as the source of language humor (see, for example, tale 60). This same form of joke, however, can be traced far back into Indian history, to a time when Sanskrit had a prestigious position similar to that which English enjoys today. The *Kathasaritsagar,* a literary work of the eleventh century, draws heavily on oral tales. In it the following account is recorded: King Satavahana, who was not as learned in Sanskrit as his wife, one day sported with her in the water. Soon his wife cried out, *"Rajan, mamodakai stadaya!"* which means, "Oh, king, don't pelt me with water." But he thought she was asking for *modaka,* meaning sweets. So he had some brought for her immediately. She then laughed at his mistake and teased him for bringing her sweets while she stood in the water.

A TELUGU TEACHER, an English teacher, a history teacher, and a mathematics teacher went to a restaurant. The Telugu teacher was the only one among them who didn't know any English. But he pretended to know something about it anyway, for fear of showing his ignorance. After they had sat around a table, the English teacher yelled to the server, "Table clean!" [an expression used in Indian restaurants to mean "clean the table"]. When the server came up to them, the Telugu teacher thought that the English teacher had ordered a special dish. He then said in Telugu, "I'll take two of them."

· 81 · *Dropping, Rolling, Tail-Peeler (Karala)*

A number of folk stories all over India revolve around a misunderstanding of something said. The next several tales give a small sample of the kinds of linguistic humor involved. In this first and delightfully picturesque Malayali tale, the foolishness of animals is revealed through their limited knowledge of language. This particular tale has at least twenty-seven variants and has been reported from every corner of the subcontinent under number 177 in the Aarne-Thompson type index.

ONCE THERE WAS an old woman who lived all alone in a big old house. This house sat on a lonely spot, near the edge of a forest. As a result, the woman never came out and the house was now falling apart for lack of care. Its roof had caved in and the courtyard was full of weeds and bushes. Over time it had become the home of wild animals, especially of lions and tigers. Late one evening the old lady was sitting in her room. The sky was full of clouds. There was thunder and lightning. A storm was coming. As she looked up she could see the sky through what was left of the roof. Soon she said to herself, "I am afraid of nothing in the world—not leopards nor tigers—except one thing; *uttal* [rain coming in through the roof]." The reason she said this, of course, was that once rain came into her room and flooded it she would have no place else to retreat to.

Now a leopard was sitting in the other room and overheard the old woman's words. He became frightened, so he said, "There is no one in this world who is not afraid of tiger and me. And she is afraid only of uttal! Who is this uttal? If this uttal comes, what will be my plight?" With this on his mind the leopard fell asleep. As he dozed, a horseman came in search of his horse. In the semidarkness he mistook the leopard for his horse and jumped on its back. He was very angry at having lost his steed, and in his rage he pricked the leopard's ears. The leopard, thinking that it was uttal that had come, started up in fright. It then raced out into the forest at full speed.

After a short time the rider realized that the animal he was on was not his own horse, but a leopard. He was overcome with fright. So, as the leopard raced through the forest, the man sought some means of escape. Finally he saw a low branch of a tree overhanging the path and clutched onto it and hung there as the leopard ran past. Then the leopard shouted to his forest friends, "Save yourselves! Run! Uttal is coming."

Soon all the forest animals were running for their lives. First the leopard came upon a fox and shouted, "Run, fox. If you want to save your life, run!" Now the fox wanted to find out what was going on, so he calmed the leopard and asked what was actually happening. The leopard explained, "I just overheard an old woman say from the next room that she is not afraid of anything in the world—not even me—except uttal. I was half asleep there, when uttal fell upon me and started pulling my ears. I ran as fast as I could, but uttal clung to my back the whole way. Finally uttal jumped off me and onto a tree and is now clining to a branch. I ran to save my life!" Hearing this, the fox had a strong desire to see the uttal. But the leopard didn't want to go back and argued against this plan. Finally, however, the fox convinced the leopard to show him the tree.

All this time, the horseman was still hanging onto a forest limb. He was unable to climb into the tree and too scared to drop down and make his way through the jungle. Soon he saw the fox and the leopard coming toward him. He feared his end was near and believed that the leopard was coming to attack him. Indeed, he trembled so much that he lost his grip on the branch and fell. When the horseman hit the ground, he rolled pell-mell down the slope of the hillock on which the tree stood. At the bottom of it he fell into a depression at the base of another large tree. By now it was quite dark and the leopard and the fox could not make out what had happened. All they knew was that something had fallen with a loud thud, rolled rapidly down the slope, and jumped into a dark hole. They could hardly contain their fright, and they quickly sped away from the place. "Run, Uncle Leopard. It is not an uttal, but an *urulicha* [a rolling]." As they ran through the forest, they called to the other animals, "Run, friends, if you wish to save your life, run! Urulicha is coming! Run for your life!"

Without any doubt about the gravity of their situation, all the animals of the forest started running as if their lives depended on it. As they ran, the leopard and the fox saw a monkey. "Run for your life, monkey. Urulicha is coming! Run!" they said. Soon the monkey stopped his friends to try to find out what exactly had happened. The leopard once again narrated the story. "While I was lying in the next room I overheard an old woman say she was not afraid of anything in the world—not even me—except uttal. Then, as I slept, uttal fell upon me and began pulling my ears. I ran away but it clung to my back. As I ran under a branch the uttal grasped a limb and hung there. When fox and I went back to see, we realized it was not uttal, but urulicha," the leopard explained.

Hearing this, the monkey also wanted to see. He soon persuaded the fox and the leopard to accompany him to the spot. Off they went, the monkey in front, then the fox and the leopard, all trembling with fear. Meanwhile, the horseman was still struggling to get out of the deep hole. He groped around in the dark for something by which to pull himself up with. Several times he climbed and jumped in an effort to reach the edge. But try as he would he couldn't get out. Finally, tired, the horseman rested.

Just then, the animals approached. The fox pointed to the spot and said to the monkey, "It is yonder, in that hole." The three crept up and looked in. But it was too dark to see anything. The monkey was disappointed. The other two animals wanted to leave, but he wanted to stay. Finally, fox told the monkey about a trick he knew. "When I want to catch a crab, I slowly put my tail into the crab's hole. When it grabs onto it, I slowly pull my tail out. Then I catch hold of it and eat it. Now my tail is too short to reach down into this deep hole, but yours is long enough. Put your tail into the hole. If an urilicha is still there, it will certainly catch hold of it."

The monkey liked this plan and was anxious to see what was in the hole. By this time the horseman had again begun groping for something to pull himself out with. His hand now felt what he thought to be a vine. So he grabbed at it and started to pull himself out. But the monkey, on whose tail the entire weight of the horseman now hung, screamed out in pain. "Uncle Leopard, Uncle Fox! Save me! I am being pulled down!" Leopard and fox rushed to the monkey's aid and kept him from falling into the pit. With the horseman on one end and the leopard and the fox

on the other, both sides pulled with all their strength. The poor
Monkey suffered unbearable pain. But at last, the monkey's body
was pulled up onto level ground by his friends. He then leapt up,
howled, and ran through the jungle shouting, "Not uttal, not
urulicha, but *valuri* [tail-peeler]. Run for your lives!" Stripped of
its skin, the monkey's tail bled and bled as he ran. The leopard
and the fox ran, too, shouting, "Run, run for your lives! Valuri is
coming! Run." And all of the animals in the forest started to run.

Meanwhile, the horseman remained in the hole, the bloody
skin of the monkey's tail still in his hands. Finally, the next
morning, he was able to climb out. But by then, there wasn't a
single animal in that part of the forest. The horseman walked
back to the village, weary and bewildered.

· 82 · *Panikar's Blunder*
        (Karala)

This tale makes fun of its main character, who is an astrologer
by profession, and his gross physical incompetence in practical
matters, particularly agricultural ones. The story resembles a
whole genre that make fun of Brahmans such as "The Rupee
Note" (tale 59) and "The Brahman's Lime" (tale 61). It is
reminiscent of tale type 1250, where a man falls out of a tree
because he lets go of a branch to clap his hands for a friend's
song, (motifs J2133.5.3 and J2133.13). Three tales of the
latter type have been reported in North India. This is the first
known southern variant to be published in English.

LONG AGO, in central Kerala, there lived a Panikar who was more
interested in growing fruit trees than in pursuing his own traditional occupation as an astrologer. This Panikar was very proud of
his plantain grove, and he used to walk around in it with great
pleasure. But one day, he noticed that almost all of the bananas
on one tree had been eaten or destroyed. The Panikar was very
annoyed and wanted to find out who was responsible for this
mischief. Walking a little further, he saw a squirrel eating a
banana in the next tree. Now the Panikar was seized with anger,

and he pounced at the squirrel hoping to kill it. But as this animal heard the sound of the Panikar coming, he jumped nimbly to the next tree and then to the next. The Panikar was so furious that he ran after the squirrel like a mad man.

Soon the Panikar saw the squirrel climbing a coconut tree so he also began to climb the same tree. But when the Panikar reached the top branches the squirrel jumped again. Of course the Panikar could not jump so nimbly from tree to tree. Instead the weight of his body made the branches bend down and the Panikar was left helplessly hanging onto a branch of leaves. Not knowing what else to do, he now cried out to his wife for help. The wife reached the plantain garden almost immediately and was quite taken aback by the peculiar scene. The Panikar asked her for a stack of hay so that he could jump down safely. His wife inquired as to how much was needed. So he let go of the bunch of leaves in order to show his wife what quantity he had in mind. No sooner had the Panikar relaxed his grip on the branches, however, than he fell to the ground.

· 83 ·   *The Fox and the Crow*

This tale, known virtually throughout the world, needs no comment other than to say it is very popular in India as well. Its message and imagery are simple and universal. Known as an Aesop fable, it is possible that this account reached India via English school textbooks.

THERE ONCE WAS a crow who had brought a piece of meat from somewhere and was sitting in a tree. By chance a fox passed under him. Seeing the crow, he said, "I have heard that you sing very sweetly, Crow. Please sing a song for me so that I can enjoy your voice."

Hearing this pleased the crow greatly and he immediately began to cry "caw, caw." As soon as he opened his bill, however, the piece of meat dropped from his mouth and the fox gobbled it up.

· 84 ·   *The Greatest Fool of All*
   (West Bengal)

One of the most popular of Indian numskull stories involves a
contest between several fools. At least eleven versions of this tale
type (no. 1332) have been previously published in English,
including one taken from the famous *Panchatantra* collection.
The frame for all these contests is the same: a passerby greets a
group of four men as they walk down a road. The four then begin
to argue over who received this special honor. When asked, the
stranger claims his respects were meant for the greatest fool. Thus
the contest starts, each man trying to tell a story about himself
that makes him appear more foolish than the next. Here, the
resemblance between versions ends. The actual incidents the four
men describe vary from tale to tale. The ones reported in this
Bengali version appear to be novel among accounts thus far
noted. Most mention the role of a wife in at least one incident,
however, and proceed to describe at least one marital scene in
slightly raucous tones. Parallels among endings are also interesting. Some versions leave the four arguing or suggest that where
stupidity is concerned no one is the winner. In the present
account the first man to speak is selected as victor, though no
reason is given. When asked, the collector explained that the first
man suffers the greatest physical hardship of the four, namely
hunger.

ONCE FOUR MEN were walking together along a village road.
Soon a fifth person approached them from the opposite direction.
This last man saluted the small group as he passed by. After the
four men had advanced a few paces, however, they then began to
quarrel among themselves. Each claimed that the passerby had
saluted him alone and not the other three. Finding no solution to
their argument, the four men resolved to call the passerby back
and ask him who he had intended to greet. The man replied to
their question by saying he had not saluted any of the four. After
some cajoling, however, the stranger agreed that he must have
saluted the greatest fool among them. On hearing this the men
started quareling again, each claiming to be the fool in question.
The first man in the group said, "I am the greatest fool for the

following reason. Once my father sent me to my maternal uncle's home with a *ghati* [a container with a narrow opening]. He asked me to bring back some clarified butter. On the way, however, I became very hungry. I therefore purchased one anna's worth of parched rice from a person in a village along the way. I put that rice in my pot, but soon I wanted to eat it. When I put my hand into the pot, I had to clench my fist to grasp the grains. But when I clenched my fist I was unable to get my hand out. For this reason I suffered from hunger all the way to my uncle's home. I want to know if anyone could be a greater fool than that. It must have been me, therefore, that you saluted."

The second man then said, "No. I am the greatest fool. Let me explain. One day, my wife requested that I call the washerman and ask him to take our dirty clothes. But instead of calling him to my home I carried the clothes to his place on my own head and threw them in his courtyard. This makes me the biggest fool of all. I must have been the one saluted."

The third man then said, "No, I am the greatest fool. One day I went to bed and had my two wives lying on either side of me. I had one wife hold each hand. But at that very moment an ant started to bite me in the eye. I could not use either hand to drive away the ant, however, for fear that one wife or the other would become angry. I, therefore, must be the fool the person saluted."

The fourth man then said, "No, I must be the greatest fool. One day I called my wife and asked her to bring some tobacco to me in the sitting room. But she refused saying that the water on the floor of the courtyard might wash off a special lac dye she was wearing on her feet. So I had my wife hold the tobacco in her hand and I then carried her on my shoulders across the courtyard. This makes me the greatest fool of all."

The question of the story is who was the greatest fool? The answer: the first man who spoke.

· 85 ·   *A Jackal and a Fox*
(Uttar Pradesh)

Stories of tricksters are frequently linked to the animal world,
where both the jackal and the fox appear in manipulative roles.
In this tale we have an unusual duel of wits between them. It is
not exactly clear, however, what the fox had in mind when
suggesting to the lion that they be tied together. As can happen
with folktales, this one seems to have lost some key element of
its logic structure during transmission. The basic theme, however, seems to be that of tale type 1149, where a larger,
stronger being is frightened away by the children's supposed
desire for its flesh.

ONE TIME, there lived a jackal and a fox. But soon the jackal
forcibly took possession of the house of the fox and sent her away.
On being turned out, the fox went to the lion saying, "Oh, you
who are the greatest of us all. Oh, you who listens to any who
wish to speak to you. Please be kind enough to listen." So the
lion said, "What do you wish to say?" The fox complained, "My
house has been forcibly taken over by a jackal who has turned me
out." The lion answered, "OK, wait a little. Tomorrow I will
decide what to do."

The next day the fox again approached the lion and asked that
he decide her case. The lion now agreed to go to the house of the
jackal. But the fox argued that they could not go as they were.
Instead she asked that the lion tie her up with a rope and then tie
that around his own waist. The lion did as he was told. Somehow
the jackal came to know about these events. He then said to his
wife, "You must make the children weep bitterly. Afterwards, I
will ask you, 'Why are our children weeping?' Then you should
say, 'The unfresh flesh of the lion is already spoiling. The children want fresh lion flesh.'"

Soon the lion and the fox approached. The jackal gave the sign
to his wife and she caused her children to weep bitterly. As the
lion came near, the jackal next asked his wife, "Why are the
children crying?" The wife replied, "Don't you know why? We
only have spoiled lion flesh, but they want fresh flesh. Where am
I to find some?" To this the jackal responded, "I made the fox,

your *mausi* [mother's sister], agree to bring a lion here. She said she would bring the beast even if she had to have herself tied to it. See, now the two are approaching." On hearing this conversation, the lion flew into a rage. He said to the fox, "Oh, wretched animal, you have deceived me!" Then he sprang high into the air and took off, dragging the fox behind him. The fox cried out as she was pulled along, "Oh! People who tell on others are pulled and dragged like me." She received so many injuries that she was soon half-dead. This is how the cunning jackal was saved.

· 86 ·   *A Jackal and a Crocodile (Uttar Pradesh)*

This story is about a jackal who dupes a crocodile into ferrying him across a river. It has been reported from many different parts of India and always shows the crocodile to be stupid. In most variants, the jackal is a trickster who falsely promises to marry the crocodile at some later date, or as is the case in this version, he serves as a false matchmaker, procuring the skeleton of a buffalo instead of a true woman. In a different *Panchatantra* version, the trickster of the story is a monkey. There the two are both males and good friends. Furthermore, in that rather unusual account, the central river-dwelling figure is manipulated and scolded by a collaborating crocodile wife. In a tribal variant from Orissa, furthermore, a man plays the role of trickster and the story serves to explain the origin of crocodile eating. In one other account, the jackal is male and the crocodile female. In that version, the jackal promises marriage, but the crocodile responds by trying to eat him. Later it cleverly escapes. The general tale type is identifiable as no. 58, and nine versions have been previously indexed under this heading. However, this story also exhibits some similarity with tale types 5 and 66 A and B. All in all, like the previous tale, this one involves a small and clever trickster and a larger but more gullible one. Their relationship always becomes troubled by events that concern food, eating, marriage, sex, defecation, and/or death. In each case the desires of the crocodile get subtly manipulated along these dimensions, to the ultimate advantage of the smaller figure.

THERE ONCE LIVED a jackal who was very fond of a certain kind of ripe plum that could be found in the forest. But then these plums became very scarce. The jackal began looking for other foods, and he noticed a farmer's fields on the other side of a small river. The farmer had sown melon and cucumber seeds, and these were just beginning to ripen on the vines. So the jackal began to scheme about how he might cross the river in order to taste this delicious harvest.

Now it happened that a crocodile lived in this river, and so the jackal went to him and asked very sweetly, "Oh! mother's brother. If you agree to take me across the river, I will find you a wife." The crocodile agreed to the jackal's proposal and said, "All right, please jump on my back." So the jackal jumped on the crocodile's back and he soon found himself on the other side of the river. Reaching the opposite bank, the two went together into the farmer's field. The jackal took a huge melon and tore it into small pieces. In this way he soon quenched both his hunger and his thirst. But one melon was not nearly enough to satisfy the crocodile. When the jackal had finished eating, it said to the crocodile, "Oh, mother's brother! Now I feel an urge to howl." The crocodile begged the jackal to wait to make this noise until he had also finished eating. But the jackal replied, "I cannot keep myself from howling any longer."

The farmer who owned the field heard the racket in his garden. Grabbing his scarf, he ran to the garden to chase the animals away. He first attacked the crocodile; meanwhile the jackal ran off very quickly. The farmer was upset and said, "Oh! That jackal has escaped! But I vow that I will punish him another way." While the farmer spoke to himself thus, the crocodile slipped back into the river. Later the jackal returned to the riverbank and called to the crocodile again. "Oh, mother's brother! I am about to bring you a wife." In fact, the jackal had robbed a young girl of her head scarf. He had also brought with him the skeleton of a dead buffalo. He covered those bones with the scarf and now he laid these out neatly on the bank of the river. After doing this he approached the crocodile and said, "Oh, mother's brother! I have brought you a wife. She is there on the river bank. But she is very shy and will not come over here by herself. You must go and fetch her. But please, please, take me back across the river first." The crocodile agreed and took the jackal back across the water. He then swam to the bank to fetch his wife. The crocodile first called out, "Please come here lovely lady! There is nothing to be ashamed of." But she did not respond and he thus approached a bit closer. Again he called out and asked her to come. But of course the dead body of the bullock could not speak. At last the crocodile became very angry, and imagining that the body was alive, he kicked it very hard. In fact he kicked so hard that he hurt his own leg. Then, discovering his error, the crocodile said to himself, "OK, Mr. Jackal! I will repay you for this someday!"

It was the jackal's habit to come and drink water from the river at the roots of a particular banyan tree. One day, while he was drinking, the angry crocodile approached and grabbed his leg. Knowing that he was caught, the jackal quickly thought of a trick. He said to the crocodile, "Oh! Look! I am standing here while you, you foolish one, are holding onto the root of a banyan tree with your mouth." Believing the jackal, the crocodile let go with its mouth and instead grabbed the root of the tree. The jackal immediately ran off saying, "Just see if you can catch me now. You are a fool to hold onto the root of a tree rather than my leg." The crocodile was very ashamed and again thought to himself, "All right! I will see to it that you are punished one day!"

Sometime later, the crocodile pretended to be dead and lay motionless in the sand. By this time he had acquired a wife, and she now began to weep. When the jackal passed by he asked the woman, "Why are you weeping, oh, my mother's brother's wife?" The woman replied, "Oh, my! Your dear mother's brother has just died!" So the jackal approached the body and sniffed it carefully. He soon came to realize that the crocodile was only pretending to be dead. So he thought of another trick. The jackal now turned and said to his mother's brother's wife, "It is usual for a person to fart at the time of his death. Has my mother's brother done this yet?" To this the woman replied, "No, not yet." Just then the crocodile somehow managed to fart. Then the jackal ran off saying, "Oh, body lying in the sand! No one can rival you! Is it possible that anyone else who was dead could fart?"

At this the crocodile felt very ashamed. Meanwhile the jackal ran off into the forest and escaped.

· 87 · *Chamdan and Yuthung (Manipur)*

The heroes of tales told by the peoples of Manipur are often mischievous. Chamdan and Yuthung are true to form. The villagers of this area delight in seeing a youthful prankster cunningly entrap others through their words and deeds. While not exactly innocent, such Manipuri heroes are rarely guilty of true wrongdoing. Revenge and social justice often provide an unstated background for their actions. Even with this in mind, it is clear that the bravado of a young man provides part of this heroic image, too.

CHAMDAN AND YUTHUNG lived in a certain village. Both of them were known far and wide for their mischievous activities. One day, an old woman of the village told them, "Dear Chamdan and Yuthung, I am very old and weak. There is nobody to help me. Both of you are strong and in good health. There is no place where I can feed my pigs. Will you please make me a big wooden trough?" The two men agreed to build a trough for the old woman. In exchange they were fed with whatever meat and liquor the old woman had.

After eating and drinking what the old woman had offered them, Chamdan and Yuthung went to the riverbank to make the wooden trough. On the bank of the river they found many crabs among the stones. They soon started catching crabs and ate them one by one. After eating the flesh, the men collected all the hard shells in one place. But they were so busy eating that they forgot about making the wooden trough for the old woman. When they finally returned home they brought all the hard shells with them. They put these in a corridor of the old woman's house. The old woman was happy to see the two men and asked if they had prepared a trough for her. They answered that they had and showed her the hard crab shells. The old woman kept silent, not knowing what else to do.

Sometime later, beside a stream near the village, a local priest was seen sacrificing pigs and fowls for the welfare of some villagers. Chamdan and Yuthung now decided to play a trick on him and eat what had been prepared for the propitiation. Chamdan said, "I shall play the part of the deity that inhabits the upper reaches of the stream. You play the part of the deity inhabiting the lower portion. In order to look like deities, let us dip ourselves in sugarcane juice and then roll in cotton. When I call you from upstream, you must reply, and when you call from the lower stream I will reply." Having completed the preparations, the two men arrived at the riverbank. One went upstream and the other went downstream. Soon the priest had completed his sacrifice and cooked everything he planned to offer to the deity. After all the preparations were finished he chanted the name of the village deity. As this was being done, both Chamdan and Yuthung appeared in their new guise and ate up all the offerings. The priest was dumbfounded and the villagers who saw the event were awestruck.

In this way, both men continued their mischief in the village. One day, they decided to steal the peppers in the garden of a villager. One of them walked on all fours like a bull and the other rode on top of him. They both agreed that the one walking like a bull should not pluck even a single pepper with his hand and the one riding on the other should not put his feet on the ground. Thus the two entered the garden and took all of the peppers available. The master of the garden was very angry, feeling sure that this was the work of Chamdan and Yuthung. He soon complained to the village *thourei*.[1] The thourei summoned both of them and said, "Look here, Chamdan and Yuthung, this man says that both of you stole peppers from his garden. So, both of you are to be fined for taking the property of others." But Chamdan answered, "No, sir, I never stole any peppers. If these hands of mine ever plucked a single one of his peppers, let them be cursed and let all ten fingers fall away." Yuthung answered, "I also plead innocent, sir. I did not steal any peppers either. If ever my feet took part in stealing his peppers, let the ten toes of my feet fall off." In this way, both men escaped punishment.

One day the two men also stole a pumpkin from one house and a chicken from another. They cooked the pumpkin with the chicken using an earthen pot found by the bank of the village stream. Before the cooking was over, both men started tasting the broth by taking some from the pot. But a hole suddenly appeared at the bottom of this earthen vessel. All of the broth leaked out and then each angrily blamed the other for taking it. The two came to blows. From that day onwards the men parted company, and the village finally had some peace.

· 88 · The Sparrow and the Sweet Pudding (Tamilnadu)

In a previous story, the little ant was a clever helper, but in this next tale the small guy is a genuine trickster. Here a tiny sparrow not only causes others to suffer undeservedly, but experiences rather exaggerated and peculiar difficulties himself.

While one may appreciate this tale as a simple, straightforward sequence of ludicrous events, another possible interpretation takes into account Hindu notions of purity and pollution. The tale starts off with a sweet food, moves onto water and a swollen stomach, and ends with an emphasis on defecation. Hence it becomes progressively more impure and improper. By contrast, the sparrow's choice of subjects to tease or embarrass gradually gains in ritual status. First there is a woodcutter, then a merchant selling cooking vessels, next a man selling brown sugar, and finally a cow that apparently yields milk. Each of these has a progressively greater importance to the basic human nutritive process, the last being a sacred animal and source of the purest food of all. These opposite lines of development meet at the climax of the tale when the cow eats from the trickster's anus, causing a flood. This incongruity can be further interpreted to symbolize the general destruction of human order and thus a return to some kind of precivilized condition. In the resulting flood, foods, cooking processes, and eaters are merged. The trickster sits high on a tree, above all this, and laughs at what he has done to food rules. Signifi-

cantly, perhaps, this tale is often heard in Brahman homes but
is not popular with lower-status castes. In non-Brahman groups,
food restrictions are a far less salient issue.

THERE ONCE LIVED a grandmother who had a sparrow in her
backyard. One day, this sparrow was scraping around in a rub-
bish heap with his beak when he found a grain of rice. He took
this grain to the grandmother and asked her to store it safely. But
one day, this grain of rice got lost when she swept the house. The
very next morning, the sparrow came to the old woman and asked
for that grain. The grandmother explained what had happened.
The sparrow then demanded a whole handful of rice in compensation for losing his one grain. The woman agreed and gave the
sparrow a large handful.

Soon afterwards the same sparrow developed a great desire for a
sweet called *payasam*. So while he sat on a branch of a tree he
thought of a trick. When he saw a woodcutter carrying a bundle
of firewood on his head pass beneath the tree, he called out to him
saying, "Woodcutter! Don't you know that your mother has just
died in her house?" The woodcutter reacted with immediate
shock and grief. He threw the bundle of firewood on the ground
and ran home. Then the sparrow took the firewood for himself
and hid it safely. A little while later, a merchant who sold vessels
passed under the same tree. The sparrow now cried out to him
saying, "Vessel seller! Don't you know that your mother has just
died in her house?" The man reacted with great shock. He
dropped his vessels he was carrying and ran home crying, "My
mother, my mother!" The sparrow then selected a fine vessel
made of bell metal and set it aside for the making of payasam.
Next a man selling hardened brown sugar passed under the tree.
The sparrow again played the same trick and managed to obtain
brown sugar for his plans.

Having collected all the needed materials, the sparrow now
began to cook his feast. First he put his metal vessel on the earth-
en stove and began to mix up the payasam. But as it cooked, a
great desire came over him to taste it. When the sparrow stuck
his finger into the hot liquid and licked it, however, he burned
both his fingers and his tongue. He was so disappointed that he
quickly threw the hot vessel into a well. Then he waited, think-

ing it would eventually cool down. After awhile, the sparrow dived into the well and lifted the vessel out. A bit of payasam still stuck to the brim of the pot and he licked this thinking, "If this little morsel is so tasty, what would the whole lot of payasam have been like?"

The sparrow soon began to drink the well water and found that this was sweet too. So with great gusto he drank all of the water in the well. This caused his stomach to swell like a balloon. He then took some hay and inserted it into his anus. Outfitted in this way he went to the old woman and requested that she give him a place to sleep. However, the grandmother had no room in her house. So she offered the sparrow a place in the cowshed at the back. The sparrow thanked the grandmother and fell asleep in the shed. But the grandmother had forgotten to feed her cow. That night it became very hungry. Soon the cow looked around and noticed that the sleeping sparrow had some hay inserted in its anus. At once it pulled the hay out and began to chew on it. This released the water from the sparrow's stomach. It now ran out like a great river into the shed. The cow, the house, and finally the grandmother herself began to float in this flood. But the sparrow sighed with great relief. Then he flew to a nearby tree and watched the scene with amusement from its very highest branch.

Part VIII
Origin Tales

*O*UR final group of stories concerns origins. The Hindu view of time posits great cycles, both of death and of rebirth. It thus makes sense to conclude with tales about "beginnings." But there are many kinds of origin tales. We try to present a wide range of examples. The Indic tale indexes clearly indicate that stories about how specific things came to be are more popular with tribal populations than with peasant groups. Why this is so is not fully clear. But it does seem to be the case that India's caste communities, particularly those who are well-integrated into mainstream Hindu life, have more to say about human relationships and focus less on the physical environment. One can perhaps link this difference to otherworldly values in Hinduism more generally. But the material probably also reflects certain simple facts of life in more crowded, complex, institutionally regulated environments. In any event, only three of the eleven stories in this section have been collected in non-tribal settings. All of the latter (92, 93, and 99) come from persons of priestly background, and all utilize a clearly Hindu frame. The eight other stories do not exhibit mainstream attitudes so vividly, although tale 94, told by a Bhil group in Gujarat, does utilize some familiar Hindu imagery. These linkages seem to reflect the Bhil's own partly castelike, partly tribelike status.

This section has been subdivided into four tale clusters: (1) origins of man and of the environment, (2) origins of specific

sacred sites, (3) origins of particular social customs, and (4)
origins of specific actions or events. The first tale is from a Mao
Naga tribal area in Manipur. It describes how the three categories of active being (man, beast, and god) came to occupy
separate domains. This important story contains multiple images of human culture which help to contrast the Naga's present
life-style with that of an imagined prehuman period, their concept of the "original" human state. A second Naga tale follows.
It outlines the origin of the hilly tract called Nagaland. In this
short description one finds clear evidence of this group's sen-
sitivity to their own political and cultural subordination. There
is a metaphoric equivalence found in this account between local
social status and their own homeland: a rough-hewn, marginal,
geographic territory.

A third tale, collected in a remote area of Gujarat, provides a
contrastive example: it is an animal origin story (see also tale
36). Here we learn how the porcupine got its human cry, rather
like the classic just-so story "how the tiger got its stripes." But
one can also see several social functions being served by this
account. The story justifies communal claims to land and to
farming skills made by a particular social group, the Wagher.
And it also explains a distinctive custom whereby these contemporary farmers agree to let the porcupine graze freely in their
fields (for a parallel see tale 18).

The next group of tales consists of two examples. Both are
about temples; one was collected in West Bengal and one in
Gujarat (see also tales 21 and 44). In the first a cow recognizes a
lingam, the phallic symbol of Lord Siva, buried in the earth. It
then begins to exude milk on this sacred spot. This provides the
classic scenario for an account about the building of a temple.
Hundreds of similar examples are known to exist (see Shulman
1980). The second tale, from Gujarat, utilizes this same motif
in reverse. Here a false shrine is first set up with inglorious
motives. But when the founder later kicks the implanted stone
to "prove" its insignificance, the rock begins to "bleed" milk.
The spot is immediately declared sacred. Again, a temple is
built. These are two prime examples of Hindu shrine myths;
their emphasis on particular sacred spots makes for a meaningful

contrast with the more generalized and secular concerns of the
three tales placed in the preceding group.

The third tale cluster in this section is concerned with the
origin of human customs. Now the focus shifts back to tribal
areas. First in the sequence is an account collected among the
Bhils of Gujarat. It describes the origin of a popular alcoholic
beverage, manufactured exclusively by this group. That story
approaches, though it does not fully parallel, pan-Hindu story
themes (see tale 50). The two others that follow, by contrast,
outline typically tribal concerns. Both accounts were recorded in
the Naga area, and both focus on animal motifs. One explains
the origin of head-hunting in terms of a strategy used by ants.
The other deals with dogs, and recounts how these beasts became so useful to and so dependent on mankind. Here hunting
is the key theme. This is what traditional accounts of Naga life
would lead one to expect.

Finally, the reader will encounter a sequence of three stories
(tales 97, 98, and 99) which concern the nature of causality
itself. All three, furthermore, have a special subgenre form: they
are cumulative tales. In such accounts one quite ordinary event
begins a long sequence of surprising results. A complex chain of
actions unravels until some quite unforeseen outcome is reached.
In the first two stories, both collected in tribal areas, this chain
is reversed. Thus, at the end, the story's initial motif is regained. Such tales raise broad philosophical questions: how are
we to explain life experience? Why do animals or people do
what they do? In these first two tales, each outcome is traced to
a nonhuman source; one to the fruit of the *ow* tree, the other to
a hungry crab. But the third and final tale is different. It does
not depend on a similar set of reversals. Instead, this account
pushes forward inexorably, repeating all that has gone before
each time a new event appears. The topic differs too. Each actor
in the chain is thwarted. All that occurs is due to the death of
one mosquito. Even the beggar throws away his begging bowl
at the end. The images are all ones of destruction. The tale
eventually winds down to nothingness, and thereby captures a
central Hindu theme. This orthodox view of cosmic dissolution
appropriately concludes our tale collection.

The Origin of Man
    (Manipur)

Tale 91 concerns the origin of several human conventions popular in a specific area of Gujarat (caste rights to land, respect for
the porcupine). This tale, from the Mao Nagas of Manipur,
deals with the origins of the elements of all existence: God,
Beast, and Man. As in a Hindu myth about the marriage of Siva
(tale 20) discussed earlier, this tribal parallel also posits the
birth of three sons from a cosmic pregnancy involving a great
mother. Like the Hindu goddess Sakti, this woman also lives on
a high mountain peak. In contrast to many Hindu origin
myths, however, the present one does not dwell on the issue of
asexual or incestuous reproduction. Instead, this tribal myth
concentrates on the death of the world's great cosmic mother
and on how her three sons decide to divide their inheritance
when her unifying influence has faded. The universal quality of
this myth springs from its focus on the development of logical
categories and how things came to be gradually separated after
an initial period of unity.

It is significant that the metaphor for cosmic evolution used
in this Naga tale is one about the division of inheritance among
brothers. This gives the whole set of cosmic developments described an attractive familial form. It is also interesting to note
that Man is said to be the youngest of the three brothers. He
also has the closest bond, of the three brothers, with his dying
mother. This reflects a common South Asian concern with the
close bond between a mother and her youngest son. The mother's grave, furthermore, is poignantly linked to the origin of a
human fireplace and of cooked human food. The fact that the
elder sons, God and Animal, never find their mother's burial
site suggests their basic ignorance of fire, cooking, and kinship.

The race that is depicted at the end of this myth provides a
neat device for explaining how the world came to be physically
divided between the three brothers. Man ultimately wins the
right to the valleys and hence (by implication) to agricultural
activities. Furthermore, Man wins this rich patrimony through
his use of a hunting tool and his general cleverness. The Animal
(tiger) who excels in physical prowess, wins the right to roam in

the forest though he is given certain other limitations (an immobile neck). God, however, is assigned the deepest mountain
ravines. This implies that He resides only in the darkest places,
and He takes care that man does not see Him there. This cosmic
separation of man and god, of course, provides a key step in the
general evolution from a state of oneness toward a true human
state of culture. The separation of Man and Animal is also at
issue, and this soon becomes linked to various symbols of eating
and of being eaten. The mention of man's need for sleep is also
significant. If the manipulation of eyesight helps separate Man
and God, so does the manipulation of sound help to separate
Man from Animal. Music and powerful ritual noises, too, find
their place in man's cultural world at this point. Finally, certain
striking geographic features of the area serve as markers of these
final separation events.

LONG AGO there was a great woman named Jilly Mosiro. She
lived on a flat and windy peak of a high mountain. One day, a
patch of clouds moving from south to north passed across her and
she became pregnant. After a time she gave birth to three sons,
Ora, who was a god, Okhe who was a tiger, and Aliyu who was a
man. Jilly Mosiro took great care in bringing up her sons. In the
course of time they all became full-grown. Then the mother realized that she loved her youngest son, Aliyu, more than either of
the other two.

After some years Jilly Mosiro became old and weak. Her three
sons now began to discuss among themselves how they could care
for their aged mother. They decided to keep her in the house, and
each one would look after her in turn. But one day when the
mother was under the care of the eldest son, Ora, she began to
feel uneasy. Indeed, she developed a high fever. The next day, she
was under the care of her second son, Okhe, and her fever and
nervousness continued. But when her youngest son Aliyu came to
care for her, she became happy. Aliyu treated his mother with
great care and the mother wished that she would die while she
was under his protection. Aliyu also wished that his mother
would die while under his care. To accomplish this wish Aliyu
thought of a means to quicken his mother's death by using some
poisoned peppers. He boiled a handful of these peppers in water

and asked his mother to drink the liquid which he had prepared
for her. Surprisingly, however, the mother regained her health
after taking this drink, rather than dying as had been expected.

The mother then asked for more and more of the pepper liquid. Though she improved, she never did manage to regain her
health entirely. Then a second time she felt she was nearing
death. Now she began to think ahead, asking her son, Aliyu, to
bury her body quickly in such an event and to keep the chosen
place a secret. She also asked Aliyu to convert her grave into a
fireplace that would be used for cooking food. One fine and auspicious day, Jilly Mosiro finally died in the arms of her son Aliyu.
Man immediately buried his mother's body as she had instructed
him to do. When this was finished, he dug a number of other
places near his house which would also look like burial sites.
When the second son, Okhe or tiger, returned and could not find
his mother, he started looking for the dead body. He was very
anxious to locate her grave. The eldest brother, Ora or God, consoled him and advised him not to worry. Still the middle son
continued his search. Ultimately the eldest brother reached out
and touched his second brother with his hand. From that day
onwards, the second brother, Okhe the tiger, was unable to move
his neck sideways or backwards. From then on, furthermore, the
tiger's neck has had only a single bone. If a tiger wants to look in
any direction except in front of himself, he has to turn his whole
body around.

Tiger finally stopped his search for the body of his mother.
Now all three sons shared the sorrow of their mother's death.
After she was gone, they also realized it would no longer be possible to live together. So they began to discuss where each of them
would go. All three wanted to live in the finest place, considered
to be the valley. They failed to reach agreement on this and hence
decided that they would have a race. The one to win would stay.
A tuft of grass was then tied at the end of a pole and this was
erected at a place called Chabulophi. It was to mark an end point
for the race. The brother who could touch the tuft of grass at the
end of the pole first would be the victor. God, the eldest, and
Man, the youngest, were both disappointed to find Okhe, the
middle brother, winning this race. They then proposed a rematch
and the middle brother agreed. But God secretly wanted his

younger brother to win the race, as he himself did not wish for
victory. So God covertly advised his younger brother to hide. He
then told him to shoot an arrow at the grass at the top of the pole.
Man did as his elder brother advised him. During the race, his
implement reached the goal first, and as a result he won. The
prize was the right to live in the valley, the best land in the
world. Okhe, the tiger brother, was now given the forest. He was
to live there and roam about as he wished. The eldest, God, was
to remain in the deepest and steepest ravines of the mountains.

From the beginning, the eldest brother, God, did not like to
confront his youngest brother, Man, face to face. He did not like
any person to physically see him. So before he left for his abode in
the ravines, God decided to test the sharpness of Man's observa-
tional skills. Thus God stood at a distance and then asked his
youngest brother if he could see him. Man said that he could.
God exchanged the eyes of his youngest brother with those of a
dog. Consequently, men can no longer see in the dark but dogs
can. Man also became unable to see God directly. It is said that if
men could see God there would be frequent fights between them.
This is because God often uses devils to attack and kill men.

The middle brother, the tiger, also did not have much feeling
for his younger brother, Man. Indeed, he simply wanted to devour him. The youngest brother knew this and was afraid that he
would be eaten one night while he slept. In order to deceive his
middle brother, Man told him that he would sleep on the floor.
He then prepared a big wooden tray and filled it with water. He
made it look like a bed and covered this tray with a piece of cloth.
When Tiger returned, he saw the bed and believed it was his
youngest brother's bed. Tiger pulled off the cloth and pounced on
the tray. But Man was actually sleeping elsewhere. When he saw
how wet his elder brother was, he asked what he was doing in the
tray of water. Tiger answered that he had simply been playing.
After this Man felt very uncomfortable about staying with Okhe
and tried to find a means to get rid of him. He thus asked Tiger
what was the one thing in the world he dreaded most. At first
Tiger would not answer. But ultimately he admitted that he was
afraid of the sound "crack, crack." Man knew that this was the
sound of a big drum and horn. He thus decided to drive his
brother away by using these special musical instruments.

One day Man was making a mat. Okhe the tiger asked to join him but soon fell asleep, using the mat to cover himself. When Tiger was deep in sleep Man then tied the mat around his brother firmly. He also attached a pitcher to Tiger's tail. He then found a hollow piece of bamboo and made a harsh sound by blowing it. Tiger woke up with a start and ran off with the pitcher still tied on his tail. As he ran, the things that had been tied to him gradually dropped off. These became named places on the road between Chajikhro and Ojhakhro.

· 90 · *How Lijaba Created the World*
           (Nagaland)

The Nagas are made up of a welter of different tribes, some twenty of them, each having a different language or dialect. They therefore use Nagamese as their link language. These groups are thought to have migrated to the jungly hills of northeastern India from Southeast Asia over a very long period of time. Their westward movement was finally arrested at the edge of the Brahmaputra River valley by some strong, well-organized Hindu kingdoms. Most of the Naga peoples believed in a creator-god that has an immense, anthropomorphic form. There is a touch of pathos in this tale about how the creator left the land of the Nagas unfinished and imperfect, while he so carefully carved the lands of others.

LIJABA created the world. At first he worked slowly and carefully, making broad, even valleys, and level plains. But, as he started work on Nagaland, a giant cockroach appeared and told him that some enemies were coming to attack him. Lijaba quickly put together a jumble of hills and valleys, not taking time to level and smooth them in his haste to finish his work. This is why today Nagaland consists of steep mountains and cliffs, unlike the broad, smooth plain of the Brahmaputra valley.

· 91 ·   *The Porcupine Daughter*
(Gujarat)

There are many origin tales in India that purport to explain how
a particular custom or feature of the environment came into
existence. This type of tale is found with particular frequency
among tribal groups located in India's more remote areas. This
becomes clear when one studies the sources of "origin" motifs
given in the major motif indexes available for Indian folklore.
The present example of such a story comes from the Wagher, a
remote, tribe-like community that lives in Saurastra, western
Gujarat. The Waghar reside in an area containing forty-two
villages near the town of Dwarka, on the seacoast. The story
helps to justify how a local group called the Kunabi become
important landowners in this region. As in many tales already
discussed, a junior figure (the Kunabi) here wins a contest with
a powerful landlord (*jamindar*) by employing a simple but clever
trick. He has someone hide in a hole, and she shouts unexpect-
edly so that it sounds as if the land itself is speaking.

   This tale resembles the "Voice From The Grave" (tale type
1532), which is clearly popular in India but is reported nowhere
in European tale collections. It also resembles stories where a
person pretending to be a god answers a dupe from behind a tree
or a temple idol (tale type 1380). In more specific details, such
as the hidden person being described as a daughter of the man
planning the trick, or the girl turning into a porcupine permanently, this story is unique among those currently reported from
South Asia. This story attempts to explain two things: caste
rights to land and the porcupine's special, sacred status in this
local area. As a tale about rights to land, it resembles other
stories reported by similar farming castes elsewhere in India.
Burial under the earth's surface provides the linking motif.

LONG AGO there lived a jamindar in a small town of Saurastra. He
had plenty of land. In fact he had so many fields that he could not
cultivate them all. So he decided to give some of his uncultivated
land to a Kunabi, a member of a caste that practiced farming.
The Kunabi soon began to cultivate his new land, making it very
fertile. He watered it daily and gave it ample doses of cowdung as

fertilizer. As a result, his harvest grew better each year. After a time, this man became quite rich and prosperous.

One day, the Kunabi began to think to himself about the arrangements he had made for cultivating his land. He had agreed to give half the crop to the jamindar each time he harvested his fields. Now he began to regret this, realizing that the jamindar benefited from his half share even though he contributed no labor to the cultivation process. Thus the Kunabi wanted to own the land outright. But, at the same time, the jamindar had also begun to think about his piece of land. He noticed the fine harvests the Kunabi was reaping and began to think it might be better if he took back this fertile section to cultivate on his own. Ultimately, the jamindar decided to go to the Kunabi farmer and speak to him directly. Approaching him he said, "You have worked on this field for many years. Now you have become rich and prosperous. It is time that you give me back my piece of land." The Kunabi at once answered saying, "Yes, I agree with you. But I have one condition." The jamindar asked, "What is your condition?" The Kunabi answered, "You must call out to the land. If the land replies to you it will be yours. If it does not answer you, but it does reply when I call out, then I shall own the land." The jamindar agreed to this proposal. The Kunabi then asked that this agreement be written down. The jamindar again agreed and a paper was signed. Four persons were called from a nearby village to witness the contract and a writer was employed to record it.

Soon a day was fixed to execute the test agreed on. The time chosen was a full-moon night when everything would be maximally auspicious. In the meantime, however, the Kunabi began to scheme. He was very keen to possess this piece of land. So he instructed his young daughter, "Oh, flower of my eyes! Be the savior of my clan." The daughter replied, "Please order me and tell me what to do, dear father." The Kunabi continued and explained to his daughter, "A big pit will be dug in a nearby field. I want you to hide in that pit in such a way that nobody will know you are there." "Well and good, father," replied the daughter. "Of course I will arrange some small holes so that you can breathe while you are in the pit," explained the father. "I understand," replied the faithful daughter.

The Kunabi then continued with his instructions. "Tomorrow night the jamindar and I will come to the field where you are hiding. A few villagers will come along as witnesses. First the jamindar will call out to the field. But you must not reply to his call. The second call will come from me. You must then respond immediately shouting, "Oh, Oh" twice. Your voice should be so loud so that it can be properly heard by all of us who are standing by the side of the field." "I understand you, father," said the daughter. Then the Kunabi continued, "Please be sure to follow my instructions exactly." "I will obediently follow your directions," said the daughter.

So a big pit was dug in the middle of the field in question and the Kunabi's daughter was carefully hidden inside it. Some holes were also pierced in the cover of the hiding place so that she could breathe. Then the critical moment arrived. All the villagers gathered along the edge of the field. They stood beside the jamindar and the Kunabi. As planned, the jamindar was to call out first. He did this but there was no reply. This made him dejected and silent. Next came the Kunabi's turn. He called out to the field and there was an immediate and loud reply, "Oh, Oh." All of the villagers who were standing around clapped their hands. "The land now belongs to the Kunabi," they cried. "He is now the true owner of the field. The land favored him with its reply and shouted, 'Oh, Oh.' " With a broken heart the jamindar left the field. The Kunabi was acknowledged as the new and complete owner. All the other villagers now dispersed as it was getting late.

At midnight the Kunabi returned alone to his field and opened the pit. But when the cover of the hole was removed, he had a great shock. Instead of his daughter he now found a porcupine hidden there. "Oh, my! Where is my daughter?" he cried. Seeing her father in such a distraught mood, the porcupine opened her mouth and said, "Dear father, you have cheated our mother land. This field cursed me when I uttered 'Oh, Oh.' As a result of this curse I have become a porcupine. I must now live out my life in animal form." The Kunabi father sobbed softly and said, amidst his tears, "Oh, my dear daughter! Henceforth, let no Kunabi beat you or kill you. You must be allowed to eat anything you like from the fields around our homes."

Since these events occurred, porcupines have always been allowed to eat sugar cane, beans, peas, and millets from the fields just as men eat them. Porcupines are never killed nor do men hunt them. And the porcupine's cry is said to sound like the weeping of a human child.

· 92 · *The Origin of the Temple at Tarakesvar (Bengal)*

Stories about temple origins (*purana, mahatmya*) constitute a popular genre in all of the languages of India. Often these are developed by the literary community into more formalized myths and then are woven into pan-Indian story traditions. But even where this happens, informal narratives such as this one continue to coexist alongside an "authorized" version. The function of these less formal accounts is to explain to visitors (pilgrims) how a particular place became known for its sacredness. Typically, an informal version reports a story using a very factual, historic tone. Like this one, informal accounts emphasize the particularistic rather than universalistic aspects of the temple history.

How are the elements of this story related to what the visitor wants to know? The presence of the *sannyasi,* a person with mystical insight and magical powers, lends authority to such claims of sacredness. Great minds and sacred animals (the cow) recognize the power of place and are inspired to perform miracles. Even the king, highest temporal authority of the land, may be convinced of the sanctity of such a shrine and then becomes its patron, granting it land and building a temple. In this story, such a monarch eventually renounces his throne in order to subordinate himself to a religious master.

I CANNOT SPEAK with certainty about the history of the Tarakesvar temple, but what I do know has come from '*purani kahini*' [ancient stories]. In the beginning, this place was covered by a dense forest. In the forest lived a sannyasi by the name of Dhumropan Giri. He belonged to the Joshi Mattha. This man lived in the forest and worshipped Baba [Siva]. The house of the king of the area was only three miles from where this sannyasi stayed, and the king often heard about the holy man living in his vicinity. Sometimes local villagers reported to the king that certain bad incidents in the village had been caused by this sannyasi. So the king finally sent his men to fetch the sannyasi and had him imprisoned. But soon afterwards, it was noticed that the cell of the sannyasi was empty during the day despite his having been locked up. He was only to be found there at night when he returned to rest. This man came and went at will, as if unbarred. This was reported to the king, who now became anxious. He soon went to meet the sannyasi and asked him how this was possible. The sannyasi then explained that he was a devoted man whose only occupation was performing a daily *puja* [worship] for Baba. What the villagers had said was untrue. The king believed him and immediately ordered his release. The sannyasi returned to his place in the forest. The king then became a frequent visitor there, often requesting some needed advice.

The sannyasi had a horse with three legs. He looked after this horse like his own child. Now the villagers again started rumors that something was unusual about a sannyasi taking such good care of a useless beast. This horse excited their suspicion. When the king asked the sannyasi about these reports of his behavior, a hot argument ensued. The sannyasi maintained that, even though three-legged, this horse was not a useless animal. He rode him frequently, far and wide. The king then offered the man a deal. If the sannyasi could ride this horse, the king would give him all the land which the beast could cover. The sannyasi then mounted his horse and began to ride. He rode from Burdwan to Midnapore and from there to Hooghly, to Amdanga Mattha, and to Gorbeta [Midnapore]. From there he returned to Tarakesvar again. The king verified the sannyasi's journey, found that he had visited the entire area, and then, as he had promised, he gave the sannyasi all of the land which he had covered with his horse. Hence the sannyasi became the first Mohanto of this place, the owner of the land. The people called him Dhumropan Giri because he was fond of *ganja* [opium]. This name means "He who is always smoking."

In this jungle there was a stone or, rather, a solid stone mound (*pashan*). It happened that the same king had a herd of cattle. In that herd there was a cow of the variety called *copila,* which used to visit that pashan every day and stand just over it. It would then pour its milk onto the stone. The chief cowherd, whose name was Mukundu Gowalla, noticed this one day. He then told the king, who thought that there must be something supernatural about such behavior. So he decided to take the stone to his own place. When his workers began digging it up, however, they could find no base to it. During the night, several days after the digging had begun, the sleeping king had a vision of Lord Siva. Siva spoke to him and said, I have no limits, and so you will not find the end of me [in that stone]. You must build a temple on that spot.

The stone had a slight depression on the top because it had frequently been used by local cowherd boys for beating paddy husks. This use of the stone was also known to the king.

Soon the king had a temple built. It came to stand in the area which he had given to the Mohanto, so he handed the temple over to that man. The king then gave up his throne, came to Dhumropan Giri, became the Mohanto's disciple [*sisya*], and took the vows of a sannyasi. His queen tried to convince him to give up these vows and return to the palace. Failing at this, she committed suicide.

The temple was built about two hundred and fifty years ago, according to the history and facts which we know. We cannot be certain. These events could have taken place earlier, but we are sure of its existence for at least the last two and a half centuries.

· 93 · Bhimnath Mahadev (Gujarat)

This next story is representative of a whole genre of Indian folktales that flourish as spinoffs from India's two great epics, the *Mahabharata* and the *Ramayana*. Sometimes such tales resemble accurate retellings of excerpts taken from well-known literary versions. More often, however, they are imaginative elaborations or additions to especially popular episodes these great civilization-wide frame stories contain. The latter is the

case for this next story. It takes as its inspiration that general
section of the *Mahabharata* where the five Pandava brothers
wander in the forest together, waiting out a period of exile from
their family kingdom. But like many accounts that make use of
this frame, the tale then goes on to narrate a fresh incident.
Only the three oldest Pandavas are described, a pattern quite in
keeping with their relatively greater development as figures in
the epic.

The general personalities of the three, Dharma (or
Yudhisthira), Bhima, and Arjuna, are well preserved in this tale.
But one interesting modification does occur. In more orthodox
versions of the *Mahabharata,* Bhima is occasionally critical of his
elder brother Dharma. Nowhere, however, does he speak out
against his junior, Arjuna. This restraint is in keeping with the
general moral norm that an elder sibling should act as a model
for younger ones. In this account, however, Bhima focuses his
frustration on Arjuna. Indeed Bhima tries to trick Arjuna concerning a serious, ritual matter. These are folk themes shared by
many other types of local tales, but not patterns seen often in
India's more learned story literature. This subtle shift in
Bhima's behavioral style makes him more boisterous, more daring, and more iconoclastic. These rebellious traits mildly mock
India's very restrained, Brahmanical culture. Such bits of color
are especially popular with rural, peasant groups.

This present Gujarati tale was collected in a typical rural
setting. It comes from Bhimnath, a small village named after
the key character, Bhima, just discussed. This settlement has a
temple dedicated to Lord Mahadev (a name for Siva) located near
a local Piludi tree. Nearby residents claim it is the very shrine
described in this story. The Nilaka river, also mentioned, flows
nearby. Hence this tale links the great *Mahabharata* epic to the
tellers' very own village and helps to sanctify and aggrandize its
identity. This is a typical pattern for epic-framed folk accounts,
and examples from all over India abound. The motif of striking
a sacred stone with a hard blow and finding that milk flows
forth is extremely common in Hindu temple origin myths. The
finding of a hidden lingam (phallic symbol of Lord Siva) in such
situations is also widely recounted. These aspects of the story,
plus Arjuna's insistence on bathing and worshiping before he

eats, help to link this account with much that is familiar in pan-Indian Hindu traditions.

DURING THE TIME when the great Pandava heroes were in exile for twelve years, they once stopped to rest on the banks of the river Nilaka. The whole area was heavily forested at that time. Lovely neem trees, *piludi* trees, Indian fig trees, and many others all grew nearby. As soon as Arjuna, the famous young Pandava, saw this beautiful site he became enthralled. Arjuna was tired and fatigued by the great distance they had all walked. So he asked his elder brother, Dharma, if the group could rest there for a while. Dharma agreed and said, "This is a beautiful spot. The river water is crystal clear, and there are small fishes darting about here and there. We can also watch the cranes, the storks, and admire the greenery." But the middle brother, in the group, Bhima, was uncomfortable. He was extremely hungry, befitting his reputation for having an enormous appetite. Bhima thus started to murmur, "What is so beautiful about nature? Things look the same all over this country. The trees are the same, and the water never changes its color." The eldest brother then spoke out, "You are right, Bhima, but we are all exhausted. We want to stop here to rest." "All right, we will rest. But shall we at least begin cooking?" asked Bhima. "Indeed, let us begin cooking," replied Dharma. Draupadi, the wife of the brothers, was then asked by the brothers to begin preparations for a meal.

Then Bhima began thinking to himself and suddenly remembered that his younger brother, Arjuna, would never eat unless he first worshipped Lord Siva. But there was no temple dedicated to Lord Siva anywhere in sight. Bhima began to worry that the meal might be delayed. So he set out in search of a Siva temple. Dharma and Arjuna remained on the river bank to bathe, and Bhima went alone into the jungle. The latter carried with him a small earthen pot filled with river water. After he entered the forest he wandered here and there, but he was unable to find a Siva temple anywhere. Meanwhile, Bhima had become very, very hungry. He was also angry with his brother Arjuna for always insisting on so many ritual procedures. He was trying to think of some way he could arrange for Arjuna to worship Lord Siva before taking his food. He knew that as long as Arjuna did not worship Siva, his elder brother Dharma would refuse to eat. And he knew that as long as his elder brother refused food, he could not eat either. Being so hungry, Bhima had a real problem. Then Bhima found a large piludi tree where he decided to sit down to think.

At last Bhima got an idea. He now stood up quickly and over-turned the earthen pot he had been carrying. He then fixed it firmly to the ground by surrounding it with earth. Next, he found a small spring and poured some water from that over the pot. He then adorned it with leaves of the bili, or woodapple tree, and with wild flowers. He thus created something that looked like a small shrine dedicated to Lord Siva. It even looked as if it had been freshly worshiped by some devotees who had recently passed that way. Now Bhima was happy. He had found a clever way to solve his problem. So he returned to the riverbank and called to his brother saying, "Oh Arjuna. Come out of the water! I have brought good news." "What news do you bring?" asked Arjuna. "Did you not want to worship Lord Siva, my brother?" "Of course, I must worship Lord Siva," replied Arjuna. "Come out of the water then. I shall accompany you and show you the place where I have found a shrine. It lies on open ground, under a piludi tree."

Then Arjuna came out of the water and joined his brother Bhima. His clothes were still wet as he proceeded to fill a small pot with water. He also collected a few flowers and leaves. These were to be used in the worship of Lord Siva. Bhima was smiling, and he kept thinking all the while of how he was managing to fool his brother Arjuna. After a time, the two brothers arrived at the spot where the shrine had been built. Arjuna now worshiped it with great respect and decorated it freshly with the leaves and flowers he had brought. He also sprinkled water over it from his little pot. When the ceremonies were finished, Bhima turned to his brother and asked, "Arjuna, have you finished your worship?" "Can there be any doubt about that?" replied Arjuna. "No, I have no doubt about it," replied Bhima. "Then why do you both-er to ask me such a silly question?" said Arjuna. Bhima then said, "My question actually concerns whether you worshiped Lord Siva at all." "Yes, of course I have worshipped Lord Siva," said Ar-juna. "Your Lord Siva?" said Bhima and he burst into laughter. "Why do you laugh?" asked Arjuna.

Bhima then raised a wooden stick over his head and gave a great blow to the earthen pot which he had so carefully arranged under the tree. But to his great surprise, milk now started to flow from the broken pot. "What a mystery!" cried Bhima. He was amazed to see milk flowing from this makeshift shrine. He then removed all the leaves and flowers that were on top of the pot and found a lingam, the very image of Lord Siva hidden underneath. But this lingam had been broken into pieces because of the force of his blow. Then Bhima also decided to worship Lord Siva.

Henceforth this small shrine became known as the Bhimnath shrine. It is the place where Bhima discovered Lord Siva. The temple can be seen today on the banks of the river Nilaka. It is overshadowed by an old piludi tree, a very special sight in this dry area of Gujarat.

· 94 · The Carpenter's Tale (Gujarat)

This is a tale about the origin of an intoxicating drink popular in the Gujarat area. The tale circulates among the Rathwa Bhils, a tribal community living in the Baroda hills of Gujarat state. These people are known for their preparation of alcohol, and the present myth establishes their special claim to the secrets of this lucrative occupation. It also depicts the Rathwas as able in felling and carving trees, skills appropriate to forest dwellers. More interesting, however, is the myth's portrayal of a key Bhil ancestor as a trickster figure who tried to outsmart the gods so as to win a world without death. This man fails in his efforts, as a greater lord proves even better at devising tricks. In this process, the consumption of liquor becomes an alternate way for men to deal with death. If humans cannot prevent death, at least alcohol can be used to ease sorrows and thereby to smooth death's way.

Many details in this Bhil story are unique. Nonetheless, several general themes link it to wider Hindu traditions. For one, the carpenter (as Visvakarma) is an important figure in Hindu mythology at large. Visvakarma is the general artificer of the

gods. Among other things, he created a great sacred image of
Lord Jagannath at Puri using a rough-hewn log. By developing
the carpenter theme, the Rathwas seem to be claiming a similar
status for themselves. Implicitly, the myth seems to place these
artisans in opposition to peasant landowners on the plains, people who have often encroached on Bhil territory. This kind of
farmer and artisan rivalry is well known in South Asian tradition. The positive attitude expressed toward drink and its
pleasures also contrasts the Bhils with ambivalent attitudes toward liquor associated with high-status landowners. The fact
that death helps to control population and crimes of violence is
another theme found in mainstream Hindu myths as well.

THERE ONCE LIVED a carpenter who was very skilled at his trade.
He was also a very clever man, and no one was able to deceive
him. As the carpenter grew old, he realized that the time would
soon come when the god of death would take him to some
faraway place. The carpenter planned for this day by going into
the forest and cutting down a large tree. The trunk of this tree
was very bulky, and with his special instruments, he was able to
carve a large hollow inside it. He then designed a kind of door for
this secret cavity so it could be closed at will. Once the door was
closed, no trace remained of the empty space inside.

One day, the god of death came to fetch the carpenter, just as
this man had anticipated. The artisan then told his visitor about
the hollow he had carved inside the trunk of a tree. His guest
expressed an interest in seeing this special achievement. The carpenter was eager to oblige and soon asked the god of death to
climb into the hollow so that he could see its full extent properly.
As the visitor entered, however, the carpenter quickly shut the
door. Once it was closed, of course, no one could tell the hole was
there. In this way, the carpenter succeeded in imprisoning the
god of death in his secret cave.

The carpenter was very pleased with his trick and delighted
with the results. Furthermore, he took great care never to tell
anyone about his achievement. He also did not point out to others that people on earth were not dying. Meanwhile, however,
the relatives of the god of death noticed his absence. They soon
went to Bhagwan, the Almighty, to complain. They pointed out

that the god of death had gone to fetch a man on earth but had not returned. Bhagwan tried his best to trace the movements of this missing divinity, but all attempts failed to locate him. After a while the Almighty became dejected. He lost faith in his ability to ever recover the god of death. Again his relatives appealed. They began to cry and lament the loss of a close family member. Furthermore, the earth was becoming overcrowded with human beings. Soon there would be no place for people to live happily anymore. Many hideous crimes were being committed by men made desperate by overcrowding.

The Almighty now became more and more worried about the absence of the god of death. He also worried about how to punish criminals. Then, suddenly one day, a thought sprang into Bhagwan's mind. He now took some *mahua* flowers in a big pot, boiled them, and subsequently prepared a special drink. This drink would intoxicate any man who partook of it and cause him to lose control of himself. Then the Almighty descended to earth with his pot and offered his drink to everyone he could find. Those who drank it became very talkative and they expressed their thoughts freely. People enjoyed the drink enormously. Finally the carpenter came to hear about this potion and expressed an interest in tasting it. Bhagwan handed him some which he drank with eagerness. Thus the carpenter also became intoxicated and began to talk. He soon lost his control of mind and expressed his most secret thoughts while the Almighty listened attentively. He began to brag saying, "You, Almighty, don't know who I am. Do not try to open my cave, because if you do I will imprison you!"

Bhagwan took up the challenge and said to the carpenter, "How would you imprison me?" The carpenter then opened the door of this cave and Bhagwan watched closely. As soon as the mouth of the cavity opened the god of death leapt out. He was half dead from suffocation, but the Almighty soon revived him. The great lord then took the carpenter away to the land of the dead. Next, Bhagwan himself taught the people of the Rathwa community in Gujarat to prepare his drink properly for human consumption. The use of the Lord's intoxicating drink has enabled people to better prepare for death.

· 95 ·   *The Origin of Head-Hunting*
           (Nagaland)

Humans often rationalize their cultural practices by references to
nature. This Ao Naga folk theory of the origin of head-hunting
focuses on the immediate causes of the custom: quarreling, killing a dangerous enemy, and pride of victory. Anthropological
accounts stress somewhat different issues. The Nagas believe
that a person has several different "souls." One "soul" travels to
the realm of the dead, while another remains associated with a
man's head, or skull. This latter "soul"—or special power—can
be manipulated by the living for various useful purposes. It is
for this reason, as well as for the others cited above, that Nagas
were once keen on returning home with their victim's head
(they no longer practice head-hunting). The beginning of this
tale is curious. The trouble which leads to head-hunting initially involves a property dispute between birds and a lizard.
What precipitates the fight is not an original theft, but the fact
that the lizard bore false witness against the ants.

IN THE BEGINNING of the world, there was only one plant: a
large tree which produced an abundance of fruit. All of the birds
made nests in its branches and ate its fruit. Even though these
fruit were plentiful, the harvest was barely enough to feed all the
birds. If even a single fruit was mistakenly dropped, someone
quickly flew down and ate it.
   One day, as all of the birds were eating, a redstart dropped a
fruit on the ground by mistake, and a passing lizard quickly gobbled it up. The redstart, accompanied by other birds, flew down
to retrieve the fruit. This time, however, they searched and
searched but could not find it. Seeing that the lizard was the only
animal around they swooped down and charged at it, accusing
the poor thing of being the thief. The lizard defended itself by
telling the birds that the fruit had been taken by the red ants
which had a hole at the base of the tree. The ants denied this
accusation, and a fight quickly developed. Thousands of red ants
now emerged from the hole and attacked the lizard. The lizard
killed many ants, but in the end, the ants overcame it, and it

died. With their sharp teeth the ants cut off the lizard's head, and carried it to their nest in a triumphant procession. The birds flew away, and all became normal once again.

Some men passing by happened to see all of this. They watched the fight with keen interest. They were impressed when they saw the ants cut off the lizard's head and carry it back to their home while leaving the body behind. Thereafter, men imitated the behavior of the ants.

· 96 · *Friendship between Man and Dog (Manipur)*

The next story is about the origin of man's close relationship to and reliance on domesticated dogs. In this sense, it is about the bond between man and his key helper or pet. This account was provided by a Mao Naga in Manipur State. One can see in it the influence of jungle animals and also the traditional use of the dog in hunting. The story turns on the importance of the dog's bark and how humans are different from other beings for their appreciation of this unusual canine trait. It also mentions a local custom of feeding one's hunting dog the right foreleg of each captured animal. This provides an interesting link to a widespread Hindu ritual custom. When a buffalo, sheep, or goat is beheaded at a Hindu temple, the right foreleg of this sacrificial beast is often severed immediately and put in its mouth. The animal head, forced to hold its own leg, is then set in front of the main idol at a discrete distance as a sacred offering. In general, this ritual custom parallels Naga usage: a temple victim submits (in principle) to its own sacrifice. Next, it offers itself to a god to be consumed symbolically. Similarly, the dog accepts the submission of its hunted prey by eating a right foreleg.

THERE ONCE LIVED a bitch that had two young pups. When these children were grown, however, the mother was killed one day by a deer. The pups were very sad about this and wanted to take revenge. They quickly decided to approach the mighty elephant to help them punish the deer. When they asked, the elephant agreed. But the two dogs did not realize that their habit of barking at the slightest sound was something the elephant could not bear. In particular, the elephant feared that if a tiger heard a dog bark nearby, he might find them both and threaten their lives. So the elephant drove the two dogs away in order to save himself from this danger.

Having been driven away by the elephant, the two dogs next approached the tiger. They now requested his help to avenge the death of their mother. The tiger listened patiently and finally agreed to help. But the two dogs continued their usual habit of barking randomly at any unusual sound. The tiger was afraid that if the dogs barked in his presence, man might be able to find him in the forest. If this happened, a lone tiger could easily be killed. So the tiger, to save himself from this threat, asked the dogs to leave him, saying he would be unable to help them. Next the dogs went to man and earnestly requested his help in punishing the deer. Man listened carefully and was very sympathetic. He also provided the dogs with food and shelter. Each night the two animals barked at unusual sounds and man was pleased by this habit. Instead of chasing them away he encouraged them in this behavior. The dogs were both pleased, and they decided to stay with man.

The dogs soon became accustomed to man and to his care and affection. Soon they became both strong and obedient. Then one day, the dogs reminded man of his promise to punish the deer. So the man took them both hunting. After wandering through the forest, they finally found the deer and began to chase it. The dogs ran very fast, while the man hid behind a bush. When the deer ran past the bush, man threw his spear and hit one of the deer squarely. The dogs were very happy and they came toward the man wagging their tails. They also bit off the right leg of the slain deer. So from that day onward man agreed to feed any dogs that accompanied him in hunting. He now offers them the right front leg of each animal victim. The dogs, in return, agreed to stay in man's house. They have done so until this day.

· 97 · *Why the Ow Fruit Drops (Falls) in March (Assam)*

This tale (Type 2042) provides an example of a popular Indian genre usually called a cumulative or chain story (see also tales 69, 70 and 81). It resembles the "Lady That Swallowed a Fly" type of tale in English and is rather like a mental version of a tongue twister. However, in Indian folklore, by contrast to English, these stories are often used to explain the origin of something. Hence, they provide more food for thought than does a simple chain play on words. In this particular example, the tale purports to explain the reason why the fruit of the *ow* tree always ripens at a particular time of year. In passing, it also mentions how the jackal and the tiger acquired their reddish spots. All of the animals referred to, except the deer, have tricksterlike personalities, both in this tale and in other story contexts. But the jackal is the most renowned of all for roguishness. Perhaps this makes its death, at the end of the sequence, significant. The chain reverses its direction at that point. Opposite of the jackal is the innocent and immobile ow tree, which eventually suffers the entire blame for the untoward incidents that occur. The animal council, furthermore, eventually transfers responsibility for such exaggerated and un-predictable behavior to something outside its own sphere, seasonal cycles in the world at large.

IN THE MONTH of March, locally called Phagun, the sun is rather hot. One day, during this month, a deer was resting in the shade of an ow tree.[1] As it was standing there, an ow fruit happened to drop on its back. This startled the deer and it ran off. While running away, it knocked the nest of a weaver bird off its branch. The startled bird flew away and dropped [sat] on the head of a stork. The stork lost its scalp and, having been startled, flew away and dropped [sat] on the back of a tiger. The tiger was so startled that it ran and sat on the hole of a crab. The crab pinched the tiger's tail, and the beast again began to run. But soon, the tiger met a jackal. The latter inquired what the matter was. The tiger explained, "I just sat over there and something bit me." The jackal said, "What could have bitten you, I wonder? Come, let us go back and investigate carefully."

The tiger had now become so scared that he would not go back. So the jackal said, "Let us both go together. Come, we will tie our tails together with a rope of thatch so that one does not leave the other." The tiger agreed to the plan and the two of them went back together. The tiger showed the jackal how it had sat down. The crab, however, again pinched his tail hard and the tiger ran away again. But the jackal was tied to him and was dragged over the rough ground. The jackal soon lost its life, and blood began to spurt from its body. Those parts of the jackal and the tiger on which the drops of blood fell turned reddish, while the other parts remained dark.

Soon afterwards, the birds and beasts of the forest called a meeting and took up the matter of the jackal's death. The animals now addressed the tiger and asked, "Why did you kill the jackal?" The tiger laid the blame on the crab, saying it had pinched him. When the crab was asked why it had pinched the tiger, it said, "The tiger sat on my hole." The tiger then explained that it had sat there because the stork had frightened it. The stork said that the weaver bird had sat on its head and that it had lost its scalp. The weaver bird explained that the deer had knocked it off its nest and frightened it. And the deer said it had been startled because an ow fruit had dropped on its back as it rested in the shade of the tree. The animals now decided to lay the blame on the ow tree. This was the verdict of the assembly: "In the month of March your fruits will drop at the slightest breeze." Since then ow fruits have always dropped from their branches at this time of the year.

· 98 ·   *Sharpening the Dagger (Manipur)*

This cumulative tale is very similar to the last one. This time the account "explains" why a whitish crab turns red in hot water and submits to being eaten as a tasty human food. The present sequence parallels the earlier one that started with the ow tree. This time, however, a man who is cutting a tree begins the chain reaction. Again, the reversing of this sequence requires a death.

In the last story, a community of animals gathers to ask why the
jackal died. In this story, a community of relatives gathers to ask
why a woman has died. As before, the victim in this tale belongs
to a category quite separate from the jury judging him. Like the
ow tree, the crab does not really deserve the enormous blame that
is heaped upon him. This tale is meant to be funny and raucous,
particularly the description of the woodcutter's testicles. But it
also serves as a commentary on the nature of fate. Causation is a
difficult matter to pinpoint and blame even more difficult to
apportion. Though external forces often act at random, one often
has little choice but to live with the results. The fact that a bat
flies into an elephant's trunk, furthermore, is reminiscent of the
ant's behavior in tale 68.

THERE WAS ONCE a man who lived in a small village situated in
the middle of a thick forest. One day, when he was out in the
forest with his dagger, his instrument became blunt while cutting the branches of trees to make a path. He then stopped on the
bank of a stream and picked up a stone in order to sharpen it.
While he was working on this, the man's body swung to and fro
with the movement of sharpening. This happened in such a way
that his testicles also began vibrating. While he was working at
his sharpening, a crab came up on the bank of the stream in
search of food. The scrotum of this man swaying back and forth
made the crab think of a sumptuous meal. So the crab crept up to
the man silently and grabbed his scrotum from behind. The man
felt a great pain, and in panic he cut off the branch of a creeper
that was just in front of him.

As the man cut this creeper, a fruit that had been hanging
from it suddenly dropped down and fell on the back of a wild
hen. The hen was surprised by this blow. In a panic, it began to
scratch with its feet. This disturbed a nest of ants, and they all
began to run from their nest. The ants then bit whatever they
found on their way. In this manner they soon disturbed the sleep
of a wild boar. The boar felt so much pain that he jumped up and
began to run. It then collided with a plantain tree that was lying
across his path. A bat was living happily in a nest on this plantain
tree. When the tree fell, the bat was surprised. It flew away in
great haste. In his sudden escape, the bat flew unwillingly into an

elephant's trunk. Inside, in the darkness, the bat felt constricted. It could find nowhere to go. In his predicament this creature began scratching the delicate lining of the trunk with his sharp claws. Then the elephant felt great pain and started to run amok. In its course, it trampled a pregnant woman to death. When the relatives of this woman found that she had been killed by an elephant, they asked the elephant why it had behaved so rashly. The elephant replied that it had felt great pain because of the unbearable scratches of a bat that had entered its trunk. The bat was then asked why he flew into an elephant's trunk. The bat said that he had flown out of his nest when the tree in which he lived had suddenly been felled.

These same people then went to the plantain tree. They asked it why it had suddenly fallen down. The plantain tree explained that it had been bumped by a wild boar running across its path. The wild boar, in its turn, explained that he had been bitten by an army of ants. The ants in their turn explained that their nest had been disturbed by the scratching of a wild hen. The wild hen then explained that a fruit had fallen on her back and had given her a great fright. When the fruit was asked why it had fallen, it explained that a certain man had suddenly cut the creeper which had supported it. Finally when the man was asked why he had cut the creeper, he explained that a crab had pinched his scrotum. The crab was finally caught, and it confessed its guilt. For the mischief it had committed the crab said, "As long as I remain in the water I shall have a whitish color. But if I am taken out of water and dropped in a hot liquid, my color will turn red and I shall provide a very tasty food for children."

· 99 ·   *The Death of Mosquito*
         (Tamilnadu)

This third cumulative tale was told at the opposite end of India from the last two. However, this one does not have quite the same form as the two chain stories just reported from northeast India. In particular, the sequence of events is never reversed. Instead, each time a new action takes place the entire set of previous happenings is recounted, making this story similarly difficult to recite. The corpse this time belongs to a slain mosquito. Like the jackal, she is a tricksterlike character. More important, however, is the fact that the mosquito's death occurs at the beginning of the long chain of events, all caused by a rat's sneeze. This whole scenario is ridiculous enough, but matters get worse when the mosquito is mourned by the rat, by a pond, by an elephant, by a tree, by a stork, by a wall, and finally by a saintly beggar. And the story ends with a second interesting inversion of the pattern just established by two foregoing tales. Instead of explaining how a food (ow fruit and crab) came to take its present form, this tale explains why a beggar broke his eating bowl. If the preceding two tales concern the provision of man's food, this last tale pertains to the refusal or denial of food. It also explains a human action, not a natural state of animal or vegetal being.

Noting that this cumulative tale is from southern India may not be so important in explaining the differences just listed as the fact that it was collected in a Brahman community. A concern with the mosquito's cremation, bathing the mourner, and the pollution of a pond, all link closely to Brahmanical ritual concerns. Even the breaking of the beggar's food bowl can be seen in this light. Any holy man would refrain from requesting food at a house where a funeral is in progress. Like tale 87, "The Sparrow and the Sweet Pudding," which was collected in the same setting, the present account contains a rush of images linked to death and dissolution. One again finds a possible hint of the larger Hindu concept of cosmic cycles here, the ultimate ending of all sensations and all things. In the same spirit, this is the last story in our tale collection.

A RAT AND A MOSQUITO once lived together as husband and wife. They loved each other very much. One day before the rat went out, the mosquito asked him, "What shall I cook you for your return?" The rat answered, "Nothing at all, I'll be thirsty when I return. So please have some fresh water ready for me." When it was time for the rat's return, therefore, the mosquito went here and there in search of some good water. Unfortunately, however, all the wells and lakes in the area were dry. "Oh God, what can I do now?" cried the mosquito. Her tears overflowed like a river, and she realized that she could indeed fill a drinking pot with them.

The rat then returned home and called to his wife. He asked her to bring some water. When the mosquito brought this liquid, the rat drank it. He then asked why it was so salty. The wife answered, "I was unable to find even a drop of water nearby. I cried and cried about this, and at last my tears were flowing like a river. I thus decided to fill our drinking pot with my own tears." "My darling!" replied the rat. He then embraced his wife. As he kissed her, however, the mosquito slipped inside the rat's nose. That made the rat sneeze with a loud sound, "hunch." The mosquito came out of his nose at once, but alas she was dead. "Oh honey! What will I do without you?" cried the rat. He then took her body to the cremation ground and saw to its burning. Afterwards, he went to bathe in a tank where there was a little water. After he had his bath, the water was stirred up and became very muddy. There was an elephant that used to visit this tank every day, and when he saw the muddied water, he asked what had happened. The tank replied, "Don't you know my story? The wife of the rat, Madam Mosquito, died recently. The honorable rat took his bath here after he cremated her body. That is why I am in this muddy condition."

The elephant was very sad upon hearing this news, and he went to a tree and dashed his trunk against it. In this way he lost one of his tusks. The tree then asked the elephant, "Oh honorable elephant! Why have you dashed against me and broken your tusk?" The elephant replied saying, "Don't ask me any more about it. The wife of the rat, Madam Mosquito, just died. Her husband, the honorable rat, bathed in my tank, and the water became muddy. This made me sad, and I broke my tusk." The tree then shed its leaves in sadness. But there was a stork that used to come and sit on the branches of this tree. When it arrived, as usual, it noticed that its favorite tree was without leaves. It then asked, "Oh honorable tree! Why did you shed your leaves?" The tree responded quickly to the stork saying, "Don't ask me any more about it. The wife of the rat, Madam Mosquito has died. Her husband, rat, bathed in the tank after the funeral and the water became muddy. It made the elephant sad, and he broke his tusk against me. This made me shed my leaves."

On hearing of these tragic events, the stork at once pierced his own eyes out and began to stand near a ruined wall. The wall then asked the stork, "Why did you pierce out your eyes?" The stork replied, "Don't ask me any more about it. The wife of the rat, Madam Mosquito, just died. Her husband, the rat, bathed in the tank after the funeral. The water in the tank became muddy, and this made the honorable elephant mad. He broke his tusk against a tree, and the tree shed its leaves. I pierced out my eyes in sympathy for the tree." On hearing about these distressing events, the ruined wall at once collapsed. But there was a beggar who used to sit at the foot of the wall and lean against it. The next time he arrived, the beggar found it collapsed and asked, "Oh ruined wall, why did you collapse?" The wall answered, "Oh! Don't ask me any more about it. It is a long story. The wife of the rat, Madam Mosquito, just died. Her husband, the rat, bathed in the tank after the funeral, and this made the water muddy, which made the elephant sad. He broke his tusk against the tree, and the tree shed its leaves. The stork pierced out his eyes in sympathy for the tree, and I fell down in an expression of sympathy for the stork. Upon hearing about these many tragic events, the beggar at once broke the earthen pot he had used daily for many years in collecting his food.

Notes to the Tales

PART I
SUITORS AND MAIDENS

· 1 · *The Goddess of Mahi River*

This tale was collected by Professor Pushker Chandervaker in the village of Dhuvaran, which lies on the banks of the Mahi river in the Kaira district of Gujarat. It was told in May 1962 by Sendhabhai Sendha, an uneducated Rajput of forty-five years who worked as a watchman at the local Public Works Department bungalow, and was well-known as a narrator. The collector wrote the tale down by hand in Gujarati and later translated it into English.

· 2 · *The Girl Who Was Loved by a Tree Spirit*

This story was collected by Dulal Chaudhuri and J. T. P. Ao from the Makong Chung area of Nagaland between 1975 and 1977. They have jointly translated this tale from the original Ao into English.

· 3 · *The Rain Prince's Bride*

This tale was told by Hana Bhota, a Bhil leader in Sanali, a settlement of Dungri Bhils located in the Aravalli Hills of the Banerskantha district bordering the Mewar district of Rajasthan. It was collected by Professor Pushker Chandervaker in October 1948. At that time, he was surveying a large body of folk songs popular in this tribal area. The tale was first rewritten in Gujarati from the Bhil, and in 1971 the collector translated it into English.

· 4 ·   A Farmer's Son

This story was recounted by Sengotayan, a farmer of about thirty belonging to the local Vellalar Kavuntar community and himself still a bachelor, due to poverty. This tale was second in a sequence of stories collected at a tale-telling session and was later translated into English by Brenda Beck.

· 5 ·   The Man Who Was in Love with Two Girls

This story was collected by Dulal Chaudhuri and J. T. P. Ao in the Makong Chung area of Nagaland between 1975 and 1977. They jointly translated the tale into English from the Ao.

· 6 ·   Love between Two Birds

This story was collected from Nagaland by Dulal Chaudhuri and J. T. P. Ao between 1975 and 1977. They jointly translated the tale into English from the Ao.

· 7 ·   Four Clever Men

This story was tape recorded on 5 March 1966 by Brenda Beck. It was told by a traditional storyteller named Marimuttu who lives in the village of Sudamani, near Chinna Dharapuram, in Tamilnadu. Marimuttu is a Vedan by caste and was about forty years old at the time. Marimuttu accompanied himself on a ritual drum called *pombai*. The tale was told at the collector's request and later translated into English by her from the Tamil. Four adults were present for this midday telling session.

· 8 ·   A Poor Man

This story was collected by Hal Schiffman of the University of Washington and Brenda Beck of the University of British Columbia. It was tape-recorded in 1966 at a storytelling session at Beck's local home in Olappalayam, near Kangayam, Tamilnadu. Seven adults (including the ethnographers) and two adolescents were present. The teller was a thirteen-year-old girl who belonged to the Vellalar Kavuntar farming community. Members of several other castes were present. This story was the seventh told in a sequence of twelve. It was later translated into English from the Tamil by Beck.

PART II
NEW BRIDES AND GROOMS

· 9 · *The Girl Fated to Die by Snakebite*

This story was collected by Mr. J. Tsuknung P. Ao in the Ao language. It comes from the Makong Chung area of Nagaland and is told by Ao Naga women. The story was contributed to this collection by Dulal Chaudhuri, who worked with Mr. P. Ao between 1975 and 1977.

1. The plants seen by the girl's father were special ones used by soothsayers for the treatment of snakebites.

· 10 · *The Yakshi's Descendants*

This Malayali tale was submitted by Raghavan Payyanad. It was collected in 1980 by K. P. Sathi as told by K. P. Balasubramaniam, a 25-year-old man of the Nayar caste living in Punchappatam village, Palghat District, Kerala.

· 11 · *A Marriage in the World of the Dead*

This tale was collected by J. P. T. Ao from the Makong Chung area of Nagaland in 1977. It was later translated into English for this collection by Dulal Chaudhuri.

· 12 · *A Dead Husband*

Professor Praphulladatta Goswami collected this tale in December of 1954 from Mrs. Subhadra Goswami, a 52-year-old Brahman woman of Nahir village, Kamrup District, Assam. Mrs. Goswami told the story to illustrate the power of destiny to her daughter-in-law.

· 13 · *Four Friends*

This tale was provided by Susan Wadley, of Syracuse University. It was originally collected in the 1920s by William Wiser, a well-known missionary and ethnographer, in Karimpur village, Mainpuri District, Uttar Pradesh. It was told to a Brahman male (name not known) by his aunt. This man acted as one of Wiser's local scribes. Wadley later translated the text into English from the Hindi.

1. Twelve years is a common period of penance or banishment in Indian tradition.

· 14 ·   *The Farmer and the Barber*

This story was collected in the 1920s by William Wiser. It was told by an elderly Brahman housewife of the village of Karimpur (published pseudonym), a settlement located near the town of Manipuri, about 150 miles southeast of Delhi. It was taken down in note form by the son of one of Wiser's informants and translated into English from the Hindi nearly sixty years later by Susan Wadley of Syracuse University. She is the anthropologist to whom the Wisers eventually gave their extensive fieldnotes.

· 15 ·   *The Story of a King*

This story was recounted by a farmer's daughter, a member of the Vellalar Kavuntar caste. She was about twelve years old when she participated in a storytelling session in her own village of Rettivalasu, near Kangayam, Tamilnadu, on 19 June 1966. Seven people were present for the telling, five adults and two teenagers. The story was tape-recorded and later translated into English from Tamil by the collector, Brenda Beck.

· 16 ·   *The King's Daughter*

This story was collected by Dr. Usha Nilsson, from her own mother, Priyamvada Devi, an older Kayastha woman who lives in Kanpur city, Uttar Pradesh. The collection circumstances are the same as for tale 92 which also appears in this volume. Nilsson translated the tale into English from the Hindi.

· 17 ·   *Sanykisar the Crow-Girl*

Lalita Handoo taped this tale in the village of Khonmuh, Srinagar District, Kashmir in May 1980 from a 78-year-old Muslim housewife and local storyteller named Sondari. The occasion was an informal collection session held in her house. This tale is generally told to young girls by elderly married women in Kashmiri homes and therefore seems to have important instructive functions. The human/nonhuman dichotomy, which runs through the whole tale, also seems to support this. For humans, adhering to social norm is as important as being free from them for animals. Those who attempt to violate social norms are forced into the world of nonhumans and live like them or with them as happens to crow-girl.

1. Unlike in many Indian languages, the moon is feminine in Kashmiri.

PART III
PARENTS AND CHILDREN

· 18 · *The Boy Who Could Speak with Birds*

This story was collected by Dulal Chaudhuri and J. T. P. Ao from the Makong Chung area of Nagaland between 1975 and 1977. They translated the tale into English from the Ao.

· 19 · *The Uninvited Guest*

This tale was collected in Srinigar, Kashmir, from Mr. P. N. Kaul, a 55-year-old government officer. It was tape-recorded by Lalita Handoo at home, on 25 December 1972. The occasion was a family storytelling session, as Mr. Kaul is her father. Six people, including two children, were present. Mrs. Handoo is also responsible for translating the story into English from the Kashmiri.

· 20 · *The Birth and Marriage of Siva*

This myth was told by Mr. Pratap Chandra Misra, a Brahman priest. He was seventy-six years old in 1947 when this account was recorded. It was told at the shrine of a village god, at midday, in the village of Damra, near Asansol, in the district of Burdwan, Bengal. Three men and two children were present. Professor Asutosh Bhattacharyya took the story down in note form and later translated it into English from the Bengali.

· 21 · *Chokanamma*

Raghavan Payyanad collected this tale from a 57-year-old man of the Vannan (tailor) caste named Mr. M. V. Koraperuvannan. The two met on 13 December 1979 in Kalliaseri Kannapuram village, Cannanore District, Kerala, at the house of the narrator. Mr. Payyanad later translated this tale into English from the Malayalam. Members of the Vannan community often become professional *teyyam* dancers.

· 22 ·   *The Youngest Daughter-in-Law*

This story was collected by Professor Asutosh Bhattacharyya, a folklorist from Calcutta, in July 1930. It was told by Mrs. Kumudini Devi, a Brahman housewife of about sixty years of age, a native of Jhalua village, near Mymensing, a district town in Bangaladesh. The tale was taken down in note form and later translated into English from the Bengali by the collector. This story was told at home, in the late morning, on an occasion when the whole family was worshiping the goddess Manasa. The audience was entirely female, except for the collector. Five adults and three children were present.

1. It is very common to worship snakes by offering them milk mixed with mashed bananas.
2. Manasa is considered the goddess of serpents. Snakes are thought to move with magical ease between her place in heaven and their own homes on earth.
3. The sij or Cactus Indious is also sacred to the Bedo Kacharis of Assam and there represents the chief male god, Mahadeva.

· 23 ·   *The Wicked Mendicant*

This tale was collected by Ashutosh Bhattacharyya. He heard it many years ago, in 1930, in the village of Jhalua, Mymensing District, Bangaladesh from his grandmother, Mrs. Braja Sundari Dev, who was seventy-five years old at the time. The occasion was evening story time.

· 24 ·   *Akanandun the Only Son*

This tale was collected in Kashmir by Lalita Handoo, a folklorist at the Central Institute of Indian Languages. The story comes from Dimal, an 84-year-old Brahman housewife and taleteller who lives in Srinagar. It was recounted for the sake of collection and tape-recorded in Dimal's home. It was told in her native language, Kashmiri, on 22 June 1971 in the middle of the day. Mrs. Handoo later translated the tale into English for use in this volume. Mrs. Dimal commented that a teller must have a heart of steel in order to tell this particular story.

· 25 ·   *Lord Siva and the Satwaras*

This story was collected by Professor Pushker Chandervarker, director of the Folklore Research Institute of Gujarat. The myth was told by Shri Karsanbhai Jiwabhai Nakum, a Satwara farmer of about sixty years of age who works at the Associated Cement Company in Dwarka, a town in the Saurastra region of Gujarat. It was taken down in note form on 8 October 1968. Professor Chandervarker later did the translation into English from the Gujarati.

· 26 ·   *An Old Man's Wisdom*

This tale was provided by Dulal Chaudhuri and J. T. P. Ao from the Makong Chung area of Nagaland and was collected between 1975 and 1977. They translated the tale into English from the Ao.

PART IV
SISTERS AND BROTHERS

· 27 ·   *Seven Dumb Daughters*

This story was collected and translated by Lalita Handoo, a native of Kashmir and now a folklorist at the Central Institute of Indian Languages. She tape-recorded it in her native tongue, Kashmiri, in December 1978. The tale was told at her home during a family chat by her mother, a Brahman woman, Smt. Laxmi Kaul, who is a housewife in the city of Srinigar. Two men, three women, and two children were present.

1. Normal speech demands that a girl say *maji kya dopuy,* but because of the stammering, this came out as *maji ka bobuy.* Roughly translated, this would be like changing the English "what did mother say?" into "what bid mother hay?"

· 28 ·   *The Clever Old Man*

Professor Praphulladatta Goswami collected this tale during May 1959 in the village of Jhargaon, Kamrup District, Assam. It was evening and Professor Goswami and the narrator, Ratikanta Brahma "Member," a 60-year-old farmer of the Bodo-Kachari tribe plus five or six other men were sipping rice beer together by a wood fire. Professor Goswami first transcribed the tale by hand and then later translated it into English.

· 29 ·   *Thabaton*

Dr. Iram Babu Singh tape-recorded this tale in February 1980 from Tombi Devi, a Hindu woman, 70 years old. She was a native of the village of Keinou, Manipur. The tale was translated by Dr. Singh for this volume.

1. These two words mean "precious as gold" and "upright as can be."

· 30 · *Kini Mulki*

This tale, told by Kargi Mundaldi (see the note to tale 44), was recorded in 1976 and translated for this volume by Peter Claus. What recalled the tale for Kargi, in conversation, was a reference to the caste of the characters of this tale in one of the folk songs (*paddana*) she had been recording for the ethnographer.

· 31 · *Greed Can Be Perilous*

This story was contributed by Raghavan Payyanad, a researcher in folklore at the Central Institute of Indian Languages. He is a native of Kerala, and this tale was first recorded in longhand in his native Malayalam. It was collected in November 1979 at the home of the narrator Madhavi Kathalam, a housewife, aged fifty-eight, who belonged to the Tiyya community in Cannanore town. Payyanad later translated the tale into English.

· 32 · *The Monkey-Son*

This story was told in the small village of Rettivalasu, near Kangayam, in the Coimbatore District of Tamilnadu. The milieu was a storytelling session in the home of a large landowner of the area. It was told at night by a local washerman called Mutali, who was about forty years of age at the time. Five other adults and three children were present. The story was tape-recorded in Tamil and later translated into English by the collector, Brenda Beck.

1. Marriages between men and their paternal aunt's daughters are viewed very favorably in the area of India where this story was collected. The refusal to marry such a girl is symbolic of monkey-boy's assertion of personal autonomy and his refusal to bow to family pressure.

· 33 · *Monkey-Boy's Story*

This story was collected in Olappalayam village, near Kangayam, in the Coimbatore District of Tamilnadu by Brenda Beck. It was told by a local nineteen-year-old girl, Sarasu, who belongs to the toddy tapping community. The tale was recounted during a storytelling session arranged in the collector's house. Five other adolescents and four adults were present. It was originally taped and later translated into English from the Tamil by Beck.

· 34 · Tolerance and Jealousy

This story was told in Madurai, Tamilnadu, by a Brahman housewife named Mrs. Vasantha. It was part of a conversation among friends in a local house and occurred during a daytime local social visit in late July 1979. The tale was later written down and translated by one of the teller's friends, Dr. Saraswathi Venugopal. She and two other women were present at the time of its telling.

· 35 · The Story of a Brother and a Sister

This story was collected by Dr. Usha Nilsson. It was tape-recorded in the city of Delhi in 1975, at the home of Priyamvada Devi, a Kayastha housewife who was seventy-four years old at the time. There were two other women present, her sisters, who corrected and corroborated the story. Usually this story is told on the day of "Brother's Second."

1. "Brother's Second" is a special day when all married women are supposed to receive and honor their brothers. This festival is especially popular in the Hindi speaking areas of North India.

· 36 · The Origin of Different Water Animals

This tale was submitted by Dulal Chaudhuri and J. P. T. Ao and collected in the Makong Chung area of Nagaland between 1975 and 1977. They translated the tale into English from the Ao.

· 37 · The Man Named Unige Mada

This tale was collected in the Nilgiri Hills of South India by Paul Hockings. It was told by N. Lingaiah, a Badaga singer and retired school master, in the Badaga language and tape-recorded during a special session in which only the teller, the ethnographer, and a research assistant were present. Hockings later translated the story into English with the help of an assistant, M. N. Thesingh.

1. Bani is still in existence, being a small hamlet of the Palu Kurumba tribe located on the southwestern slopes of the Nilgiri Hills. Rhythm and alliteration are important in the original poem, but not rhyming, and the translation follows suit. The Badaga language, how-

ever, allows for considerable play on similar sounding words—more so
than does English.

2. Despite the monsoons, this area is somewhat in a rain shadow and
periodically has suffered severe droughts, such as the one this tale
describes.

3. Notice the repetitions in this tale, e.g., "His legs on the stump
of a jagged jujube bush." What may seem like padding, however, relates to a general need to spin out tales like this, as this kind of poem is
sung to pass the time when a crowd of visitors is present for a funeral, or
perhaps is just waiting for the imminent death of a relative. A similar
effect is achieved by putting repeating parts of the narrative into the
mouths of different characters.

4. Until this century, tigers were a common nuisance in the
Nilgiris; today they are nearly extinct. Buffaloes can be very fierce and
have occasionally killed a marauding tiger.

5. Coins were hardly ever used by the Nilgiri tribes until the 19th
century. This sentence, therefore, reflects the modernization of the traditional barter arrangements between Todas and Kurumbas.

· 38 · *Mamo Jalwalo*

This tale was collected by Professor Pusker Chandervarker, director of
the Folklore Research Institute of Gujarat. He heard it and wrote it
down while visiting a village named Chandarva, which has a population
of roughly 1,500. Chandervaker translated the tale into English from
the Gujarti.

Chandarva lies on the east bank of a rivulet named Nilaka in the
Saurastra area of Gujarat and is the site of the collector's family home.
On the opposite bank of this stream there is a thicket. On the outskirts
of this thicket is a wasteland that has very salty soil. There are no trees
growing there except for one very big, old Piludi. This tree has two
large branches and a large hollow trunk. It is believed that the god
Mamo lives in that hollow trunk. No other tree has ever succeeded in
growing on this inhospitable soil.

PART V
DOMESTIC STRIFE

· 39 · *The Fish Head*

This tale was told on 9 December 1967 by Mrs. Dipali Sarma, a
Brahman housewife about twenty-three years old. She told the story in a

private home in a village near Patacharkuchi, Kamrup District, Assam, in the context of a discussion about humorous tales with the collector, Professor Praphulladatta Goswami. Mrs. Sarma had heard the tale from her mother-in-law who hailed from Barpeta, in the same district. Goswami later used his fieldnotes to translate the story into English from the Assamese.

· 40 · *The Cruel Daughter-in-Law*

This Malayali tale was collected in 1980 by Eyangod Sreedharan, translated by T. V. Gopalan, and sent to us by Raghavan Payyanad, of the Department of Folklore, Mysore University. It was told by Mrs. Chellachi, a 68-year-old Irava woman from the village of Vadavanoor, Phalghat District, Kerala. Payyanad said that several versions of this tale circulate in Malayalam.

· 41 · *A Flowering Tree*

This story was collected by a Kannada folktale specialist named Dhavalasri. It was told to her by a woman called Siddamma, from the town of Tumkur, Karnataka. The story appears in a collection of Kannada language tales by Dhavalasri entitled, *Janapada Kathamrta,* vol. 3. (1968), 32–42. It was translated by Professor A. K. Ramanujan at the University of Chicago.

· 42 · *Two Sisters-in-Law*

Usha Nilsson collected this tale in April 1975, from her cousin, Mrs. Pramila Hans (Kayastha caste), aged fifty-five, a schoolteacher in Aligarh, Uttar Pradesh. The story was told in Mrs. Hans's house. One other woman was present in addition to the teller and the collector.

· 43 · *Kecha Nahar*

Praphulladatta Goswami collected this tale when Jibeswar Goswami came to his home on a social visit in 1969. Jibeswar Goswami is a retired civil servant, aged 61 and a Brahman. He lives in Shillong, the former capital of Assam, but visits his son-in-law in Dispur, near Gauhati, the present capital of Assam. J. Goswami is a specialist in a tradition of medieval Vaishnavite music and dance.

1. Paniya Danr means the watery rudder; Kecha Nahar refers to the green ironwood tree; and Mukuta is the word for pearl.

· 44 ·   *Lord Krishna's Wives*

Several Tulu versions of this story were collected in song (*paddana*) and narrative form (*katha*) by Peter Claus in 1977. This particular version was provided by Kargi Mundaldi, a 60-year-old Mundalda woman of Hiriyadka, South Kanara District, Karnataka.

1. The *parijata,* or Indian coral tree (Erythrina indica), is said to be one of the trees found both in heaven (*swarga*) and on earth.

2. The town of Udipi is famous for its Krishna temple (here called a *matta*) and as the center where the renowned sage of Vedanta philosophy, Madvacharya, made his home.

3. The *ettayi* flower is yellow and appears on a rapidly growing. clinging vine, associated here with feminine qualities. The *tulsi* plant is sacred to Vishnu.

· 45 ·   *Sandrembi and Chaishra*

This tale was translated and sent to us by Iram Babu Singh of the Department of Folklore, Jawaharlal Nehru University, Imphal, Manipur. He taped it in February 1980 as it was told by W. Tomba Singh, a 52-year-old Hindu male. The recording session was held on the veranda of W. Tomba Singh's home at the request of the collector.

1. A *long* is a kind of fishing instrument made from very thin and pliable bamboo pieces shaped into a net. It has only one opening and curved into a long funnel rather like the English letter *U*.

2. A *tungon* is a potlike container used for carrying fish.

3. A *phiruk* is an indigenous box used to hold clothing. It is made from finely cut, pliable bamboo pieces. It is long and has a round head made of two pieces.

4. The first several sounds are the sounds of the forest bird. The last word means "almost empty."

· 46 ·   *The Tale of the Mouse*

This tale was told in Srinigar, Kashmir, on 25 June 1971 by a Muslim male of about fifty-two years of age named Gulam Rasool. It was told in a house to a circle of his friends during a storytelling session. Rasool is a domestic servant by occupation. The group he spoke to included three adults and eight children. The story was tape-recorded by Lalita Handoo, who later translated it into English from her native Kashmiri.

· 47 ·   *As Long as You Keep Your Legs Up*

This story was collected by Jawaharlal Handoo in 1978 from Sudhindra Kumar, a male teacher of Hindi literature of about forty years of age. Handoo is responsible for the translation into English from the Braj dialect of Hindi.

· 48 ·   *Siva and Parvati*

This tale was collected in 1970 by Amrit Someshwar from Annu Nalke, who was about 50 years old at the time, in the village of Kanoji, in South Kanara District, Karnataka State. It was originally told in Tulu. Someshwar, a prominent folklorist of that district, first translated it into Kannada. In 1975 he and the American anthropologist, Mimi Nichter, translated the tale into English and she in turn sent it for inclusion in this collection. The narrator, Annu Nalke, is renown for his performances in spirit possession cults which require knowledge of an extensive repertoire of myths, ballads, and legends.

1. *Cenne* is a game played in many parts of southern India. It is similar to the African game usually referred to as *mancala*. It is played on a board consisting of two rows, each with seven small bowl shaped depressions.

2. Women of the Koraga forest tribe are addressed and referred to as Korpalu.

· 49 ·   *The Story of a Man Who Had Awful Lips*

This story was collected by Saraswati Venugopal from an Ayyar Brahman woman, Mrs. Rajalakshmi, in 1950. She was thirty years old when she told the story at dinnertime, in a family house. The tale was etched on the collector's memory due to hearing it frequently. It was later written down by her and then translated into English. Four children were present for the telling, of which Mrs. Venugopal was one. Mrs. Rajalakshmi is her elder sister. Similar tales focus on other physical deformities such as a hunched back.

1. Many Indians like to chew betel leaves along with arecanuts and lime after dinner. The combination of these three is believed to be very good for the digestion.

· 50 · *Vayanatu Kulavan*

This tale was collected, translated, and sent to us by Raghavan Payyanad.
Members of the Vannan caste tell many mythological tales about local
deities in this same style. This one comes to us from Kannaperu Vannan,
age sixty, of Poonkavu village, Cannanore District, Kerala. Kannaperu,
like many men of his caste, participates in the spirit possession rituals of
this area.

· 51 · *The Enchanted Water Hole*

Iram Babu Singh, Department of Folklore, Jawaharlal Nehru University,
Imphal, Manipur, taped this tale in June 1980 from Dr. H. Kam-
khenthang, a research officer in the Tribal Development Department of
the Manipur Government. It comes from the southern part of Manipur
where the Maities live.

PART VI
MORAL VIRTUE OR ITS LACK

· 52 · *The Prince and the Shepherd*

This tale was submitted to us by the Bengali folklorist, Ashutosh Bhattacharyya. It was told on request to one of his students, Gauri Bhattacharyya, in 1967. The teller was Snehabala Dandapat, a thirty-year-old
woman of an agriculturalist caste, from the village of Hatibari, near the
steel-producing town of Jamshedpur, Singhbhum District, West
Bengal.

· 53 · *Rich Girl, Poor Girl*

This tale was submitted by Dulal Chaudhuri. He and J. T. P. Ao collected it in the Makong Chung area of Nagaland between 1975 and
1977. They translated the tale into English from the Ao.

· 54 · *The Dexterity of a Squirrel*

This Malayalam tale was submitted by Raghavan Payyanad. It was collected by T. M. Mohan from T. S. Sankaram, aged fifty-five, at his home
in Vallchira village, Trichur District, Kerala. Payyanad, a student of
folklore at Mysore University, has also collected several other versions of
the same story.

· 55 ·   *The Mincemeat Spirit*

This story was collected on 14 January 1979 from Mrs. Laxmi Kaul, a
Brahman housewife of about fifty years of age who lives in Srinigar,
Kashmir. She spoke to a family audience that included six adults and four
children. The collector, Lalita Handoo, is one of Mrs. Kaul's daughters.
The tale was tape-recorded and later translated by the collector. It was
originally told in Kashmiri.

· 56 ·   *The Crane and the Crow*

This story was told by Mrs. Satya, a housewife in a village located near the
town of Alleppy, in southern Kerala. It was collected in December 1979
by V. K. Krishna, a folklorist. Later, this account was translated into
English from the Malayalam by Raghavan Payyanad. According to him,
the tale is also widely known in more northerly parts of Kerala. The story
was told in the house of the narrator.

· 57 ·   *The Tale of Bibgaraz Maj*

Mrs. Handoo tape-recorded this story while taking part in *pan* ceremonies among a gathering of her friends and relatives. The tale was told
by Mrs. Sumavati Kaul, a sixty-year-old Brahman housewife in August
1979.

  1. Dry cowdung cakes are used as fuel throughout India.
  2. The fourth day of the lunar forthnight of the auspicious month of
Badirpyth, the sixth month of the Hindu calendar. This corresponds to
August-September.
  3. On ritualistic occasions, a part of the offerings (fruit, water,
milk, etc.) made to God are returned to devotees. This is called *navid*.
  4. Literally, the "cake of the maiden."

· 58 ·   *The Children of the Crab*

This tale was told to Peter Claus during fieldwork in South Kanara
District, Karnataka, in 1977. It was narrated in Tulu by Kargi Mundaldi, a sixty-year-old woman of the Mudalda caste. Kargi, whose repertoire of stories, plant lore, songs, and legends could not be exhausted
by six months of collection efforts, told this story while resting in the
shade after a long day's work in the paddy fields.

· 59 ·   *The Rupee Note*

This story was told by Banikanta Sarma, a Brahman male of about thirty-five years of age, hailing from Gamerimuri village near Kaithalkuchi in the Kamrup District of Assam. A clever person, he belongs to a family of scholars specializing in Sanskrit studies. He teaches Assamese and has done work on missionary contribution to Assamese language and literature in the last century. This story was collected at midday, on 23 December 1969, in an office at the University of Gauhati. The teller was a university teacher, and the collector was a colleage of his. The story was told over a cup of tea and written down by hand. The collector, Praphulladatta Goswami, of Gauhati University, translated the tale into English from the Assamese. Sarma is known as a very dependable informant for folktales.

· 60 ·   *The Value of an American "Thank You"*

This tale was told to Jawaharlal Handoo by a garage mechanic named Raja, in Mysore, Karnataka. Raja, aged thirty-five, works in the garage Handoo brings his car to for repairs. He told him this story in broken Hindi while working on the car.

· 61 ·   *The Brahman's Lime*

This story was collected by Bisweswar Hazarika, B.A. It was told by his mother during a winter evening in 1954 in a family house in the village of Barpathar, near Golaghat town, in the state of Assam. The occasion was an important children's ceremony. Three of four children were present for the telling besides Hazarika. The teller's name is not known, but she was a housewife belonging to a peasant family of the Ahom community and was about forty-five years of age at the time. The tale was later translated into English by Praphuladatta Goswami. Hazarika is now a college professor at Gauhati teaching Assamese. His special field of study is linguistics.

· 62 ·   *The Feast*

This tale was told to Praphulladatta Goswami by Banikanta Sarma on the same occasion as when tale 76 was told.

· 63 ·   *Borrowed Earrings*

Professor Narayana Rao of the University of Wisconsin Center for South Asian Studies in Madison recollects this tale from the days of his youth in Andhra Pradesh. It is part of his own repertoire of Telugu tales he tells to friends. He was the informant and translator of this tale for the collection.

· 64 · *Oh! Calcutta*

Jawaharlal Handoo collected this tale in Hindi from a 42-year-old native of Uttar Pradesh who prefers not to be named. This man spent more than a decade in Calcutta and reports that his story is popular among Hindi speaking immigrants in Calcutta and also widespread in the neighboring states of Bihar and Orissa.

· 65 · *Dala Tarwadi*

This tale was collected by Pushker Chandervaker. It was told to him by the late Dahima, mother of one of his cousins. Dahima, a Brahman widow eighty years of age, narrated the story in her native village of Chandarva, Ahmedabad District, Gujarat State. She often told the tale at night to the children of her own family and also to youths living in neighboring households. The tale was first written down by hand in Gujarati, in October 1934. Pushker Chandervaker later translated these notes of his work into English from the Gujarati for this volume.

· 66 · *The Story of Pebet*

This story was recounted on 6 January 1980 by K. Chaoba Singh, belonging to the Meitie community. He is a retired government servant of about sixty-five years of age. It was told during the evening in a house in Keishamthong, in the neighborhood of Impal, the capital of Manipur State. No other persons were present except the teller and the collector, Irom Babu Singh. The story was tape-recorded and later translated into English from the Manipuri by Dr. Singh, a folklorist and university teacher living in Impal City.

· 67 · *The Outlaw Babar Deva*

This legend was collected by Pusker Chandervarker in Goral, Kaira District, Gujarat, the village of Babar Deva's birth. During December 1962, Babar's brother Rama Deva, and others in Goral at the time, told Chadervarker what they themselves had heard of this famous outlaw during their own association with the Gandhian movement. The additional persons who spoke were Sharva Sri Shivabhai and Ambalal Patel. Both live in Borsad Chavani. Chandervarker took extensive notes on the Babar legend and later translated these into English from the Gujarati.

PART VII
KNOWLEDGE AND THE FOOL

· 68 ·   *The Elephant and the Ant*

This tale was narrated by the late Abhabha Hadabha Ker of Gorinjal
village in Okhamandal, a coastal area in western Gujarat. Abhabha Ker
was a local historian and stylish teller of heroic tales. He could even
recite folk legends in verse. He was sixty-five years old and an illiterate
farmer in 1968 when the collector met him. This legend was written
down in the Jadeji dialect in October 1968 by Pushker Chandervaker
while the latter lived with the teller in his farm cottage. It was translated into English in 1968 during the period when this collector served
as professor of Gujarati literature, in Dhrangadhra town, Zalawar,
Saurastra.

· 69 ·   *The Crow and the Sparrow*

Usha Nilsson collected this tale in Delhi from Mrs. Janakidevi, a housewife, now deceased. She was about sixty-five years old in 1975 when she
told the story to Nilsson during an informal visit. Nilsson translated the
tale into English.

· 70 ·   *The Parrots and the Carpenter's Scale*

Raghavan Payyanad collected this tale in 1979 from Kunhamma, age
sixty-two, a housewife of Vypinkara village, Ernakulam District, Kerala. Kunhamma is a Christian.

· 71 ·   *The Potter and the Wagher*

Puskar Chandravakar collected this tale from Viraji Hadabha Ker, a 46-
year-old man of the Wagher caste, as the two walked along enroute to
visit the site of a fortress historically connected with a local heroic ballad. The narrator is a skilled raconteur of local ballads, folktales, songs,
and caste histories. He lives in the village of Gorinjal, in the Okhamandal region of Gujarat State. Puskar Chandervaker translated the tale into
English from the Jadeji dialect of Gujerati spoken by the Wagher caste
people of western Saurastra.

· 72 ·   *The King of Delhi and the King of Turkey*

This story was collected in the 1920s in the village of Karimpur
(pseudonym) near Mainpuri, about one hundred and fifty miles south-

east of Delhi, in Uttar Pradesh. It was told by a Brahman man and recorded in note form by his brother. The story forms part of a collection of folktales made by William Wiser, a missionary then working in the area. The stories in his ethnographic library were later bequeathed to Susan Wadley of Syracuse University. She translated this one into English from the original Hindi.

· 73 · *The Single-Wit*

This tale was narrated by the late Mashru Mava, a member of the Chunvalia Koli (or, so-called "outlaw") caste, or Chanderva village in Ahmedabad District of Gujarat State. Though of relatively low-caste status, Mashru was locally recognized as a man of great wisdom. Once Mashru saved his village from outlaws who came to loot it. He was a good hunter and used to while away time and amuse other villagers by telling stories and relating his hunting experiences. Pushker Chandervaker collected this tale from him in October of 1939 and later, in 1967, translated it into English.

· 74 · *Tenali Ramalingadu*

This tale was submitted by Professor V. Narayana Rao of the University of Wisconsin, Madison. This tale is part of Rao's own wealth of tales he tells to friends and colleagues in both Telugu or English. He is thus both informant and translator for this tale for the collection.

· 75 · *The Ghost of a Brahman*

This tale was told by Hamsheswar Sain, a sixty-year-old Hindu male belonging to the Aguri community. It was told in his house, in the village of Silipur, near Durgapur, in Burdwan District, West Bengal, late one evening in May 1947. Mr. Sain is a grade school teacher. The tale was collected by Professor Asutosh Bhattacharyya of Calcutta University and taken down in handwritten Bengali. Bhattacharyya later translated it into English. The story was told at the collector's request. About ten children, of both sexes, were present at the time.

· 76 · *The Daily Measure*

This tale was collected in 1961 by Praphulladatta Goswami. It was told by Banikanta Sarma, a 35-year-old Brahman colleague of his at Gauhati University in Assam. The occasion was a tea break. This shows that the tradition of telling folktales continues to be enjoyed in India, even in the most urban intellectual settings.

· 77 · *Badsah the Great King*

A 65-yr-old Brahman male told this story. Siva Bayu, the teller, was a temple priest in Awantipora near Anantnag, in the state of Jammu and Kashmir at the time. This story was told on 14 June 1970 in his house at an informal storytelling session that was organized for the collector. No one else was present. Lalitta Handoo recorded the story on tape and later translated it into English from the Kashmiri.

· 78 · *The Foolish Gujjar*

This tale was collected by Lalita Handoo, on 25 December 1972. She tape-recorded it from her father, P. N. Kaul, during an informal evening storytelling session at the family home in Srinagar, Kashmir. Mr. Kaul is a government official, aged fifty-five, and a Brahman.

· 79 · *Our Wife*

Professor Narayana Rao of the University of Wisconsin Center for South Asian Studies recollects this tale from the days of his youth in Velcuru village, Andhra Pradesh. See note for tale 63.

· 80 · *I'll Take Two*

This tale was submitted by Professor Velchuru Narayana Rao, who also recalled the parallel story in the Sanskrit literary tale collection, *Kathasaritsagar*. In that story a parallel play on the Sanskrit term *modaka*, a type of sweet, is important. This folktale, however, is part of Rao's own extensive repertoire of tales he tells to friends and colleagues in Telugu or English. He does not recall where he first heard it.

· 81 · *Dropping, Rolling, Tail-Peeler*

This tale was collected and submitted by Raghavan Payyanad. He arranged to have Kunhambu Swami tell it to him in a house in Kuttuparamba village, Cannanore District, Kerala. A friend, T. V. Gopalan, later translated the story into English.

· 82 · *Panikar's Blunder*

This story was told by M. K. Velappakutty, secretary of a rural co-operative society in Kerala. It was told in the village of Panamkulam, near Karunannoor, Trichur District, on 4 May 1980. The collector was T. M. Mohan, a folklore student. He visited the narrator's house and wrote the account down in note form. It was later translated into English from the Malayalam at the Folklore Department of the Central Institute of Indian Languages by Raghavan Payyanad.

· 83 · *The Fox and the Crow*

This is one of the tales from the Wiser Collection, translated by Susan Wadley. Wiser's notes do not indicate who told this particular tale. See note for tale 85.

· 84 · *The Greatest Fool of All*

This tale was told by Bankim Mahato, a Hindu agriculturalist of about sixty years of age, who lives in the village of Jhargram, in Midnapore District, West Bengal. It was collected by a folklore student named Sanat Kumar Mitra in midafternoon, 6 April 1966. There was no audience except for the collector, who requested the story and took it down in note form. The tale was later translated into English from the Bengali by Professor Asutosh Bhattacharyya of Calcutta University.

· 85 · *A Jackal and a Fox*

This tale was written down by a Brahman male after his mother narrated it to him in the village of Karimpur (a ficticious name), in Manipuri District, Uttar Pradesh. The request to collect this and similar stories came from William Wiser sometime during the 1920s. Susan Wadley, who had been analyzing the Wiser collection, translated the account and sent it for inclusion in this collection.

· 86 · *A Jackal and a Crocodile*

This tale was recounted by an unknown Brahman housewife, sometime in the 1920s, in the village of Karimpur (pseudonym), near Mainpuri, in Uttar Pradesh, about 150 miles southeast of Delhi. It was written down by hand, in Hindi, by her brother-in-law and later translated into English by Susan Wadley of Syracuse University. The story belongs to a larger collection of tales gathered by William Wiser, a missionary and ethnographer who worked in this area during the early part of this century.

· 87 · *Chamdan and Yuthung*

This tale was contributed by Iram Babu Singh of the Folklore Department at Jawaharlal Nehru University, Imphal, Manipur. Singh heard the tale one evening at the local literary academy. It was told by Merajao Kabui, an inspector with the Manipur Road and Transportation Corporation. Kabui, forty-five years old, was well educated. Singh took notes at the time of the telling. Later, he wrote the story down and showed it to Kabui for approval. Still later, Singh translated it into English from the Manipuri.

1. A *thourei* is a village man empowered to arbitrate in disputes.

· 88 ·   *The Sparrow and the Sweet Pudding*

The collector first learned this story from her Ayyar Brahman mother, Mrs. Lakshmi, in the village of Sattur, near Virudunagar, in Ramnad District, Tamilnadu, sometime between 1945 and 1950. Mrs. Laksmi used the tale to put her children to sleep at night. The collector, Dr. V. Saraswati Venugopal, of the department of Tamil, the University of Madurai, remembered the story because of having heard it frequently. She later translated it into English from the Tamil after rediscovering it thirty years later when it was spontaneously retold by a friend at a Brahaman home in the city of Madurai.

PART VIII
ORIGIN TALES

· 89 ·   *The Origin of Man*

This origin tale was told by Linus D. Nelli, a 32-year-old male of the Mao Naga tribe. It was recounted on 8 February 1980 near a Pastoral Training Center, at Sangaiprou, near Imphal in Manipur State. Nelli is a Christian who works in a local church as a brother. He told this myth especially for the collector, Iram Babu Singh, who later translated it into English at the J. N. University Centre, Imphal. The original text was in Manipuri. The story was partially tape-recorded and partially written down in note form.

· 90 ·   *How Lijaba Created the World*

This tale was collected by Dulal Chaudhuri and J. T. P. Ao from the Makong Chung area of Nagaland between 1975 and 1977. They translated the tale into English from the Ao.

· 91 · *The Porcupine Daughter*

This story was told by Viram Hadabha Ker, a young man of the Wagher caste who belongs to Gorinja village, near Dwarka, in the Saurastra area of Gujarat. It was collected in handwritten form by Professor Pushker Chandervarker, director of the Folklore Research Institute of Gujarat, during a visit to Dwarka town on 25 October 1968. Chandervarker later translated the tale into English from the Gujarati.

· 92 · *The Origin of the Temple at Tarakesvar*

This tale was collected by Alan Morinis and was told on 11 September 1977 by Poromananda Chattopadhyay, a Brahman priest at the Lakshmi-Narayan Temple. The story was later translated into English from the Bengali by Morinis.

· 93 · *Bhimnath Mahadev*

The collector, Puskher Chandervaker, heard this story from Mrs. Champaben U. Dave, of Bhimnath. She is the wife of one of the collectors' cousins. This woman is illiterate, and she belongs to a priestly caste. Hence she shares in her family's traditional knowledge of local myths and all-India epic stories. She has a good memory and often retells incidents from the sacred texts to other village women on ritual days. Chandervaker took this story down in long hand in 1948 and translated it into English in 1967. The same account also exists in ballad form and is sung by bards of the Kunbi Patel caste, an important agricultural community in Gujarat state.

· 94 · *The Carpenter's Tale*

This tale was collected from the Rathawa Bhils by Shin Sankerbhai Tadavi, a grade school teacher from Pavi-Jelpur village in the Broach district of southern Gujarat. Sankarbhai is a Rathawa Bhil himself, and this story is part of a larger collection of tales which he assembled in his own Rathwa-Bhili dialect and then rewrote in Gujarati. Pushker Chandervaker translated the later version into English in November 1979.

· 95 · *The Origin of Head-Hunting*

This tale was collected by Dulal Chaudhuri and J. P. T. Ao from the Makong Chung area of Nagaland between 1975 and 1977. They translated the tale into English from the Ao.

· 96 · *Friendship between Man and Dog*

This tale was told by Linus Nelli, a Mao Naga male who was about thirty-two years old at the time. It was collected near Imphal, in Manipur State, at the same time and under the same circumstances as tale 89. See the note to that tale for more details.

· 97 · *Why the Ow Fruit Drops (Falls) in March*

This cumulative tale was told by Bhaben Narzi, a member of the Bodo Kachari tribe in the Kamrup District of Assam. It was collected in 1968 in Jhargaon village near Rangiya town and was told for the collector and a friend. It was originally written down and later translated into English from the Assamese by the collector, Praphulladatta Goswami. Narzi used to live the life of a farmer. Now he is a lawyer's assistant in Gauhati. Deeply interested in tribal cultural traditions, he has written on the songs, tales, and customs of the Bodo community of Assam. Narzi is one of Goswami's best informants.

   1. The ow or *Dilennia Indica* is a vegetable used to give some curries a sour taste.

· 98 · *Sharpening the Dagger*

This tale was collected by Iram Babu Singh, of the J. N. University Centre in Imphal. He heard it on 26 March 1980 from a Mrs. Lamding, a twenty-seven year old woman of the Thadou tribe located in the Kangchup Road tribal village near Lamsang town, in Manipur State. It was told in a garden, for the collector, and was tape-recorded. Mrs. Lamding is a grade school teacher. Singh later translated the tale into English from the Manipuri. He reports having collected a similar account from a member of the Meitei community in the same area.

· 99 · *The Death of Mosquito*

This chain tale was told by an Ayyar Brahman housewife of about sixty years of age who lives in Madurai city, Tamilnadu. It was told in the evening, at home, to an audience of six people, four of whom were adult women, "just having a good time." Two children were also present. Saraswathi Venugopal wrote the tale down by hand on 22 July 1979 and later translated it into English. The women present were her relatives and friends. Venugopal reports having heard another version of the tale that contains only small variations from the one supplied here.

Bibliography

AARNE, ANTTI. *The Types of the Folktale.* (Folklore Fellows Communications, no. 184). Translated and enlarged by Stith Thompson. Helsinki: Suomalainen Tiedeakatemia, 1964.

ADAMS, ROBERT. "The Tales of Greed and Punishment: A Study of an Indian Oral Tale." *Journal of the Assam Research Society* 15 (1961): 22–36.

AMORE, R. C., AND LARRY D. SHINN. *Lustful Maidens and Ascetic Kings: Buddhist and Hindu Stories of Life.* New York: Oxford University Press, 1981.

BECK, BRENDA E. F. "The Study of a Tamil Epic: Several Versions of Silappadikaram Compared." *Journal of Tamil Studies* 1 (1972): 23–38.

———. *The Three Twins: The Telling of a South Indian Folk Epic.* Bloomington: Indiana University Press, 1982.

BEN-AMOS, DAN. "Hebrew Parallels to Indian Folktales." *Journal of the Assam Research Society* 15 (1961): 37–45.

BENDALL, CECIL. "The *Tantrakhyana*: A Collection of Indian Folktales from a Unique Sanskrit Manuscript, Discovered in Nepal." *Journal of the Royal Asiatic Society of Great Britain and Ireland* 20 (1888): 465–501.

BENFEY, THEODORE. *Pantschantantra Fünf Bücher Indischer Fabeln, Märchen und Erzählungen.* Leipzig: F. A. Brockhaus, 1859.

BLOOMFIELD, MAURICE. "The Character and Adventures of Muladeva." *Proceedings of the American Philosophical Society* 52 (1913): 616–50.

———. "On Talking Birds in Hindu Fiction." In *Festschrift für Ernst Windisch,* 349–61. Leipzig: Otto Harrassowitz, 1914.

321

_____. "On Recurring Psychic Motifs in Hindu Fiction: The Laugh and Cry Motif." *Journal of the American Oriental Society* 36 (1916): 54–89.

_____. "On the Art of Entering Another's Body: A Hindu Fiction Motif." *Proceedings of the American Philosophical Society* 56 (1917): 1–43.

_____. "The Fable of the Crow and the Palm Tree: A Psychic Motif in Hindu Fiction." *American Journal of Philology* 40 (1919): 1–36.

_____. "On Overhearing as a Motif of Hindu Fiction." *American Journal of Philology* 41 (1920): 309–35.

_____. "The Dohada or Craving of Pregnant Women." *Journal of the American Oriental Society* 40 (1920): 1–24.

_____. "Joseph and Potiphar in Hindu Fiction." *Transactions and Proceedings of the American Philosophical Association* 54 (1922): 142–76.

_____. "On False Ascetics and Nuns in Hindu Fiction." *Journal of the American Oriental Society* 44 (1924): 202–42.

_____. "On Organized Brigandage in Hindu Fiction." *American Journal of Philology* 47 (1926): 205–33.

BODDING, P. O. *Santal Folk Tales.* 3 vols. Oslo and Cambridge, Mass.: H. Aschehoug and Co., 1925–29.

BØDKER, LAURITS. *Indian Animal Tales, a Preliminary Survey.* (*Folklore Fellows Communications* no. 170). Helsinki: Soumalainen Tiedeakatemia, 1957.

BROWN, W. N. "THE *Panchatantra* in Modern Indian Folklore." *Journal of the American Oriental Society* 39 (1919): 1–54.

_____. "The Wandering Skull: New Light on *Tantrakhyana.*" *American Journal of Philology* 40 (1919): 423–29.

_____. "Escaping One's Fate." In *Studies in Honor of Maurice Bloomfield,* edited by Ruth Norton, 89–104. New Haven: Yale University Press, 1920.

_____. "Vyaghramari, or the Lady Tiger-killer: A Study of the Motif of Bluff in Hindu Fiction." *American Journal of Philology* 42 (1921): 122–51.

_____. "The Silence Wager Stories: Their Origin and Their Diffusion. *American Journal of Philology* 43 (1922): 289–317.

_____. "The Tar-baby Story at Home." *Scientific Monthly* 15 (1922): 228–34.

_____. *The Indian and Christian Miracles of Walking on Water.* Chicago: Open Court, 1928.

BURLINGAME, EUGENE WATSON. "The Act of Truth (*Saccakiriyai*): A Hindu Spell and Its Employment as a Psychic Motif in Hindu Fiction." *Journal of the Royal Asiatic Society of Great Britain and Ireland* 49 (1917): 429–68.

CAMPBELL, A. *Santal Folk Tales.* Pukhuria, India: Santal Mission Press, 1891.

CHAUDHURY, P. C. ROY, GEN. ED. *Folktales of India Series.* 20 vols. New Delhi: Sterling, 1969–75.

CLAUS, PETER J. "Spirit Possession and Spirit Mediumship from the Perspective of Tulu Oral Traditions." *Culture, Medicine, and Psychiatry* 3 (1979): 29–52.

CROOKE, C. WILLIAM. *Religion and Folklore of Northern India.* London: H. Mifford, 1926.

DAY, L. B. *Folktales of Bengal.* London: Macmillan, 1883.

DORSON, RICHARD M., ED. *Folktales Told Around the World.* Chicago: University of Chicago Press, 1975.

DUMEZIL, G. *Mythe et Épopée.* 3 vols. Paris: Gallimard, 1968–73.

EDGERTON, FRANKLIN. *The Pancatantra Reconstructed.* 2 vols. New Haven: American Oriental Society, 1924.

_____. *Panchatantra.* 1924. Reprint. London: Allen & Unwin, 1964.

ELLIS, JOHN M. *One Fairy Story Too Many: The Brothers Grimm and Their Tales.* Chicago: University of Chicago Press, 1983.

ELWIN, VERRIER. *Folk Tales of Mahakoshal.* Bombay: Oxford University Press, 1944.

EMENEAU, MURRAY B. "A Classical Indian Folktale as a Reported Modern Event: The Brahman and the Mongoose." *Proceedings of the American Philosophical Society* 83 (1940): 503–13.

_____. *Kota Texts.* 4 vols. Berkeley and Los Angeles: University of California Publications in Linguistics, 1944–46.

FRERE, MARY. *Old Deccan Days; or, Hindu Fairy Legends Current in Southern India.* 1868. London: John Murray, 1870, 1881, 1889; also New York: Dover, 1967.

GHOSH, OROON, ED. *The Dance of Siva and Other Tales from India.* New York: The New American Library, 1965.

GOSWAMI, PRAPHULLADATTA. "The Cinderella Motif in Assamese Folktales." *The Indian Historical Quarterly* 23 (1947): 311–19.

_____. *Ballads and Tales of Assam.* Gauhati, India: University of Gauhati, 1960.

GRIERSON, SIR GEORGE A. *Hatim's Tales, Kashmiri Stories and Songs.* Collected by Aurel Stein, with a note on the folklore of the tales by W. Crooke. London: John Murray, 1923.

GRIMM, JACOB. *Deutsche Mythologie.* Gottingen: Dieterich, 1835. English translation by James S. Stalybrass, *Teutonic Mythology,* 4 vols. London, 1880–88.

HALLIDAY, W. R. "Notes Upon Indo-European Folk-tales and the Problem of Their Diffusion." *Folklore* 34 (1923): 117–40.

HANDOO, JAWAHARLAL. *A Bibliography of Indian Folk Literature.* Mysore: Central Institute of Indian Languages, 1977.

HART, GEORGE L. "The Little Devotee: Cekkilar's Story of Ciruttontar." In *Sanskrit and Indian Studies: Essays in Honour of Daniel H. H. Ingalls,* edited by Masatoshi Nagatomi et al., 217–36. Hingham, MA: Kluwer Academic, 1980.

_____. *The Poems of Ancient Tamil.* Berkeley: University of California Press, 1975.

JACOBS, JOSEPH. *Indian Fairy Tales.* London: David Nutt, 1892. New York: Dover, 1969.

KINGSCOTE, MRS. HOWARD, AND S. M. NATESA SASTRI. *Tales of the Sun, or Folklore of Southern India.* London: W. H. Allen, 1890.

KIRKLAND, EDWIN C. *A Bibliography of South Asian Folklore.* Bloomington: Indiana University Research Center, 1966.

KNOWLES, JAMES H. *The Folktales of Kashmir.* London: Trubner and Sons, 1893.

MAYEDA, NORIKO, AND W. N. BROWN. *Tawi Tales: Folktales from Jammu.* Vol. 57 of the American Oriental Series. New Haven: Amerian Oriental Society, 1974.

MITRA, S. C. "Folklore of the Headless Man in North Bihar." *Journal of the Anthropological Society of Bombay* 10 (1916): 495–507.

MOHANTI, PRAFULLA. *Indian Village Tales.* London: Davis-Poynter, 1975.

MÜLLER, F. MAX. "Comparative Mythology." In M. Muller, *Oxford Essays,* 1–87. Oxford: Clarendon Press.

————. *Natural Religion*. London: Longmans, Green and Company, 1907.

NARAYAN, R. K. *Gods, Demons, and Others*. London: Heinemann, 1964.

NORTON, RUTH. "The Life Index: A Hindu Fiction Motif." In *Studies in Honor of Maurice Bloomfield*, edited by Ruth Norton, 211–24. New Haven: Yale University Press, 1920.

O'FLAHERTY, WENDY D. *Tales of Sex and Violence*. Chicago and London: University of Chicago Press, 1985.

PARKER, HENRY. *Village Folk-Tales of Ceylon*. 3 vols. London: Luzac, 1910–14. New York: Arno Press, 1977.

PENZER, N. M., ED. *The Ocean of Story* (C. H. Tawney's translation of Somadeva's *Kathasaritsagara*). 10 vols. London: C. J. Sawyer, 1924–28. Delhi: Motilal Banarsidass, 1968.

RAMANUJAN, A. K. "Hanci: A Kannada Cinderella." In *Cinderella: A Folklore Casebook*, edited by Alan Dundes, 259–75. New York: Garland, 1982.

————. "The Indian Oedipus." In *Oedipus: A Folklore Casebook*, edited by Lowell Edmunds and Alan Dundes, 234–66. New York: Garland, 1983.

RHYS DAVIDS, C. A. F., ED. *Tibetan Tales Derived from Indian Sources* (originally translated from the Tibetan by F. Anton von Schiefner and from the German by W. R. S. Ralston). London: George Routledge and Sons, 1926.

RHYS DAVIDS, MRS. C. A. F., ED. *Jatakas* (Buddhist Birth Stories). London: G. Routledge and Sons, 1925.

ROGHAIR, GENE H. *The Epic of Palnadu*. Oxford: Oxford University Press, 1982.

SASTRI, S. M. NATESA. *Folklore in Southern India*. 3 vols. Bombay: Education Society Press, 1884–88.

————. *Indian Folk Tales*. Madras: Guardian Press, 1908.

SHULMAN, DAVID D. *Tamil Temple Myths*. Princeton: Princeton University Press, 1980.

STEEL, FLORA ANNIE. *Wide-Awake Tales*. Bombay and London: Trubner and Sons, 1884. Reprinted as *Tales of the Punjab, Told by the People*. London: Macmillan, 1894; London: Bodley Head, 1973.

THOMPSON, STITH. *Motif-Index of Folk Literature*. 6 vols. Rev. ed. Bloomington: Indiana University Press, 1955–58.

THOMPSON, STITH, AND JONAS BALYS. *The Oral Tales of India*. Bloomington: Indiana University Press, 1958.

THOMPSON, STITH, AND WARREN E. ROBERTS. *Types of Oral Indic Tales*. (*Folklore Fellows Communications* no. 180). Helsinki: Suomalainen Tiedeakatemia, 1960.

TING, NAI-TUNG. *A type Index of Chinese Folktales*. Helsinki: Suomalainen Tiedeakatemia Academia Scientarium Fennica, 1978.

TROGER, RALPH. *A Comparative Study of a Bengali Folktale: Underworld Helpers. An Analysis of the Bengali Folktale Type: The Pursuit of Blowing Cotton A–T 480* (trans. from the German by Heinz Mode). Calcutta: Indian Publications, 1966.

VAN BUITENEN, J. A. B. *Tales of Ancient India*. Chicago: University of Chicago Press, 1959.

WADLEY, SUSAN S. *Shakti: Power in the Conceptual Structure of Karimpur Religion*. Chicago: Department of Anthropology, University of Chicago, 1975.

WILKINS, CHARLES, TRANS. *Hitopadesa* (Fables and Proverbs from the Sanskrit). Gainsville, Florida: Scholars' Facsimiles and Reprints, 1968.

Contributors

The Editors

BRENDA E. F. BECK holds a D.Phil. in social anthropology from Oxford University, England. She has spent a total of nearly three years in southern India, first from 1964 to 1966 and again during several later trips for shorter periods. Her publications include roughly twenty articles and chapters in the folklore field. She is past president of the Canadian Sociology and Anthropology Association and author of *The Three Twins: The Telling of a South Indian Folk Epic.* Beck is currently professor of anthropology at the University of Toronto, Ontario, Canada.

PETER J. CLAUS is professor of anthropology at California State University, Hayward. His research in India was in the Tulu-speaking region of Karnataka State, where his major collection effort was devoted to paddana oral legends. He has published several paddana translations and studies on the relationship between oral literature and village ritual in various journals in India and the United States.

PRAPHULLADATTA GOSWAMI has recently retired from his position of several decades as professor and head of the Department of Folklore Research at the University of Gauhati, in Assam. The department was founded at his initiative in 1972—the first folklore department in India. He is responsible for building a fine collection of Assamese tales. Several of his many essays and books report and analyze themes found in various types of stories important to this growing library of materials. Dr. Goswami was a visiting professor at the Folklore Institute in Bloomington, Indiana, during 1966. While there, he worked closely with Professor Richard Dorson on the initial stages of the present volume. He is currently developing a special collection of short, humorous tales popular in his home district of Kamrup, Assam. Professor Goswami is also the president of the Folklore Society of Assam, Gauhati.

327

JAWAHARLAL HANDOO holds a doctorate from Kurukshetra University and is currently associate professor of folklore at the Central Institute of Indian Languages in Mysore. He has been director of the Folklore Unit there since 1970. Handoo is the founder-secretary of the Folklore Fellows of India and editor of the *Journal of Indian Folkloristics*. He has written a number of papers, three books, and has also edited two books. His special fields of interest are folklore theory, oral narrative, and folk song.

Other Contributors

ASUTOSH BHATTACHARYYA was professor and head of the Department of Modern Indian Languages at the University of Calcutta until 1977. He is currently honorary director of the Research Institute of Folk-Culture, West Bengal and a fellow at the Indian National Academy of Dance, Drama, and Music. Between 1937 and 1947, Bhattacharyya made an extensive collection of folktales in the area belonging to Bangaladesh, and after 1947 he continued this work by doing parallel field studies in West Bengal. During much of this period he was associated with Dr. Verrier Elwin, then deputy director of the Anthropological Survey of India. Bhattacharyya's interests cover all aspects of contemporary Indian folklore tradition.

PUSHKER CHANDERVAKER is a leading scholar of Gujarati folk traditions. He was a reader of folklore at Saurastra University between 1968 and 1976. He is currently director of the Folklore Research Institute of Gujarat where he spends much time developing his extensive tale collection. He is the author of numerous books and over one hundred research papers. Chandervaker's primary interest is in collecting stories, riddles, proverbs, and other folklore materials, the themes of which he often uses in writing his own original novels and one-act plays.

DULAL CHAUDHURI is a lecturer at F. C. College, Calcutta University, and director of the Akademi of Folklore, Calcutta. He has published on methodology in folklore and Chakma proverbs. His major research has been on the folklore of the Naga tribes of northeastern India. He has worked extensively with Mr. J. Tsuknung P. Ao, a an Ao Naga who has a great interest in tale collection. Mr. Ao is currently a publicity officer for the Nagaland government.

LALITA HANDOO holds a master of arts degree from Jammu and Kashmir University. She did fieldwork in Kashmir from 1970 to 1972 and again from 1978 to 1980 and is now developing a structural analysis of Kashmiri folktales for a doctoral dissertation. She is the author of a number of papers and is currently a research assistant at the Central Institute of Indian Languages. Her special interests are the folktale, riddles and proverbs, lexicography, and translation.

PAUL HOCKINGS holds a doctorate in anthropology from the University of California, Berkeley. He has done extensive work on the Badaga community of the Nilgiri Hills and has shown special interest in tribal medical practices, in Nilgiri folklore, and in ethnographic filmmaking. He is the author of three books, a bibliography, and a number of articles. Hockings is currently a professor of anthropology at the University of Illinois, Chicago.

E. A. MORINIS holds a D.Phil. in social anthropology from Oxford University, England. He spent extended periods in West Bengal during 1974–78, and 1981 where his research work focused on the relationship between popular religious practices and classical Hindu literary texts. He has a special interest in medicine and has published several articles relating to popular medical beliefs in Bengal. Morinis is also much interested in the folklore surrounding Hindu temple pilgrimages and sacred sites. He is the author of *Pilgrimage in the Hindu Tradition* (Oxford University Press, 1984).

V. NARAYANA RAO is an associate professor in the Department of South Asian Languages and Literature at the University of Wisconsin. He has specialized in Telugu materials and is himself a native of Andhra Pradesh, the state where this important language is predominant. Narayana Rao has a developed interest in Telugu folktales and also in Telugu folk epic materials. He has written several essays on topics concerned with differences between oral and written story variants.

USHA NAKSENA NILSSON is a professor of India languages and literature in the Department of South Asian Studies, University of Wisconsin, Madison. Her publications include three novels, five volumes of short stories, translations of medieval Hindi poetry, of Mirabai and Surdas, and of modern Hindi short stories. Her primary interest in folklore is feminine oral traditions, the life cycle folksongs and tale narrated at women's fasts and feasts. She has done fieldwork around the cities of Delhi and Aligarh in 1975, 1981, and 1983–84.

MIMI NICKTER has degrees in applied linguistics and communications. She has conducted several years of fieldwork in rural South India on the topic of women and health. She has also done fieldwork in Sri Lanka on indigenous notions of fertility and has worked closely with folklorist

Amrit Someshwar in collecting, analyzing, and translating Tulu
folktales and legends. Her interest is in the use of popular metaphors
and imagery found in everyday speech and in folklore in culturally responsive health education messages. She is currently working as an international health consultant in Asia and Africa.

RAGHAVAN PAYYANAD is a doctoral candidate in folklore at the Central
Institute of Indian Languages in Mysore and a lecturer in Brennen College, Tellichery, affiliated with Calicut Univeristy, Kerala. He has
made several fieldtrips through the Cannanore District of Kerala and has
collected nearly one hundred folktales in his mother tongue, Malayalam. He has also had students and friends collect tales from the Palghat, Trichur, and Alleppy Districts which are adding new materials to
his fast-growing collection.

A. K. RAMANUJAN is a distinguished scholar of South Asian languages
and literature and is currently professor at the University of Chicago.
He is a noted linguist and poet as well as a student of the folklore of
several Dravidian languages. Ramanujan is well known for his sensitive
English translations of Kannada and Tamil poetry. He has collected
folktales from Karnataka, Tamilnadu, and Kerala and has written about
these stories in several essays. Ramanujan is also the author of fifteen
books and numerous articles.

IROM BABU SINGH holds a doctorate from the University of Kalyani,
West Bengal, and is presently a member of the Department of Manipuri
Language and Literature at Manipur University in Imphal. His primary
research interest is the collection and interpretation of Manipuri
folktales, songs, and rituals. He is currently working on a large project
of this nature funded by the Indian Council of Social Science Research.
Singh has published four books and several essays concerned with the
Manipur area.

SARASWATHI VENUGOPAL holds a doctorate in Tamil folklore. Her collection of Tamil folk materials includes lullabies, funeral laments, and
numerous folktales. She has published a book on Tamil folklore and is
the author of several scholarly papers on related topics. Venugopal is
currently a reader in folklore at Madurai Kamaraj University in Tamilnadu. Her special interests include caste variations in folk beliefs and
the structural analysis of myth.

SUSAN WADLEY holds a doctorate in anthropology from the University
of Chicago. She has done extensive research on folk traditions in rural

Uttar Pradesh and has developed a large library of tales and songs that circulate in the western U. P. region. Her work is of special interest because of her collaboration with William and Charlotte Wiser, missionaries who made anthropological observations fifty years earlier on the same settlement, Karimpur, Wadley lived in. Among other fieldnotes, she has possession of the Wiser folktale collection. Wadley is the author or editor of several books and numerous papers relating to folklore topics. She is currently professor of anthropology at Syracuse University.

NOTE TO INDICES

Sources used for compiling this and the following indices are: (1) Antti Aarne and Stith Thompson, *The Types of the Folk-Tale; A Classification and Bibliography.* Revised edition. Folklore Fellows Communications no. 184. Helsinki: Suomalainen Tiedeakatemia, 1964. (2) Stith Thompson, *Motif-Index of Folk Literature, A Classification of Narrative Elements in Folktales, Ballads, Myths, Fables, Medieval Romances, Exempla, Fabliaux, Jest-Books, and Local Legends.* 2d ed. 6 vols. Bloomington: Indiana University Press, 1955–58. (3) Stith Thompson and Warren Roberts, *Types of Indic Oral Tales.* Folklore Fellows Communications no. 180. Helsinki: Suomalainen Tiedeakatemia, 1960. (4) Stith Thompson and Jonas Balys, *The Oral Tales of India.* Bloomington: Indiana University Press, 1958. (5) Laurits Bødker, *Indian Animal Tales: A Preliminary Survey.* Folklore Fellows Communications no. 170. Helsinki: Suomalainen Tiedeakatemia, 1957.

Tale types from source (1) above are denoted "AT." Tale types from source (3) are denoted "TR." Those from source (5) are denoted "Bødker."

Motifs listed are taken exclusively from source (4) [which are repeated in source (2)]; thus no designation is needed.

An asterisk (by convention) indicates suggested new tale types or motifs. (We have suggested two subdivisions of AT 750 and several new motifs.)

Index of Tale Types and Motifs by Story

Story No.	Tale Type	Motifs	Comments
1		A425.1.2	myth
		A421	
		A970	
2		H119	
		F441.2	
		T16	
		T86.2	
		T117.5.1	
3		A285	etiological myth-tale
		A287	
		C313	
		C960	
		*D43.2 Human transformed to god	
4		D812.14	
		D931	
		L161.1	
		Z71.1	
5	AT 1458	H385	cf. AT 1451–1454
6		A2431.3	
		W116	
7	AT 653	H355.4	
		T92.11	
8	AT 653B	D1155	
		D1163	
9	AT 934A	M341.2.21.1	cf. AT 336
		N101	
10		F302.2	legend
		F305	
		G259.5	
11		F81	cf. T111

(continued)

Index of Tale Types and Motifs by Story (*Continued*)

Story No.	Tale Type	Motifs	Comments
		T65.1.1	
		T211	
12	AT 412	E711.4	
		T113	
13	AT 516B + 560	D1076	
		E52	
		K1058.1	
14		H120	This and the following story
		J1112	might constitute a new type in
		K2253	India (in between AT 1405–
15		K1814	1429); it could be named: Man
		K2231	does not look at his wife; only
		T513	realizes her beauty when he thinks she's another woman.
16	*AT 750J	Q26	This story and no. 57 seem to
		P253.10	constitute a variant of AT 750 and
		Z71.5	could be designated AT 750J: "Devotion Rewarded." *Or* it might be subsumed under 750B.
17		B451.4	cf. TR 402A Ind.
		H383	
		N711.1	
		N844.2	
		R224	
		R321.2	
		T121.8	
		Z71.5	
18		B2151	cf. AT 670, 671
		C221.1.2.3	
		D217	
		N451	
19		K455.2	
		P634.0.1	
		W125	
20		A112	myth
		A1210	
		D990	
		D993	
		D1001	
		H1573	
		T512	
21		C551	
		F441.2	
		Q221	
		T511	

Index of Tale Types and Motifs by Story (*Continued*)

Story No.	Tale Type	Motifs	Comments
		T548.1	
		*T567	human daughter of animal parents
22		A137.9	see comment on #16
		B391.1.2	
		*C335 Tabu: looking south	
		K1811.2	see next story for same motif
		L52	
		N817	
		Q20.1	
		Z71.5	
23	TR 1121B Ind.	*C335	cf. AT 303
		T511.2.01	
		T561.1	
		T591.1	
		Z71.5	
		H550.1	
24	*AT 750B Ind.	E121	This widespread story could be designated as AT 750B Ind.: Only Child Eaten by Parents and Revived. Cf. AT 750***. See also no. 16.
		Q22	
		T548.4	
25		A1211	
		A1610	
		K171.1	legend of caste origin
26		J151	
		J345.2	
		J710	
27	AT 1457	Z71.5	
28	AT 1539	K301.2	
		K335.1.2.2	
		K421.2	
		K437	
		K1970	
		Z71.5	
29		G410	cf. AT 311, 312
		G501	
		G652	
		R11.1	
		Z71.5.1	
30	AT 720	E715.1	legend (?)
		P253.10	
		Q211.4	
		Q429.3	
		T181	
		Z71.5.1	

(*continued*)

Index of Tale Types and Motifs by Story (*Continued*)

Story No.	Tale Type	Motifs	Comments
31		J2411.1.1	
		K335.1.1.3	
		K2212	
		Q285	
32	AT 1535	K171.1	
		K335.1.1.2	
		K331.3	
33		L11	
		N817	
34	AT 480	L55	
		S31	
35	AT 1558	W175.1	
36		A2433.6	
		A2493	
		Q281	
37		Q45	legend
38		D991	legend
		D1400	
		F441.2	
		N815.01	
39		K2210	
		K2214.2.1	
		Q261	
		Q431	
40		J2411.4	
		K2210	
		K2214.2.1	
		N534.4	
41		D215	
		D562.1	
		D630.2	
		D766.1	
		Q2	
		Q280	
		S55	
42	AT 750B		
43	AT 403	D191	
		D721.3	
		K2222	
		P361	
		Q2	
44		D185.1	myth
		T257.2	
45	AT 403	D150	
		D190	
		D211.4	
		H220	
		S31	
46	AT 2029C	B211.2.8	No. 46 only resembles AT 2029;

Index of Tale Types and Motifs by Story (*Continued*)

Story No.	Tale Type	Motifs	Comments
		W125.2	cf. also AT 1373A
47	AT 1355	K1551	
48		K1814	myth
49			cf. AT 1365C
50		A510	myth
51		D112.1	
		D555	
		D621	
52	AT 533	H41	
		K2252	
		Q262	
		Q266	
		Q469.9.2	
53		L100	
		Q2	
		Q276	
54	AT 121 Bødker 567		
55		*K1972 Misc. Man pretends to be god; see also nos. 87, 91	
56	Bødker 918		
57	*AT 750J	D475.1.6	see comment for no. 16
		Q20	
		Q220	
58		B382	
		B478	
		Q2	
		T511.1	
		T554.2	
		T591.1	
59		*W151.1 Greedy Brahman; see also nos. 65 and 74	
60	AT 1699	J2496.2	
61		J1705.2	cf. 1542
62		J556	
63		J556	
64			
65		*W151.1	see no. 59 above, no. 74 below
		J1510	
66	AT 122B	K1961.1.5	cf. AT 122B, 113
		Z71.5	
67		K1836	legend

(*continued*)

Index of Tale Types and Motifs by Story (*Continued*)

Story No.	Tale Type	Motifs	Comments
		K2212	
		K2231	
68		B240.14	cf. Bødker 44
		L315	
69	AT 2034D		
70	AT 2034D		
71		L311	
		Q312	
72		H561.5	
		H587.0.1	
		H592.5	
73	Bødker 497 + 776		
74		J1280	
		*W151.1	see nos. 59, 65 above
75	AT 926A	J1141.1.7	
76		N101	
77		E121.4	legend
		E725	
		N848	
78		K2370	
79	AT 1699	J2460	
80	AT 1699		
81	AT 177	J1786.7	
82	AT 1250B	J2133	
83	AT 57		
	Bødker 360		
84	AT 1332		
85	AT 1149	J2132.5.1	
	Bødker 540	K1715	
86	AT 58 + 5 + 66B		
	Bødker 356		
87		J1160	
		J1705.2	
		*K1972 Misc. man pretends to be god; see also nos. 55, 91	
88		K343.1.2	
89		A1815	myth
		A1282.1	
		A2250	
		A2351	
		A2433.3.21	
		K21.8	
90		A969	myth
91	AT 1532	A2275.3	

Index of Tale Types and Motifs by Story (*Continued*)

Story No.	Tale Type	Motifs	Comments
		A2430	
		D110	
		*K1974.1 man in grave (underground) speaks as god	
		Q272	
		Q551.3.2	
92		B184.1	temple legend
		D931	
		D2188.1	
		V112	
		V340	
		V462.0.1	
93		V112	temple legend
		V340	
		V510.1	
94	AT 330	A487	perhaps the Indian instances of AT
		A1427	330 should be distinguished as
		R6	"Ind" in view of Yama's
			differences from the Christian
			Devil
95		B260	origin legend
96		A2493.4	
		A2494.4.0.1	
97	AT 2042A	J681.1.1;	
98	AT 2042A	Z49.11	
		A1515	
99	AT 2022	Z49.6.3	
		Z32.2	

Index of Tale Types

Index of Motifs

345

Motif No.		Story No.
A2493	Friendships between the animals	36
A2493.4	Friendships between man and dog	96
A2492.4.0.1	Dog driven away from other animals because of his barking	96

B. ANIMALS

B184.1	Magic horse	92
B211.2.8	Speaking mouse	46
B215.1	Bird language	18
B240.14	Elephant as king of animals	68
B260	Animal warfare	95
B382	Animal grateful for removal of bone lodged in throat	58
B391.1.2	Snake grateful because man feeds her young snakes milk	22
B451.4	Helpful crow	17
B478	Helpful crab	58

C. TABU

C221.1.2.3	Tabu: eating dove	18
C313	Tabu: woman looking at man	3
*C330.1	Tabu: looking south	22, 23
C551	Untouchables	21
C960	Transformation for breaking tabu	3

D. MAGIC

*D43.2	Human transformed to god	3
D110	Transformation: man into wild beast	91
D112.1	Transformation: man to lion	51
D150	Transformation: man to bird	45
D185.1	Transformation: man to fly	44
D190	Transformation: man to reptile	45
D191	Transformation: man to serpent	43
D215	Transformation: man to tree	41
D555	Transformation by drinking	51
D562.1	Transformation by application of water	41
D621	Daily transformation	51
D630.2	Power of self-transformation received from god	41
D721.3	Disenchantment by destorying skin	43
D766.1	Disenchantment by bathing	41

Motif No.		Story No.
H587.0.1	Enigmatic letter obtained must be explained on pain of death	72
H592.5	Donkey ruling a kingdom: king condemning man unjustly	72
H1573	Religious tests	20

J. THE WISE AND THE FOOLISH

J151	Wisdom from old man	26
J345.2	Man leaves farming for fishing—when water dries up he goes hungry	26
J556	Intemperance in honesty	62, 63
J681.1.1	Jackal and leopard tie tails together for mutual protection	97
J710	Forethought in provision for food	26
J1112	Clever wife	14
J1141.1.7	Which is man and which is a demon in man's shape	75
J1160	Clever pleading	87
J1280	Repartee with ruler	74
J1510	The cheater cheated	65
J1705.2	Stupid Brahman	61, 87
J1786.7	Lion thinks man astride him is monster; frightened	81
J2132.5.1	Other animal's tail tied to tiger's: killed when tiger flees	85
J2133	Numskull falls	82
J2411.1.1	Foolish imitation of sham death and return	31
J2411.4	Imitation of magician unsuccessful	40
J2460	Literal obedience	79
J2496.2	Misunderstandings because of lack of knowledge of a foreign language	60

K. DECEPTIONS

K11.8	Race won by deception	89
K171.1	Deception crop division	25, 32
K301.2	Family of thieves	28
K331.3	Worthless object substituted for valuable while owner sleeps	32
K335.1.1.2	Cowhide falls on robbers from tree, they flee and leave money	32

Motif No.		*Story No.*
L55	Stepdaughter heroine	55
L100	Unpromising hero (heroine)	53
L161.1	Marriage of poor boy and rich girl	4
L311	Weak (small) hero overcomes large fighter	71
L315	Small animal overcomes large	68

M. ORDAINING THE FUTURE

M341.2.21.1	Prophecy: death from cobra	9

N. CHANCE AND FATE

N101	Inexorable fate	9, 76
N451	Secrets overheard from animal's conversation	18
N534.4	Information about treasure received from overheard conversation	40
N711.1	King (prince) finds maiden in woods and marries her	17
N815.0.1	Tree spirit	38
N817	Deity as helper	22
N844.2	Fakir as helper	17
N848	Holy man as helper	77

P. SOCIETY

P253.10	Great love of brothers for sister	16, 30
P361	Faithful servant	43
P634.0.1	Customs connected with eating and food	19

Q. REWARDS AND PUNISHMENTS

Q2	Kind and unkind	41, 43, 53, 58
Q20	Piety rewarded	57
Q20.1	Reward for service of god, hero, or ascetic for a period	22
Q22	Reward for faith	24
Q26	Keeping fast rewarded	16
Q45	Hospitality rewarded	37
Q211	Murder punished	30
Q220	Impiety punished	57
Q221	Personal offenses against gods punished	21

Motif No.		Story No.
T257.2	Jealousy of rival wives	44
T511.1	Conception from eating fruit	58
T511.4	Conception from eating flower	21
T511.2.0.1	Conception from eating root	23
T512	Conception from drinking	20
T548.1	Child born in answer to prayer	21
T548.4	Charity rewarded by birth of child	24
T550.1	Monster child helps mother	23
T554.2	Woman bears dog	58
T561.1	Child born in conch shell	23
*T567	Human daughter born from animal parents	21
T591.1	Magic remedies for barrenness	23, 58

V. RELIGION

V112	Temples	92, 93
V340	Miracle manifested to nonbelievers	92, 93
V462.0.1	Kingship renounced to become ascetic	93
V510.1	God speaks in vision to devotee	93

W. TRAITS OF CHARACTER

W116	Vanity	6
W125	Gluttony	19
W125.2	Gluttonous wife eats all the meal while cooking it	46
*W151.1	Greedy Brahman	59, 65, 74
W175.1	Sister gives due honor in regard to brother only in times of his prosperity	35

Z. MISCELLANEOUS GROUPS OF MOTIFS

Z32.3	Death of the little hen	99
Z49.6.3	Man sharpening his dao is bitten by prawn (crab)	98
Z71.1	Formulistic number: three	4
Z71.5	Formulistic number: seven	16, 17, 22, 23, 27, 28, 66
Z71.5.1	Seven brothers and one sister	29, 30

General Index

Active being, categories of, 266, 269
Animal protagonists: as allowing political metaphor, 183, 210; as distancing device, 183; "human" status of, 194; imitated by man, 287; stereotyped roles of, 222; as surrogates for human characters, 167; use of symbolism with, 194
Arjuna, 280–83
Ascetics, powers of, 242

Babar: historical figure of, 213; inspired by Sayadu Minyano, 213; legendary character of, 184, 212–19
Bhima, 280–83
Bibgaraz Maj, goddess, 197–99
Bidhata, god of Destiny, 35, 240
Bluntness, as humorous response to pretense, 206
Boar, sexual connotations of, 170
Brahma: birth of, 71–73; creates parijata tree, 156
Brahmans: and deception, 208–9; food restrictions of, 262; as misers, 202–6, 234, 237; as pretentious, 206; as subjects of moral tales, 183

Bride, unenviable position of youngest, 79
British Government, as target of outlaws, 214
Brothers, as protectors of married sisters, 92, 99, 103
"Brother's Second," holiday, 121–22, 305

Cannibalism, 84, 110
Causality: and cumulative tales, 267; nature of, 267
Cenne, game of, 137, 171–72, 309
Characters, spatial placement of, 3
Children: fear of losing, 79; fear of bearing deformed, 79, 80
Cleanliness, Hindu ritual of, 182
Communication: and exorcism, 33–34; extrahuman, 60, 63, 165; with dead in dreams, 161
Courtship: and fantasy, 1; outcome of determined by women, 2–3; and premarital sex, 1; and status quo, 1–2
Cunning, as subversive undercurrent, xxx
Cumulative tales, 227, 267, 289–90, 292

Purana tradition, Sanskritic, 175
Purity, Hindu notions of, 261

Ramayana, 73, 221, 279
Ravana, and abduction of Sita,
103
Regional differences and sim-
ilarities, 184
Respectability, 67, 70
Revival of the dead, 81, 84
Rich-poor framework, contest in,
14
Riddles: and clever characters,
233; and impossible condi-
tions, 35
Ritual sacrifice, 82
Rukmini, Krishna's wife, 156–
60

Sakat, and festival of *sakat,* 152
Sakti, daughter of Dharma, 71
Sankata Mangal Chandi, goddess,
80
Sannyasi, and supernatural power,
79, 277–78
Sati, 26
Satpura Hills, parental house of
Mahi River, 5–6
Satyabhama, Krishna's wife,
156–60
Satyagraha movement, 213, 215
Satya kanni (truth-girl), 73
Self-sacrifice, 124
Sexual favors, 169–71
Siblings: collective identity of,
92; economic equality of, 121;
elder as model for younger,
280; reciprocity between, 121;
relations among, 93
Siva, 5, 61; as Baba, 278–79;
birth and marriage of, 70–73;
and clever farmers, 85–87; as

giver of wishes, 117–18; as
hunter, 175–76; as local deity,
75; as Lord Mahadev, 280,
302; and quarrel with Parvati,
171–74
Souls: multiple, 161–67, 286;
transfer of, 242–45
Status inversion and hierarchy,.
183
Surprise reversals, in tales of moral virtue, 182
Swarga (paradise), 208

Temple origins, stories of (*purana, mahatmya*), 277
Time, Hindu view of, 265
Transformations of being, and
natural imagery, 2
Trickster, animal or human, xxx;
heroic image of, 259

Untouchable roles, xxxi

Virtues: of ideal wife, 27, 189; in
human-divine and social relationships, 181; of outlaws,
212
Vishnu: birth of, 71–73; and in-
cantation, 85

Waking vision, 29
Water ritual and transformation,
142–51
Weddings, as scenes of adjudica-
tion, 12–14
Widows and widowers, 26, 32,
34, 139
Wife, virtues of ideal, 27, 189;
and conflict between natal and
nuptial families, 27, 92
Wisdom, India as an original
source of, 221;
quality/quantity of, 235